Oh My Goddess!

あぁっ女神さまっ

9

STORY AND ART BY
Kosuke Fujishima

TRANSLATION BY
Dana Lewis AND Toren Smith

LETTERING AND TOUCH-UP BY
Susie Lee AND Betty Dong
WITH Tom2K

DARK HORSE MANGA™

CHAPTER 53

Law of the Ninja

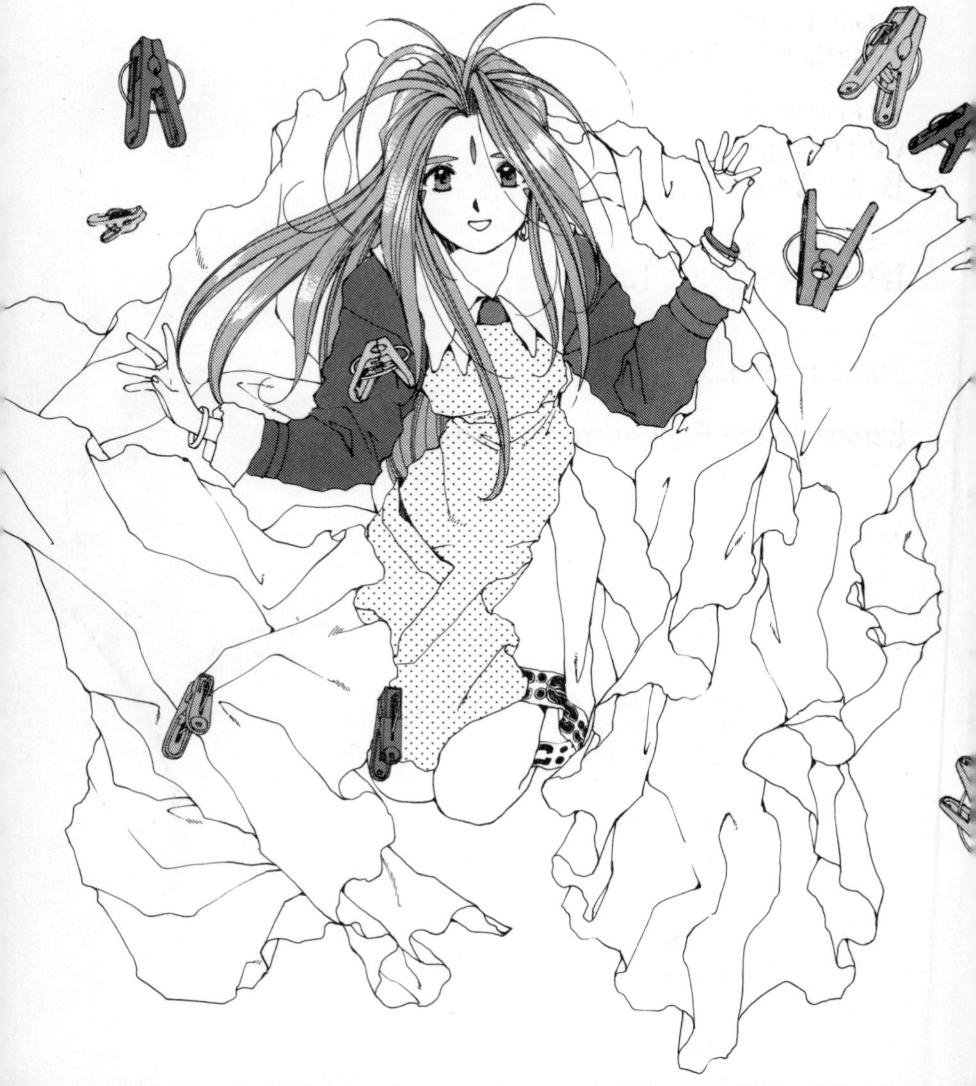

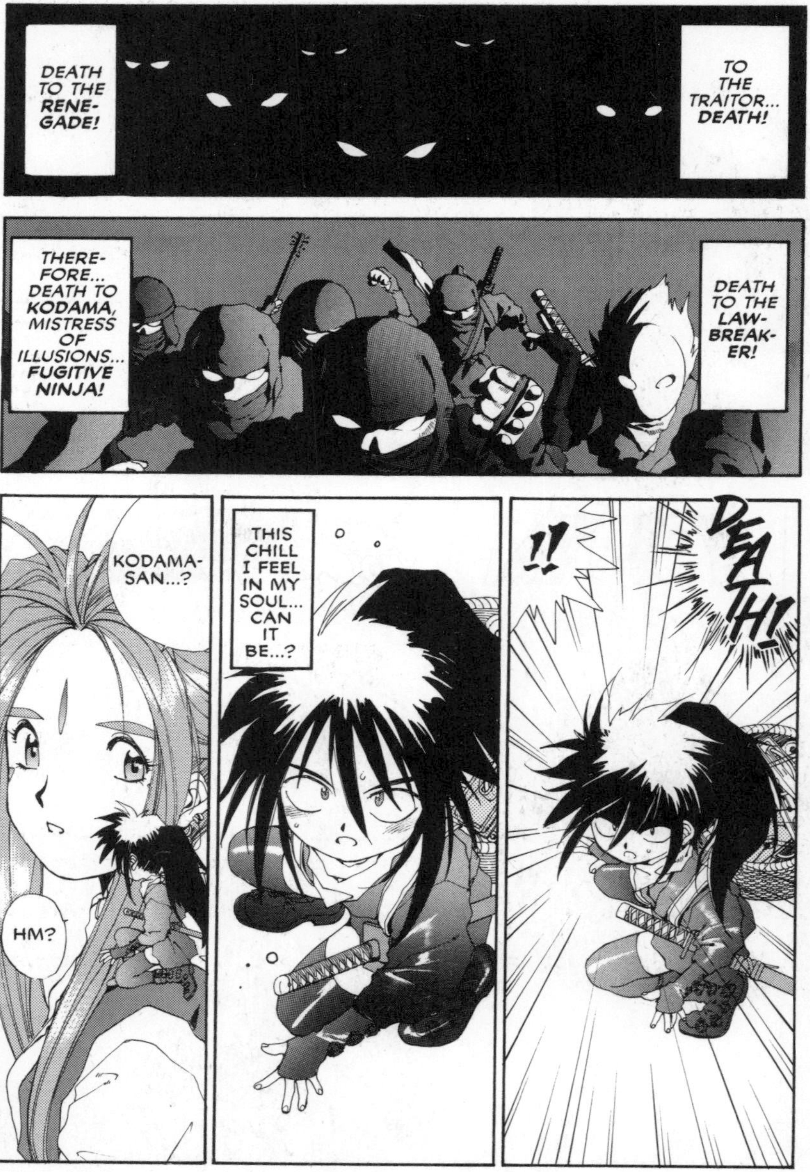

TO THE TRAITOR... DEATH!
DEATH TO THE RENEGADE!
DEATH TO THE LAW-BREAKER!
THERE-FORE... DEATH TO KODAMA, MISTRESS OF ILLUSIONS... FUGITIVE NINJA!
!!
DEATH!
THIS CHILL I FEEL IN MY SOUL... CAN IT BE...?
KODAMA-SAN...?
HM?

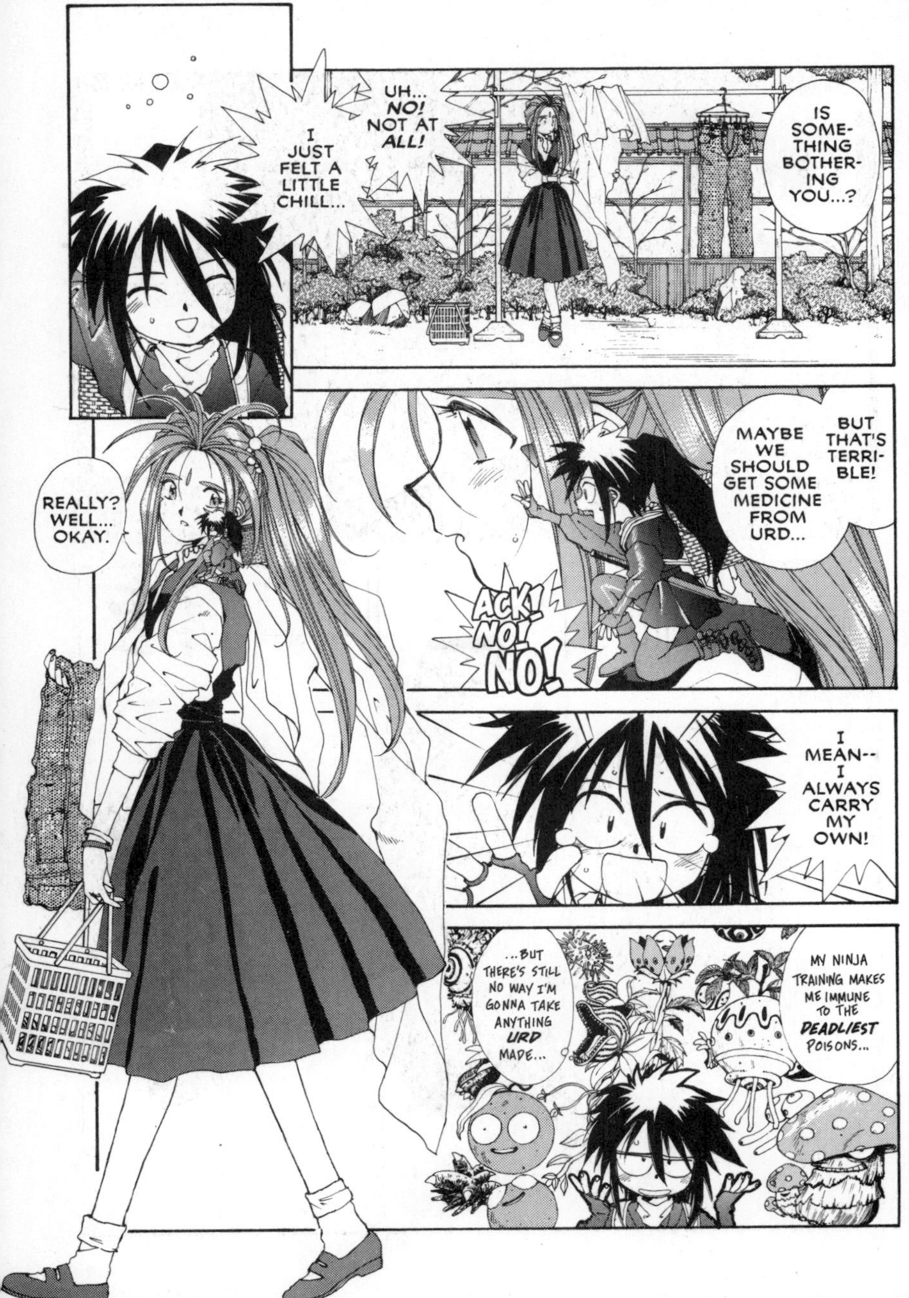
IS SOMETHING BOTHERING YOU...?
UH... NO! NOT AT ALL!
I JUST FELT A LITTLE CHILL...
BUT THAT'S TERRIBLE!
MAYBE WE SHOULD GET SOME MEDICINE FROM URD...
ACK! NO! NO!
I MEAN-- I ALWAYS CARRY MY OWN!
MY NINJA TRAINING MAKES ME IMMUNE TO THE DEADLIEST POISONS...
...BUT THERE'S STILL NO WAY I'M GONNA TAKE ANYTHING URD MADE...
REALLY? WELL... OKAY.

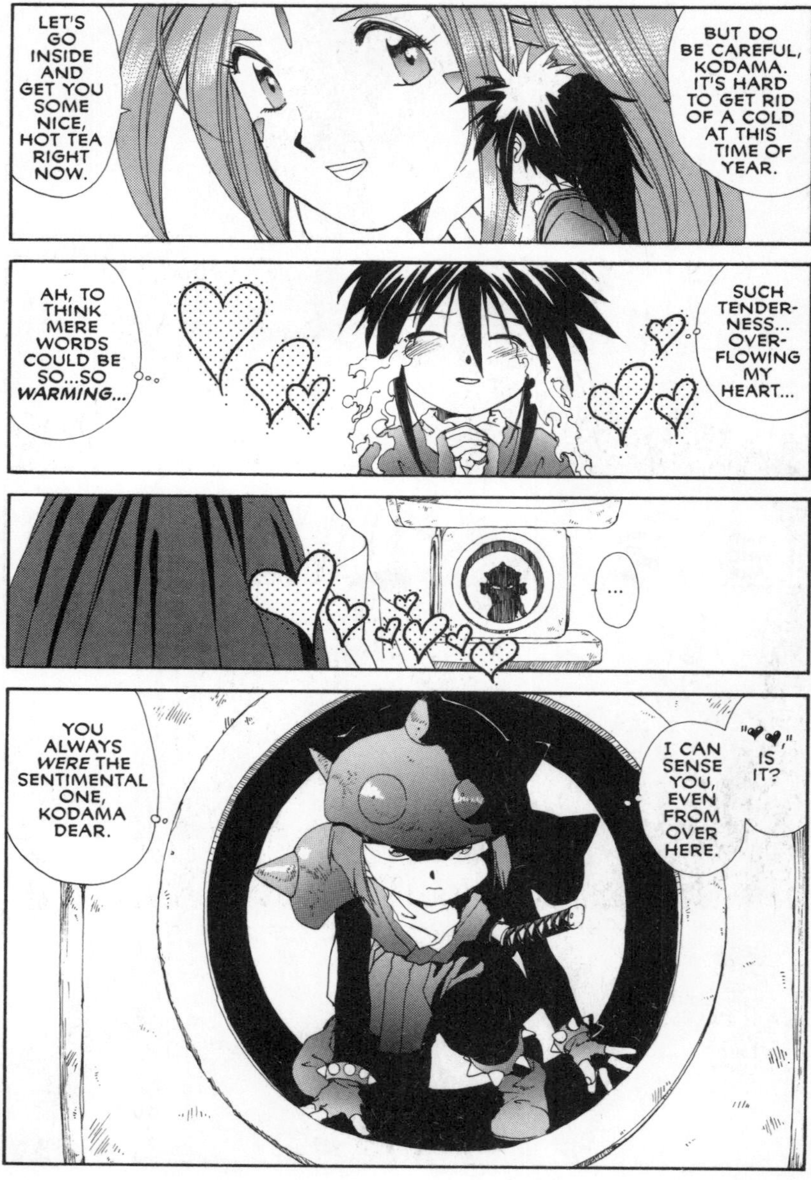
BUT DO BE CAREFUL, KODAMA. IT'S HARD TO GET RID OF A COLD AT THIS TIME OF YEAR.
LET'S GO INSIDE AND GET YOU SOME NICE, HOT TEA RIGHT NOW.
SUCH TENDER-NESS... OVER-FLOWING MY HEART...
AH, TO THINK MERE WORDS COULD BE SO...SO *WARMING*...
...
"♥♥," IS IT?
I CAN SENSE YOU, EVEN FROM OVER HERE.
YOU ALWAYS *WERE* THE SENTIMENTAL ONE, KODAMA DEAR.

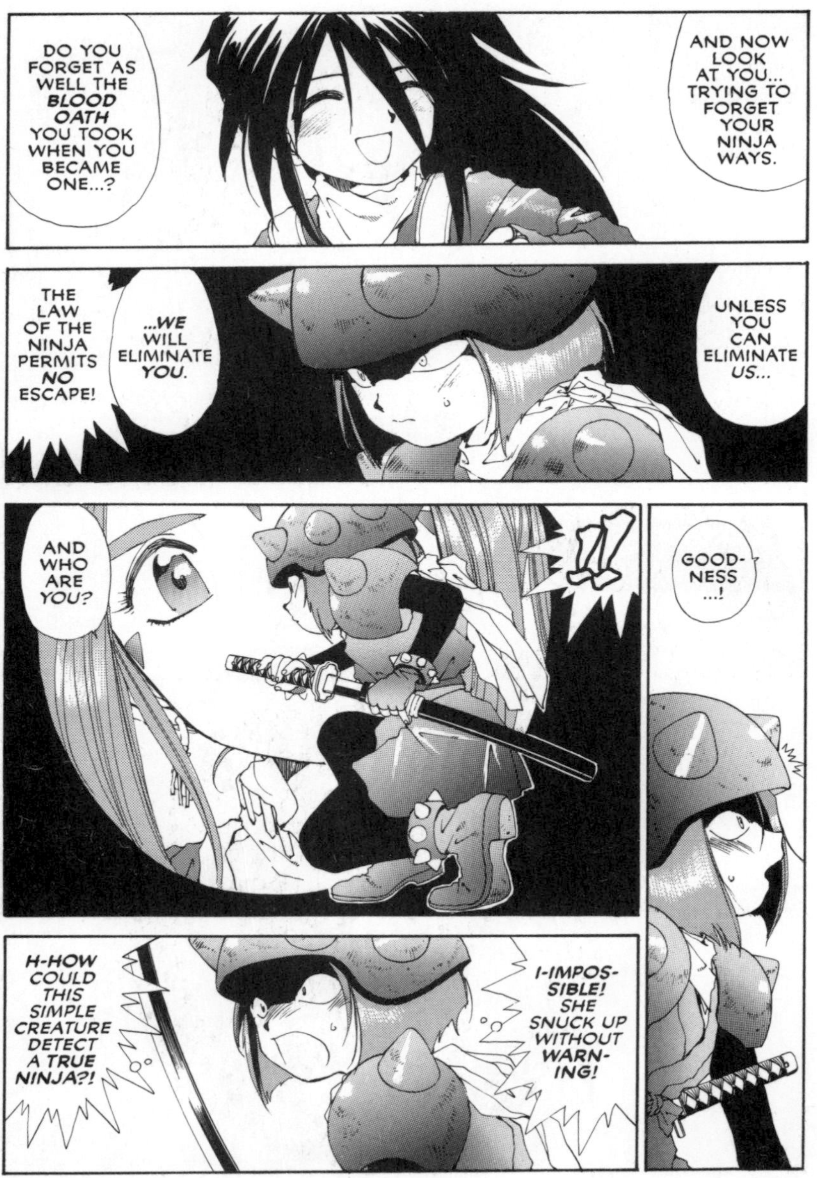
AND NOW LOOK AT YOU... TRYING TO FORGET YOUR NINJA WAYS.
DO YOU FORGET AS WELL THE BLOOD OATH YOU TOOK WHEN YOU BECAME ONE...?
UNLESS YOU CAN ELIMINATE US...
...WE WILL ELIMINATE YOU.
THE LAW OF THE NINJA PERMITS NO ESCAPE!
GOOD-NESS ...!
AND WHO ARE YOU?
I-IMPOSSIBLE! SHE SNUCK UP WITHOUT WARNING!
H-HOW COULD THIS SIMPLE CREATURE DETECT A TRUE NINJA?!

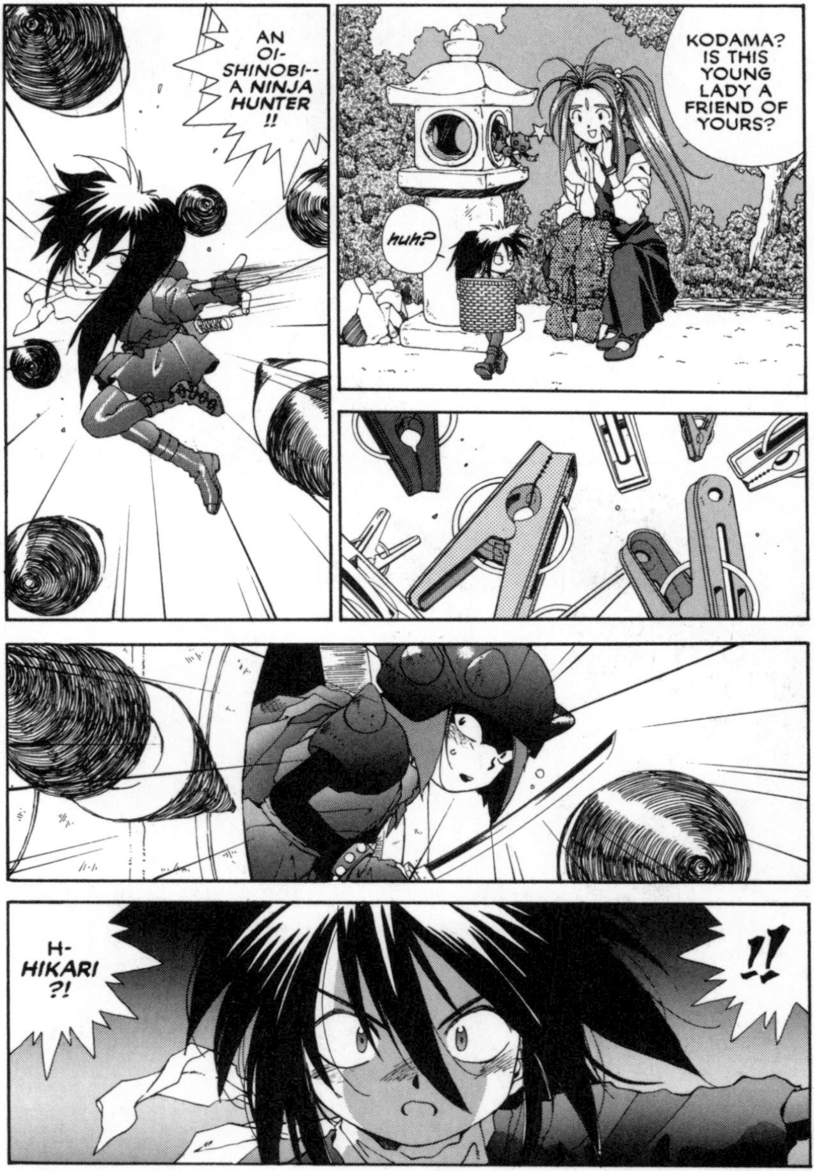
KODAMA? IS THIS YOUNG LADY A FRIEND OF YOURS?
huh?
AN OI-SHINOBI-- A NINJA HUNTER !!
!!
H-HIKARI ?!

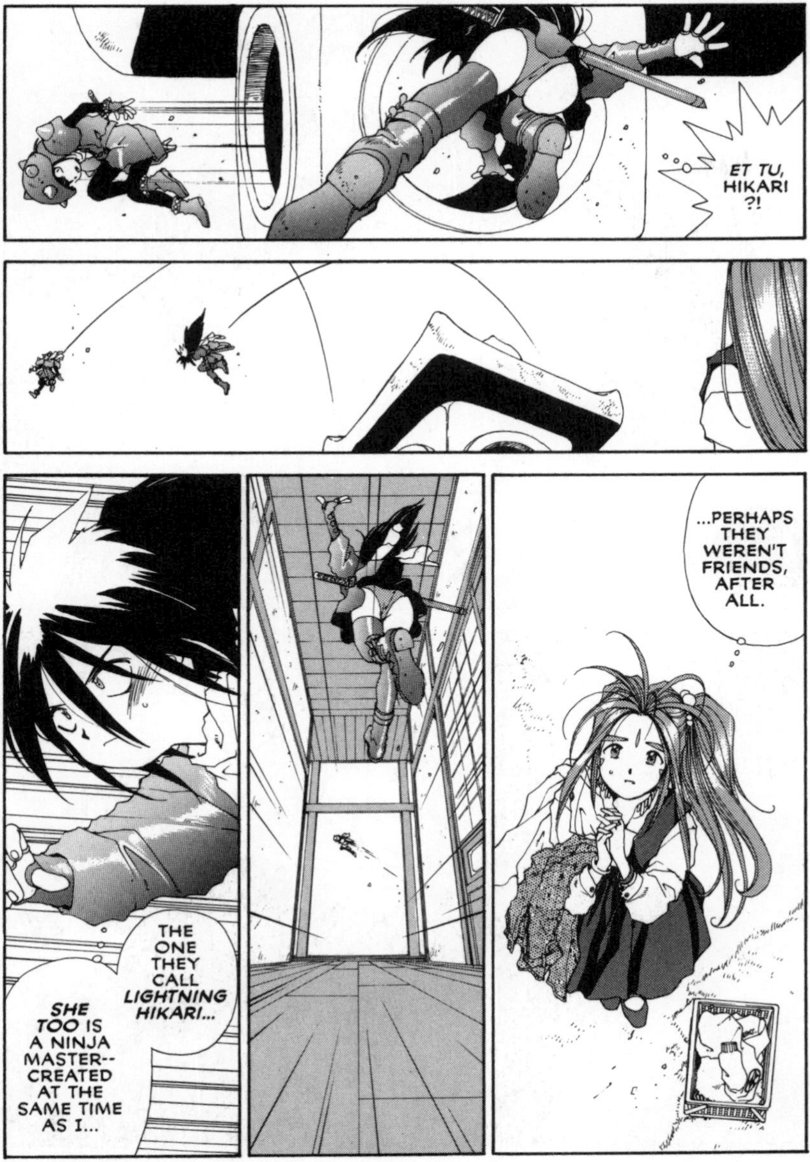
ET TU, HIKARI ?!
...PERHAPS THEY WEREN'T FRIENDS, AFTER ALL.
THE ONE THEY CALL *LIGHTNING HIKARI*...
SHE TOO IS A NINJA MASTER--CREATED AT THE SAME TIME AS I...

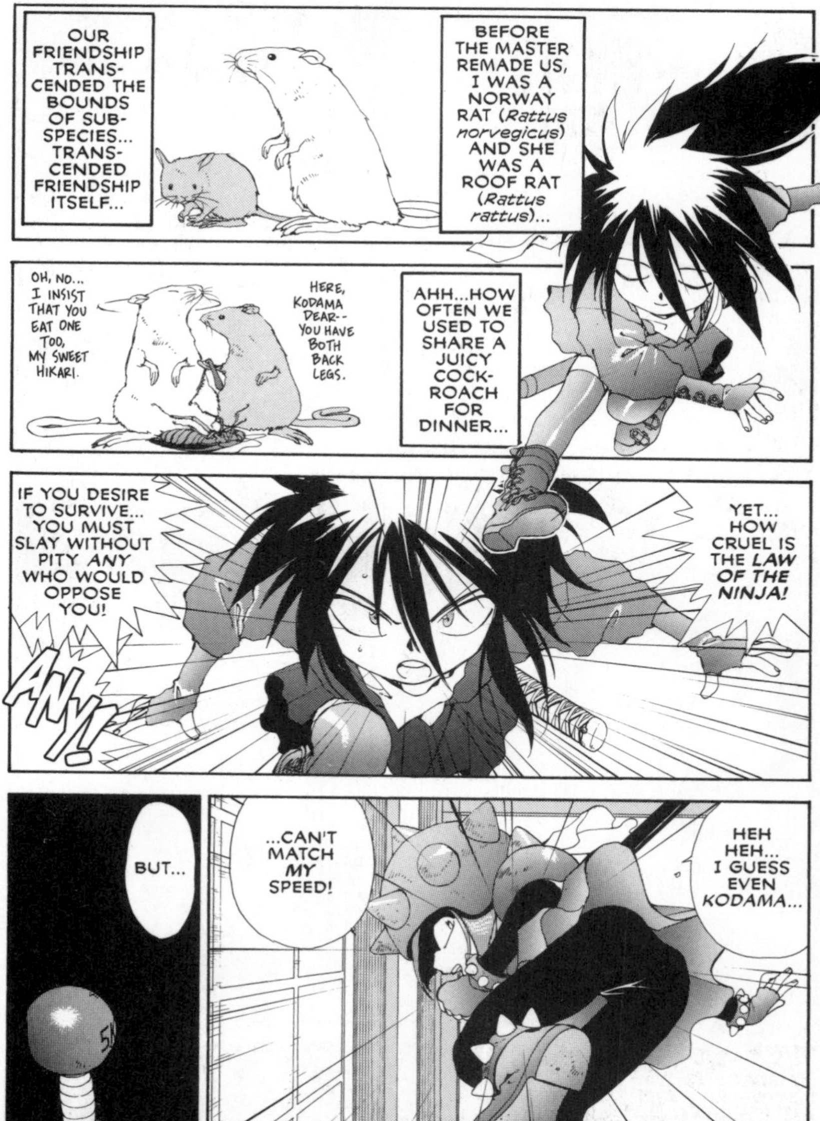
BEFORE THE MASTER REMADE US, I WAS A NORWAY RAT (*Rattus norvegicus*) AND SHE WAS A ROOF RAT (*Rattus rattus*)...
OUR FRIENDSHIP TRANSCENDED THE BOUNDS OF SUBSPECIES... TRANSCENDED FRIENDSHIP ITSELF...
AHH...HOW OFTEN WE USED TO SHARE A JUICY COCKROACH FOR DINNER...
HERE, KODAMA DEAR--YOU HAVE BOTH BACK LEGS.
OH, NO... I INSIST THAT YOU EAT ONE TOO, MY SWEET HIKARI.
YET... HOW CRUEL IS THE *LAW OF THE NINJA!*
IF YOU DESIRE TO SURVIVE... YOU MUST SLAY WITHOUT PITY *ANY* WHO WOULD OPPOSE YOU!
ANY!
HEH HEH... I GUESS EVEN *KODAMA*...
...CAN'T MATCH *MY* SPEED!
BUT...

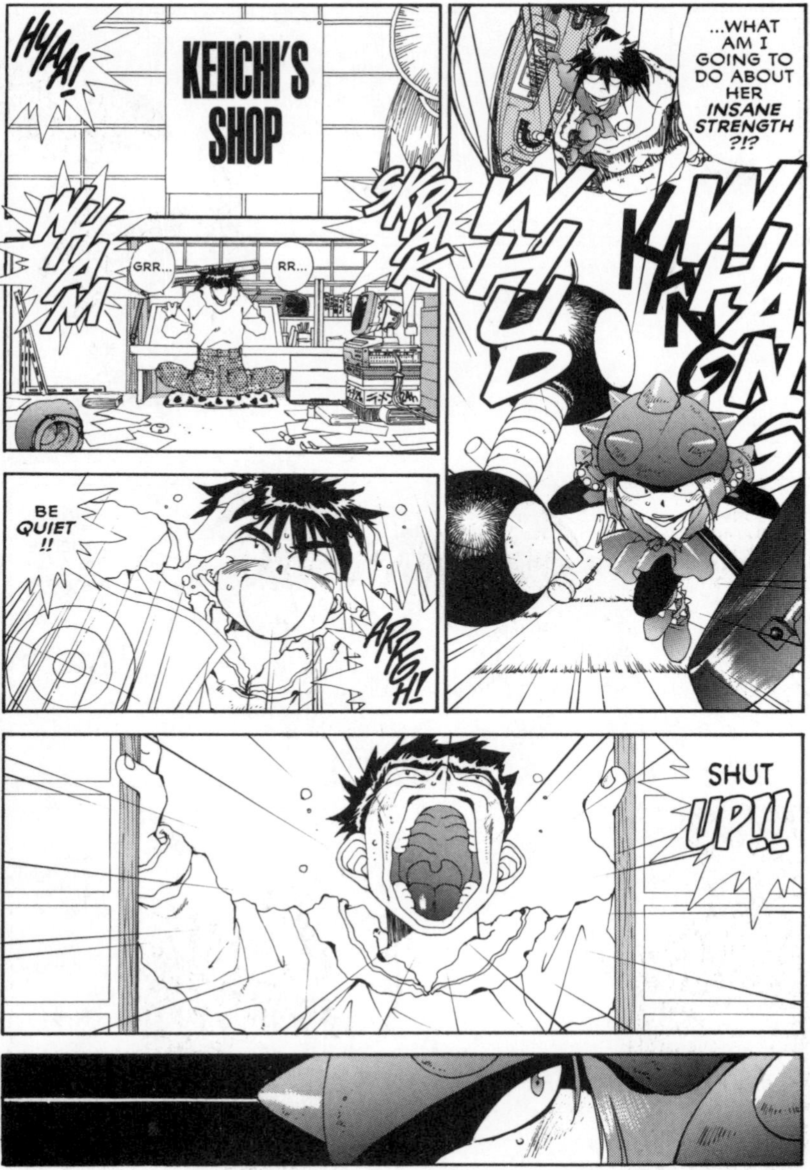
...WHAT AM I GOING TO DO ABOUT HER *INSANE STRENGTH*?!?
SKRAK
WHUD
HYAAA!
KEIICHI'S SHOP
WHAM
GRR...
RR...
BE *QUIET*!!
ARRGH!!
SHUT UP!!

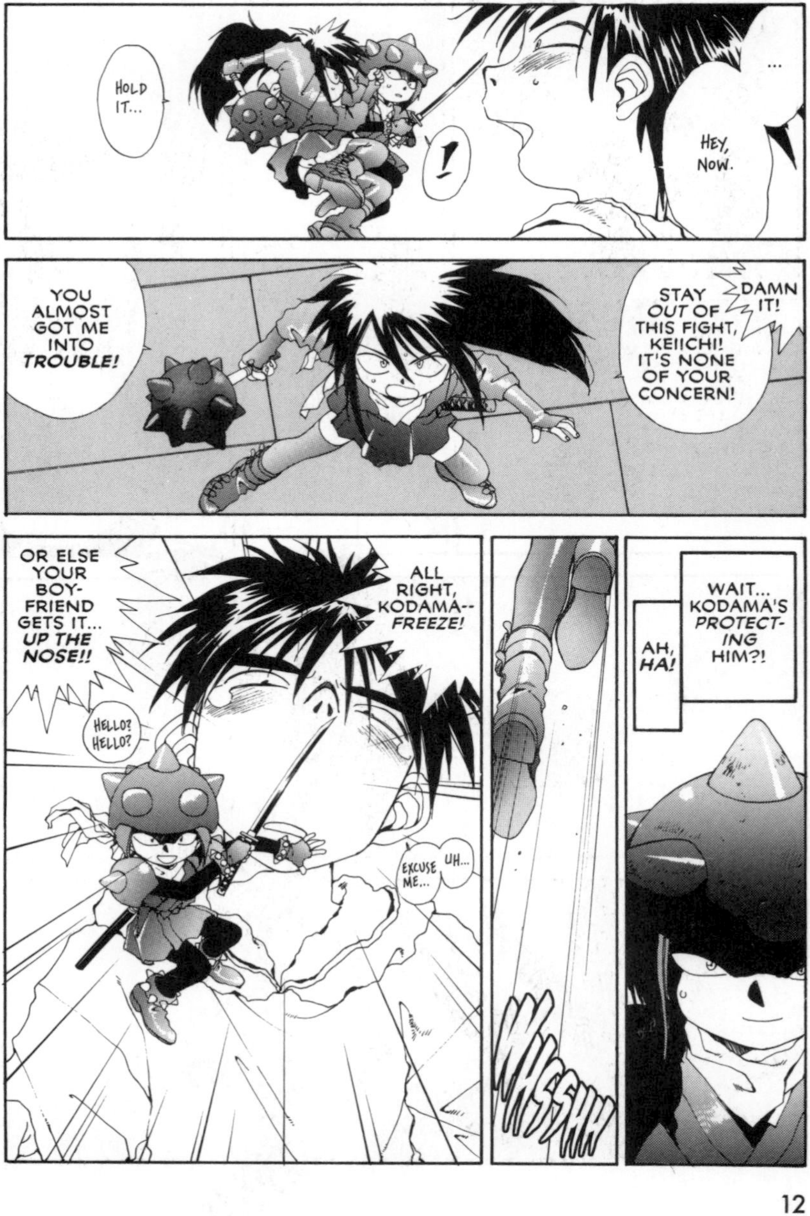
...
HEY, NOW.
!
HOLD IT...
DAMN IT!
STAY OUT OF THIS FIGHT, KEIICHI! IT'S NONE OF YOUR CONCERN!
YOU ALMOST GOT ME INTO TROUBLE!
WAIT... KODAMA'S PROTECTING HIM?!
AH, HA!
WHSSHH
ALL RIGHT, KODAMA-- FREEZE!
OR ELSE YOUR BOY-FRIEND GETS IT... UP THE NOSE!!
HELLO? HELLO?
UH...
EXCUSE ME...

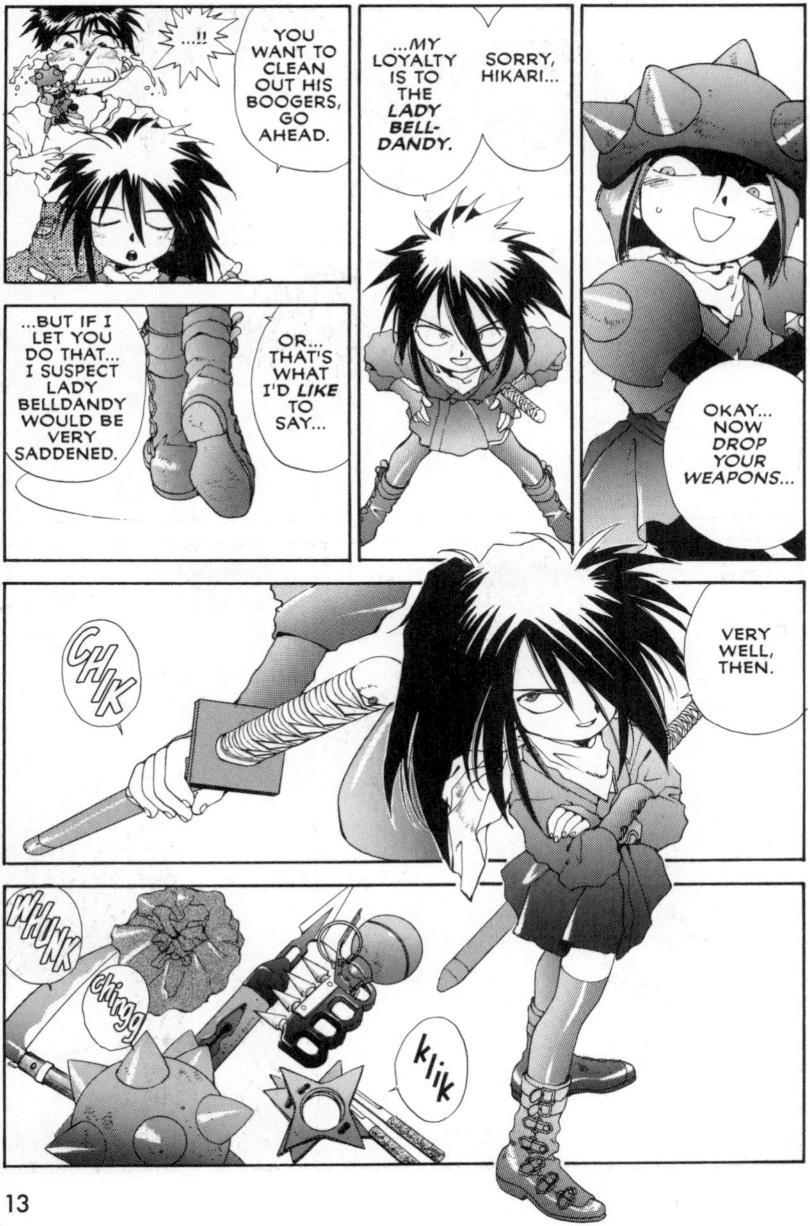
OKAY... NOW *DROP* YOUR *WEAPONS...*
SORRY, HIKARI...
...*MY* LOYALTY IS TO THE ***LADY BELL-DANDY.***
YOU WANT TO CLEAN OUT HIS BOOGERS, GO AHEAD.
...!!
OR... THAT'S WHAT I'D *LIKE* TO SAY...
...BUT IF I LET YOU DO THAT... I SUSPECT LADY BELLDANDY WOULD BE VERY SADDENED.
VERY WELL, THEN.
CHIK
klik
chingg
WHUNK

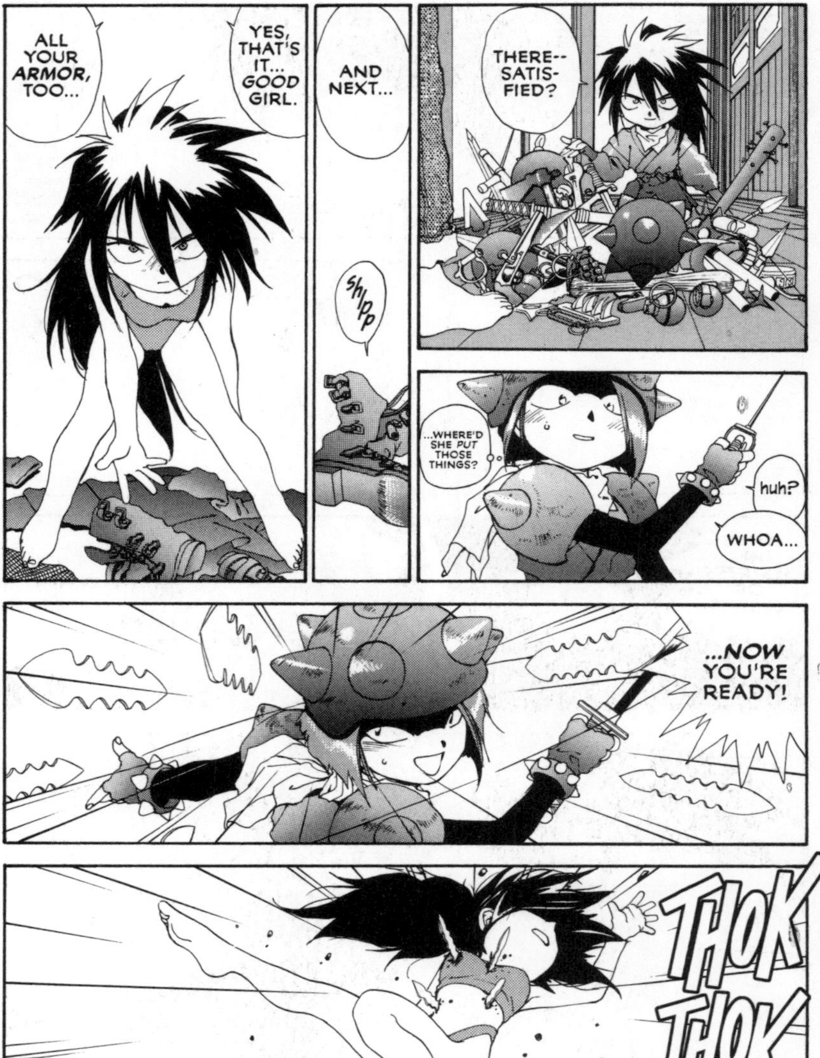
THERE-- SATISFIED?
huh?
WHOA...
...WHERE'D SHE *PUT* THOSE THINGS?
AND NEXT...
shlpp
YES, THAT'S IT... *GOOD* GIRL.
ALL YOUR *ARMOR,* TOO...
...*NOW* YOU'RE READY!
THOK
THOK
THOK

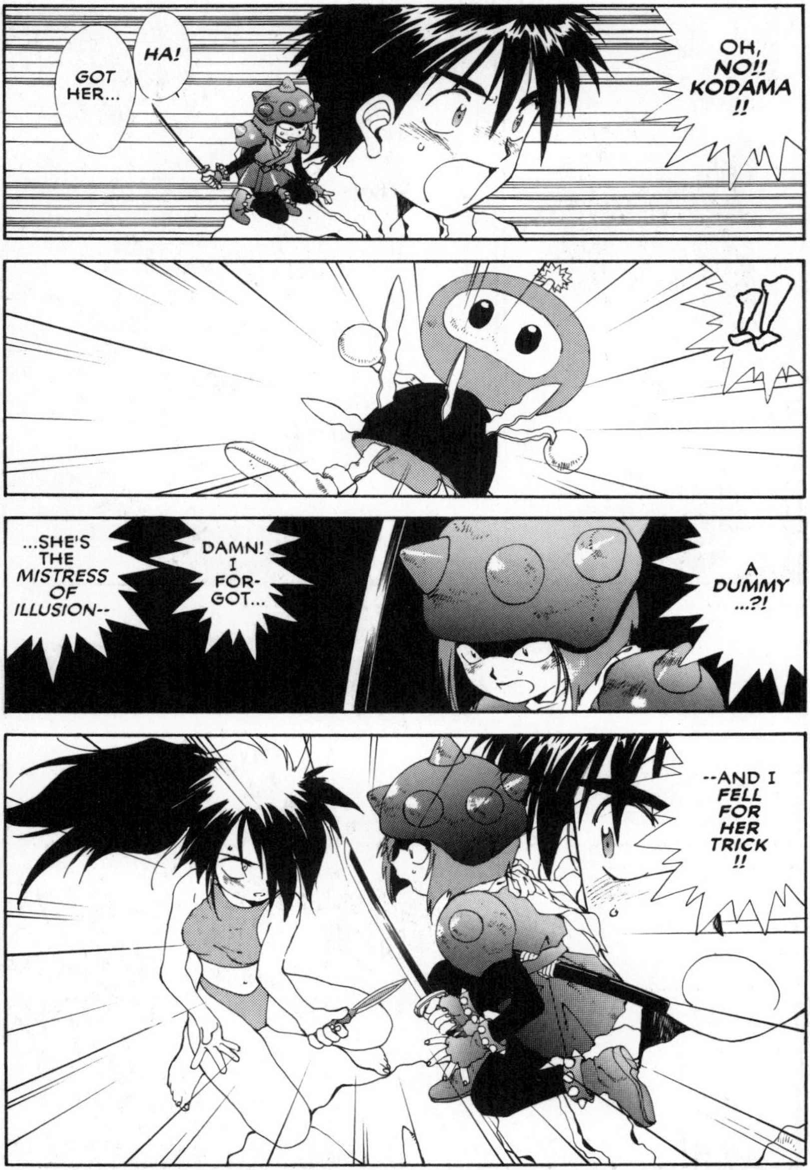
OH, NO!! KODAMA !!
HA!
GOT HER...
!!
A DUMMY ...?!
DAMN! I FOR- GOT...
...SHE'S THE *MISTRESS* OF ILLUSION--
--AND I FELL FOR HER TRICK !!

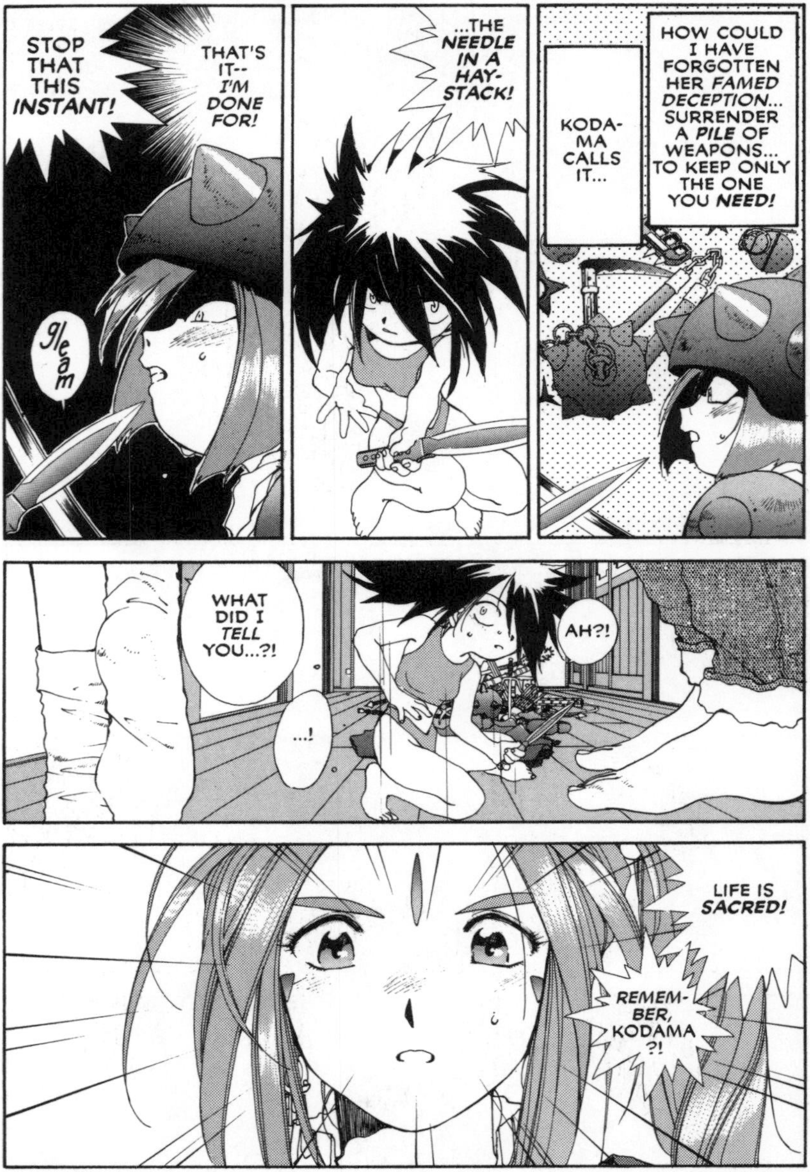
HOW COULD I HAVE FORGOTTEN HER *FAMED DECEPTION*... SURRENDER A *PILE* OF WEAPONS... TO KEEP ONLY THE ONE YOU *NEED!*
KODAMA CALLS IT...
...THE *NEEDLE IN A HAYSTACK!*
THAT'S IT-- *I'M* DONE FOR!
STOP THAT THIS *INSTANT!*
gleam
AH?!
WHAT DID I *TELL* YOU...?!
...!
LIFE IS *SACRED!*
REMEMBER, KODAMA ?!

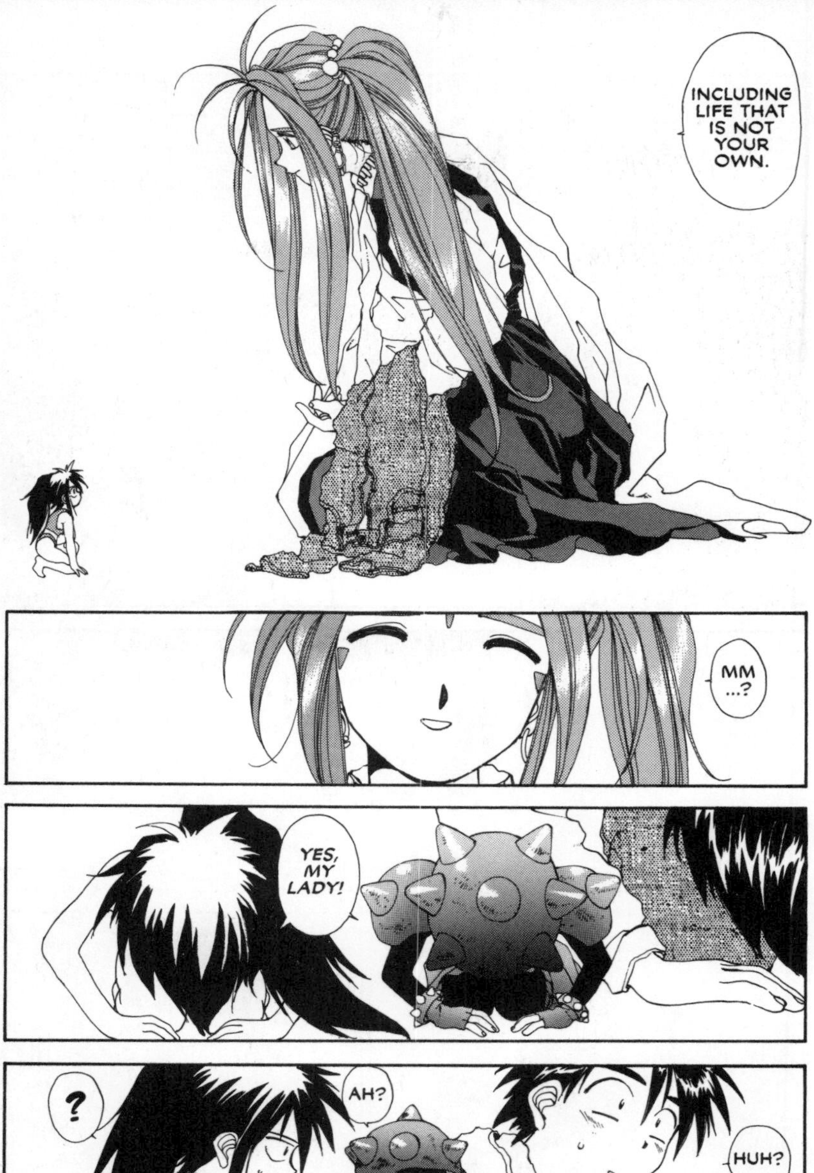
INCLUDING LIFE THAT IS NOT YOUR OWN.
MM ...?
YES, MY LADY!
HUH?
AH?
?

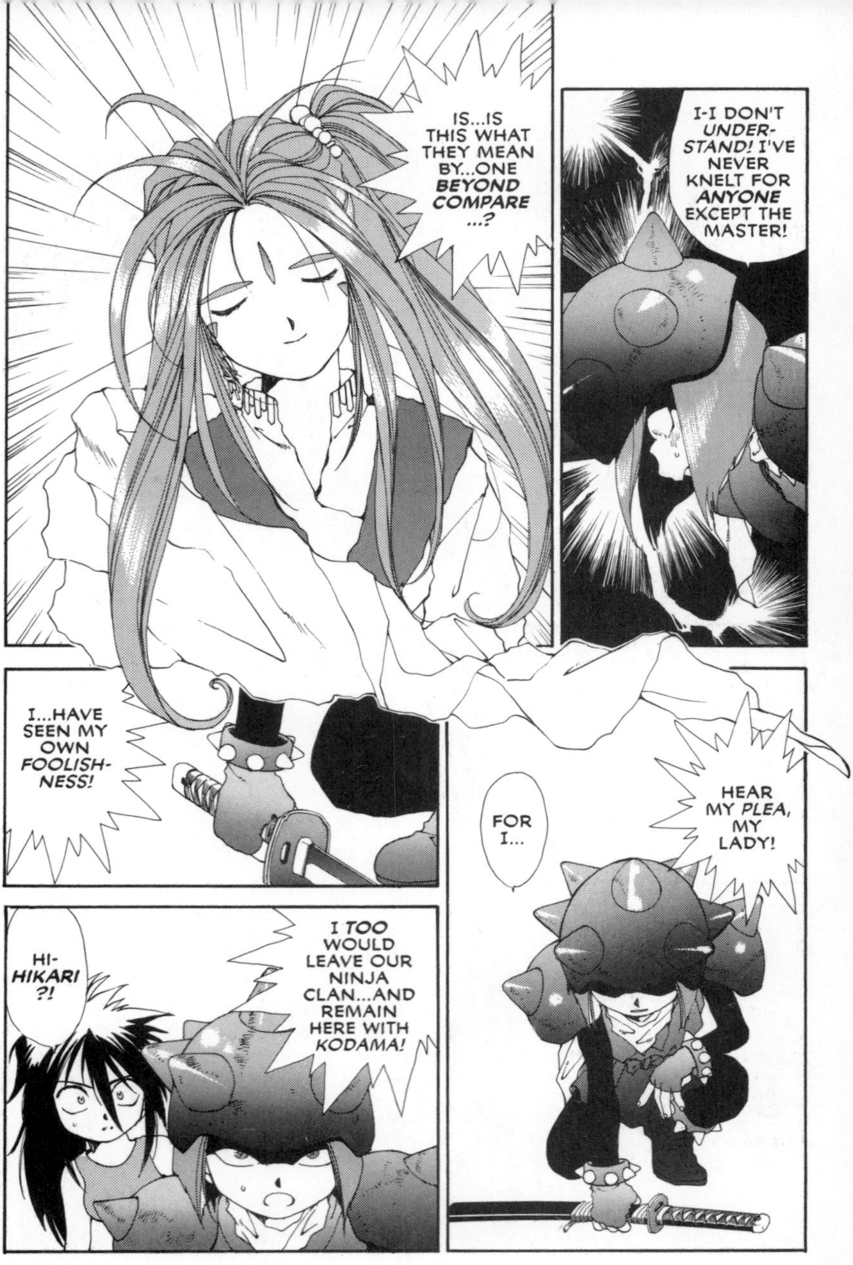
I-I DON'T *UNDER-STAND!* I'VE NEVER KNELT FOR ***ANYONE*** EXCEPT THE MASTER!
IS...IS THIS WHAT THEY MEAN BY...ONE ***BEYOND COMPARE***...?
HEAR MY *PLEA,* MY LADY!
FOR I...
I...HAVE SEEN MY OWN *FOOLISH-NESS!*
I *TOO* WOULD LEAVE OUR NINJA CLAN...AND REMAIN HERE WITH *KODAMA!*
HI-*HIKARI*?!

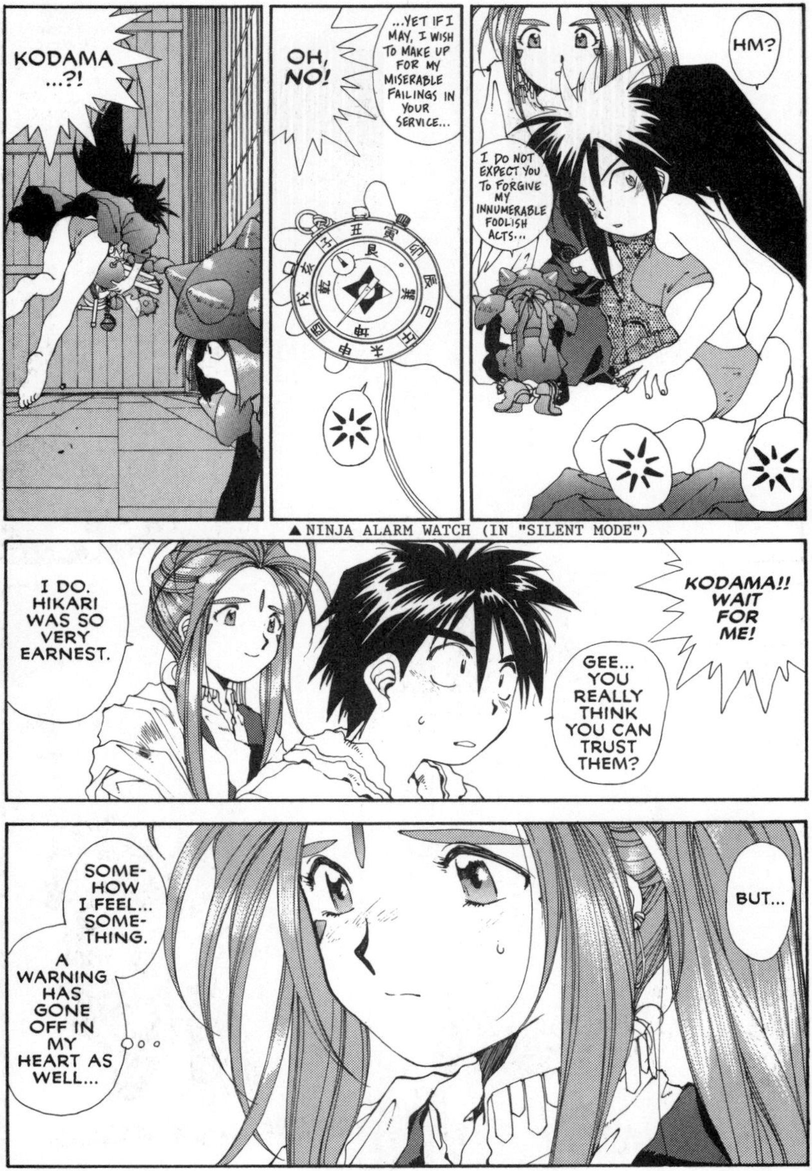
HM?
I DO NOT EXPECT YOU TO FORGIVE MY INNUMERABLE FOOLISH ACTS...
...YET IF I MAY, I WISH TO MAKE UP FOR MY MISERABLE FAILINGS IN YOUR SERVICE...
OH, NO!
KODAMA ...?!
KODAMA!! WAIT FOR ME!
GEE... YOU REALLY THINK YOU CAN TRUST THEM?
I DO. HIKARI WAS SO VERY EARNEST.
BUT...
SOME-HOW I FEEL... SOME-THING.
A WARNING HAS GONE OFF IN MY HEART AS WELL...
▲ NINJA ALARM WATCH (IN "SILENT MODE")

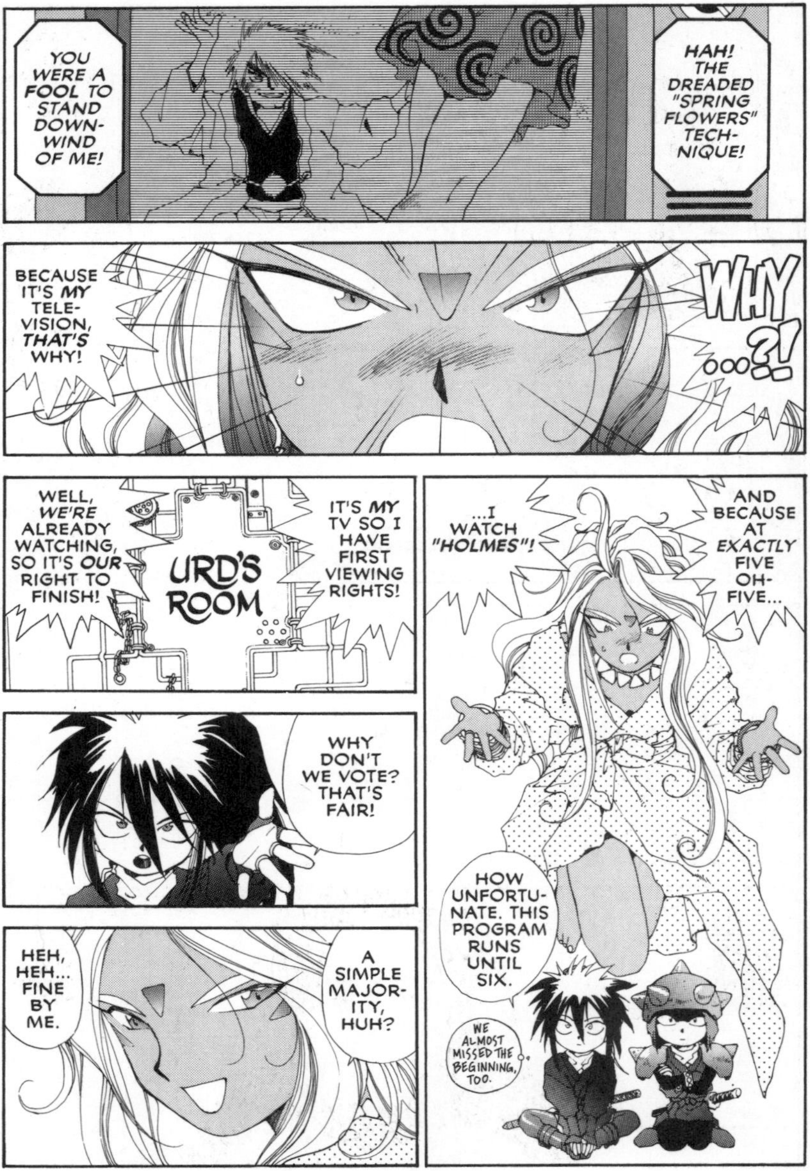
HAH! THE DREADED "SPRING FLOWERS" TECH-NIQUE!
YOU WERE A FOOL TO STAND DOWN-WIND OF ME!
WHY ?! ooo
BECAUSE IT'S MY TELE-VISION, THAT'S WHY!
AND BECAUSE AT EXACTLY FIVE OH-FIVE...
...I WATCH "HOLMES"!
HOW UNFORTU-NATE. THIS PROGRAM RUNS UNTIL SIX.
WE ALMOST MISSED THE BEGINNING, TOO.
IT'S MY TV SO I HAVE FIRST VIEWING RIGHTS!
URD'S ROOM
WELL, WE'RE ALREADY WATCHING, SO IT'S OUR RIGHT TO FINISH!
WHY DON'T WE VOTE? THAT'S FAIR!
A SIMPLE MAJOR-ITY, HUH?
HEH, HEH... FINE BY ME.

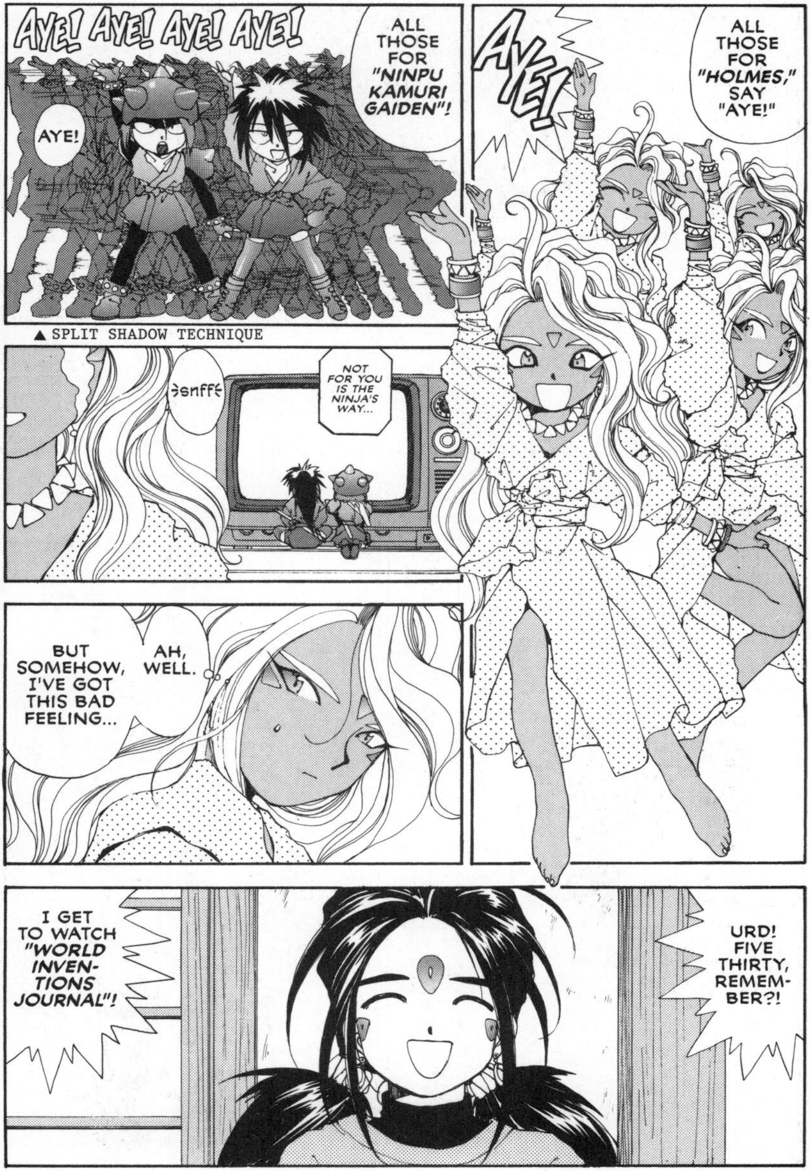
ALL THOSE FOR "HOLMES," SAY "AYE!"
AYE!
ALL THOSE FOR "NINPU KAMURI GAIDEN"!
AYE! AYE! AYE! AYE!
AYE!
▲ SPLIT SHADOW TECHNIQUE
NOT FOR YOU IS THE NINJA'S WAY...
snff
AH, WELL.
BUT SOMEHOW, I'VE GOT THIS BAD FEELING...
URD! FIVE THIRTY, REMEMBER?!
I GET TO WATCH "WORLD INVENTIONS JOURNAL"!

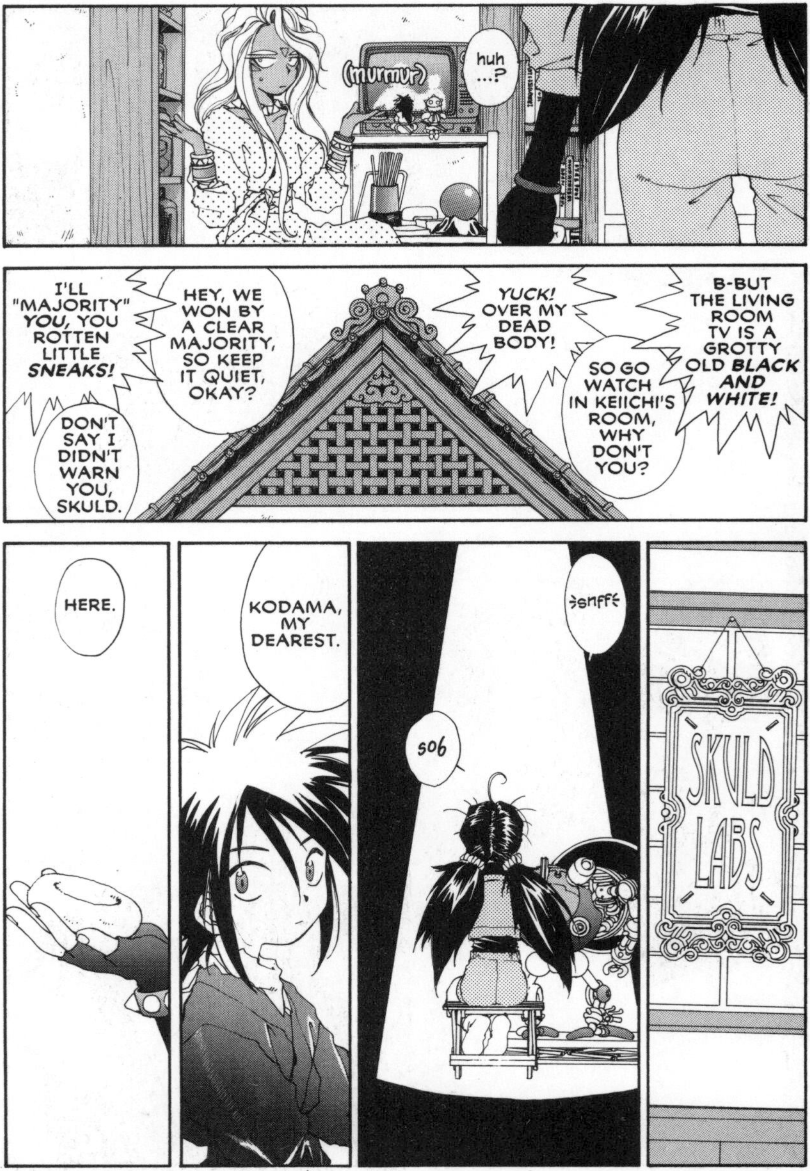
huh ...?
(murmur)
B-BUT THE LIVING ROOM TV IS A GROTTY OLD **BLACK AND WHITE!**
SO GO WATCH IN KEIICHI'S ROOM, WHY DON'T YOU?
YUCK! OVER MY DEAD BODY!
HEY, WE WON BY A CLEAR MAJORITY, SO KEEP IT QUIET, OKAY?
I'LL "MAJORITY" ***YOU,*** YOU ROTTEN LITTLE ***SNEAKS!***
DON'T SAY I DIDN'T WARN YOU, SKULD.
SKULD LABS
snff
sob
KODAMA, MY DEAREST.
HERE.

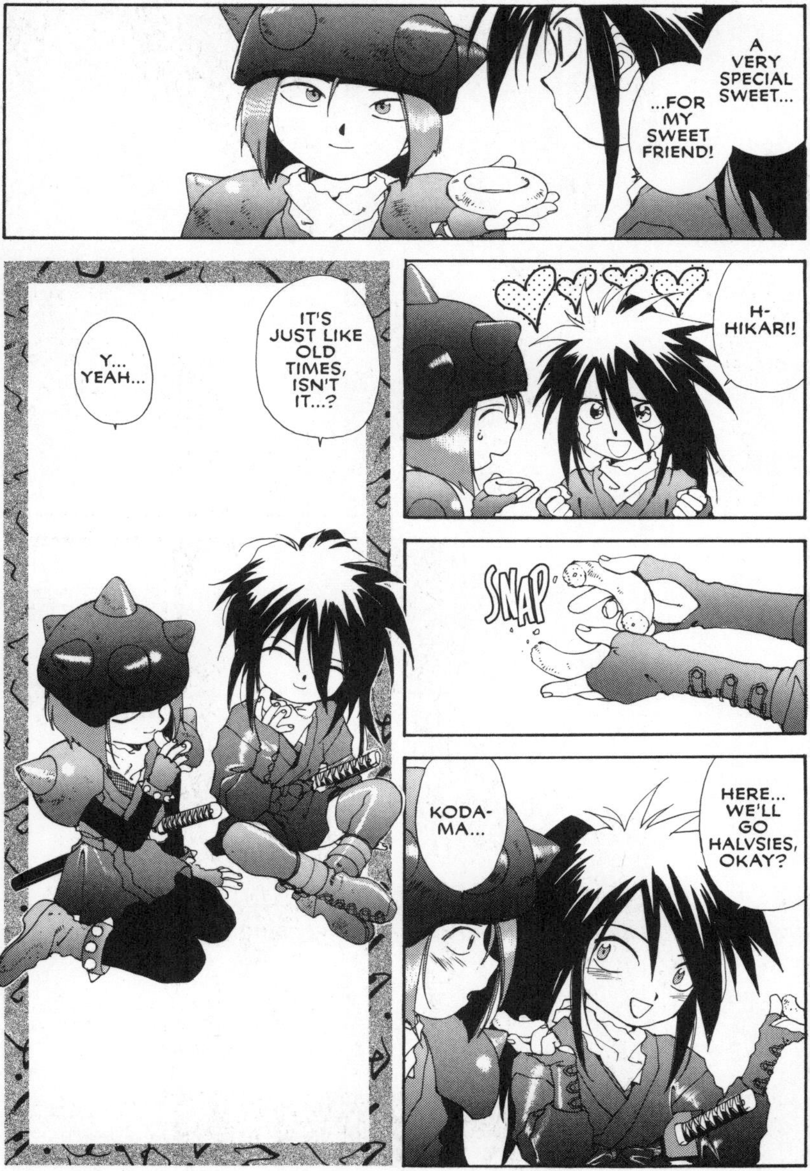

A VERY SPECIAL SWEET...
...FOR MY SWEET FRIEND!
H- HIKARI!
SNAP
HERE... WE'LL GO HALVSIES, OKAY?
KODA- MA...
IT'S JUST LIKE OLD TIMES, ISN'T IT...?
Y... YEAH...

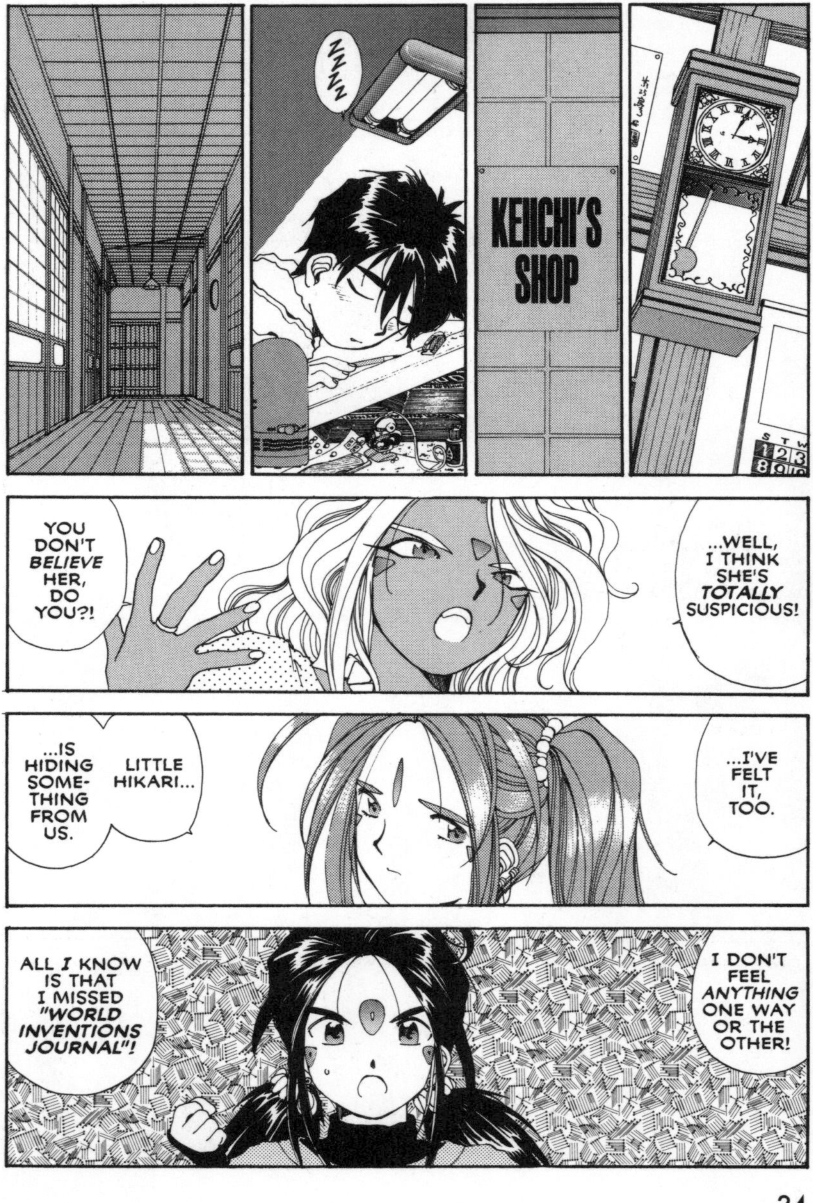
KENCHI'S SHOP
ZZZZ
...WELL, I THINK SHE'S *TOTALLY* SUSPICIOUS!
YOU DON'T *BELIEVE* HER, DO YOU?!
...I'VE FELT IT, TOO.
LITTLE HIKARI...
...IS HIDING SOMETHING FROM US.
I DON'T FEEL *ANYTHING* ONE WAY OR THE OTHER!
ALL *I* KNOW IS THAT I MISSED *"WORLD INVENTIONS JOURNAL"*!

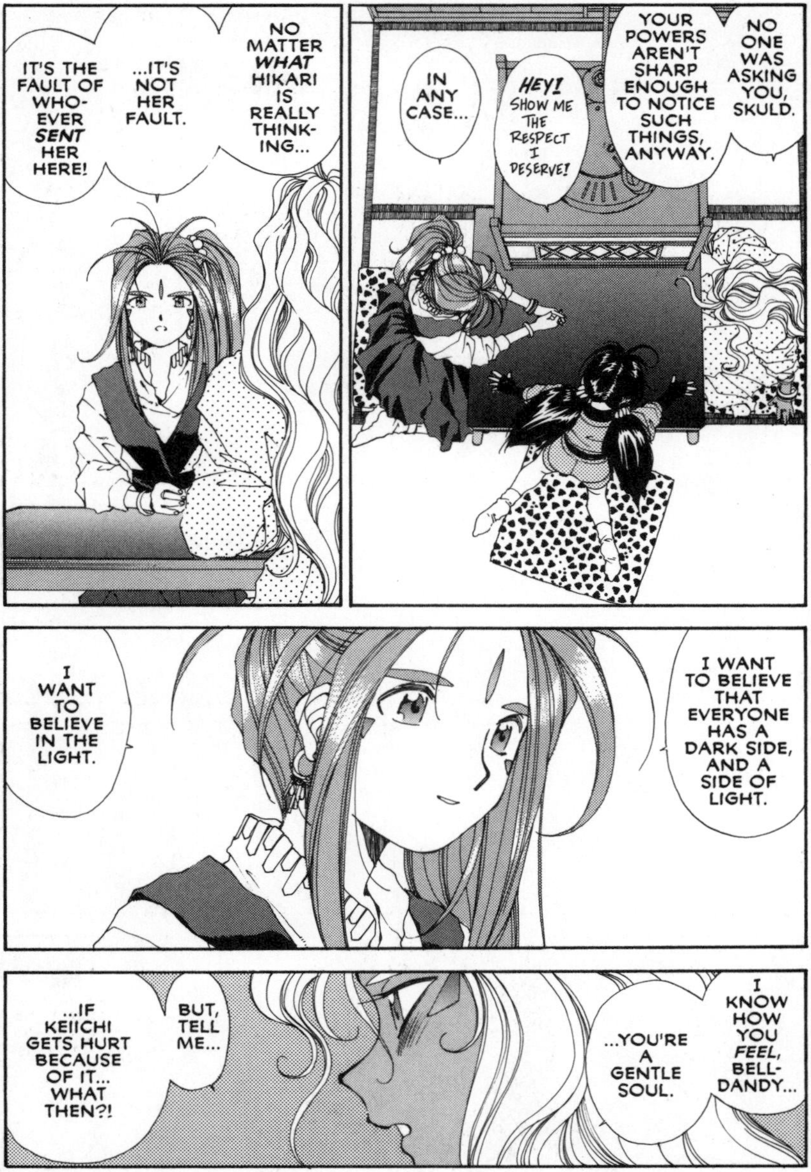
NO ONE WAS ASKING YOU, SKULD.
YOUR POWERS AREN'T SHARP ENOUGH TO NOTICE SUCH THINGS, ANYWAY.
HEY! SHOW ME THE RESPECT I DESERVE!
IN ANY CASE...
NO MATTER WHAT HIKARI IS REALLY THINKING...
...IT'S NOT HER FAULT.
IT'S THE FAULT OF WHO-EVER SENT HER HERE!
I WANT TO BELIEVE THAT EVERYONE HAS A DARK SIDE, AND A SIDE OF LIGHT.
I WANT TO BELIEVE IN THE LIGHT.
I KNOW HOW YOU FEEL, BELL-DANDY...
...YOU'RE A GENTLE SOUL.
BUT, TELL ME...
...IF KEIICHI GETS HURT BECAUSE OF IT... WHAT THEN?!

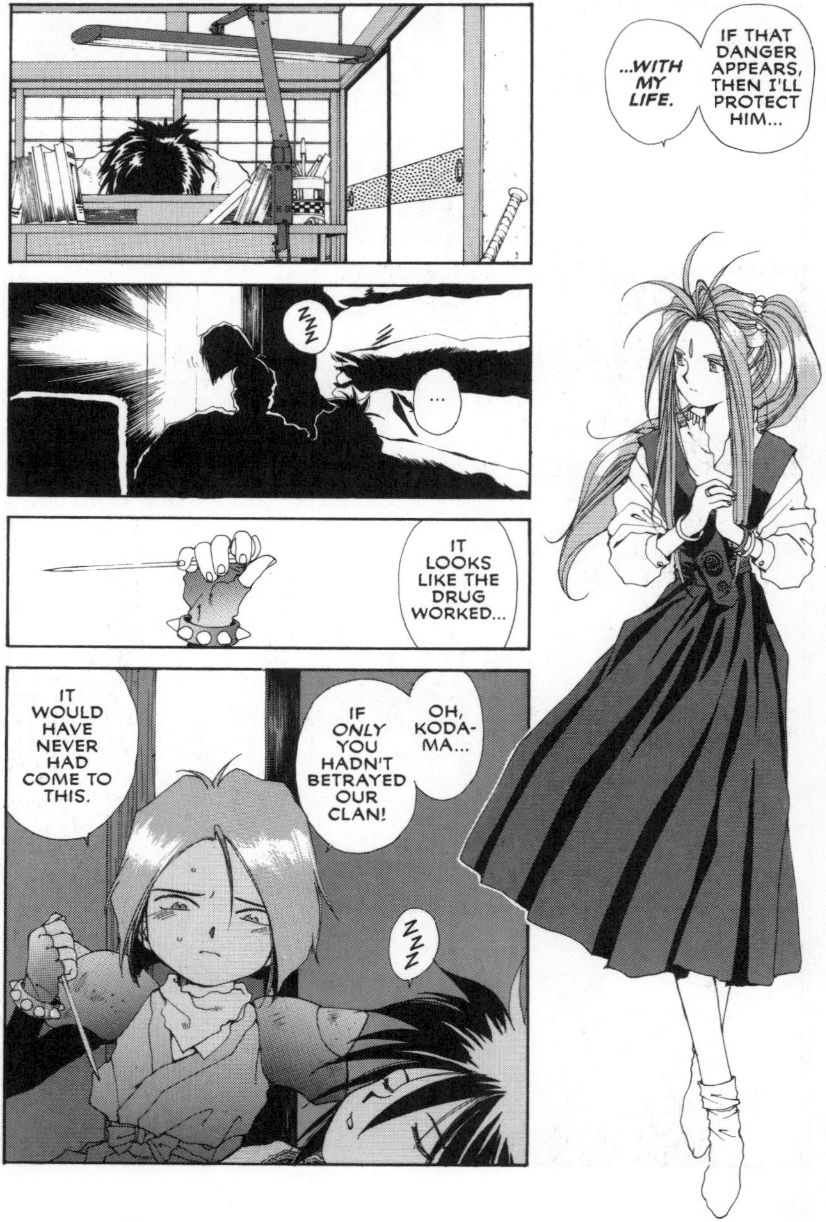
IF THAT DANGER APPEARS, THEN I'LL PROTECT HIM...
...*WITH MY LIFE.*
ZZZ
...
IT LOOKS LIKE THE DRUG WORKED...
OH, KODAMA...
IF *ONLY* YOU HADN'T BETRAYED OUR CLAN!
IT WOULD HAVE NEVER HAD COME TO THIS.
ZZZ

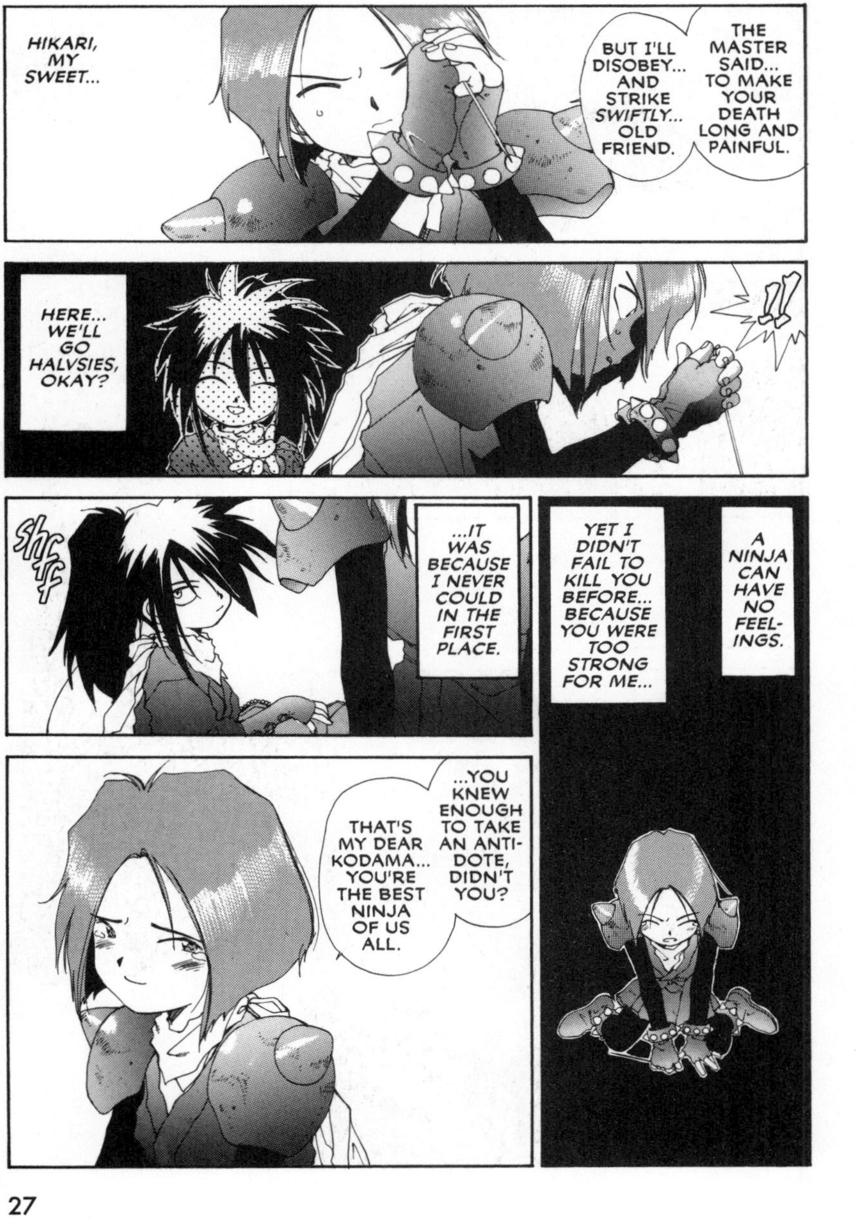
THE MASTER SAID... TO MAKE YOUR DEATH LONG AND PAINFUL.
BUT I'LL DISOBEY... AND STRIKE SWIFTLY... OLD FRIEND.
HIKARI, MY SWEET...
!!
HERE... WE'LL GO HALVSIES, OKAY?
A NINJA CAN HAVE NO FEEL-INGS.
YET I DIDN'T FAIL TO KILL YOU BEFORE... BECAUSE YOU WERE TOO STRONG FOR ME...
...IT WAS BECAUSE I NEVER COULD IN THE FIRST PLACE.
shff
...YOU KNEW ENOUGH TO TAKE AN ANTI-DOTE, DIDN'T YOU?
THAT'S MY DEAR KODAMA... YOU'RE THE BEST NINJA OF US ALL.

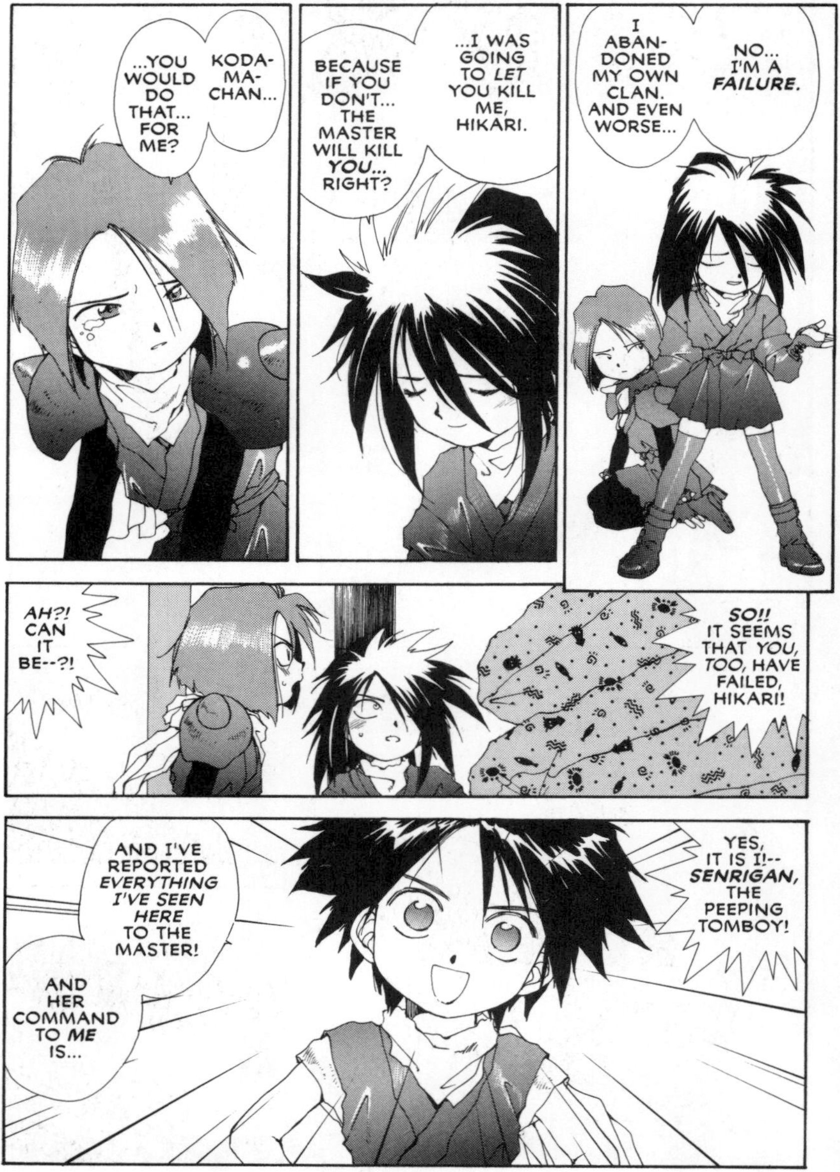
NO... I'M A *FAILURE.*
I ABANDONED MY OWN CLAN. AND EVEN WORSE...
...I WAS GOING TO *LET* YOU KILL ME, HIKARI.
BECAUSE IF YOU DON'T... THE MASTER WILL KILL *YOU...* RIGHT?
KODAMA-CHAN...
...YOU WOULD DO THAT... FOR ME?
SO!! IT SEEMS THAT *YOU, TOO,* HAVE FAILED, HIKARI!
AH?! CAN IT BE--?!
YES, IT IS I!-- *SENRIGAN,* THE PEEPING TOMBOY!
AND I'VE REPORTED *EVERYTHING I'VE SEEN HERE* TO THE MASTER!
AND HER COMMAND TO *ME* IS...

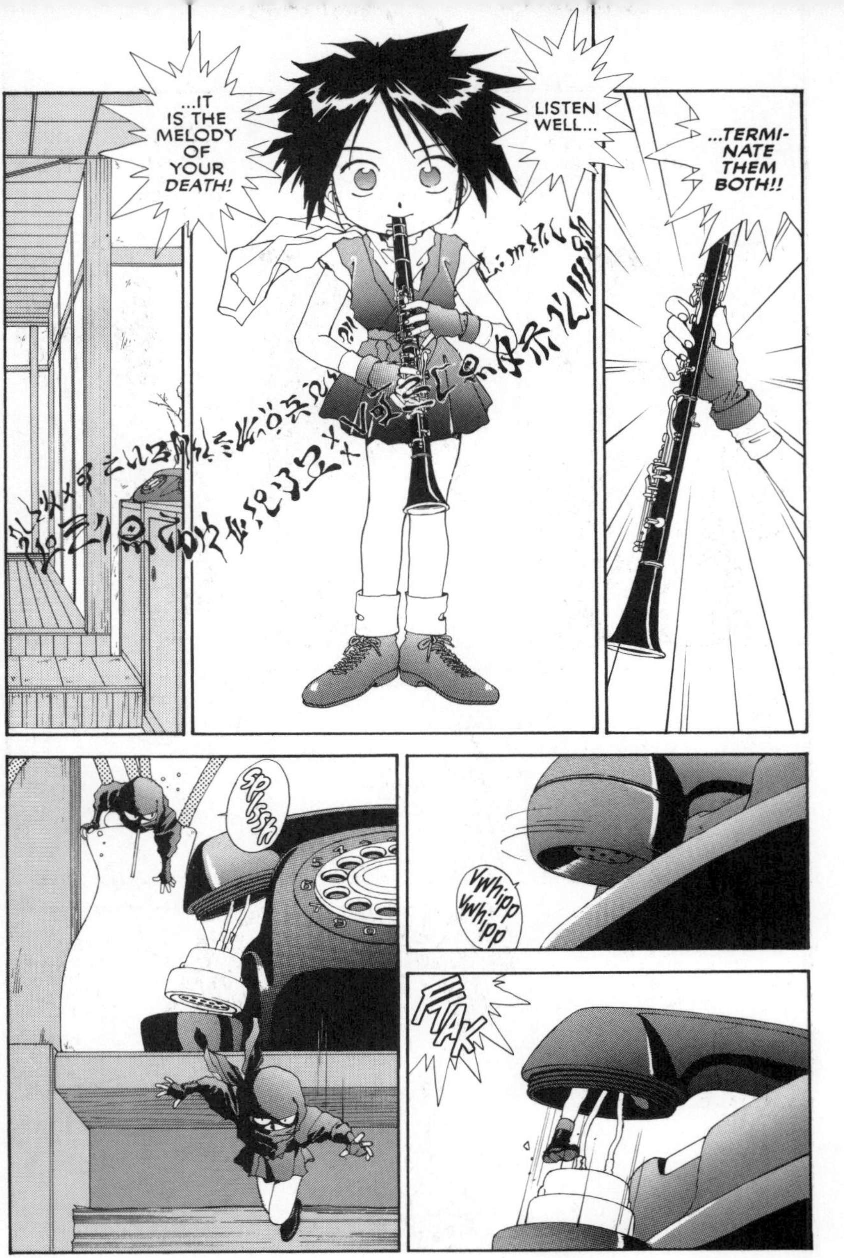

...TERMINATE THEM BOTH!!
LISTEN WELL...
...IT IS THE MELODY OF YOUR DEATH!
Vwhipp Vwhipp
FWAK
SPLISSH

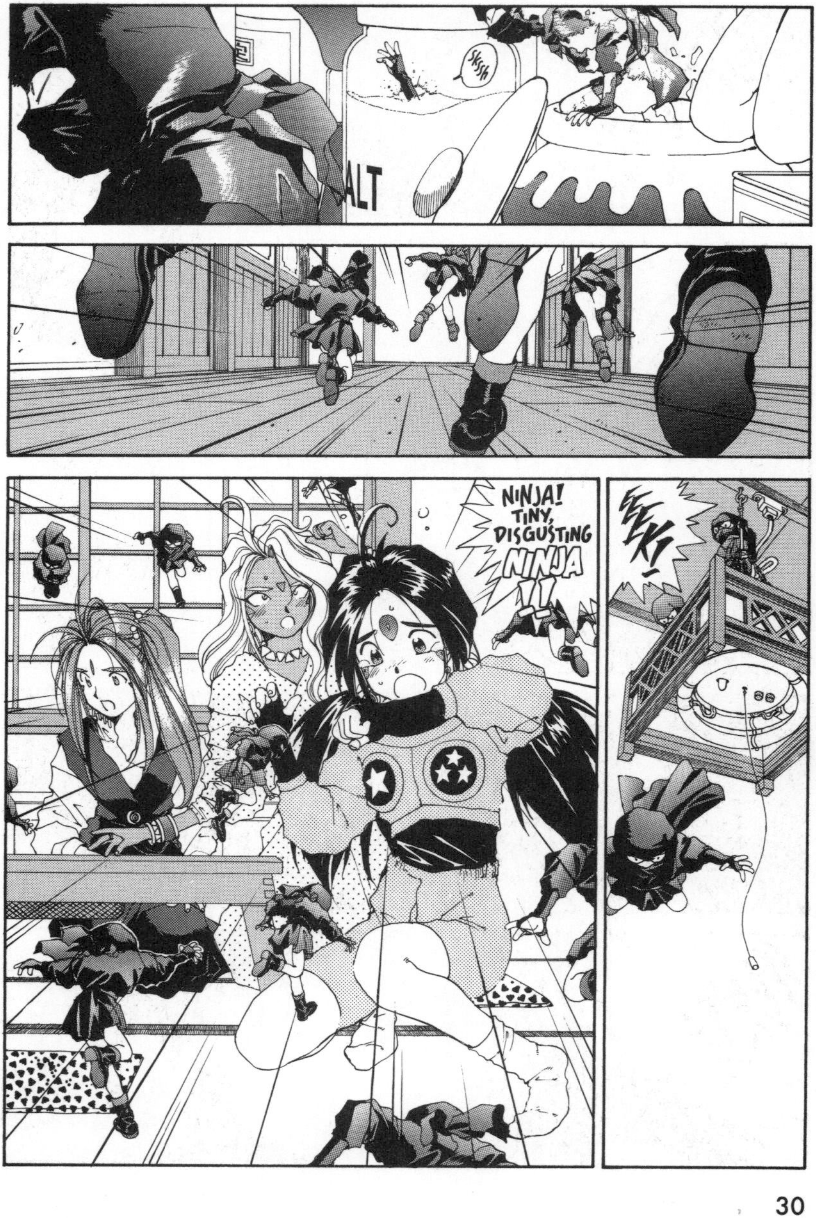

Skssh
ALT
EEEK!
NINJA! TINY, DISGUSTING NINJA!!

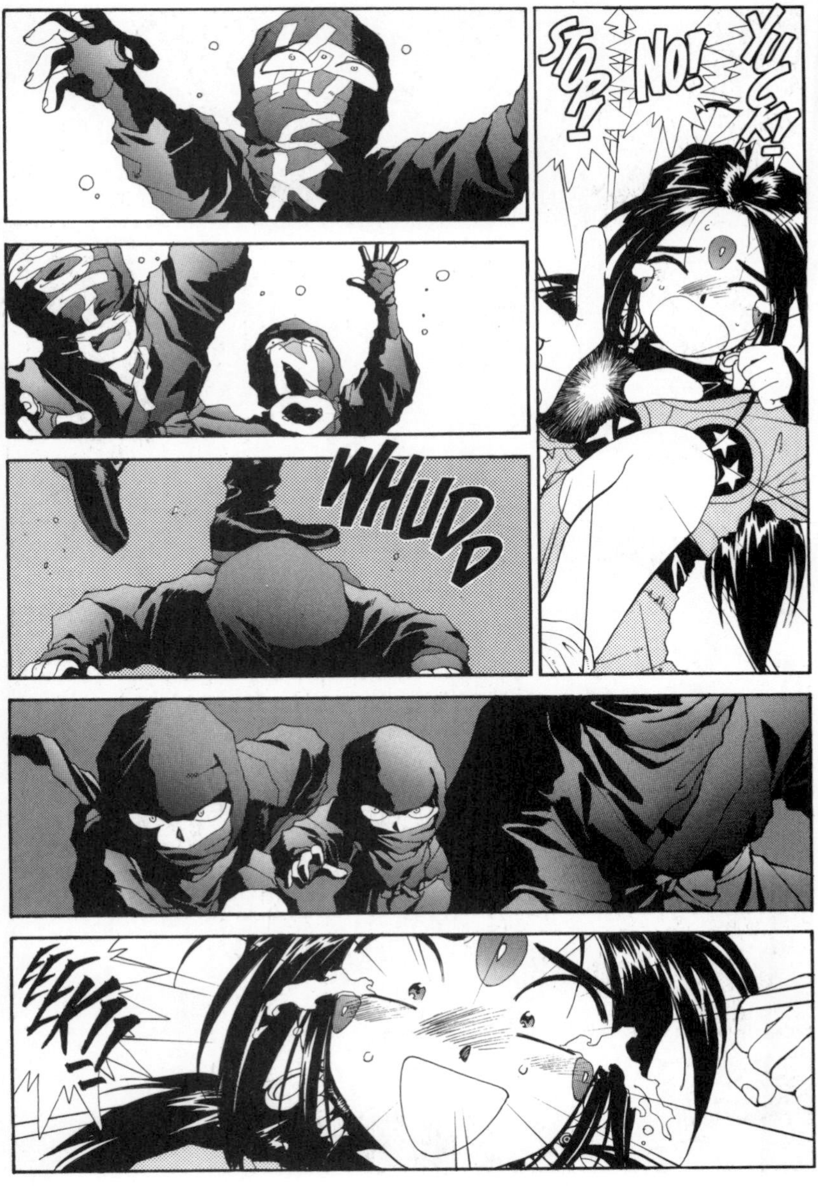
YUCK!
NO!
STOP!
HUCK
WHUDD
EEEK!!

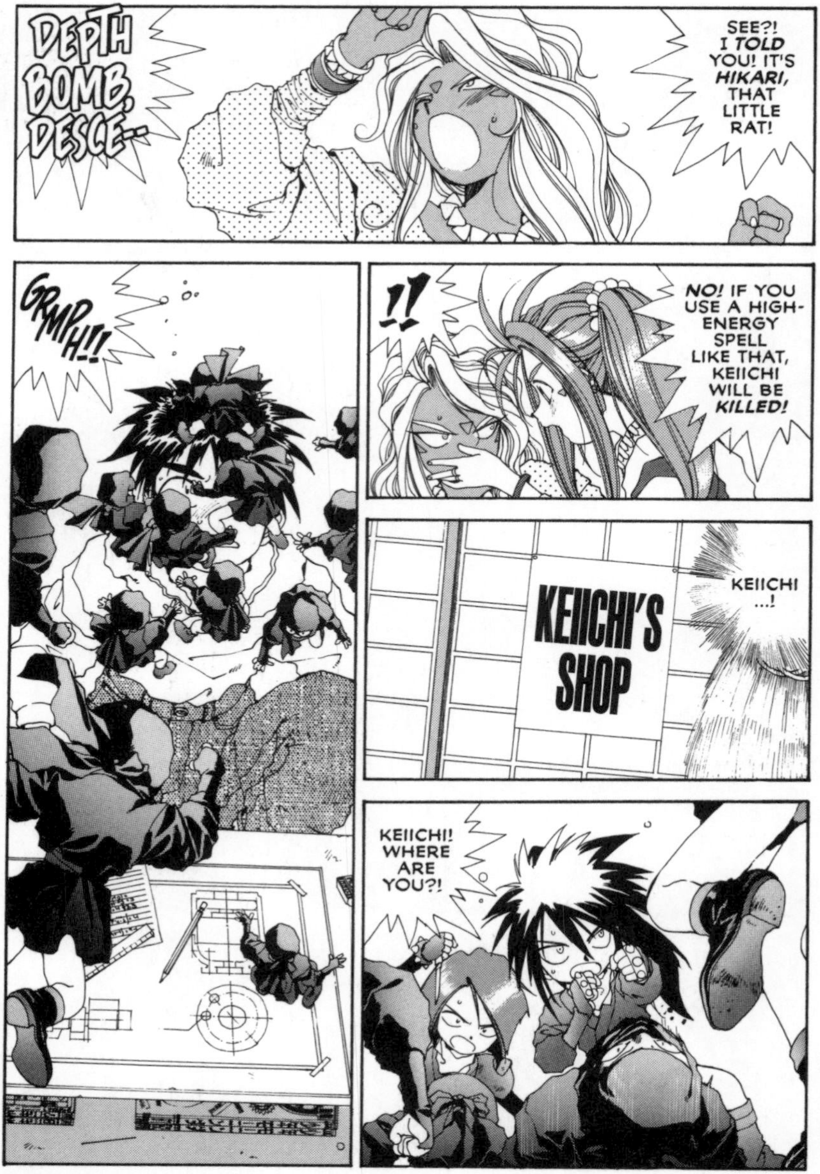
SEE?! I *TOLD* YOU! IT'S *HIKARI,* THAT LITTLE RAT!
DEPTH BOMB, DESCE--
NO! IF YOU USE A HIGH-ENERGY SPELL LIKE THAT, KEIICHI WILL BE *KILLED!*
!!
KEIICHI ...!
KEIICHI'S SHOP
KEIICHI! WHERE ARE YOU?!
GRMPH!!

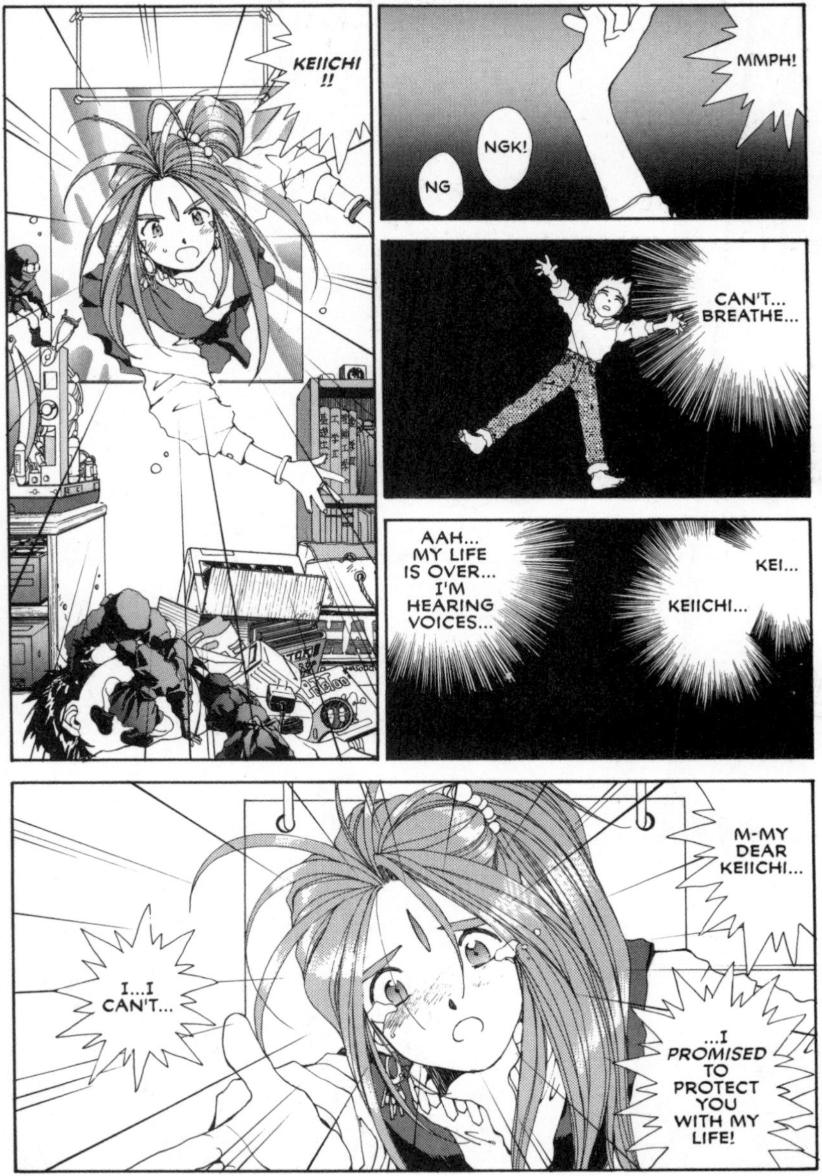
MMPH!
NGK!
NG
CAN'T... BREATHE...
KEI...
KEIICHI...
AAH... MY LIFE IS OVER... I'M HEARING VOICES...
KEIICHI !!
M-MY DEAR KEIICHI...
I...I CAN'T...
...I *PROMISED* TO PROTECT YOU WITH MY LIFE!

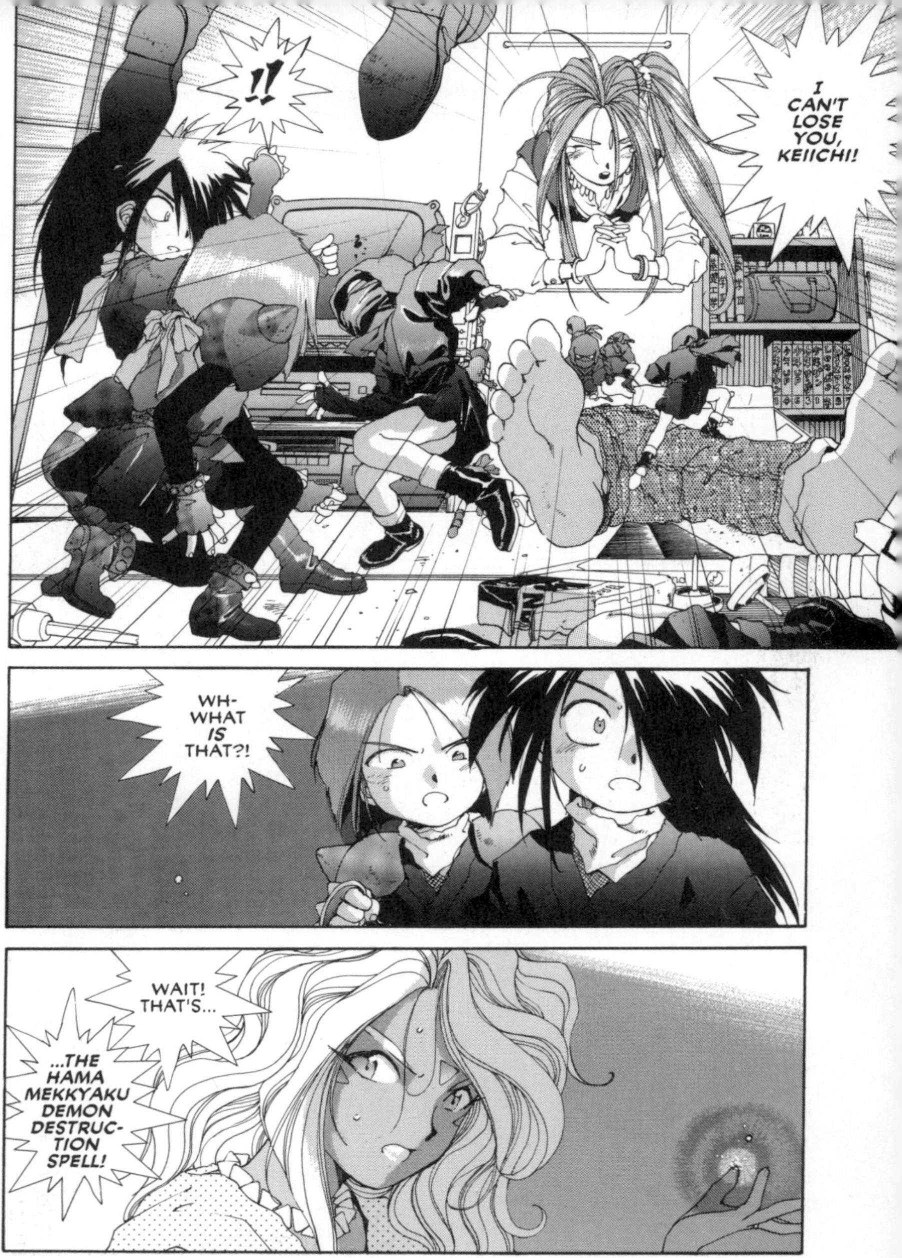
I CAN'T LOSE YOU, KEIICHI!
!!
WH- WHAT IS THAT?!
WAIT! THAT'S...
...THE HAMA MEKKYAKU DEMON DESTRUCTION SPELL!

▲URD WAS ATTEMPTING *DENKO GEKISHO*: A LOWER-LEVEL SUMMONING SPELL.

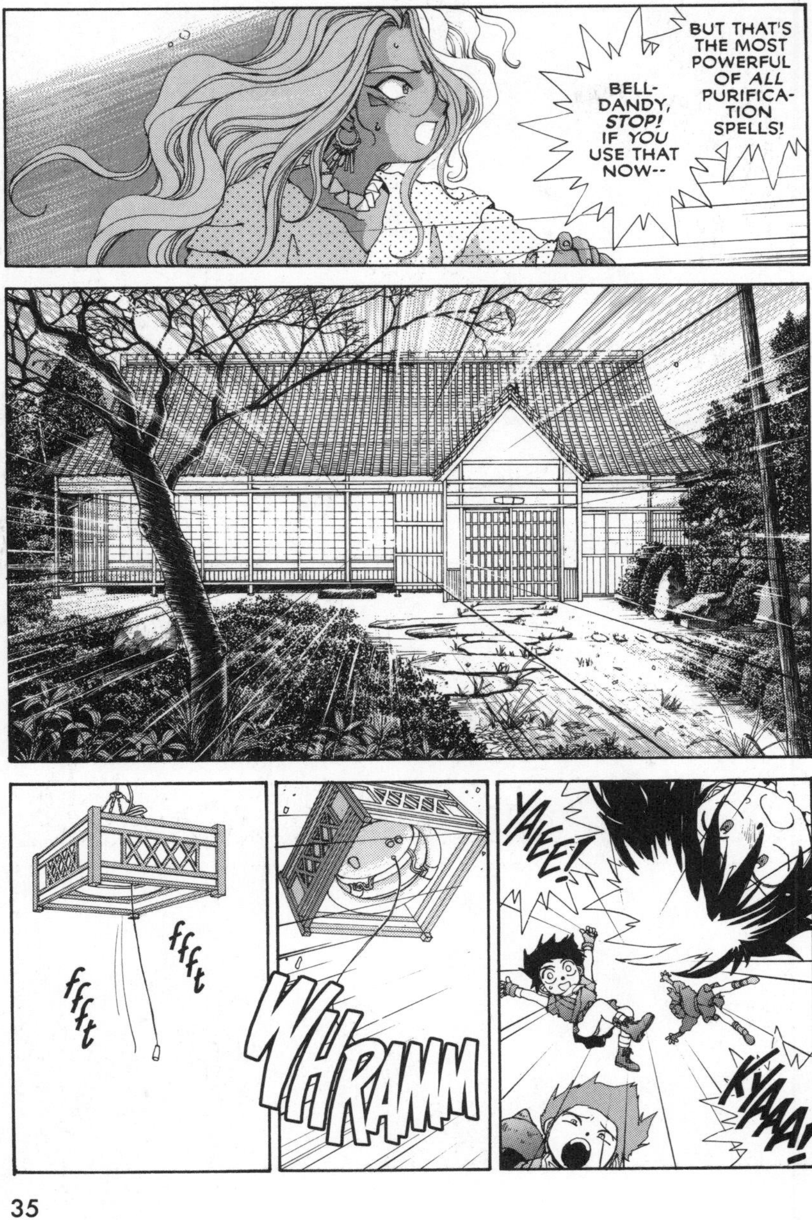
BUT THAT'S THE MOST POWERFUL OF ALL PURIFICATION SPELLS!
BELL-DANDY, STOP! IF YOU USE THAT NOW--
YAIEE!
KYAAA!
WHRAMMM
ffft
ffft

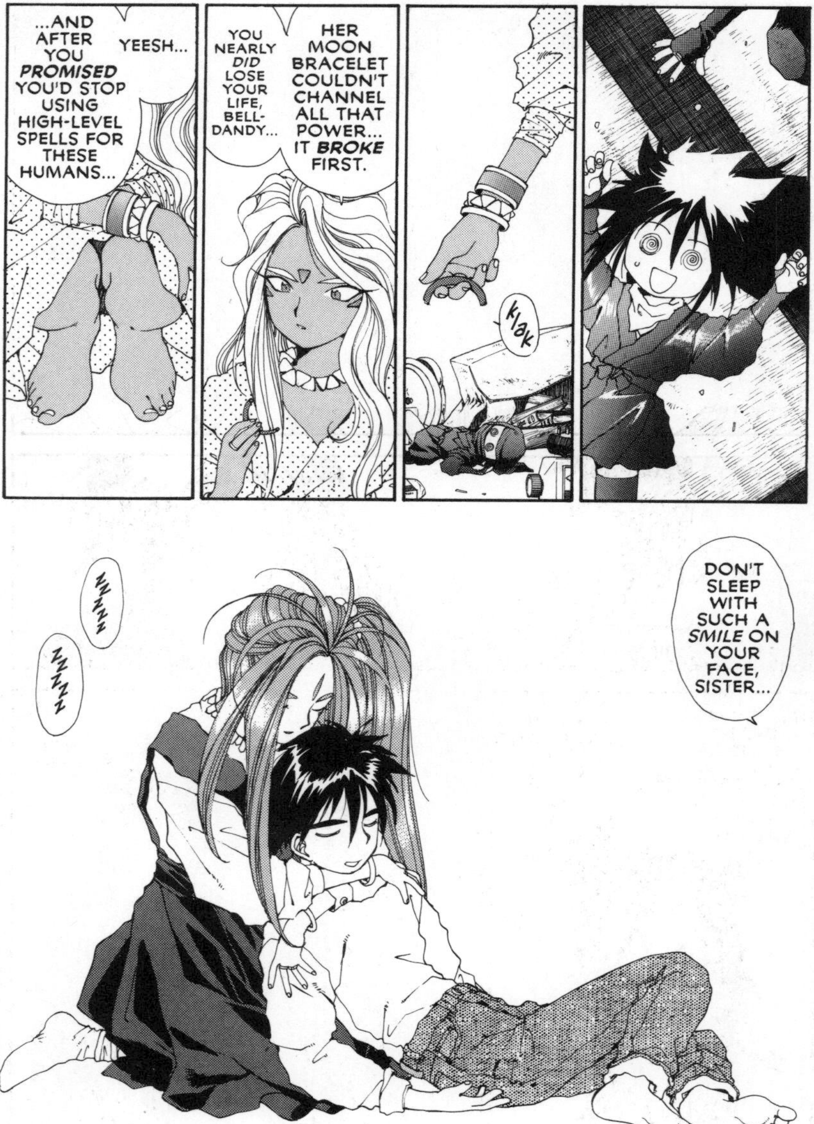
klak
HER MOON BRACELET COULDN'T CHANNEL ALL THAT POWER... IT *BROKE* FIRST.
YOU NEARLY *DID* LOSE YOUR LIFE, BELL-DANDY...
YEESH...
...AND AFTER YOU *PROMISED* YOU'D STOP USING HIGH-LEVEL SPELLS FOR THESE HUMANS...
DON'T SLEEP WITH SUCH A *SMILE* ON YOUR FACE, SISTER...
ZZZZZ
ZZZZZ

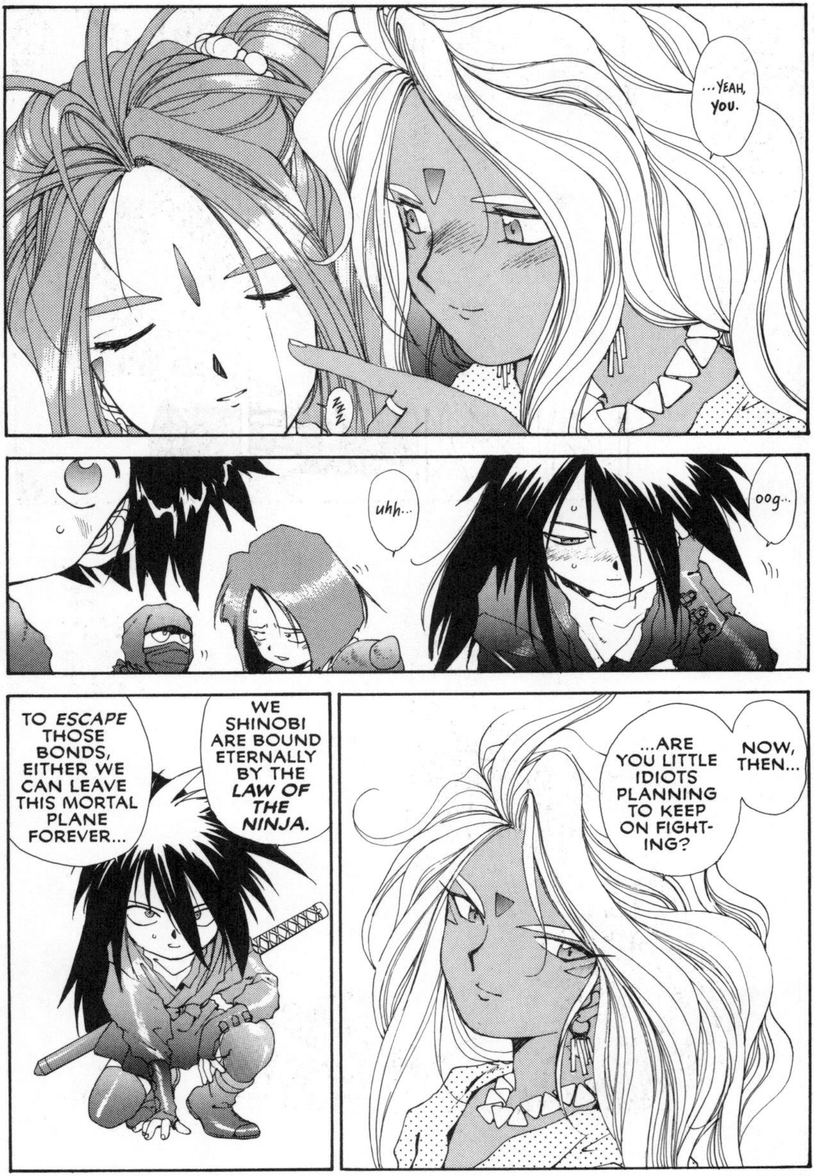
...YEAH, YOU.
zzz
oog...
uhh...
NOW, THEN...
...ARE YOU LITTLE IDIOTS PLANNING TO KEEP ON FIGHT-ING?
WE SHINOBI ARE BOUND ETERNALLY BY THE LAW OF THE NINJA.
TO ESCAPE THOSE BONDS, EITHER WE CAN LEAVE THIS MORTAL PLANE FOREVER...

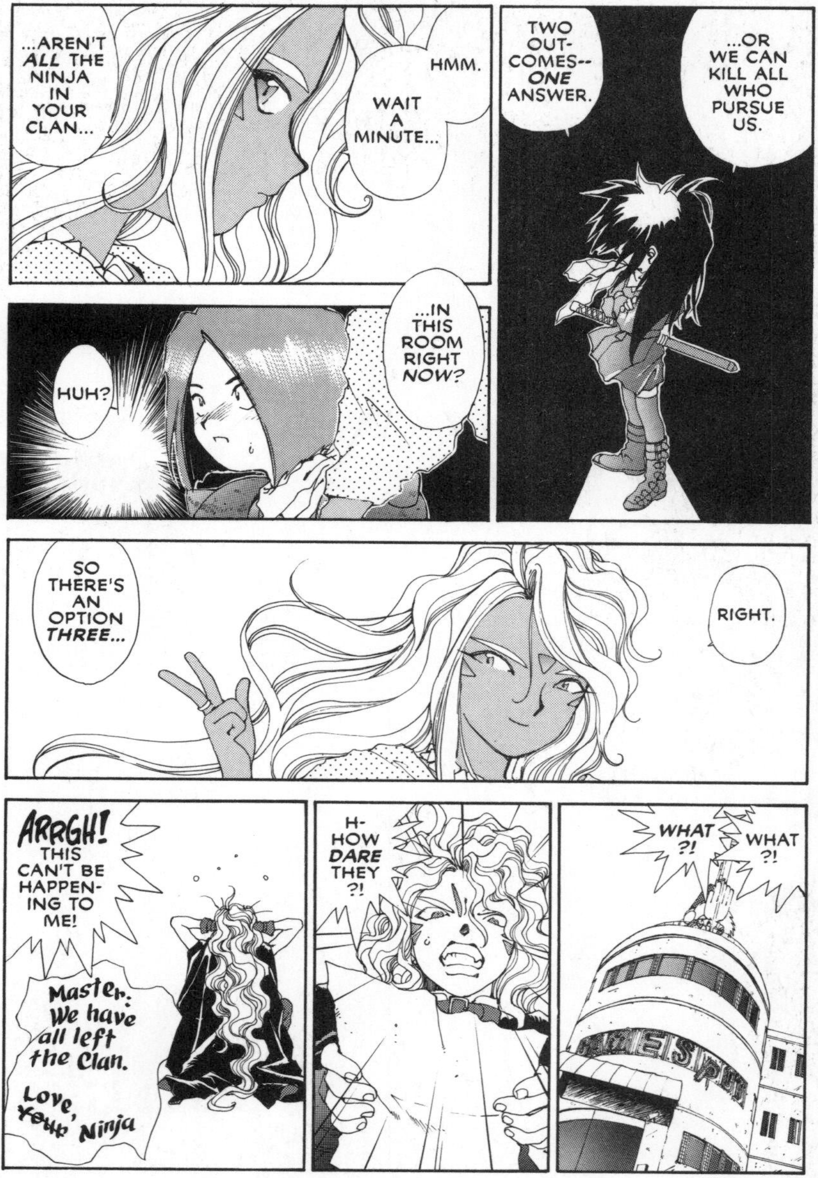

...OR WE CAN KILL ALL WHO PURSUE US.
TWO OUT-COMES--*ONE* ANSWER.
HMM.
WAIT A MINUTE...
...AREN'T *ALL* THE NINJA IN YOUR CLAN...
...IN THIS ROOM RIGHT *NOW?*
HUH?
RIGHT.
SO THERE'S AN OPTION *THREE...*
WHAT ?!
WHAT ?!
H-HOW *DARE* THEY ?!
ARRGH! THIS CAN'T BE HAPPEN-ING TO ME!
Master: We have all left the Clan.
Love, Your Ninja

CHAPTER 54

Together for Never

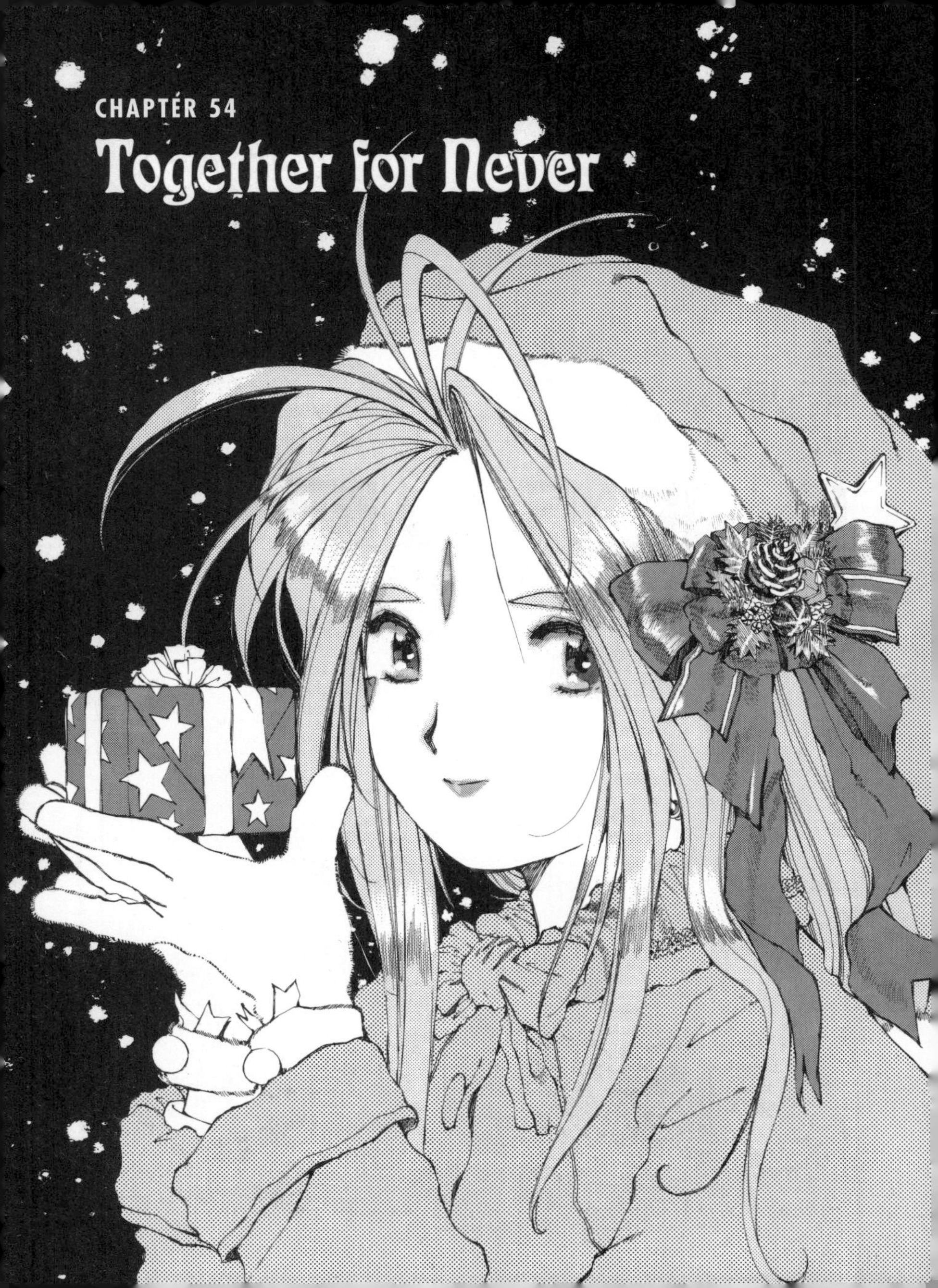

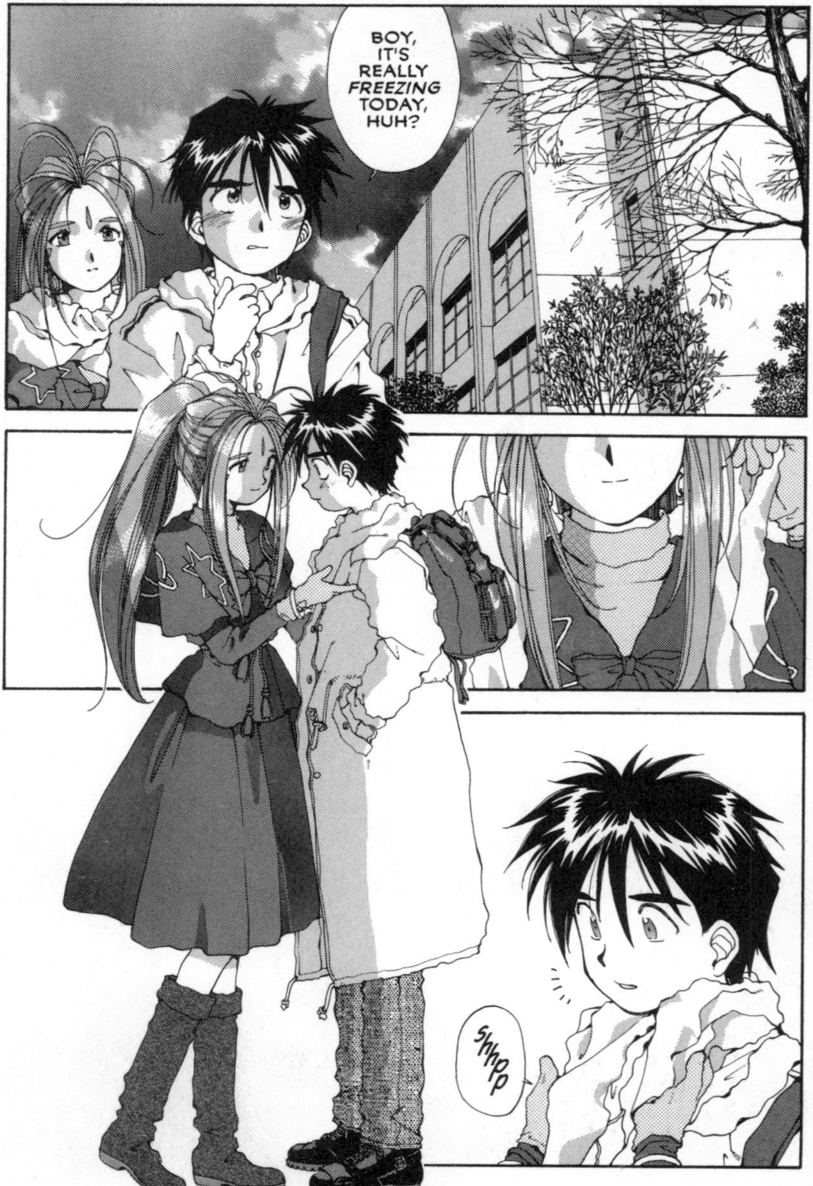
BOY, IT'S REALLY *FREEZING* TODAY, HUH?
SHHPP

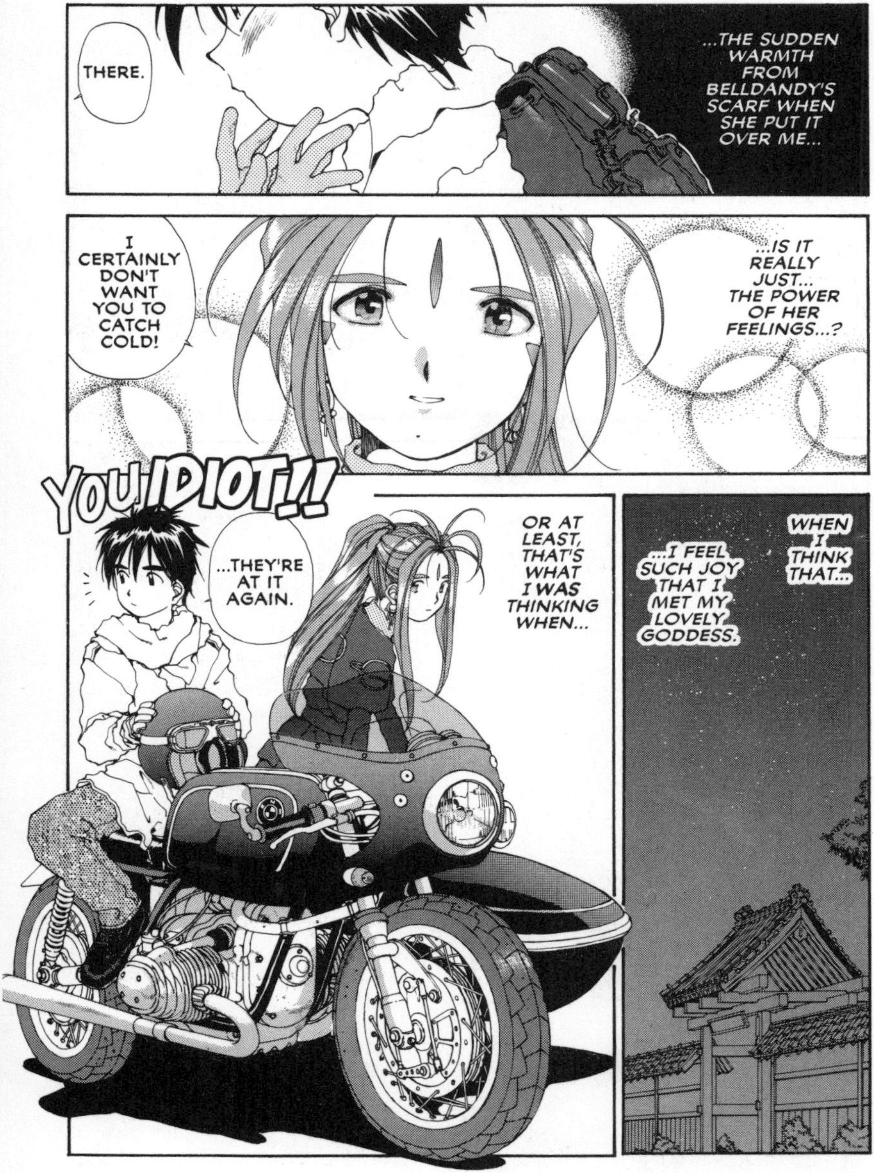
...THE SUDDEN WARMTH FROM BELLDANDY'S SCARF WHEN SHE PUT IT OVER ME...
THERE.
...IS IT REALLY JUST... THE POWER OF HER FEELINGS...?
I CERTAINLY DON'T WANT YOU TO CATCH COLD!
WHEN I THINK THAT...
...I FEEL SUCH JOY THAT I MET MY LOVELY GODDESS.
OR AT LEAST, THAT'S WHAT I WAS THINKING WHEN...
YOU IDIOT!!
...THEY'RE AT IT AGAIN.

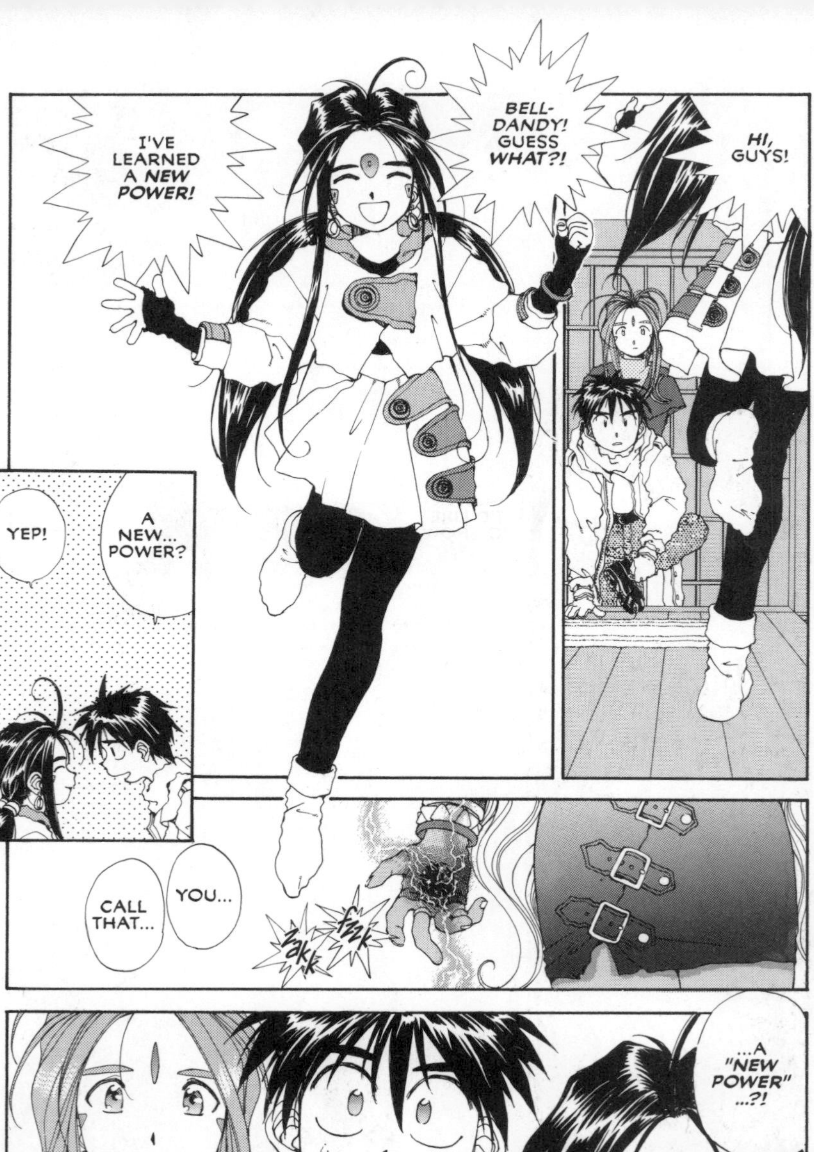
HI, GUYS!
BELL-DANDY! GUESS WHAT?!
I'VE LEARNED A NEW POWER!
A NEW... POWER?
YEP!
YOU...
CALL THAT...
fzzk
zakk
...A "NEW POWER" ...?!

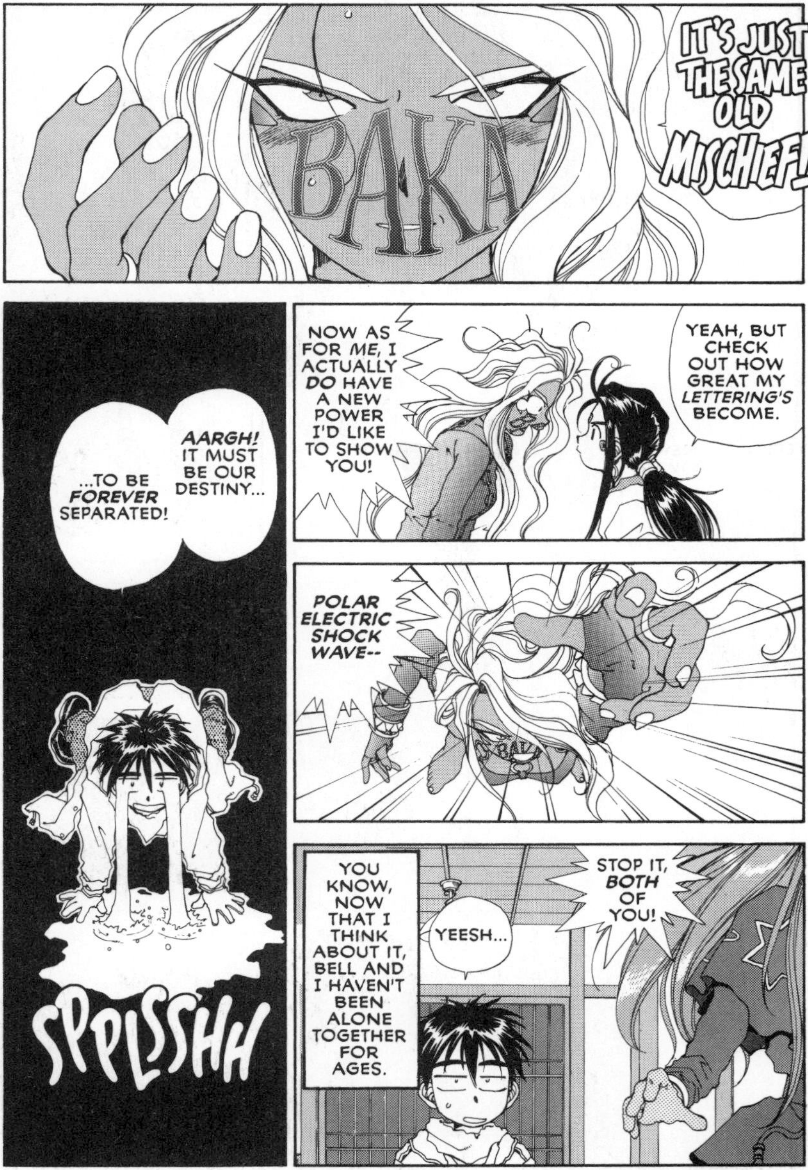
IT'S JUST THE SAME OLD MISCHIEF!
BAKA
YEAH, BUT CHECK OUT HOW GREAT MY *LETTERING'S* BECOME.
NOW AS FOR *ME*, I ACTUALLY *DO* HAVE A NEW POWER I'D LIKE TO SHOW YOU!
POLAR ELECTRIC SHOCK WAVE--
STOP IT, *BOTH* OF YOU!
YEESH...
YOU KNOW, NOW THAT I THINK ABOUT IT, BELL AND I HAVEN'T BEEN ALONE TOGETHER FOR AGES.
AARGH! IT MUST BE OUR DESTINY...
...TO BE *FOREVER* SEPARATED!
SPPLSSHH

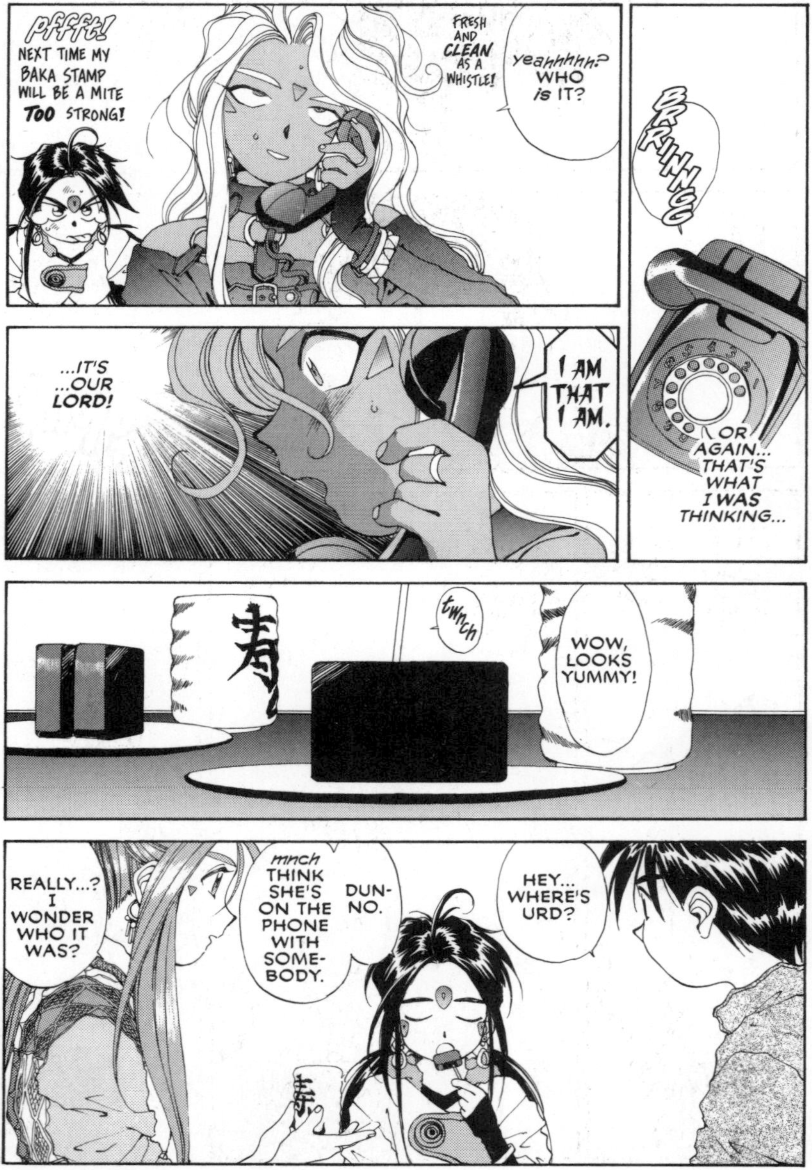
BRRINNGG
OR AGAIN... THAT'S WHAT I WAS THINKING...
yeahhhhh? WHO is IT?
FRESH AND CLEAN AS A WHISTLE!
pfffft!
NEXT TIME MY BAKA STAMP WILL BE A MITE TOO STRONG!
I AM THAT I AM.
...IT'S ...OUR LORD!
twnch
WOW, LOOKS YUMMY!
HEY... WHERE'S URD?
DUN-NO.
mnch
THINK SHE'S ON THE PHONE WITH SOME-BODY.
REALLY...? I WONDER WHO IT WAS?

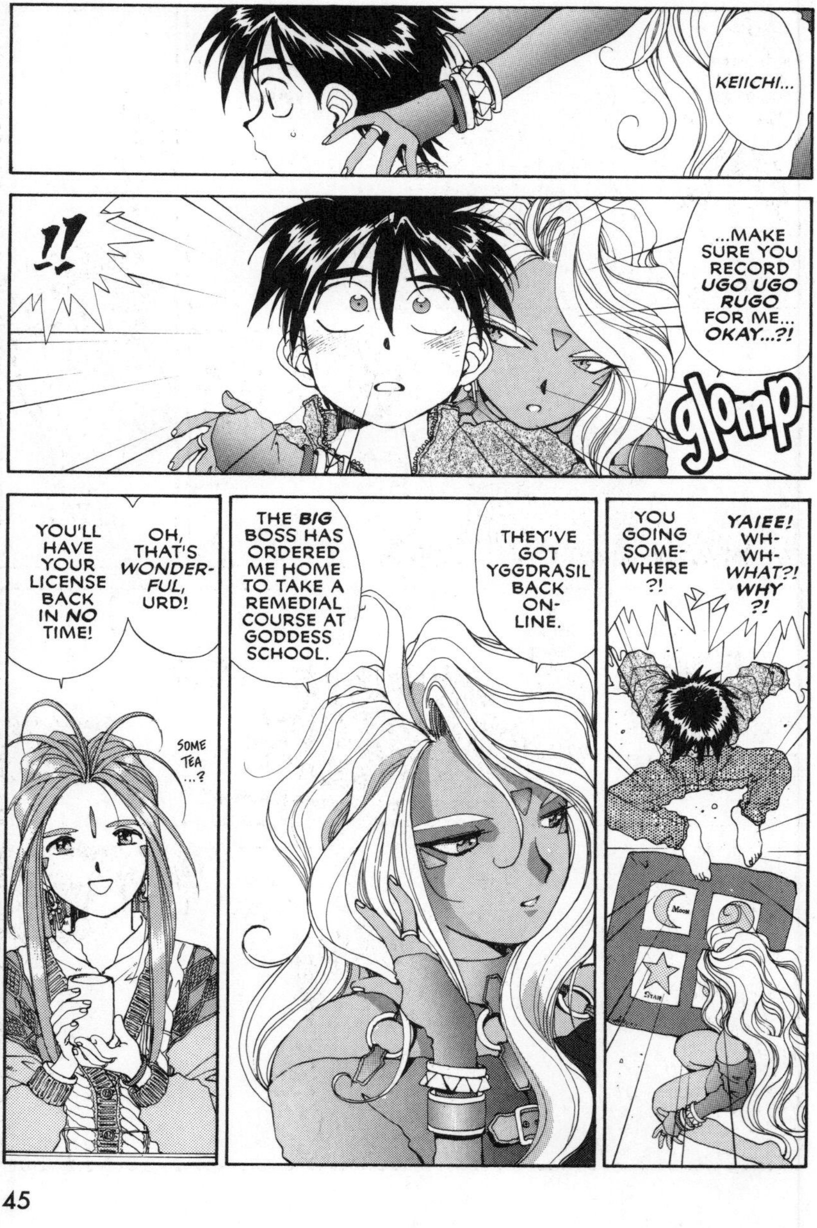
KEIICHI...
...MAKE SURE YOU RECORD UGO UGO RUGO FOR ME... OKAY...?!
glomp
!!
YAIEE! WH-WH-WHAT?! WHY?!
YOU GOING SOME-WHERE?!
THEY'VE GOT YGGDRASIL BACK ON-LINE.
THE BIG BOSS HAS ORDERED ME HOME TO TAKE A REMEDIAL COURSE AT GODDESS SCHOOL.
OH, THAT'S WONDER-FUL, URD!
YOU'LL HAVE YOUR LICENSE BACK IN NO TIME!
SOME TEA ...?

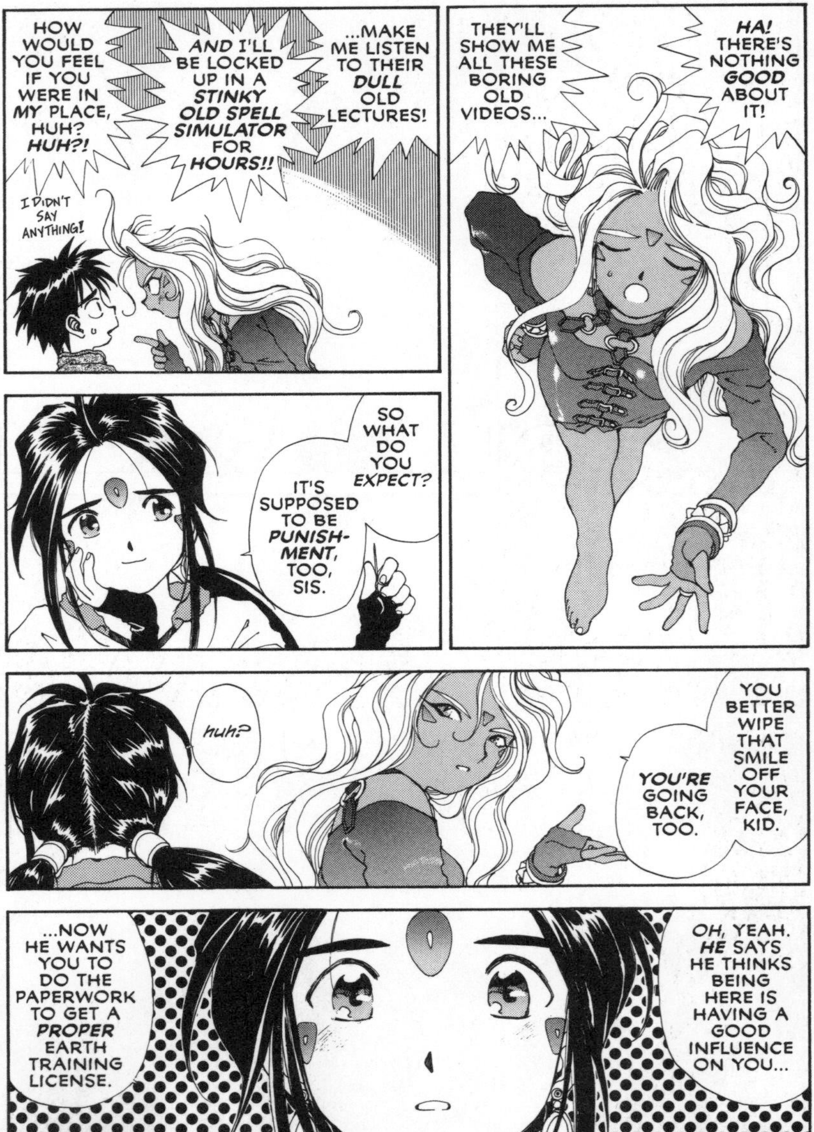
HA! THERE'S NOTHING GOOD ABOUT IT!
THEY'LL SHOW ME ALL THESE BORING OLD VIDEOS...
...MAKE ME LISTEN TO THEIR DULL OLD LECTURES!
AND I'LL BE LOCKED UP IN A STINKY OLD SPELL SIMULATOR FOR HOURS!!
HOW WOULD YOU FEEL IF YOU WERE IN MY PLACE, HUH? HUH?!
I DIDN'T SAY ANYTHING!
SO WHAT DO YOU EXPECT?
IT'S SUPPOSED TO BE PUNISHMENT, TOO, SIS.
YOU BETTER WIPE THAT SMILE OFF YOUR FACE, KID.
YOU'RE GOING BACK, TOO.
huh?
OH, YEAH. HE SAYS HE THINKS BEING HERE IS HAVING A GOOD INFLUENCE ON YOU...
...NOW HE WANTS YOU TO DO THE PAPERWORK TO GET A PROPER EARTH TRAINING LICENSE.

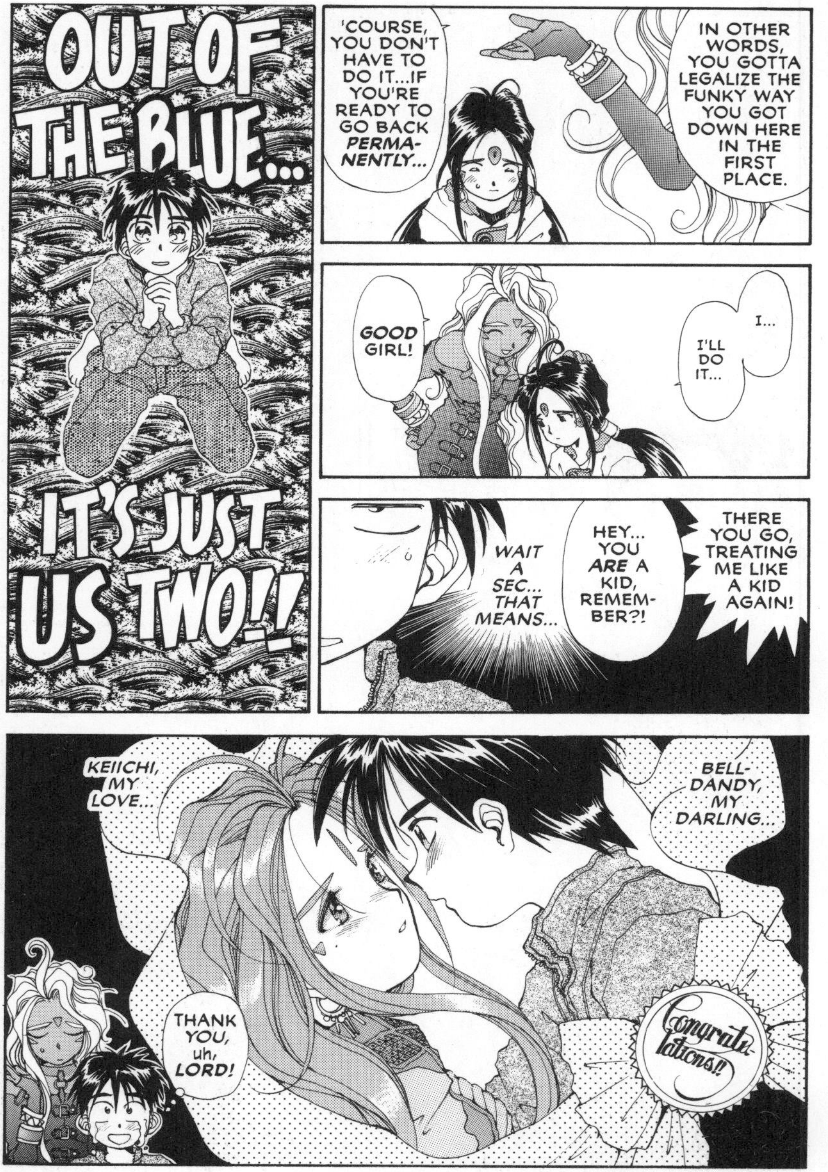
IN OTHER WORDS, YOU GOTTA LEGALIZE THE FUNKY WAY YOU GOT DOWN HERE IN THE FIRST PLACE.
'COURSE, YOU DON'T HAVE TO DO IT...IF YOU'RE READY TO GO BACK PERMANENTLY...
I...
I'LL DO IT...
GOOD GIRL!
THERE YOU GO, TREATING ME LIKE A KID AGAIN!
HEY... YOU ARE A KID, REMEMBER?!
WAIT A SEC... THAT MEANS...
OUT OF THE BLUE...
IT'S JUST US TWO!!
BELLDANDY, MY DARLING...
KEIICHI, MY LOVE...
Congratulations!!
THANK YOU, uh, LORD!

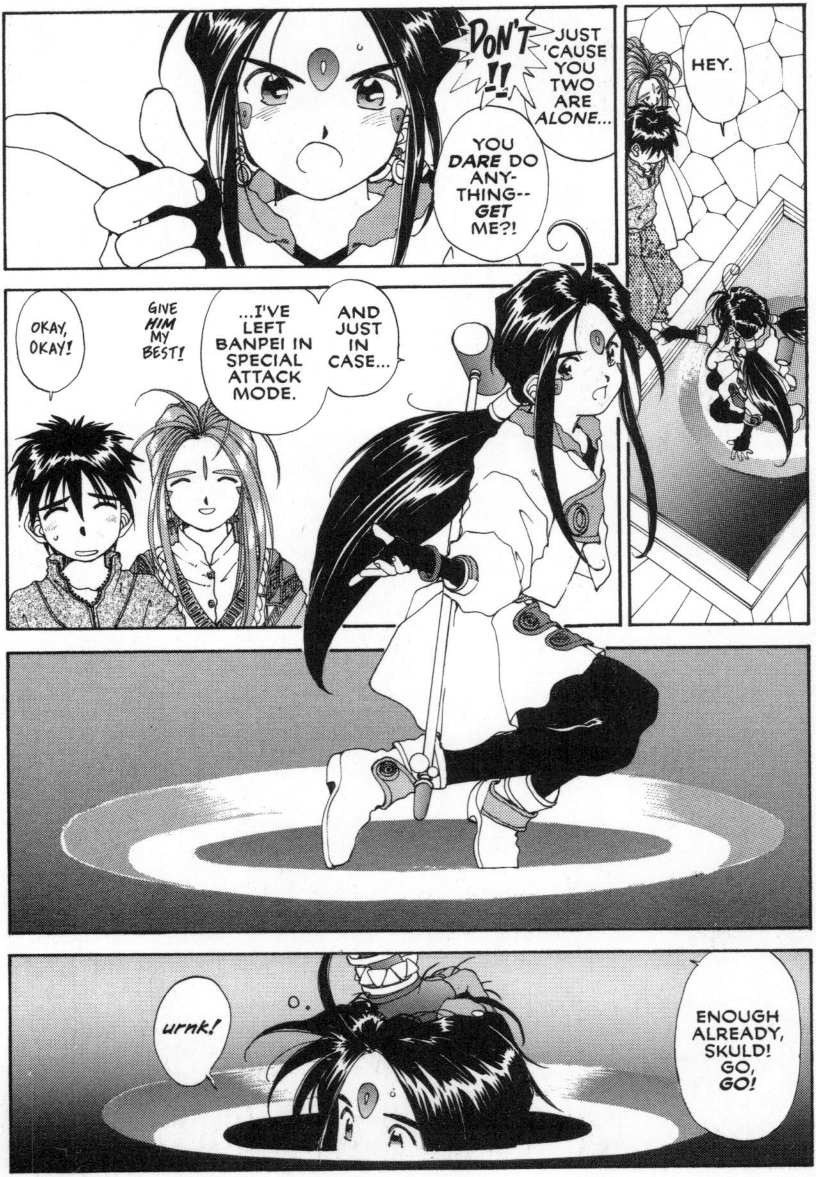
HEY.
DON'T!!
JUST 'CAUSE YOU TWO ARE ALONE...
YOU DARE DO ANYTHING-- GET ME?!
AND JUST IN CASE...
...I'VE LEFT BANPEI IN SPECIAL ATTACK MODE.
GIVE HIM MY BEST!
OKAY, OKAY!
ENOUGH ALREADY, SKULD! GO, GO!
urnk!

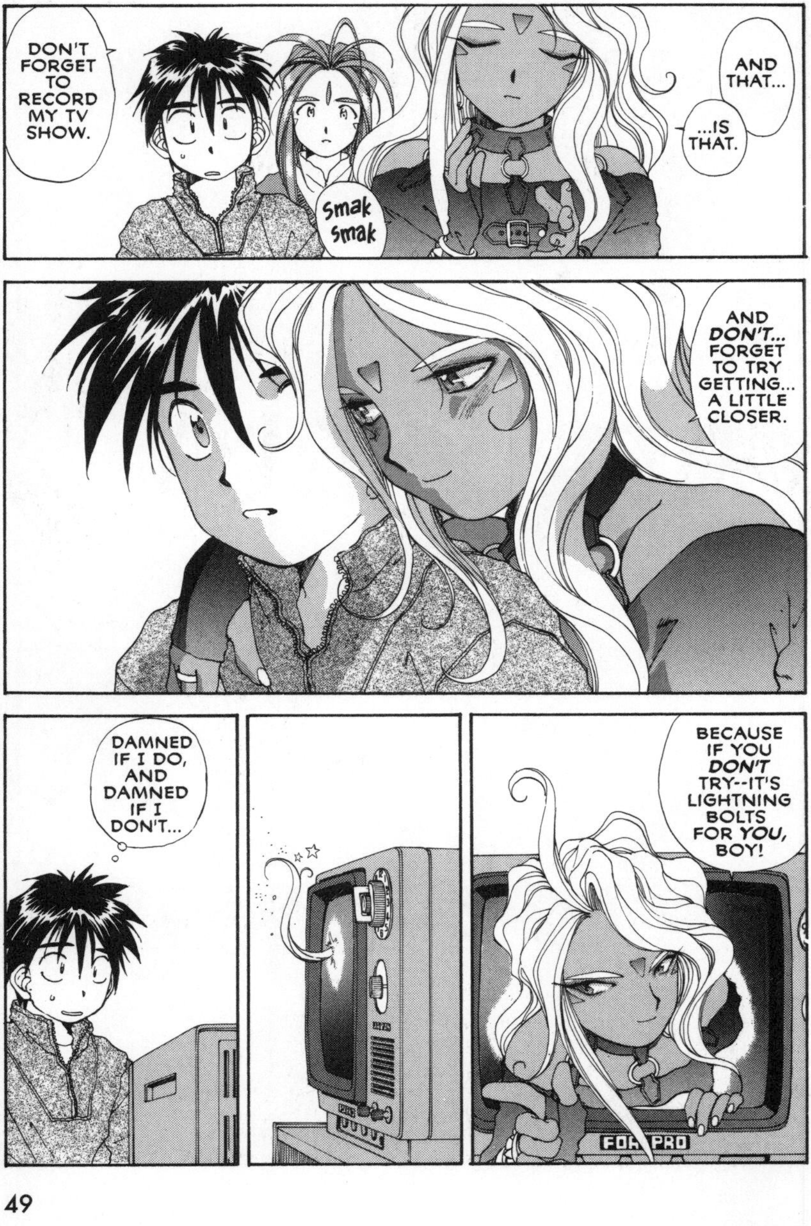
AND THAT...
...IS THAT.
DON'T FORGET TO RECORD MY TV SHOW.
Smak Smak
AND *DON'T*... FORGET TO TRY GETTING... A LITTLE CLOSER.
BECAUSE IF YOU *DON'T* TRY--IT'S LIGHTNING BOLTS FOR *YOU*, BOY!
DAMNED IF I DO, AND DAMNED IF I DON'T...

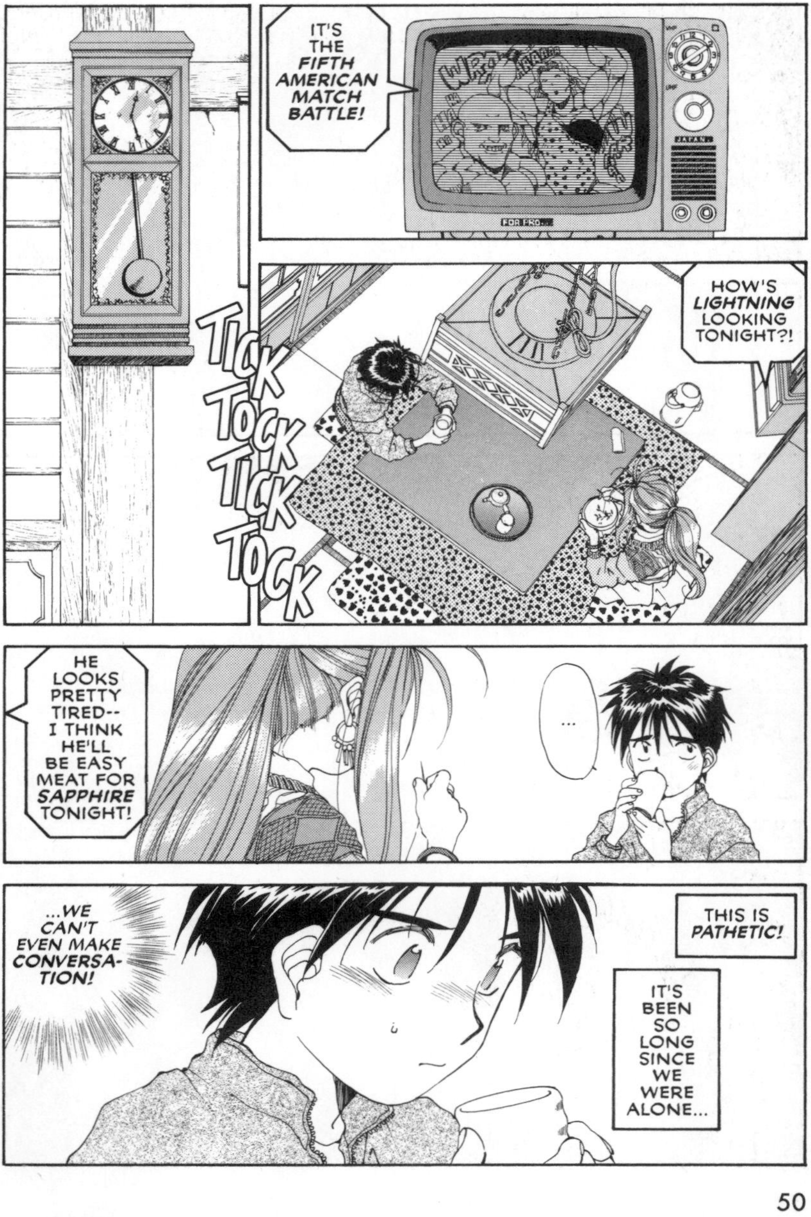
IT'S THE FIFTH AMERICAN MATCH BATTLE!
HOW'S LIGHTNING LOOKING TONIGHT?!
TICK TOCK TICK TOCK
...
HE LOOKS PRETTY TIRED-- I THINK HE'LL BE EASY MEAT FOR SAPPHIRE TONIGHT!
THIS IS PATHETIC!
IT'S BEEN SO LONG SINCE WE WERE ALONE...
...WE CAN'T EVEN MAKE CONVERSATION!

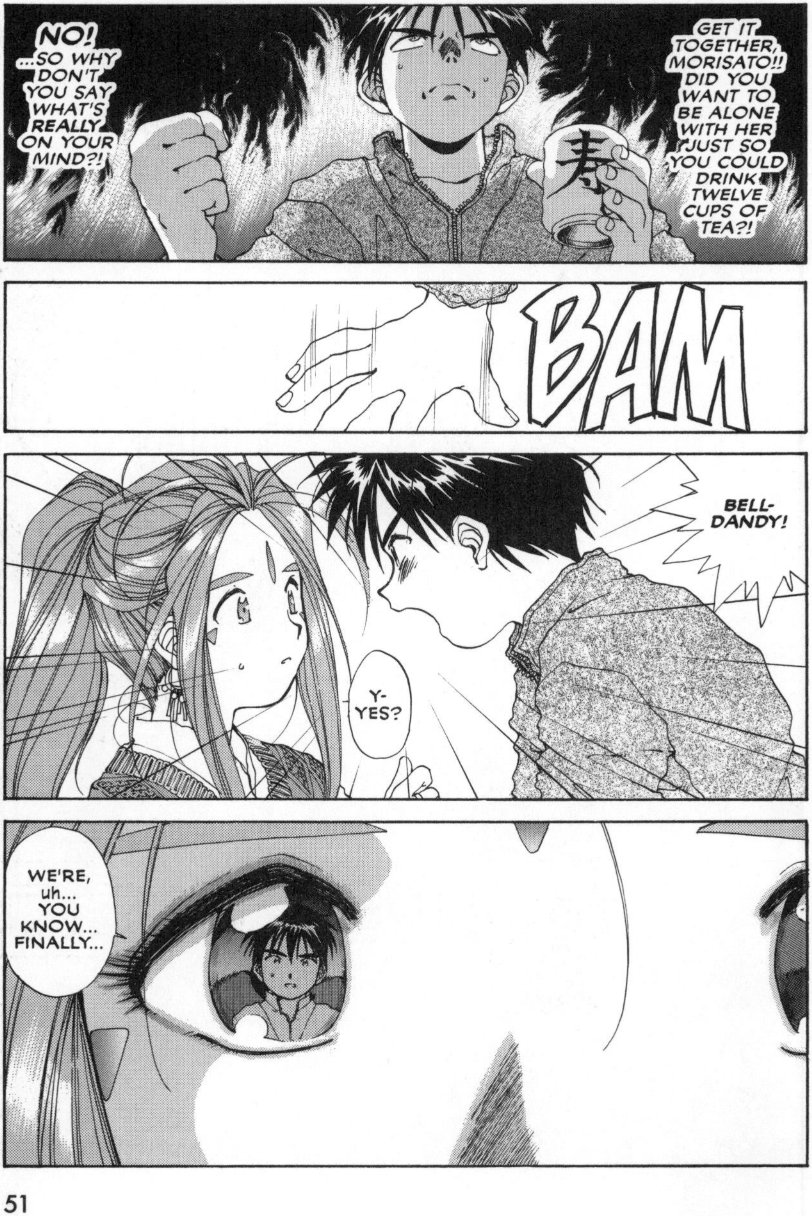

GET IT TOGETHER, MORISATO!! DID YOU WANT TO BE ALONE WITH HER JUST SO YOU COULD DRINK TWELVE CUPS OF TEA?!
NO! ...SO WHY DON'T YOU SAY WHAT'S REALLY ON YOUR MIND?!
BAM
BELL-DANDY!
Y-YES?
WE'RE, uh... YOU KNOW... FINALLY...

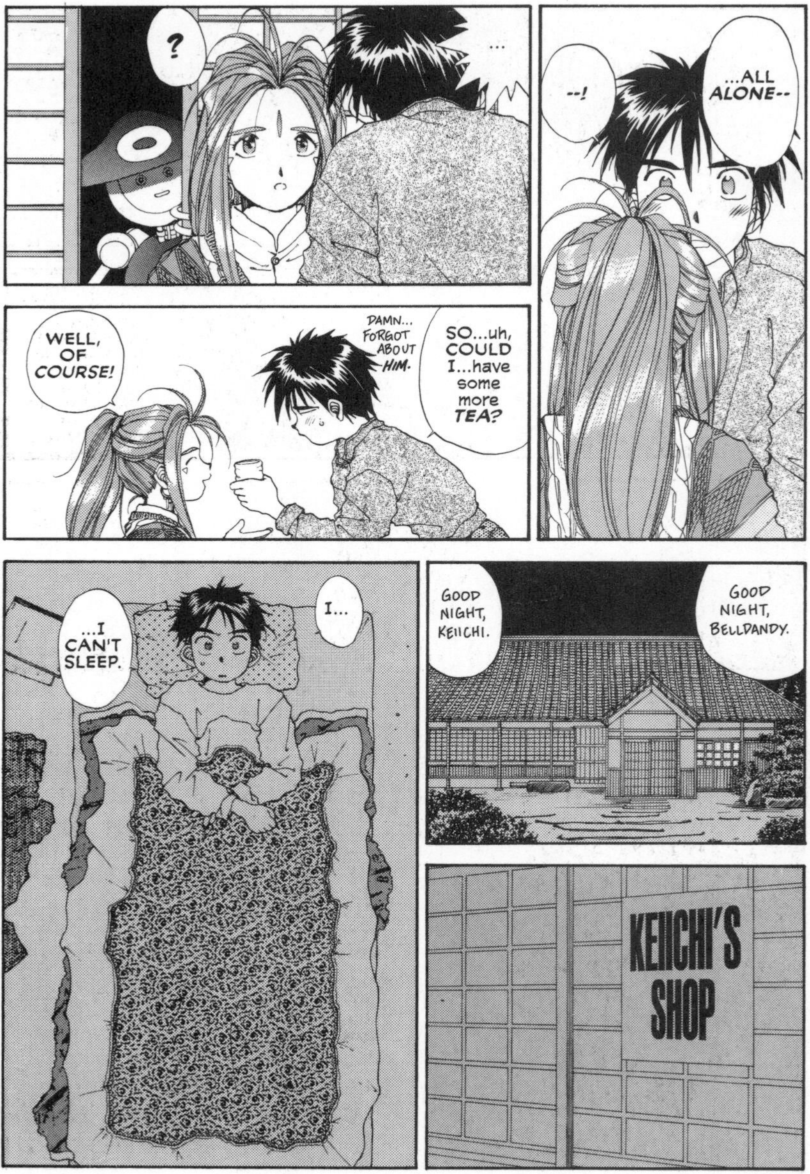
...ALL ALONE--
--!
...
?
SO...uh, COULD I...have some more TEA?
DAMN... FORGOT ABOUT HIM.
WELL, OF COURSE!
GOOD NIGHT, BELLDANDY.
GOOD NIGHT, KEIICHI.
KEIICHI'S SHOP
I...
...I CAN'T SLEEP.

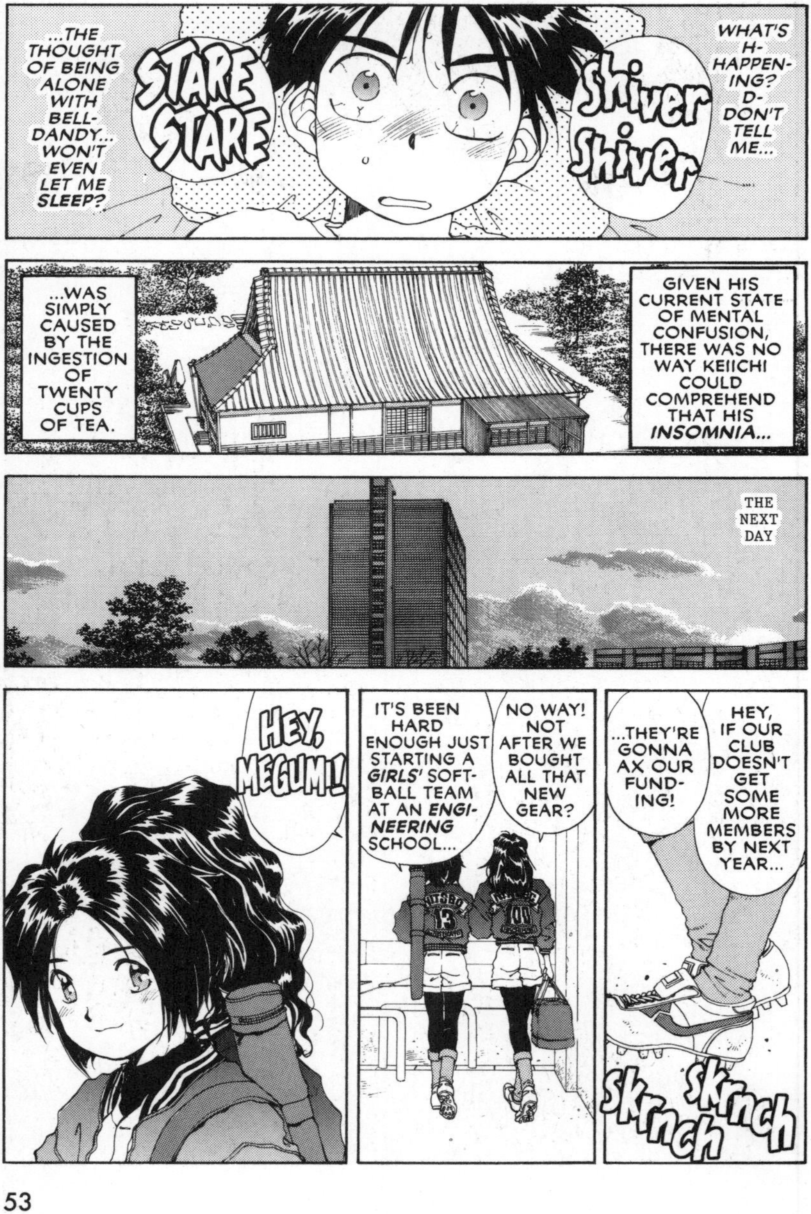
WHAT'S H-HAPPENING? D-DON'T TELL ME...
Shiver Shiver
STARE STARE
...THE THOUGHT OF BEING ALONE WITH BELL-DANDY... WON'T EVEN LET ME SLEEP?
GIVEN HIS CURRENT STATE OF MENTAL CONFUSION, THERE WAS NO WAY KEIICHI COULD COMPREHEND THAT HIS INSOMNIA...
...WAS SIMPLY CAUSED BY THE INGESTION OF TWENTY CUPS OF TEA.
THE NEXT DAY
HEY, IF OUR CLUB DOESN'T GET SOME MORE MEMBERS BY NEXT YEAR...
...THEY'RE GONNA AX OUR FUND-ING!
skrnch skrnch
NO WAY! NOT AFTER WE BOUGHT ALL THAT NEW GEAR?
IT'S BEEN HARD ENOUGH JUST STARTING A GIRLS' SOFT-BALL TEAM AT AN ENGI-NEERING SCHOOL...
HEY, MEGUMI!!

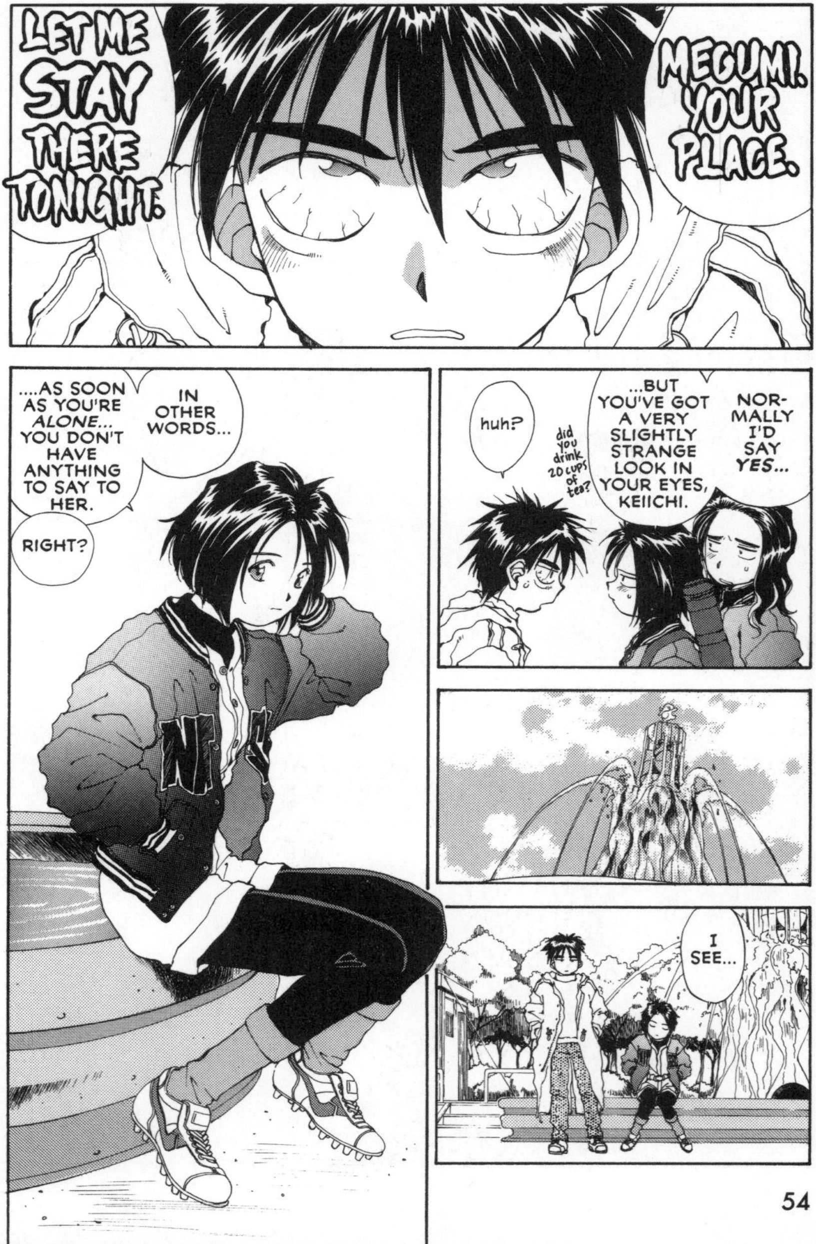
MEGUMI. YOUR PLACE.
LET ME STAY THERE TONIGHT.
NORMALLY I'D SAY *YES*...
...BUT YOU'VE GOT A VERY SLIGHTLY STRANGE LOOK IN YOUR EYES, KEIICHI.
did you drink 20 cups of tea?
huh?
I SEE...
IN OTHER WORDS...
....AS SOON AS YOU'RE *ALONE*... YOU DON'T HAVE ANYTHING TO SAY TO HER.
RIGHT?

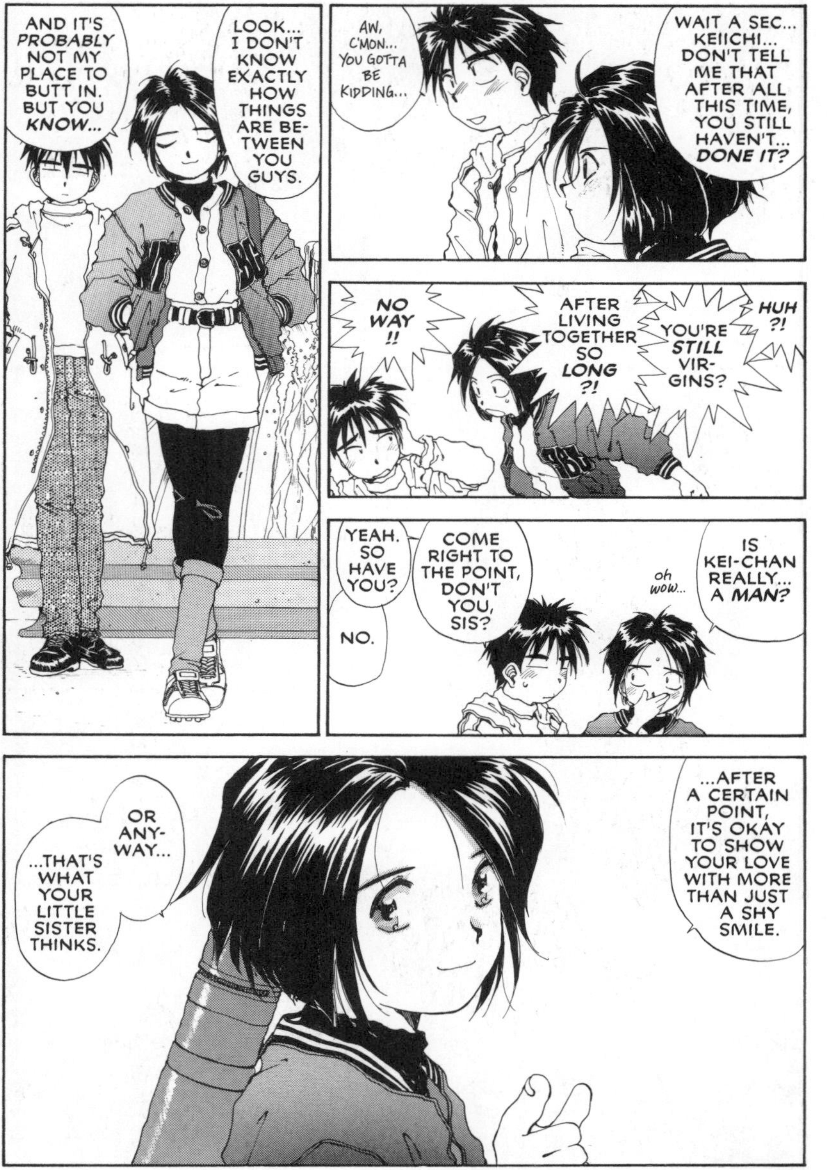
WAIT A SEC... KEIICHI... DON'T TELL ME THAT AFTER ALL THIS TIME, YOU STILL HAVEN'T... *DONE IT?*
AW, C'MON... YOU GOTTA BE KIDDING...
HUH ?!
YOU'RE *STILL* VIR-GINS?
AFTER LIVING TOGETHER SO *LONG ?!*
NO WAY !!
IS KEI-CHAN REALLY... A *MAN?*
oh wow...
COME RIGHT TO THE POINT, DON'T YOU, SIS?
YEAH. SO HAVE YOU?
NO.
LOOK... I DON'T KNOW EXACTLY HOW THINGS ARE BE-TWEEN YOU GUYS.
AND IT'S *PROBABLY* NOT MY PLACE TO BUTT IN. BUT YOU *KNOW...*
...AFTER A CERTAIN POINT, IT'S OKAY TO SHOW YOUR LOVE WITH MORE THAN JUST A SHY SMILE.
OR ANY-WAY...
...THAT'S WHAT YOUR LITTLE SISTER THINKS.

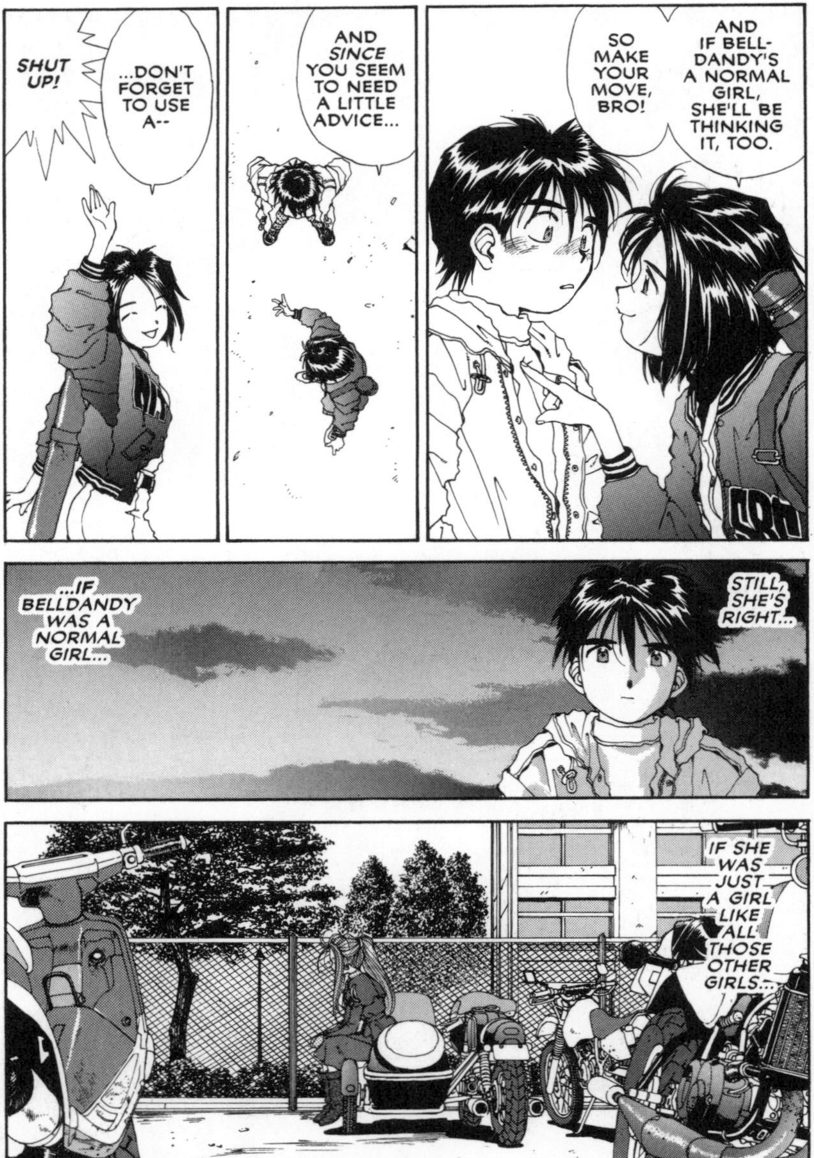
AND IF BELL-DANDY'S A NORMAL GIRL, SHE'LL BE THINKING IT, TOO.
SO MAKE YOUR MOVE, BRO!
AND *SINCE* YOU SEEM TO NEED A LITTLE ADVICE...
...DON'T FORGET TO USE A--
SHUT UP!
STILL, SHE'S RIGHT...
...IF BELLDANDY WAS A NORMAL GIRL...
IF SHE WAS JUST A GIRL LIKE ALL THOSE OTHER GIRLS...

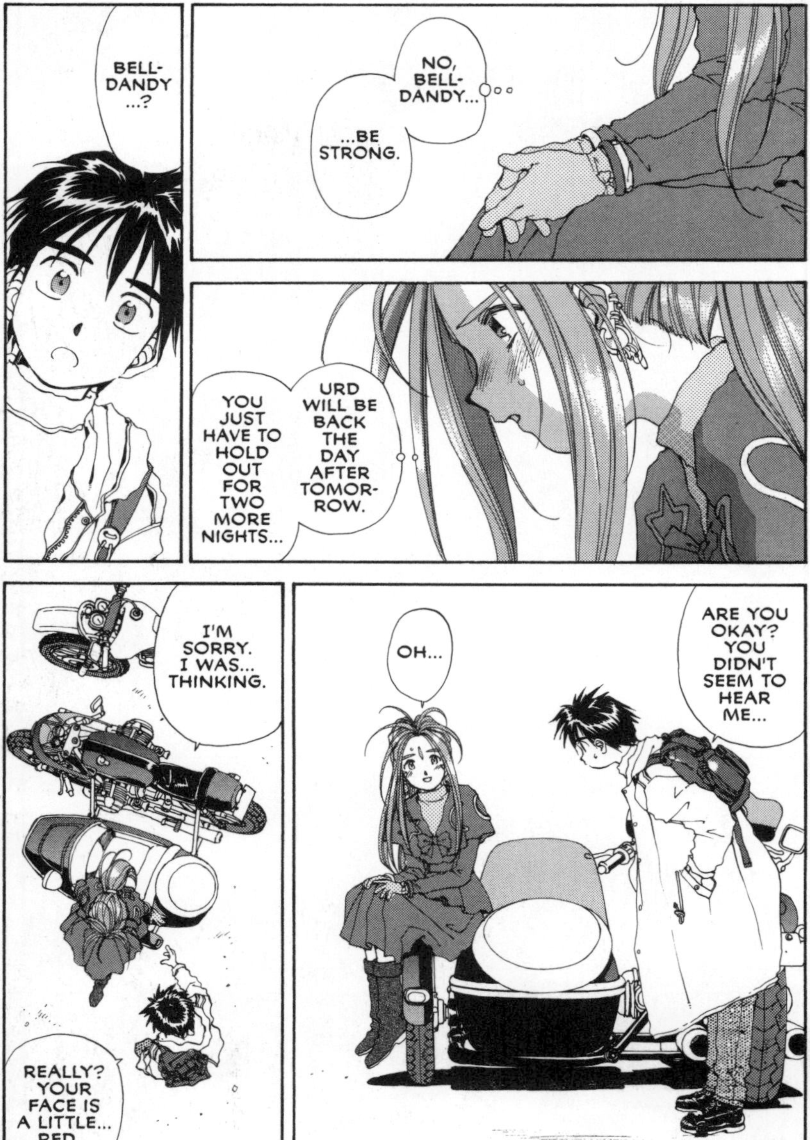
NO, BELL-DANDY...
...BE STRONG.
URD WILL BE BACK THE DAY AFTER TOMORROW.
YOU JUST HAVE TO HOLD OUT FOR TWO MORE NIGHTS...
BELL-DANDY ...?
ARE YOU OKAY? YOU DIDN'T SEEM TO HEAR ME...
OH...
I'M SORRY. I WAS... THINKING.
REALLY? YOUR FACE IS A LITTLE... RED...

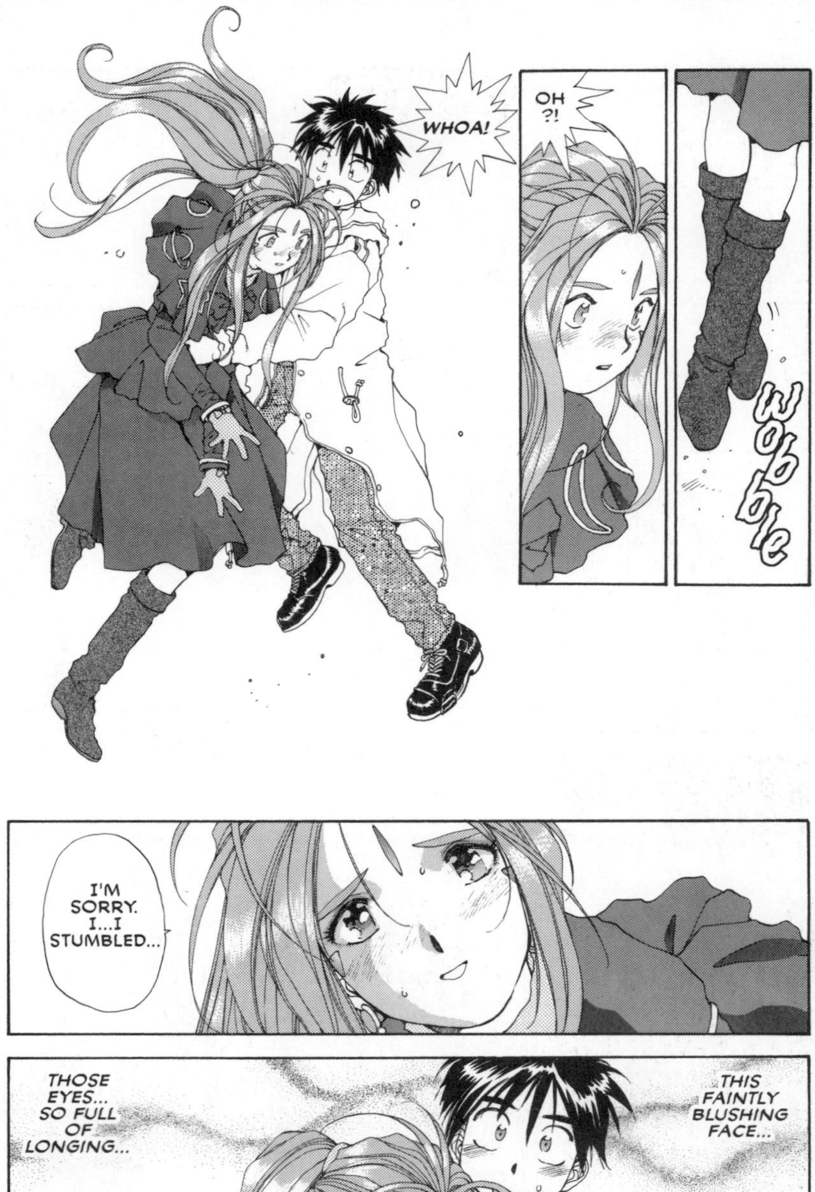
wobble
OH ?!
WHOA!
I'M SORRY. I...I STUMBLED...
...THIS FAINTLY BLUSHING FACE...
THOSE EYES... SO FULL OF LONGING...

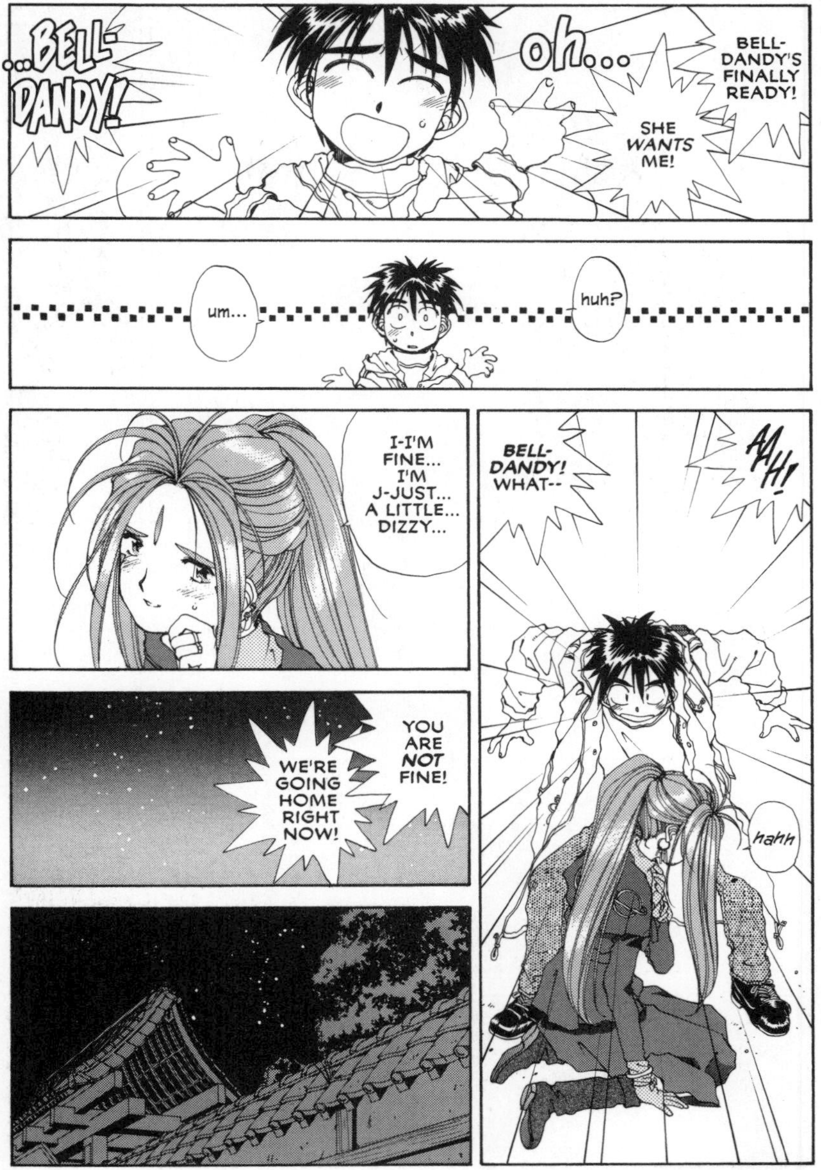
BELL-DANDY'S FINALLY READY!
oh...
SHE WANTS ME!
...BELL-DANDY!
huh?
um...
AAHH!
BELL-DANDY! WHAT--
hahh
I-I'M FINE... I'M J-JUST... A LITTLE... DIZZY...
YOU ARE NOT FINE!
WE'RE GOING HOME RIGHT NOW!

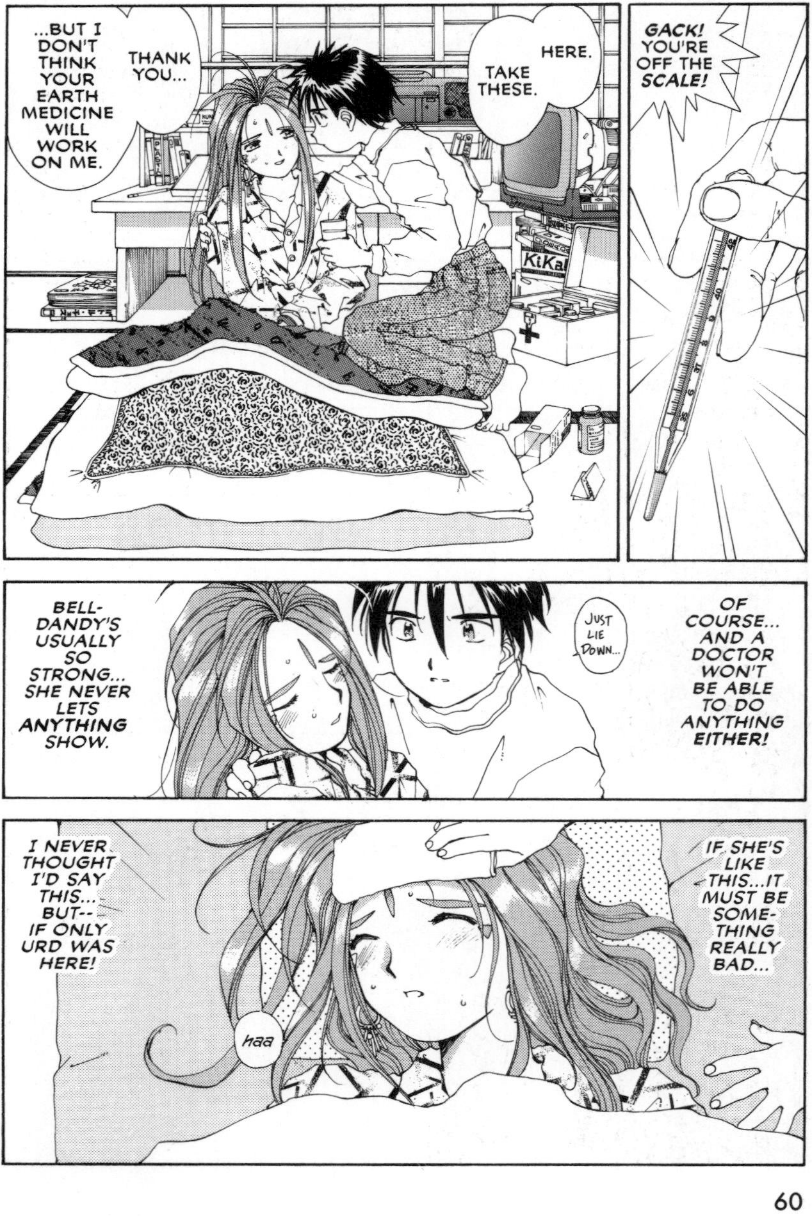
GACK! YOU'RE OFF THE SCALE!
HERE. TAKE THESE.
THANK YOU...
...BUT I DON'T THINK YOUR EARTH MEDICINE WILL WORK ON ME.
OF COURSE... AND A DOCTOR WON'T BE ABLE TO DO ANYTHING EITHER!
JUST LIE DOWN...
BELL-DANDY'S USUALLY SO STRONG... SHE NEVER LETS ANYTHING SHOW.
IF SHE'S LIKE THIS...IT MUST BE SOME-THING REALLY BAD...
I NEVER THOUGHT I'D SAY THIS... BUT-- IF ONLY URD WAS HERE!
haa

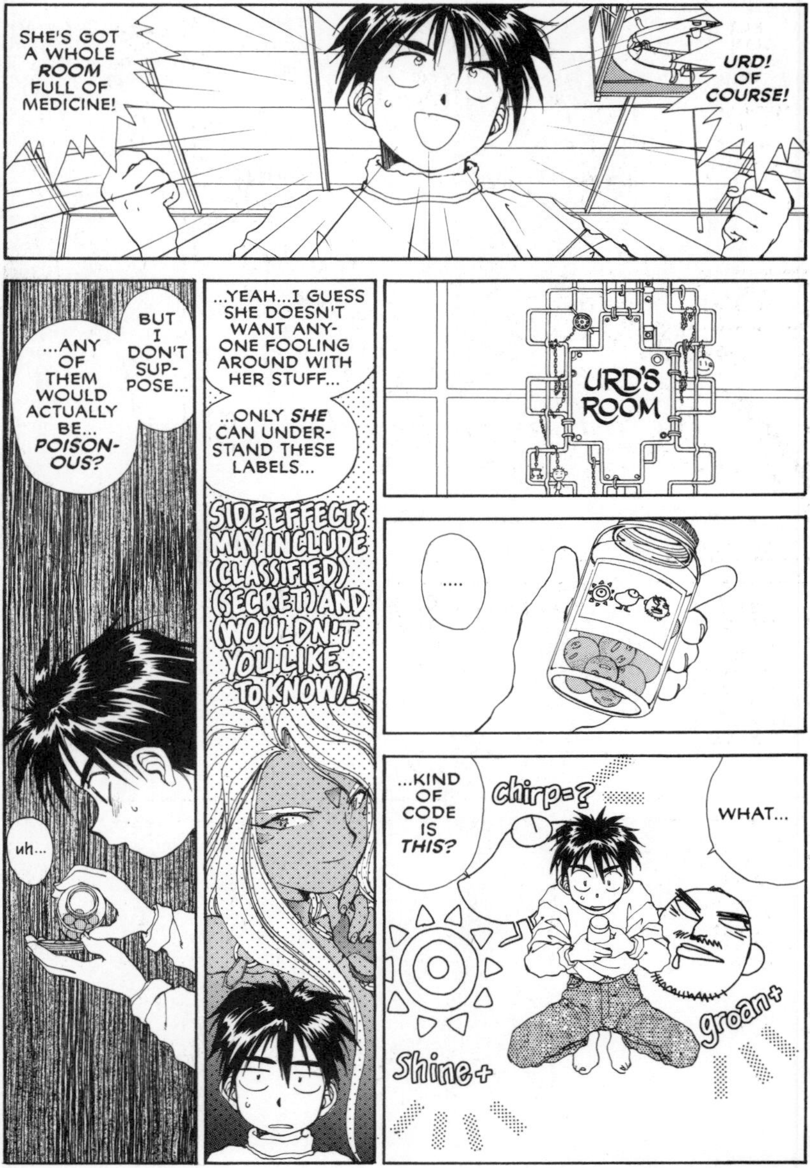
URD! OF COURSE!
SHE'S GOT A WHOLE ROOM FULL OF MEDICINE!
URD'S ROOM
....
WHAT...
...KIND OF CODE IS THIS?
chirp=?
groan+
Shine+
...YEAH...I GUESS SHE DOESN'T WANT ANYONE FOOLING AROUND WITH HER STUFF...
...ONLY SHE CAN UNDERSTAND THESE LABELS...
SIDE EFFECTS MAY INCLUDE (CLASSIFIED) (SECRET) AND (WOULDN'T YOU LIKE TO KNOW)!
BUT I DON'T SUPPOSE...
...ANY OF THEM WOULD ACTUALLY BE... POISONOUS?
uh...

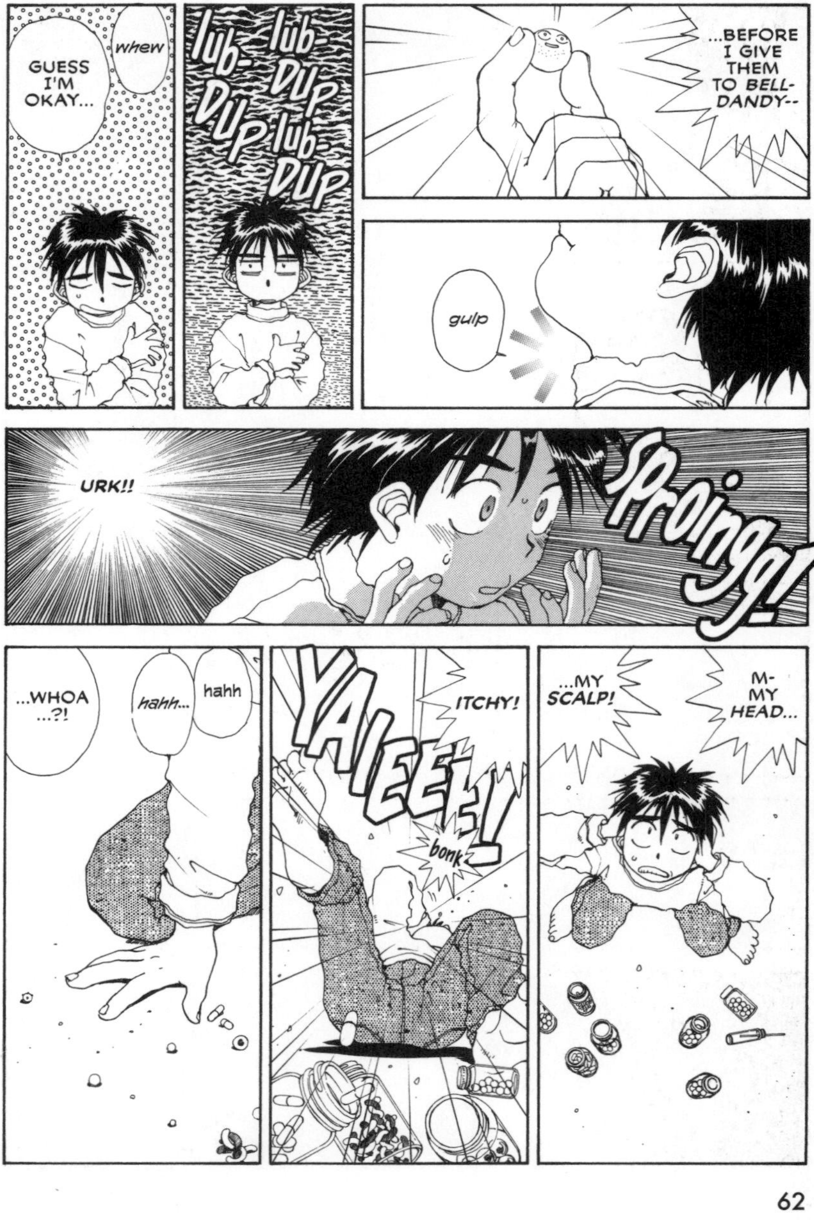

...BEFORE I GIVE THEM TO BELL-DANDY--
gulp
lub-DUP lub-DUP
lub-DUP
whew
GUESS I'M OKAY...
Sproingg!
URK!!
M-MY HEAD...
...MY SCALP!
ITCHY!
YAIEEE!!
bonk
hahh
hahh...
...WHOA ...?!

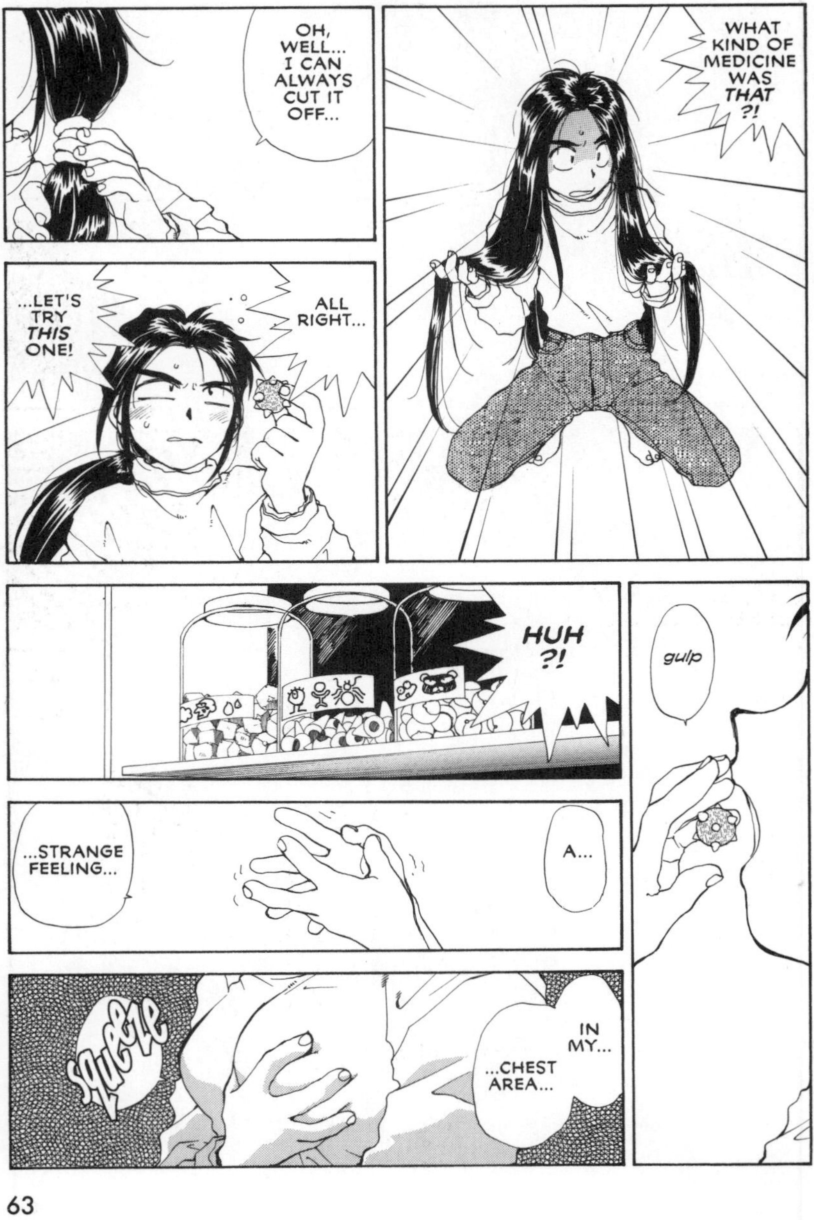
WHAT KIND OF MEDICINE WAS *THAT* ?!
OH, WELL... I CAN ALWAYS CUT IT OFF...
ALL RIGHT...
...LET'S TRY *THIS* ONE!
gulp
HUH ?!
A...
...STRANGE FEELING...
IN MY...
...CHEST AREA...
squeeze

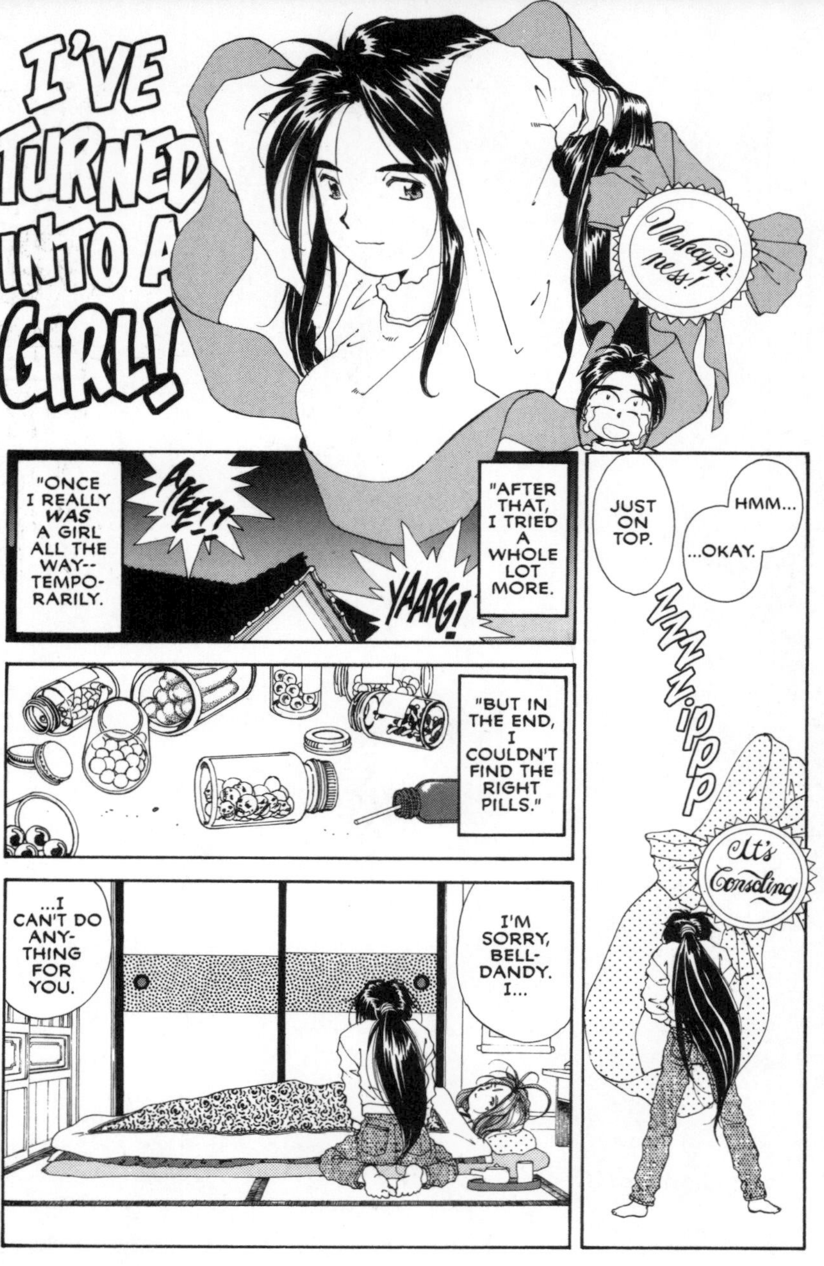
I'VE TURNED INTO A GIRL!
Unhappiness!
HMM... ...OKAY.
JUST ON TOP.
VWWVIPPP
It's Consoling
"AFTER THAT, I TRIED A WHOLE LOT MORE.
AAEE!!
YAARG!
"ONCE I REALLY WAS A GIRL ALL THE WAY--TEMPORARILY.
"BUT IN THE END, I COULDN'T FIND THE RIGHT PILLS."
I'M SORRY, BELLDANDY. I...
...I CAN'T DO ANYTHING FOR YOU.

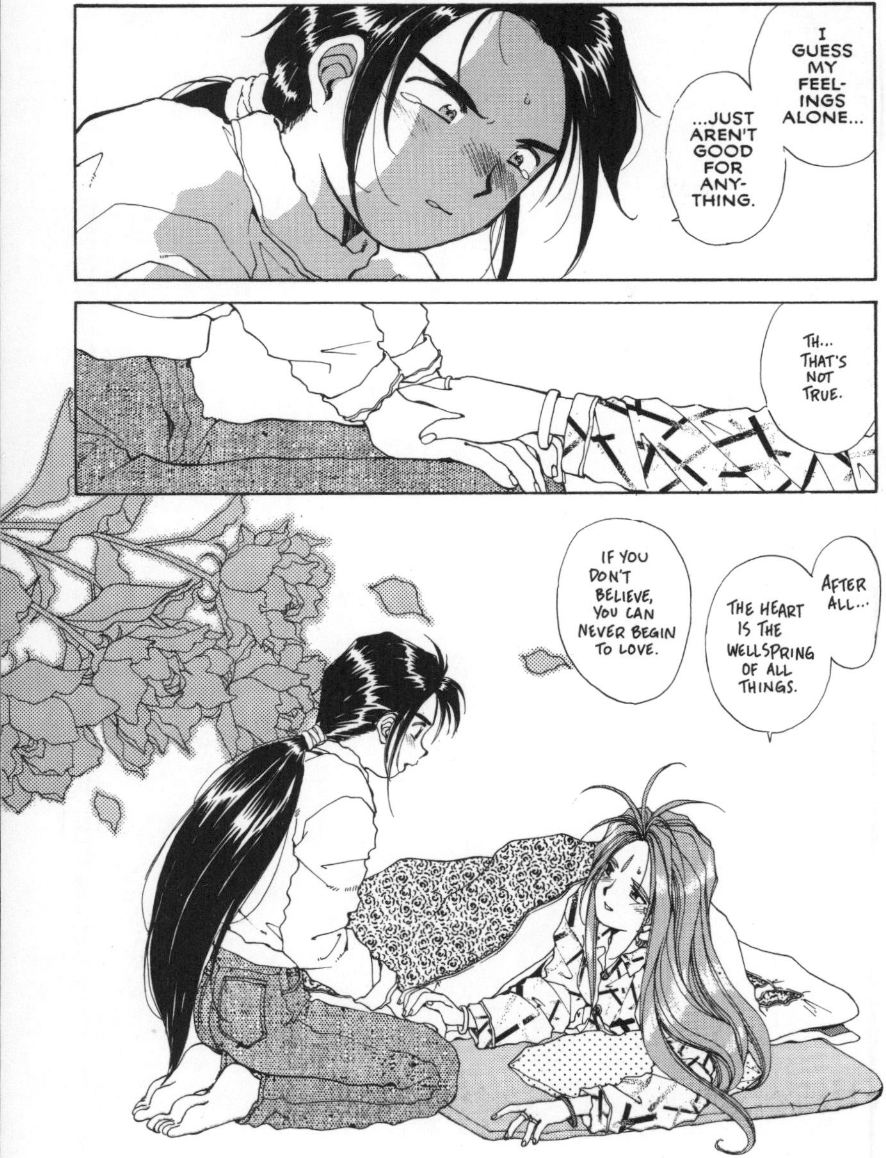
I GUESS MY FEEL-INGS ALONE...
...JUST AREN'T GOOD FOR ANY-THING.
TH... THAT'S NOT TRUE.
AFTER ALL...
THE HEART IS THE WELLSPRING OF ALL THINGS.
IF YOU DON'T BELIEVE, YOU CAN NEVER BEGIN TO LOVE.

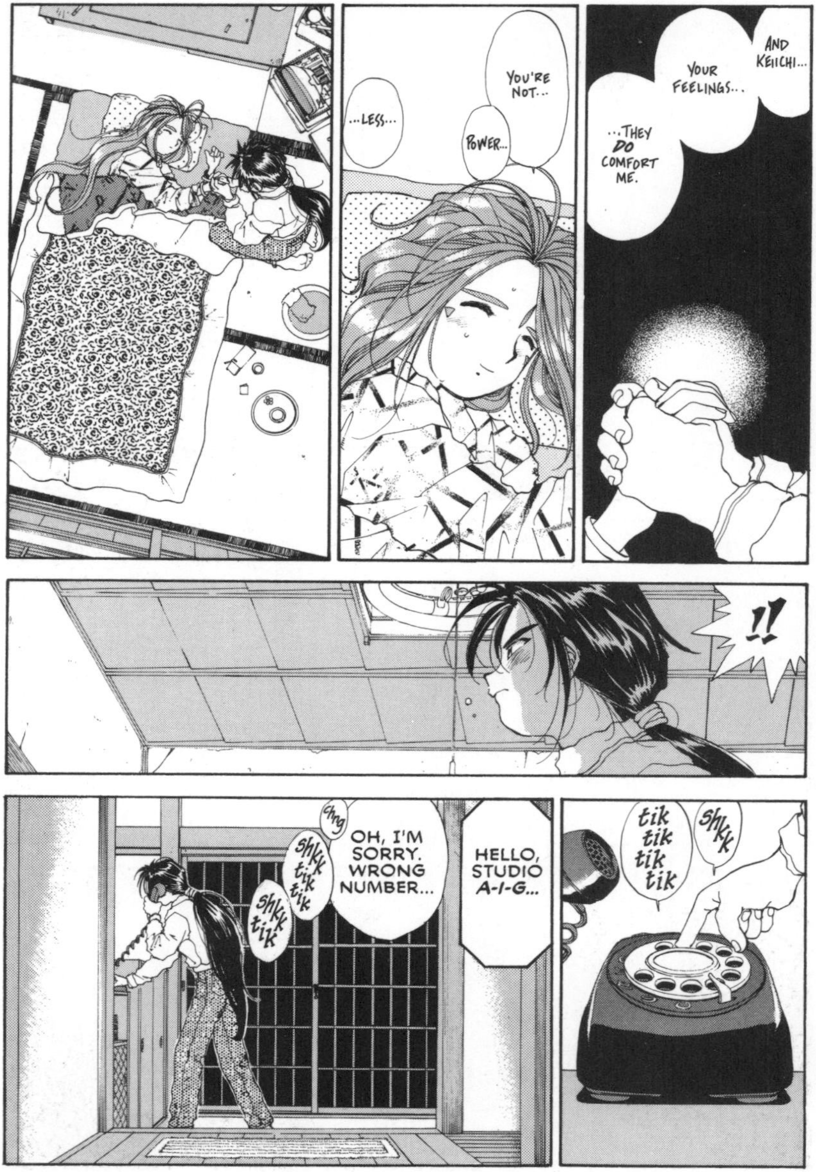
AND KEIICHI...
YOUR FEELINGS...
...THEY DO COMFORT ME.
YOU'RE NOT...
POWER...
...LESS...
!!
shkk
tik tik tik tik
HELLO, STUDIO A-I-G...
OH, I'M SORRY. WRONG NUMBER...
chng
shkk tik tik
shkk tik

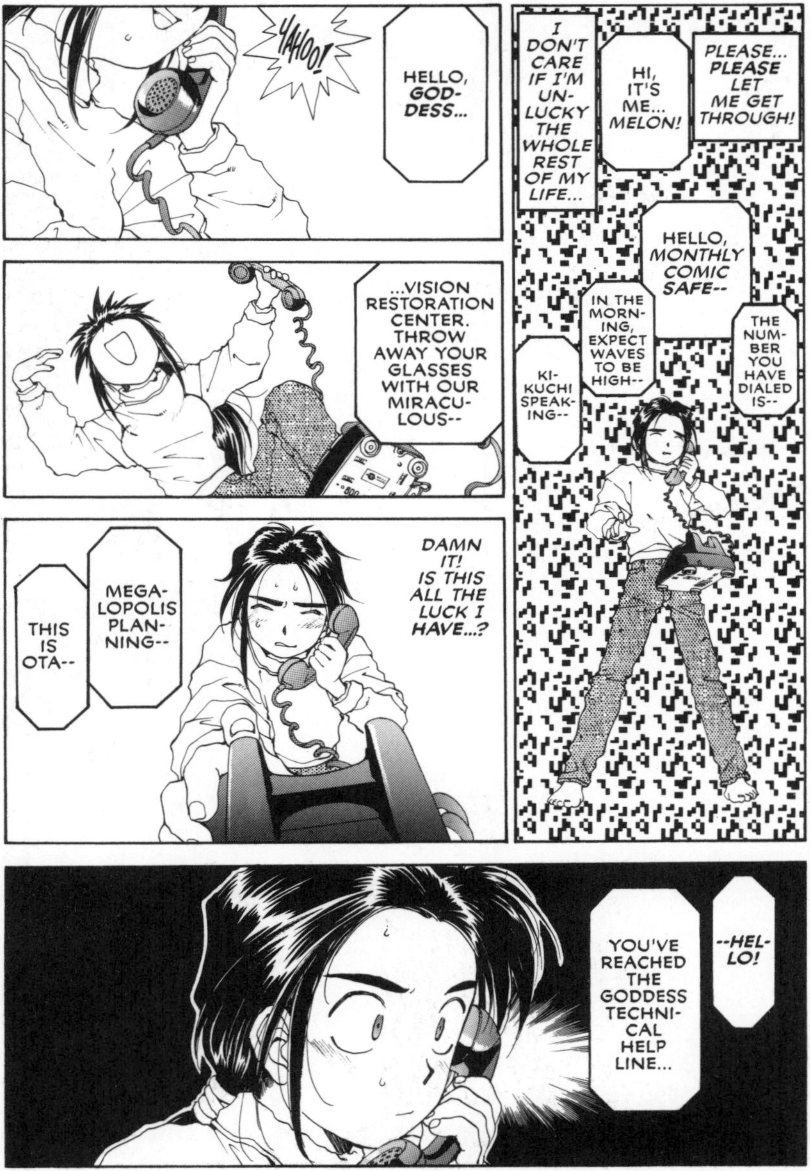
PLEASE... PLEASE LET ME GET THROUGH!
HI, IT'S ME... MELON!
I DON'T CARE IF I'M UNLUCKY THE WHOLE REST OF MY LIFE...
HELLO, MONTHLY COMIC SAFE--
THE NUMBER YOU HAVE DIALED IS--
IN THE MORNING, EXPECT WAVES TO BE HIGH--
KIKUCHI SPEAKING--
HELLO, GODDESS...
YAHOO!
...VISION RESTORATION CENTER. THROW AWAY YOUR GLASSES WITH OUR MIRACULOUS--
DAMN IT! IS THIS ALL THE LUCK I HAVE...?
MEGALOPOLIS PLANNING--
THIS IS OTA--
--HELLO!
YOU'VE REACHED THE GODDESS TECHNICAL HELP LINE...

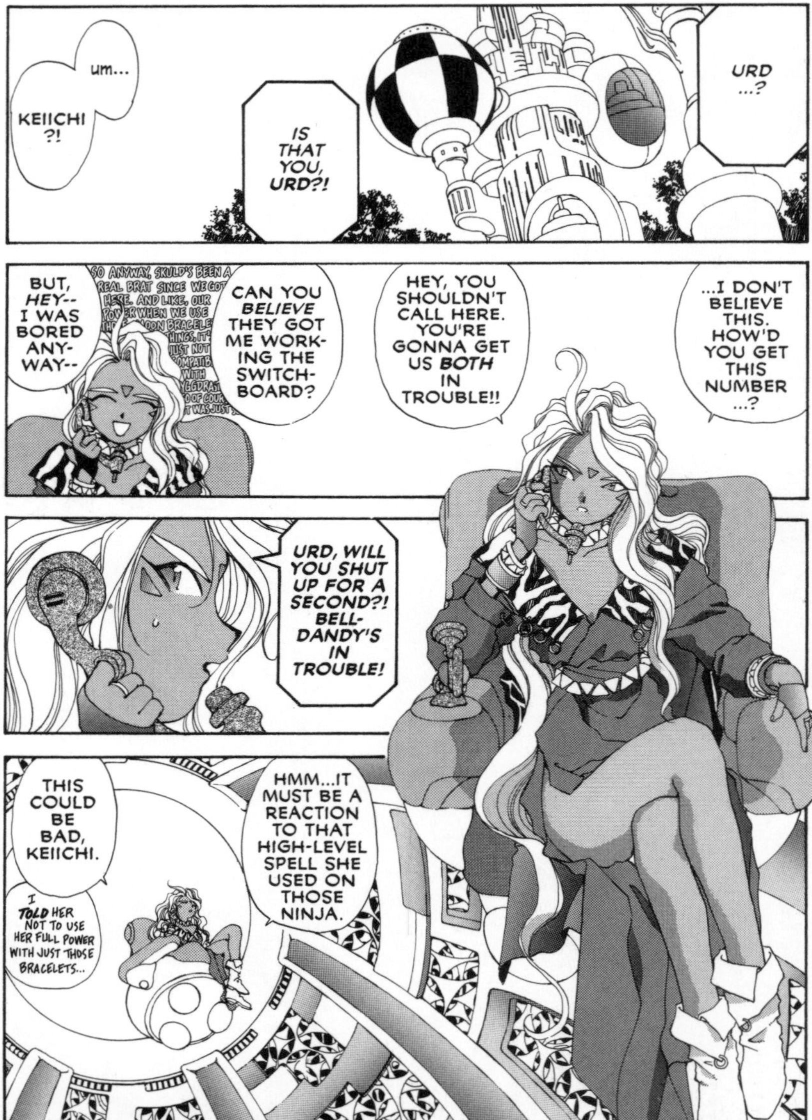
URD ...?
IS THAT YOU, URD?!
um...
KEIICHI ?!
...I DON'T BELIEVE THIS. HOW'D YOU GET THIS NUMBER ...?
HEY, YOU SHOULDN'T CALL HERE. YOU'RE GONNA GET US *BOTH* IN TROUBLE!!
CAN YOU *BELIEVE* THEY GOT ME WORKING THE SWITCHBOARD?
SO ANYWAY, SKULD'S BEEN A REAL BRAT SINCE WE GOT HERE. AND LIKE, OUR
BUT, *HEY*-- I WAS BORED ANYWAY--
URD, WILL YOU SHUT UP FOR A SECOND?! BELLDANDY'S IN TROUBLE!
HMM...IT MUST BE A REACTION TO THAT HIGH-LEVEL SPELL SHE USED ON THOSE NINJA.
THIS COULD BE BAD, KEIICHI.
I *TOLD* HER NOT TO USE HER FULL POWER WITH JUST THOSE BRACELETS...

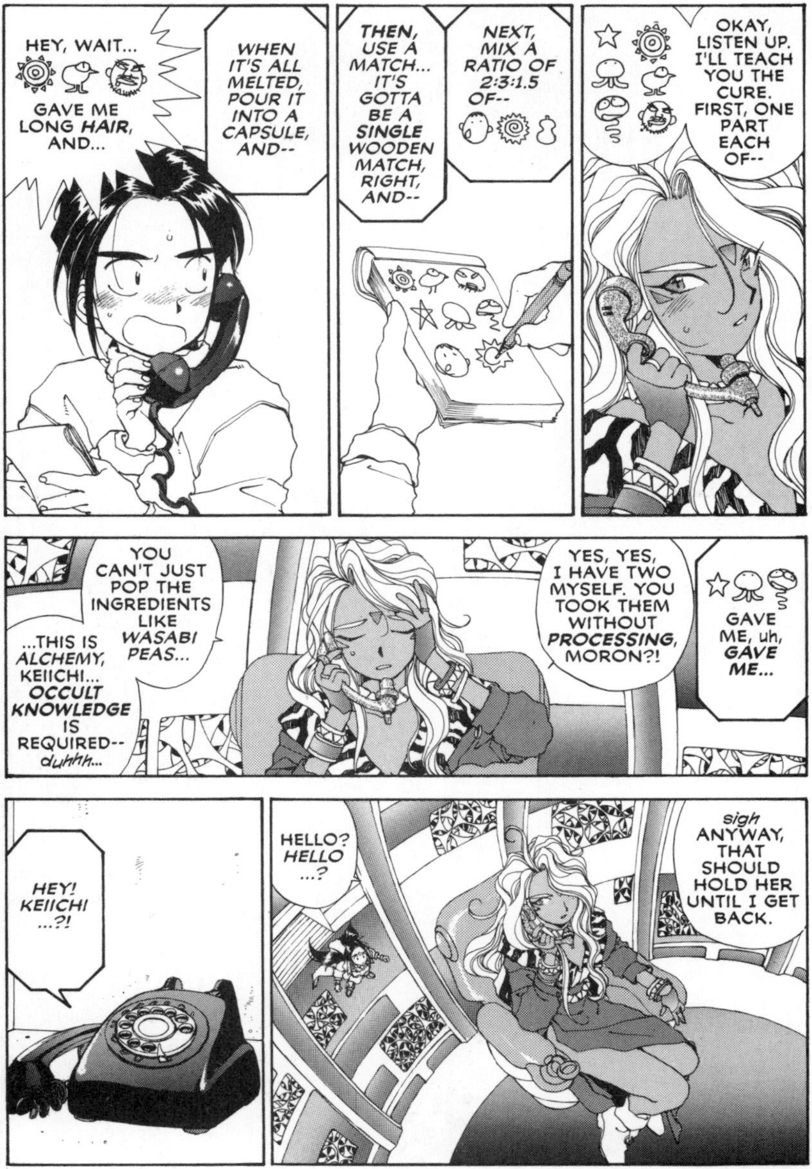
OKAY, LISTEN UP. I'LL TEACH YOU THE CURE. FIRST, ONE PART EACH OF--
NEXT, MIX A RATIO OF 2:3:1.5 OF--
THEN, USE A MATCH... IT'S GOTTA BE A SINGLE WOODEN MATCH, RIGHT, AND--
WHEN IT'S ALL MELTED, POUR IT INTO A CAPSULE, AND--
HEY, WAIT...
GAVE ME LONG HAIR, AND...
GAVE ME, uh, GAVE ME...
YES, YES, I HAVE TWO MYSELF. YOU TOOK THEM WITHOUT PROCESSING, MORON?!
YOU CAN'T JUST POP THE INGREDIENTS LIKE WASABI PEAS...
...THIS IS ALCHEMY, KEIICHI... OCCULT KNOWLEDGE IS REQUIRED-- duhhh...
sigh ANYWAY, THAT SHOULD HOLD HER UNTIL I GET BACK.
HELLO? HELLO ...?
HEY! KEIICHI ...?!

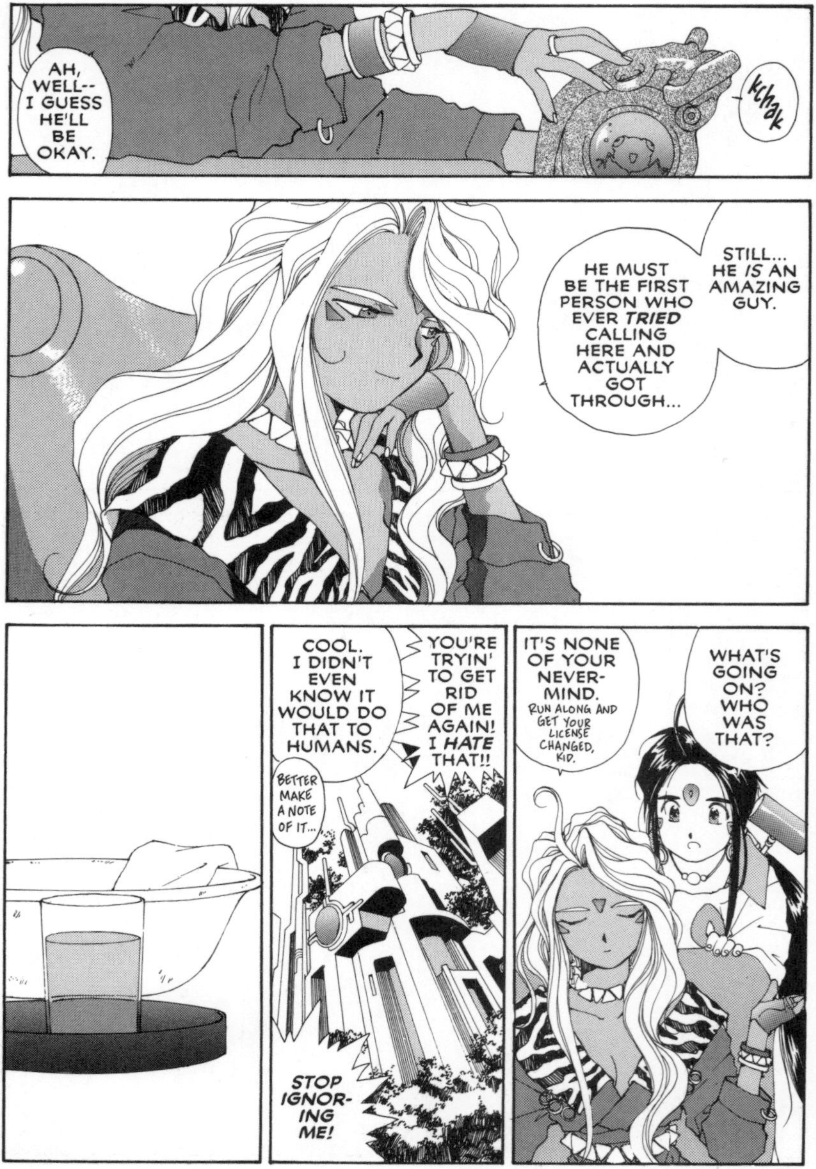
kchak
AH, WELL-- I GUESS HE'LL BE OKAY.
STILL... HE *IS* AN AMAZING GUY.
HE MUST BE THE FIRST PERSON WHO EVER *TRIED* CALLING HERE AND ACTUALLY GOT THROUGH...
WHAT'S GOING ON? WHO WAS THAT?
IT'S NONE OF YOUR NEVER-MIND.
RUN ALONG AND GET YOUR LICENSE CHANGED, KID.
YOU'RE TRYIN' TO GET RID OF ME AGAIN! I *HATE* THAT!!
COOL. I DIDN'T EVEN KNOW IT WOULD DO THAT TO HUMANS.
BETTER MAKE A NOTE OF IT...
STOP IGNORING ME!

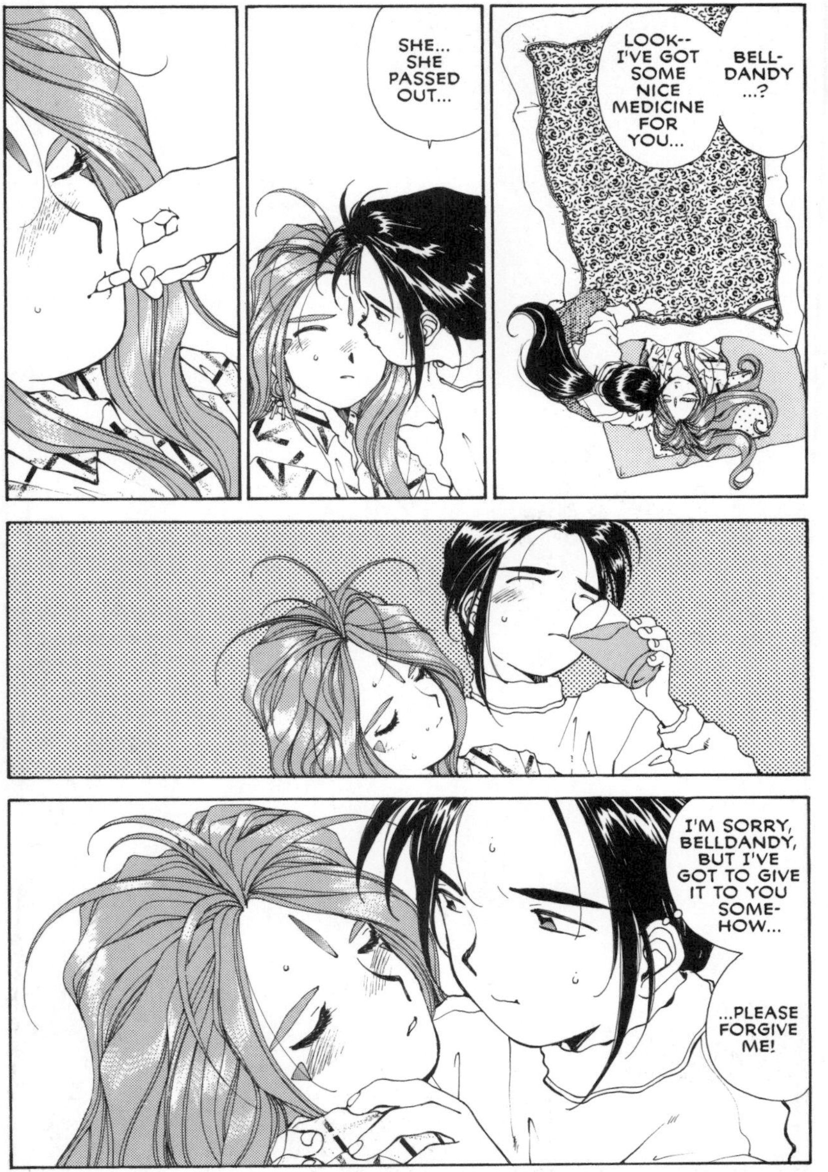
BELL-DANDY ...?
LOOK-- I'VE GOT SOME NICE MEDICINE FOR YOU...
SHE... SHE PASSED OUT...
I'M SORRY, BELLDANDY, BUT I'VE GOT TO GIVE IT TO YOU SOME-HOW...
...PLEASE FORGIVE ME!

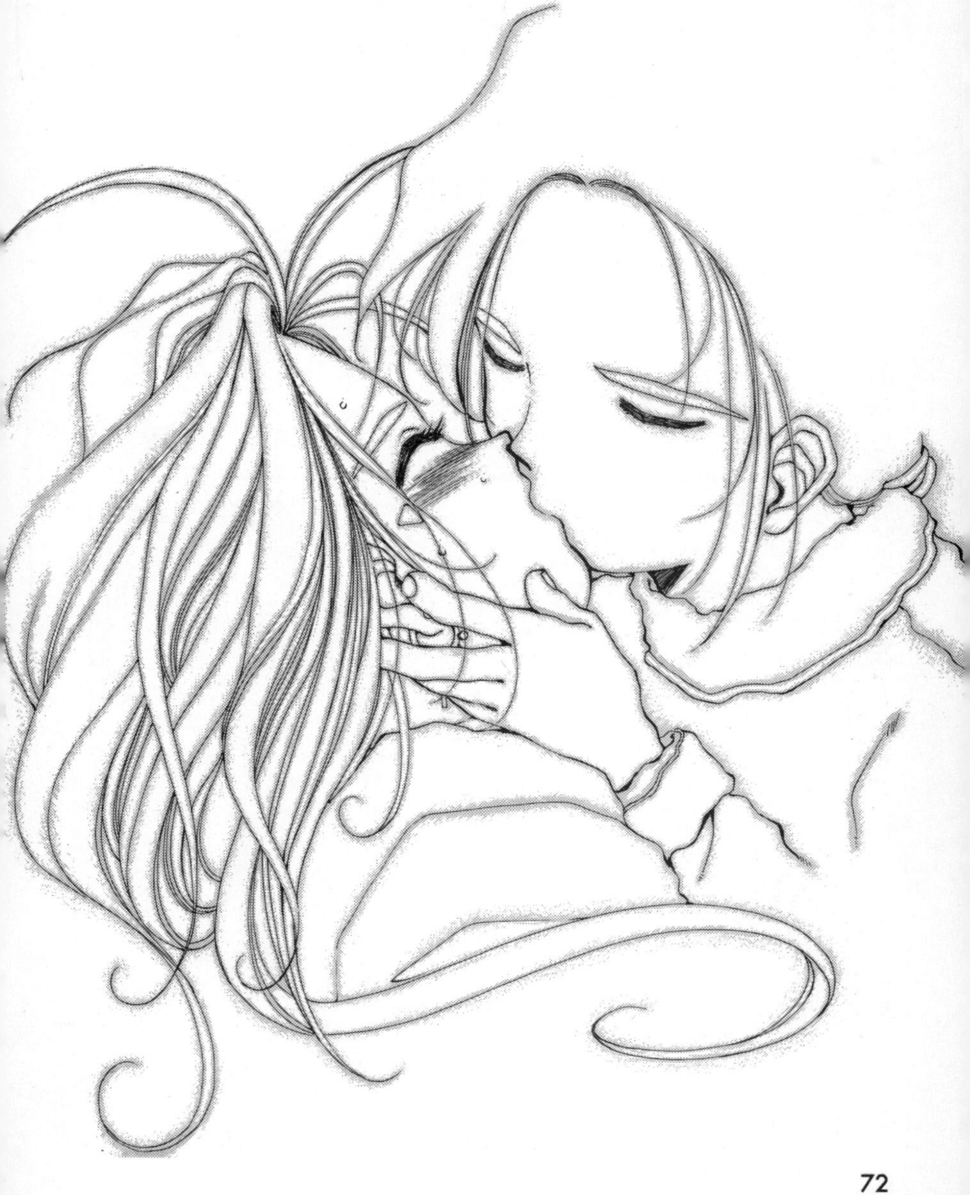

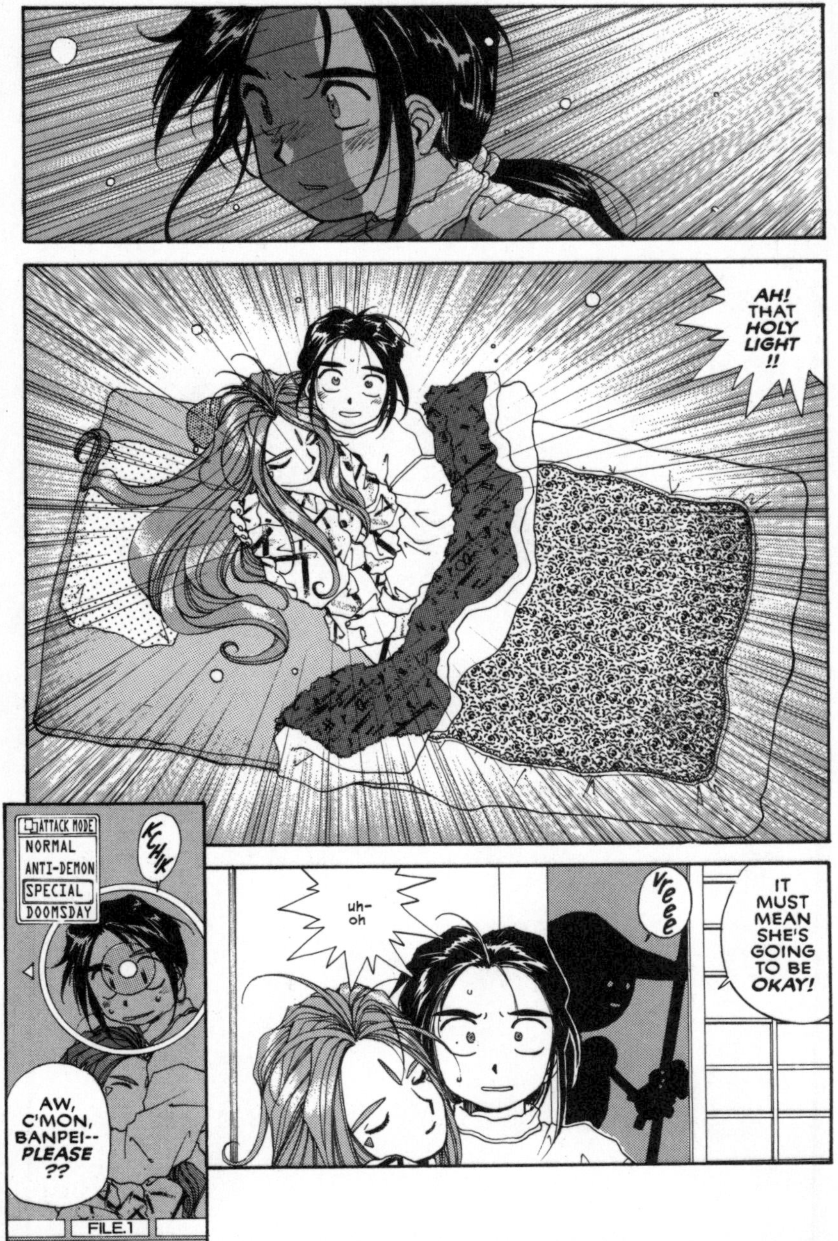
AH! THAT HOLY LIGHT!!
IT MUST MEAN SHE'S GOING TO BE OKAY!
Vreee
uh-oh
ATTACK MODE
NORMAL
ANTI-DEMON
SPECIAL
DOOMSDAY
KCHIK
AW, C'MON, BANPEI-- PLEASE??
FILE.1

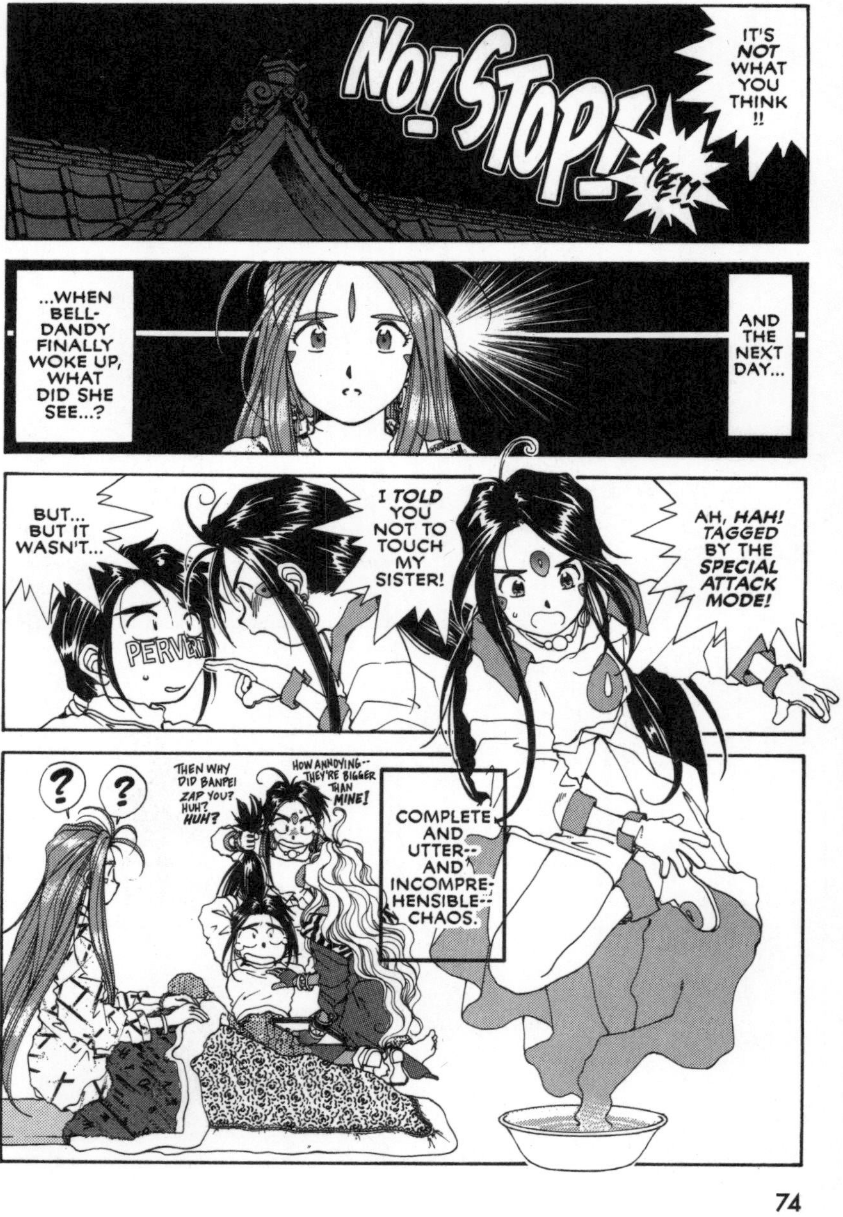
IT'S NOT WHAT YOU THINK !!
NO! STOP!!
AIEE!!
AND THE NEXT DAY...
...WHEN BELL-DANDY FINALLY WOKE UP, WHAT DID SHE SEE...?
AH, HAH! TAGGED BY THE SPECIAL ATTACK MODE!
I TOLD YOU NOT TO TOUCH MY SISTER!
BUT... BUT IT WASN'T...
PERVERT
COMPLETE AND UTTER-- AND INCOMPREHENSIBLE-- CHAOS.
HOW ANNOYING-- THEY'RE BIGGER THAN MINE!
THEN WHY DID BANPEI ZAP YOU? HUH? HUH?
?
?

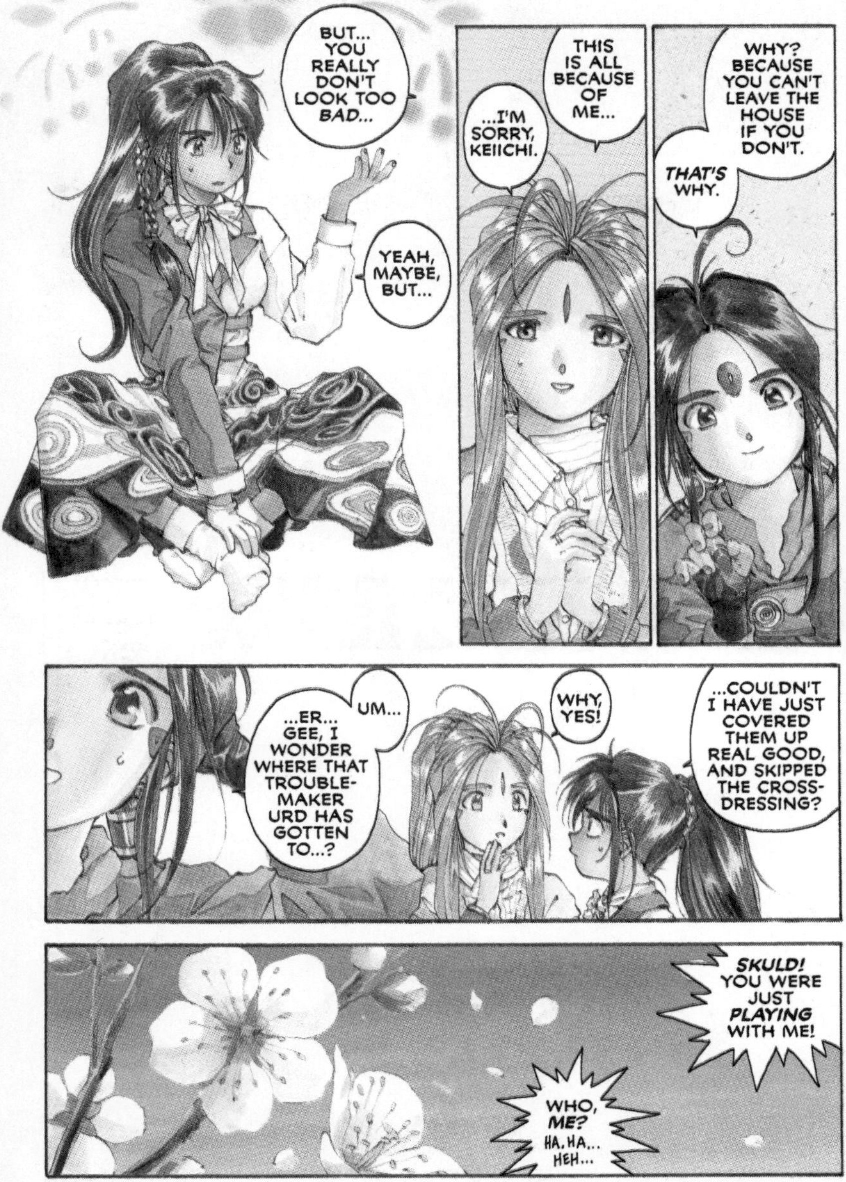
WHY? BECAUSE YOU CAN'T LEAVE THE HOUSE IF YOU DON'T.
THAT'S WHY.
THIS IS ALL BECAUSE OF ME...
...I'M SORRY, KEIICHI.
BUT... YOU REALLY DON'T LOOK TOO BAD...
YEAH, MAYBE, BUT...
...COULDN'T I HAVE JUST COVERED THEM UP REAL GOOD, AND SKIPPED THE CROSS-DRESSING?
WHY, YES!
UM...
...ER... GEE, I WONDER WHERE THAT TROUBLE-MAKER URD HAS GOTTEN TO...?
SKULD! YOU WERE JUST PLAYING WITH ME!
WHO, ME? HA, HA... HEH...

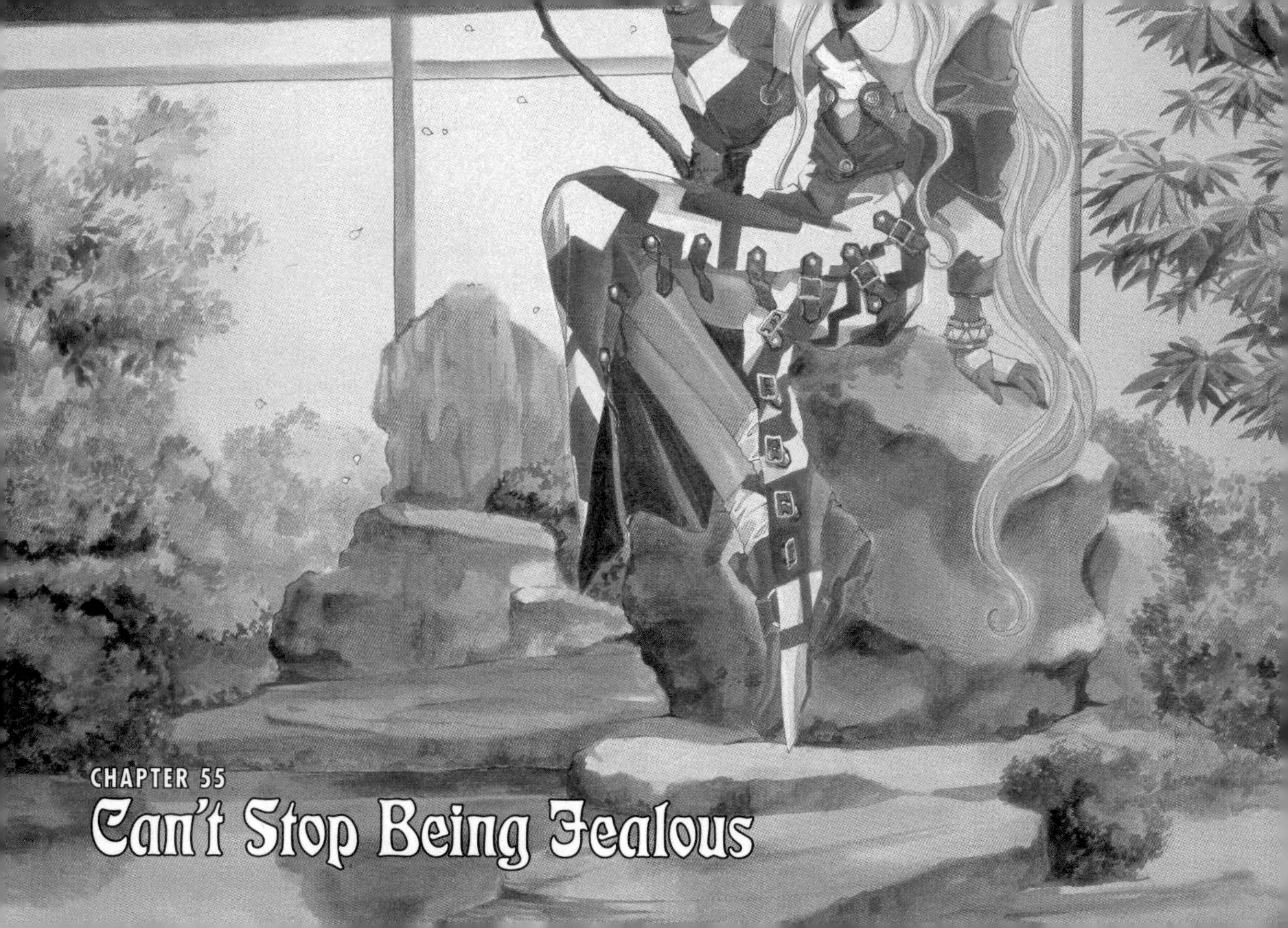
CHAPTER 55
Can't Stop Being Jealous

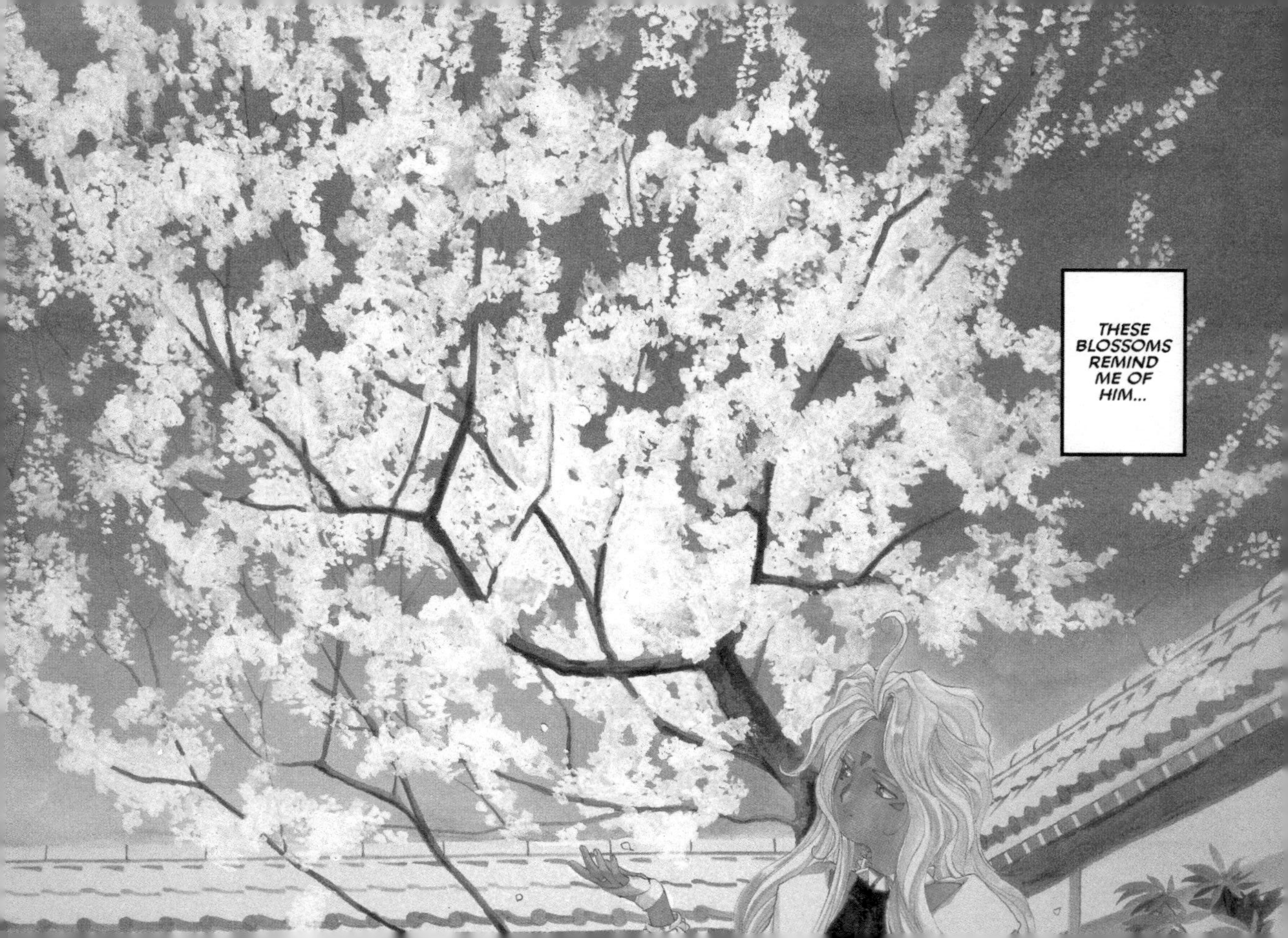
THESE BLOSSOMS REMIND ME OF HIM...

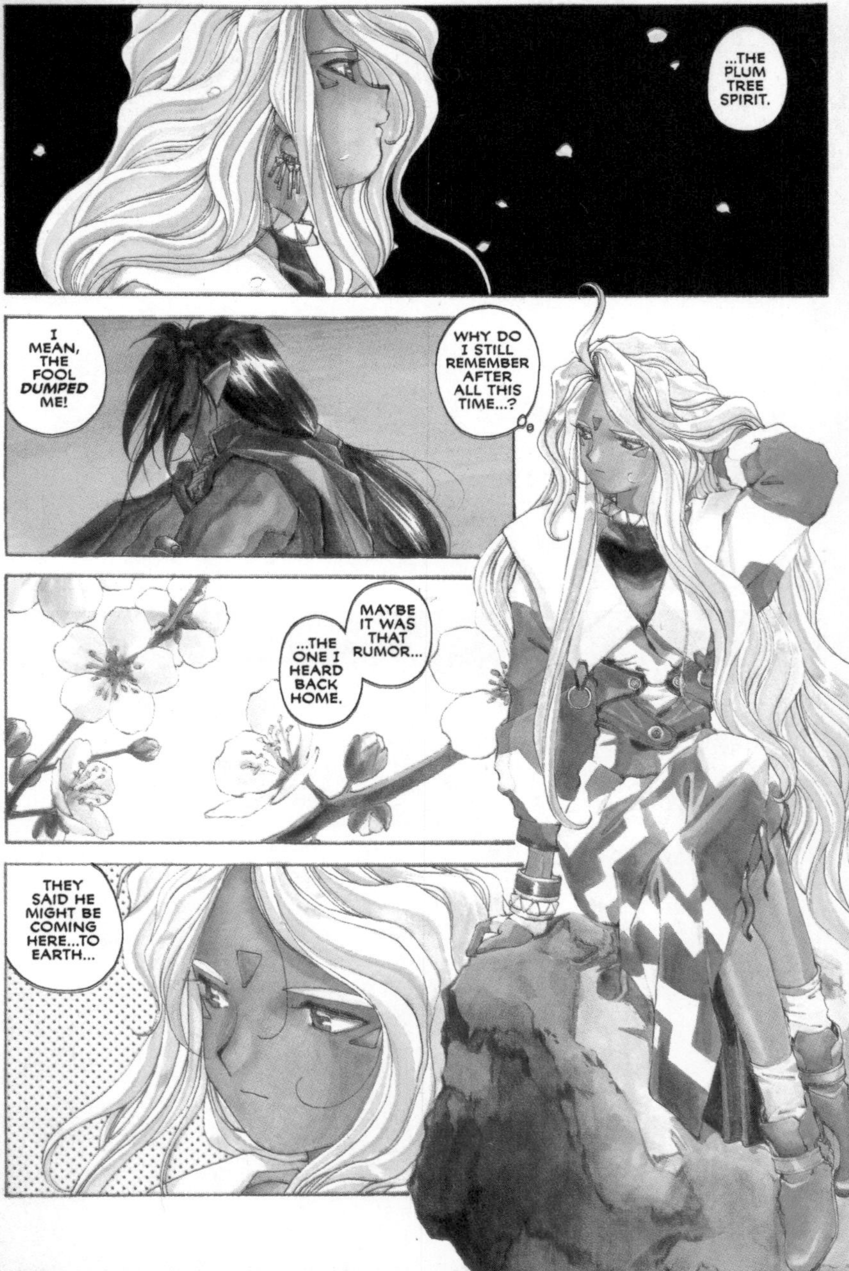
...THE PLUM TREE SPIRIT.
WHY DO I STILL REMEMBER AFTER ALL THIS TIME...?
I MEAN, THE FOOL *DUMPED* ME!
MAYBE IT WAS THAT RUMOR...
...THE ONE I HEARD BACK HOME.
THEY SAID HE MIGHT BE COMING HERE...TO EARTH...

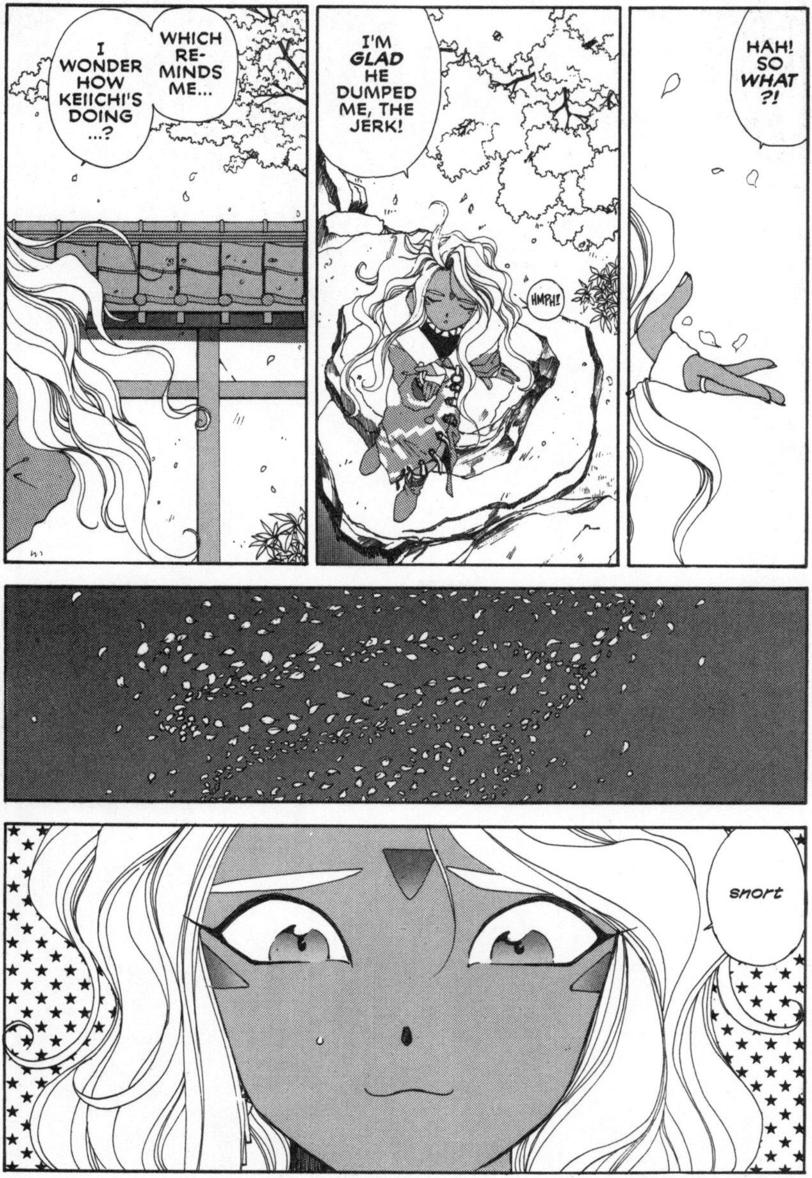
HAH! SO WHAT?!
I'M GLAD HE DUMPED ME, THE JERK!
HMPH!
WHICH RE-MINDS ME...
I WONDER HOW KEIICHI'S DOING ...?
snort

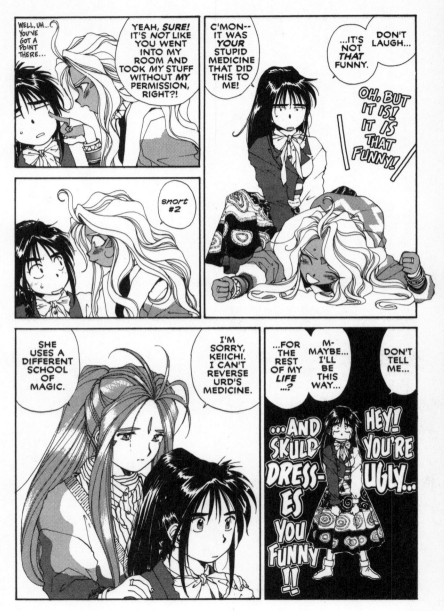

DON'T LAUGH...
...IT'S NOT *THAT* FUNNY.
C'MON-- IT WAS *YOUR* STUPID MEDICINE THAT DID THIS TO ME!
OH, BUT IT IS! IT IS THAT FUNNY!
YEAH, *SURE!* IT'S *NOT* LIKE YOU WENT INTO MY ROOM AND TOOK *MY* STUFF WITHOUT *MY* PERMISSION, RIGHT?!
WELL, UH... YOU'VE GOT A POINT THERE...
snort #2
DON'T TELL ME...
M-MAYBE... I'LL BE THIS WAY...
...FOR THE REST OF MY *LIFE* ...?
HEY! YOU'RE UGLY...
...AND SKULD DRESS-ES YOU FUNNY!!
I'M SORRY, KEIICHI. I CAN'T REVERSE URD'S MEDICINE.
SHE USES A DIFFERENT SCHOOL OF MAGIC.

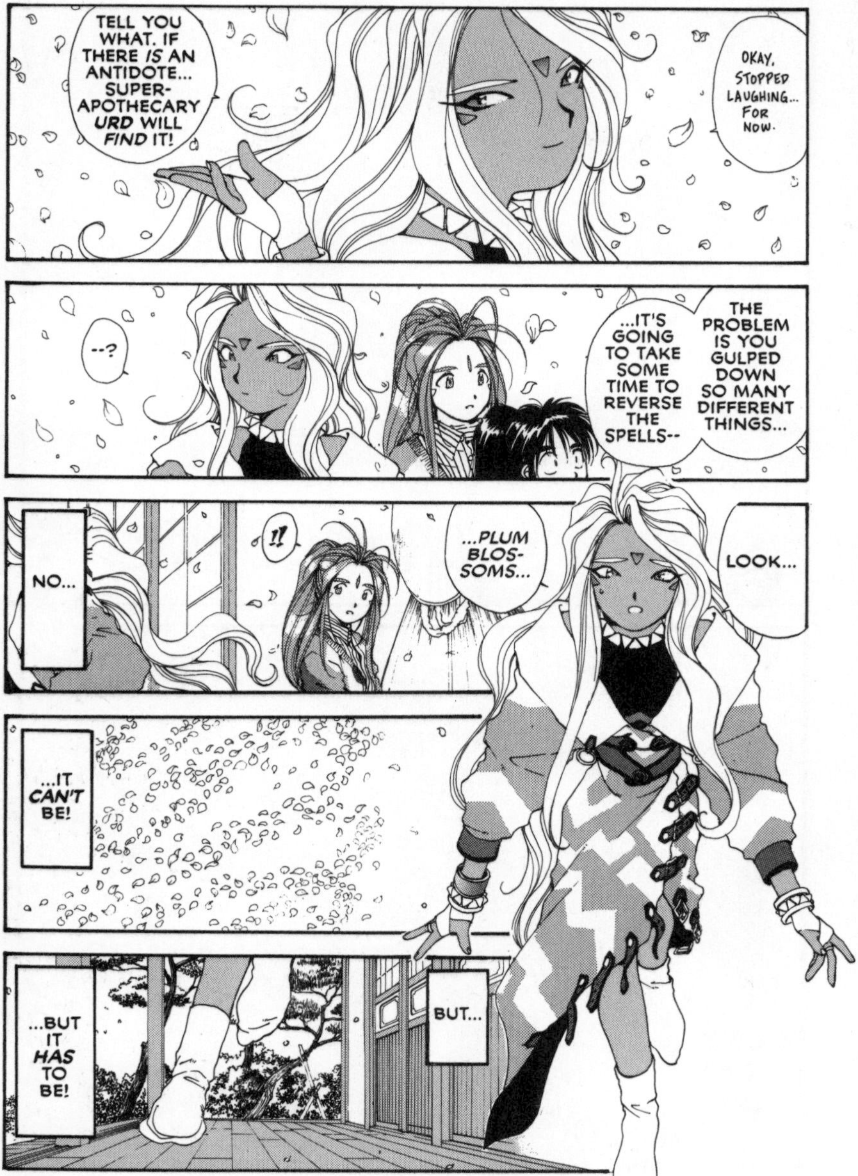
OKAY, STOPPED LAUGHING... FOR NOW.
TELL YOU WHAT. IF THERE *IS* AN ANTIDOTE... SUPER-APOTHECARY **URD** WILL *FIND* IT!
THE PROBLEM IS YOU GULPED DOWN SO MANY DIFFERENT THINGS...
...IT'S GOING TO TAKE SOME TIME TO REVERSE THE SPELLS--
--?
LOOK...
...PLUM BLOS-SOMS...
!!
NO...
...IT *CAN'T* BE!
BUT...
...BUT IT *HAS* TO BE!

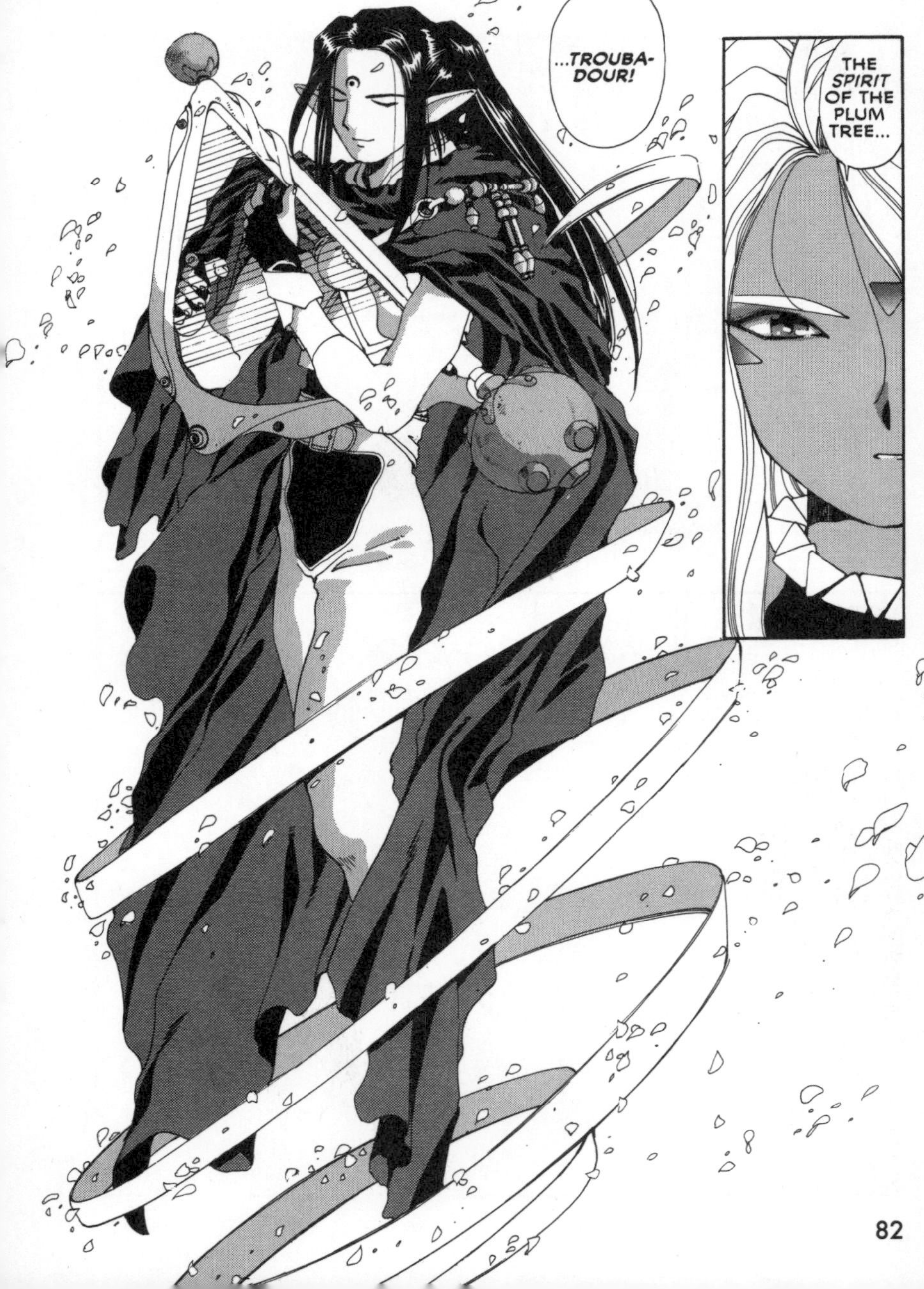
THE SPIRIT OF THE PLUM TREE...
...TROUBA-DOUR!

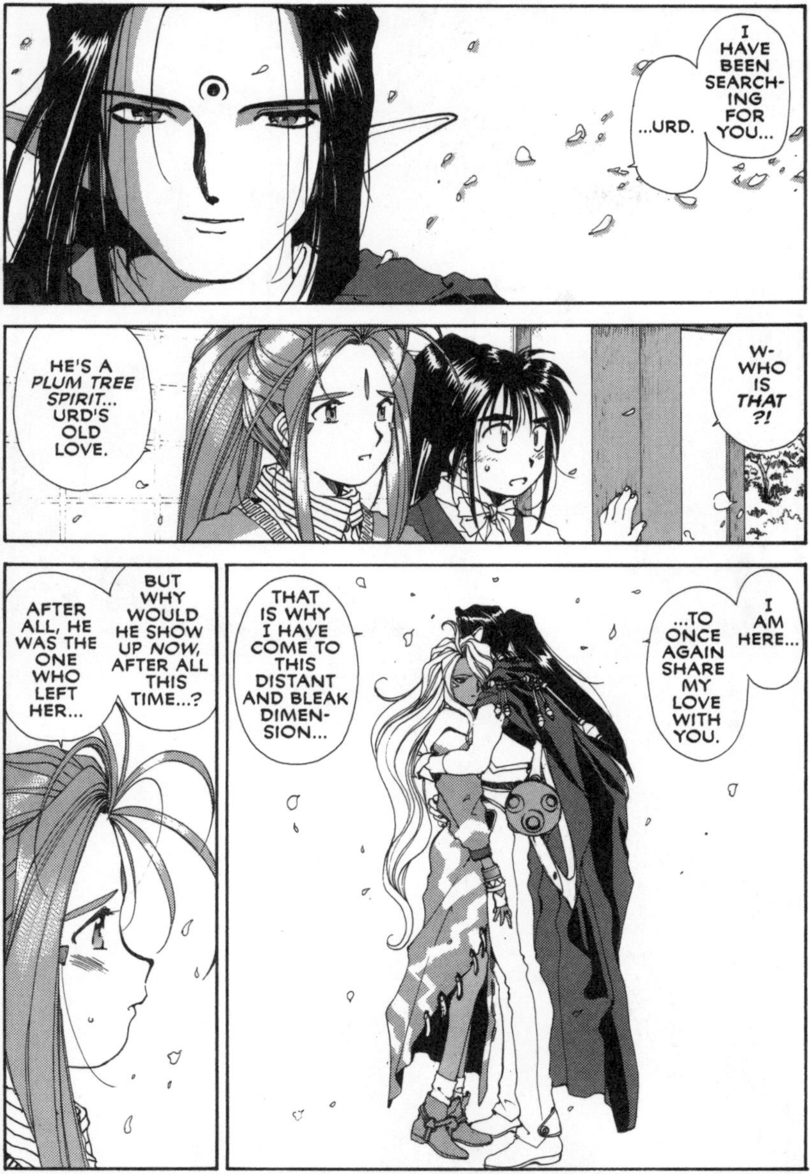
I HAVE BEEN SEARCHING FOR YOU...
...URD.
W-WHO IS *THAT* ?!
HE'S A *PLUM TREE SPIRIT*... URD'S OLD LOVE.
I AM HERE...
...TO ONCE AGAIN SHARE MY LOVE WITH YOU.
THAT IS WHY I HAVE COME TO THIS DISTANT AND BLEAK DIMENSION...
BUT WHY WOULD HE SHOW UP *NOW*, AFTER ALL THIS TIME...?
AFTER ALL, HE WAS THE ONE WHO LEFT HER...

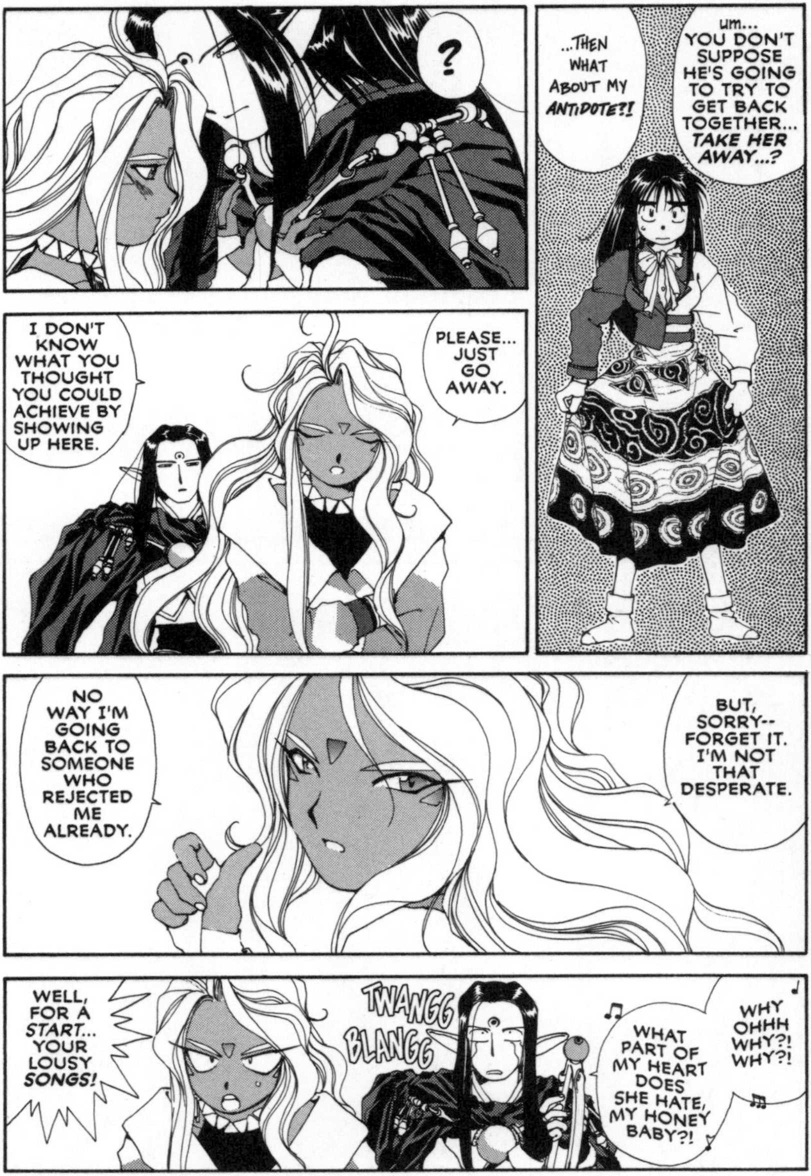
um... YOU DON'T SUPPOSE HE'S GOING TO TRY TO GET BACK TOGETHER... TAKE HER AWAY...?
...THEN WHAT ABOUT MY ANTIDOTE?!
?
PLEASE... JUST GO AWAY.
I DON'T KNOW WHAT YOU THOUGHT YOU COULD ACHIEVE BY SHOWING UP HERE.
BUT, SORRY-- FORGET IT. I'M NOT THAT DESPERATE.
NO WAY I'M GOING BACK TO SOMEONE WHO REJECTED ME ALREADY.
WHY OHHH WHY?! WHY?!
WHAT PART OF MY HEART DOES SHE HATE, MY HONEY BABY?!
TWANGG
BLANGG
WELL, FOR A START... YOUR LOUSY SONGS!

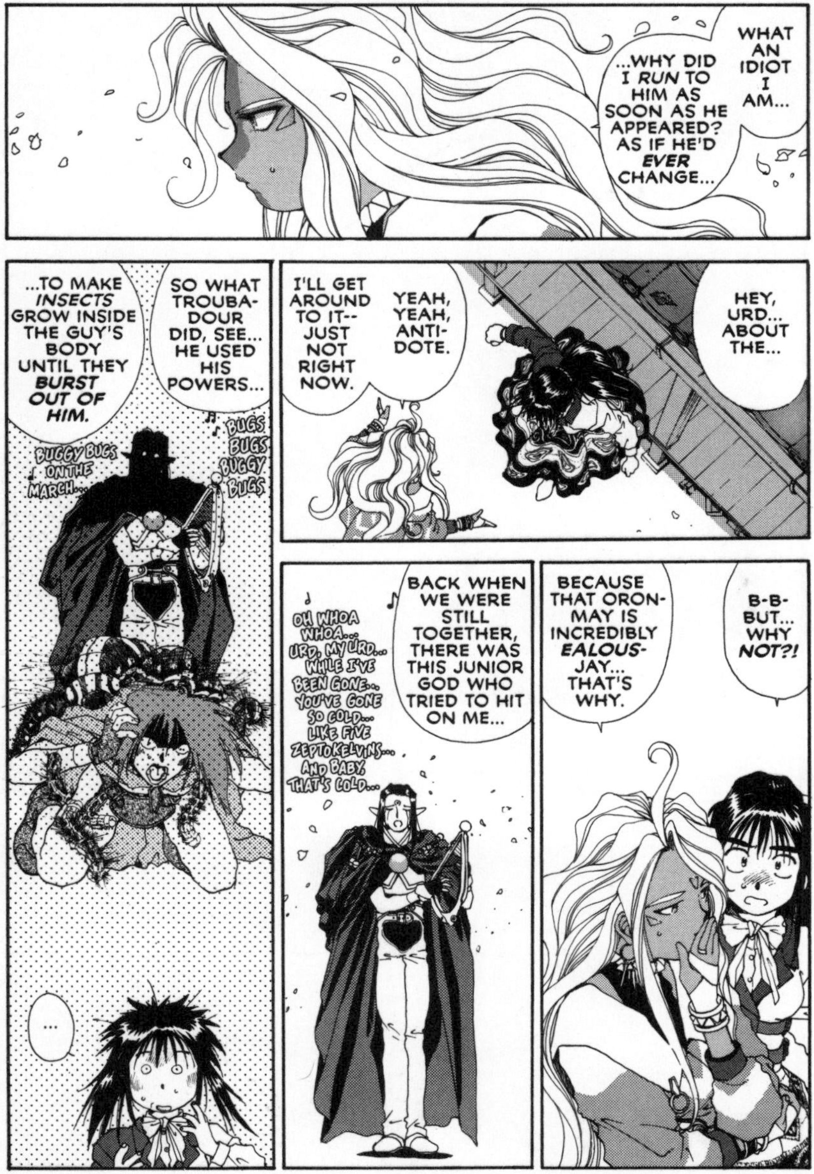
WHAT AN IDIOT I AM...
...WHY DID I RUN TO HIM AS SOON AS HE APPEARED? AS IF HE'D EVER CHANGE...
HEY, URD... ABOUT THE...
YEAH, YEAH, ANTI-DOTE.
I'LL GET AROUND TO IT-- JUST NOT RIGHT NOW.
B-B-BUT... WHY NOT?!
BECAUSE THAT ORON-MAY IS INCREDIBLY EALOUS-JAY... THAT'S WHY.
BACK WHEN WE WERE STILL TOGETHER, THERE WAS THIS JUNIOR GOD WHO TRIED TO HIT ON ME...
OH WHOA WHOA... URD, MY URD... WHILE I'VE BEEN GONE... YOU'VE GONE SO COLD... LIKE FIVE ZEPTOKELVINS... AND BABY, THAT'S COLD...
SO WHAT TROUBA-DOUR DID, SEE... HE USED HIS POWERS...
...TO MAKE INSECTS GROW INSIDE THE GUY'S BODY UNTIL THEY BURST OUT OF HIM.
BUGS BUGS BUGGY BUGS
BUGGY BUGS ON THE MARCH...
...

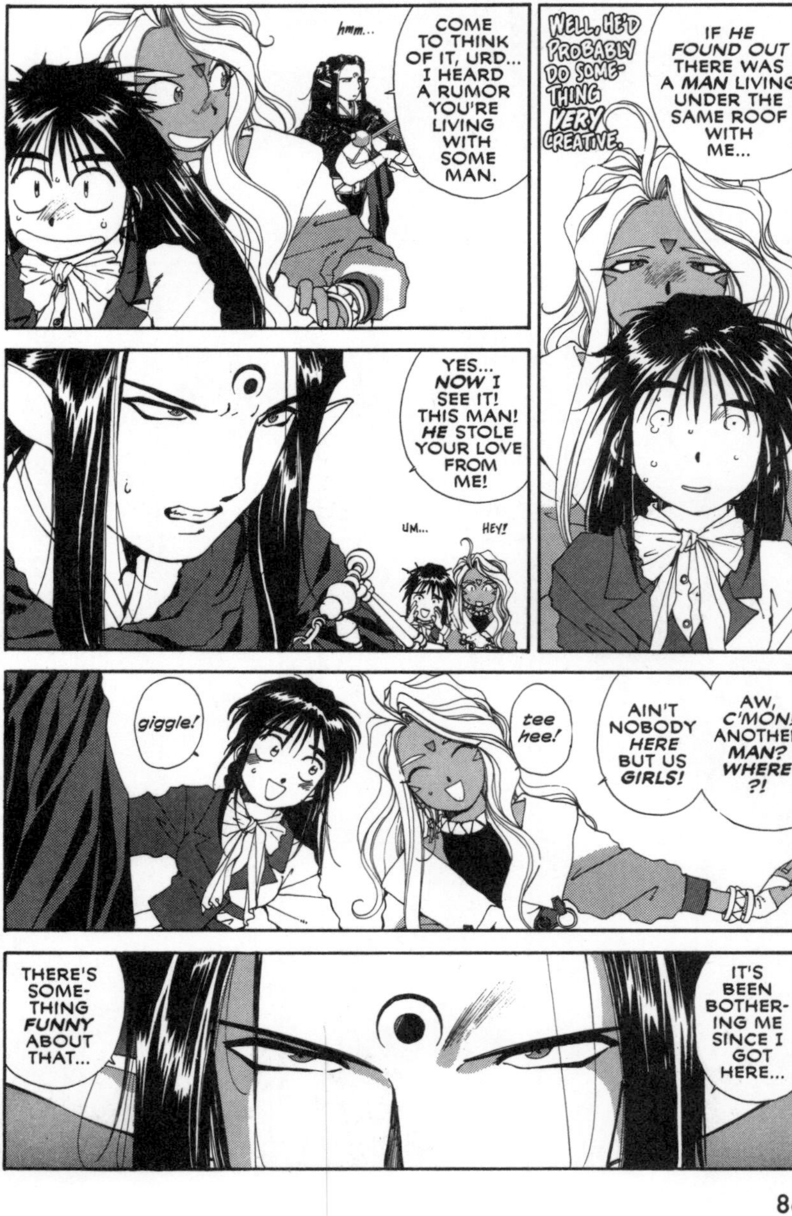
IF HE FOUND OUT THERE WAS A MAN LIVING UNDER THE SAME ROOF WITH ME...
WELL, HE'D PROBABLY DO SOME-THING VERY CREATIVE.
COME TO THINK OF IT, URD... I HEARD A RUMOR YOU'RE LIVING WITH SOME MAN.
hmm...
YES... NOW I SEE IT! THIS MAN! HE STOLE YOUR LOVE FROM ME!
HEY!
UM...
AW, C'MON! ANOTHER MAN? WHERE ?!
AIN'T NOBODY HERE BUT US GIRLS!
tee hee!
giggle!
IT'S BEEN BOTHER-ING ME SINCE I GOT HERE...
THERE'S SOME-THING FUNNY ABOUT THAT...

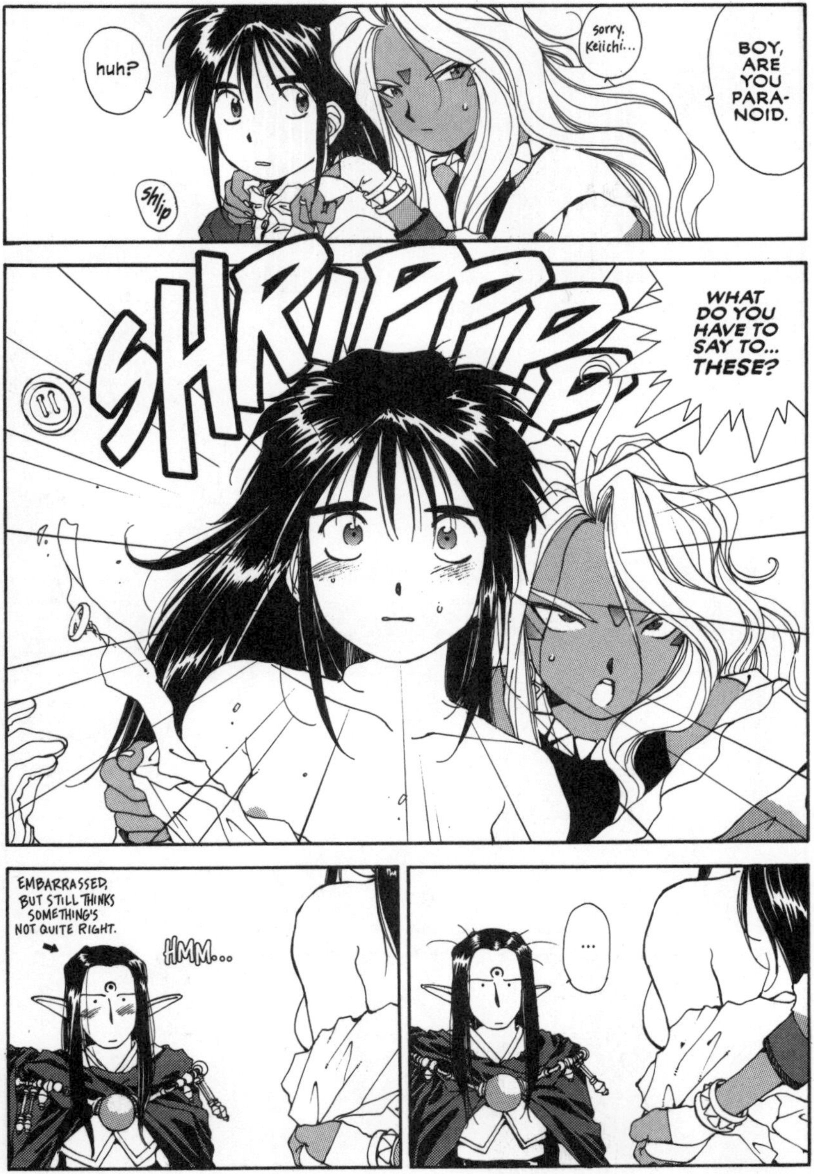
BOY, ARE YOU PARA-NOID.
sorry, Keiichi...
huh?
shlip
WHAT DO YOU HAVE TO SAY TO... THESE?
SHRIPPP
...
EMBARRASSED, BUT STILL THINKS SOMETHING'S NOT QUITE RIGHT.
HMM...

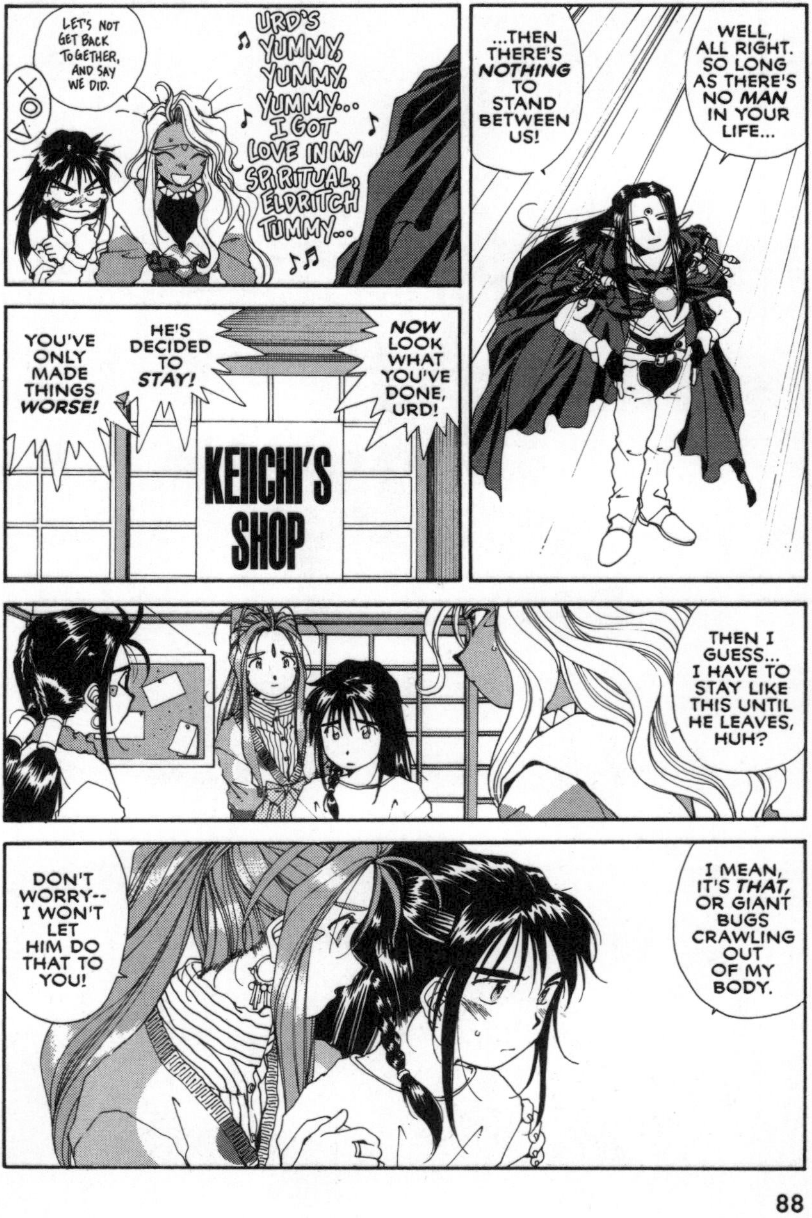
WELL, ALL RIGHT. SO LONG AS THERE'S NO *MAN* IN YOUR LIFE...
...THEN THERE'S *NOTHING* TO STAND BETWEEN US!
URD'S YUMMY, YUMMY, YUMMY... I GOT LOVE IN MY SPIRITUAL, ELDRITCH TUMMY...
LET'S NOT GET BACK TOGETHER, AND SAY WE DID.
XO△
NOW LOOK WHAT YOU'VE DONE, URD!
HE'S DECIDED TO *STAY!*
YOU'VE ONLY MADE THINGS *WORSE!*
KEIICHI'S SHOP
THEN I GUESS... I HAVE TO STAY LIKE THIS UNTIL HE LEAVES, HUH?
I MEAN, IT'S *THAT*, OR GIANT BUGS CRAWLING OUT OF MY BODY.
DON'T WORRY-- I WON'T LET HIM DO THAT TO YOU!

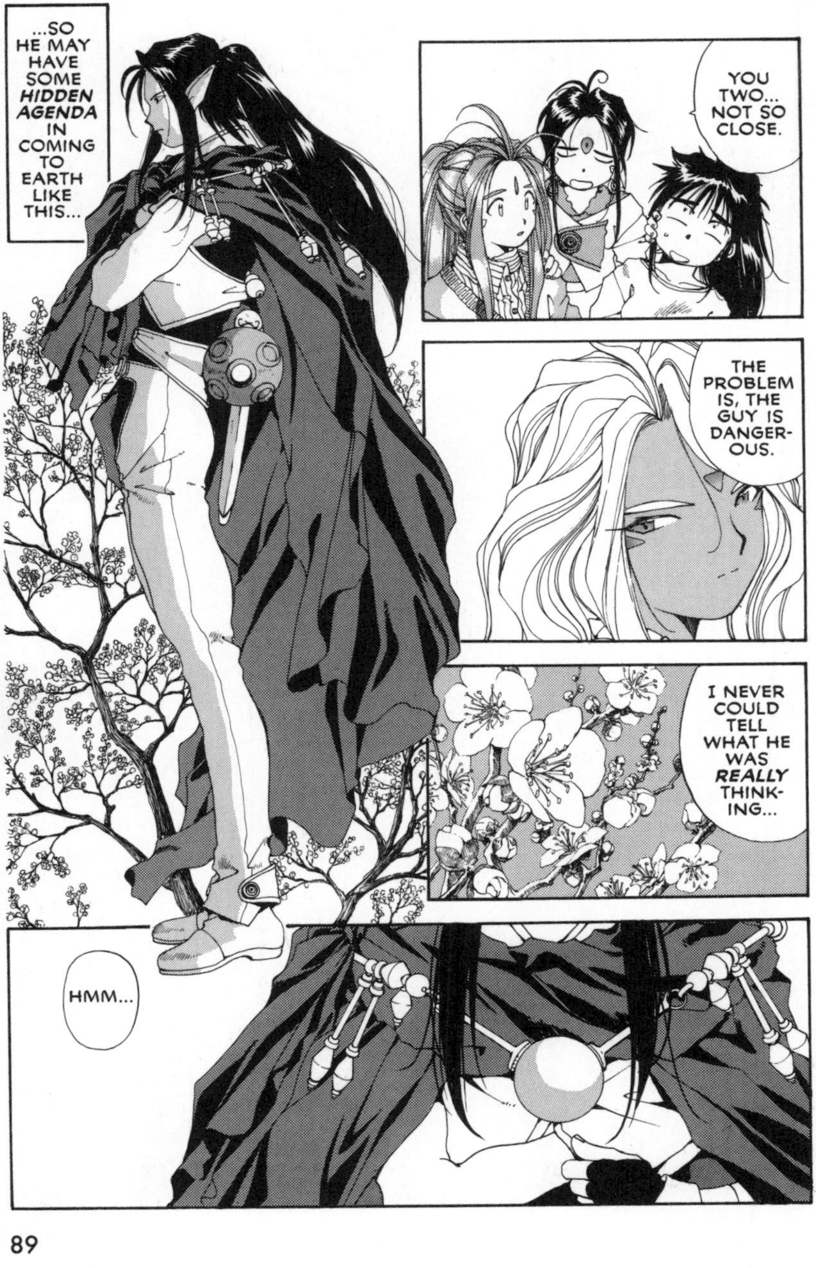
YOU TWO... NOT SO CLOSE.
THE PROBLEM IS, THE GUY IS DANGER-OUS.
I NEVER COULD TELL WHAT HE WAS *REALLY* THINK-ING...
...SO HE MAY HAVE SOME *HIDDEN AGENDA* IN COMING TO EARTH LIKE THIS...
HMM...

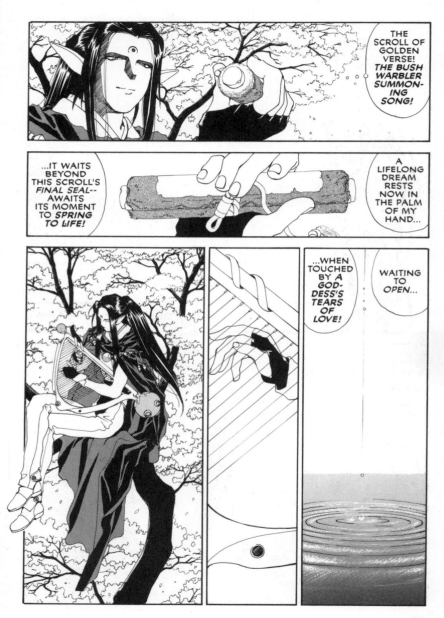

THE SCROLL OF GOLDEN VERSE! *THE BUSH WARBLER SUMMONING SONG!*
A LIFELONG DREAM RESTS NOW IN THE PALM OF MY HAND...
...IT WAITS BEYOND THIS SCROLL'S *FINAL SEAL*-- AWAITS ITS MOMENT TO *SPRING TO LIFE!*
WAITING TO *OPEN*...
...WHEN TOUCHED BY *A GODDESS'S TEARS OF LOVE!*

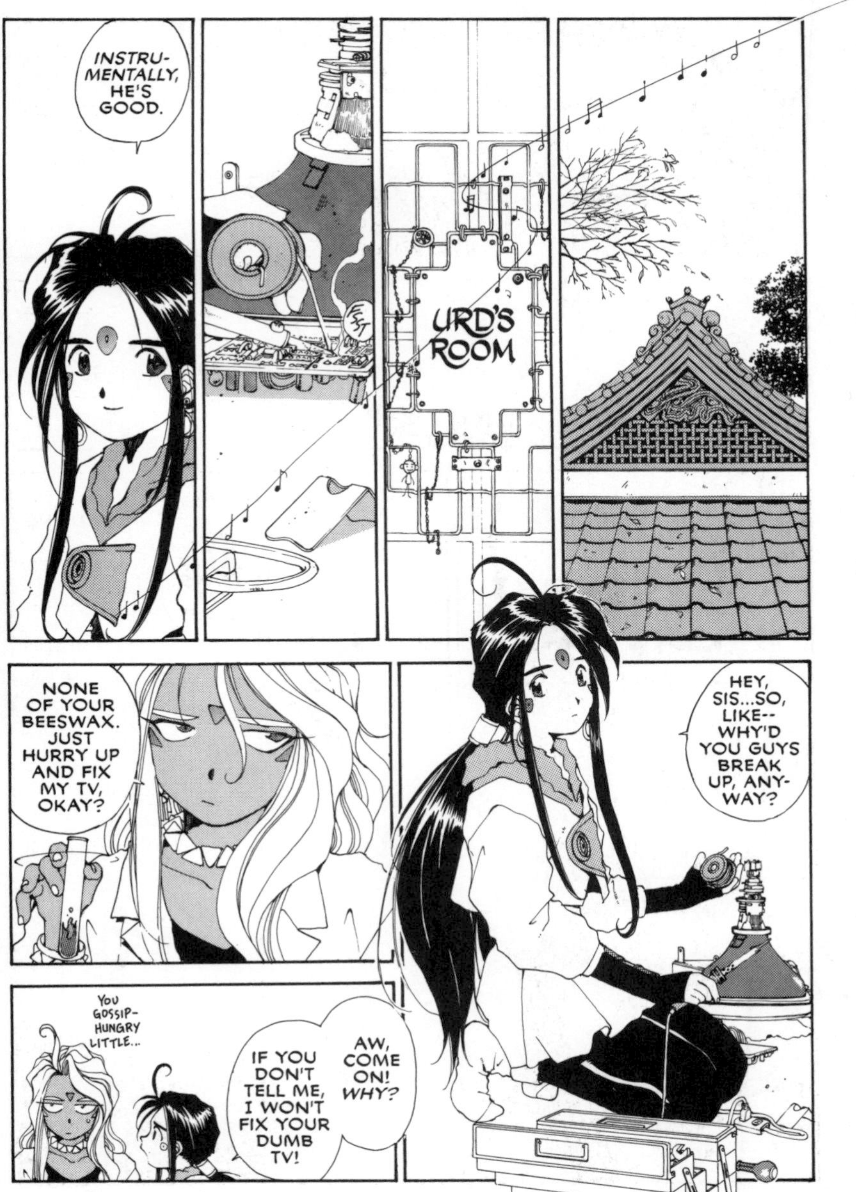
URD'S ROOM
INSTRU-MENTALLY, HE'S GOOD.
HEY, SIS...SO, LIKE--WHY'D YOU GUYS BREAK UP, ANYWAY?
NONE OF YOUR BEESWAX. JUST HURRY UP AND FIX MY TV, OKAY?
AW, COME ON! *WHY?*
IF YOU DON'T TELL ME, I WON'T FIX YOUR DUMB TV!
YOU GOSSIP-HUNGRY LITTLE...

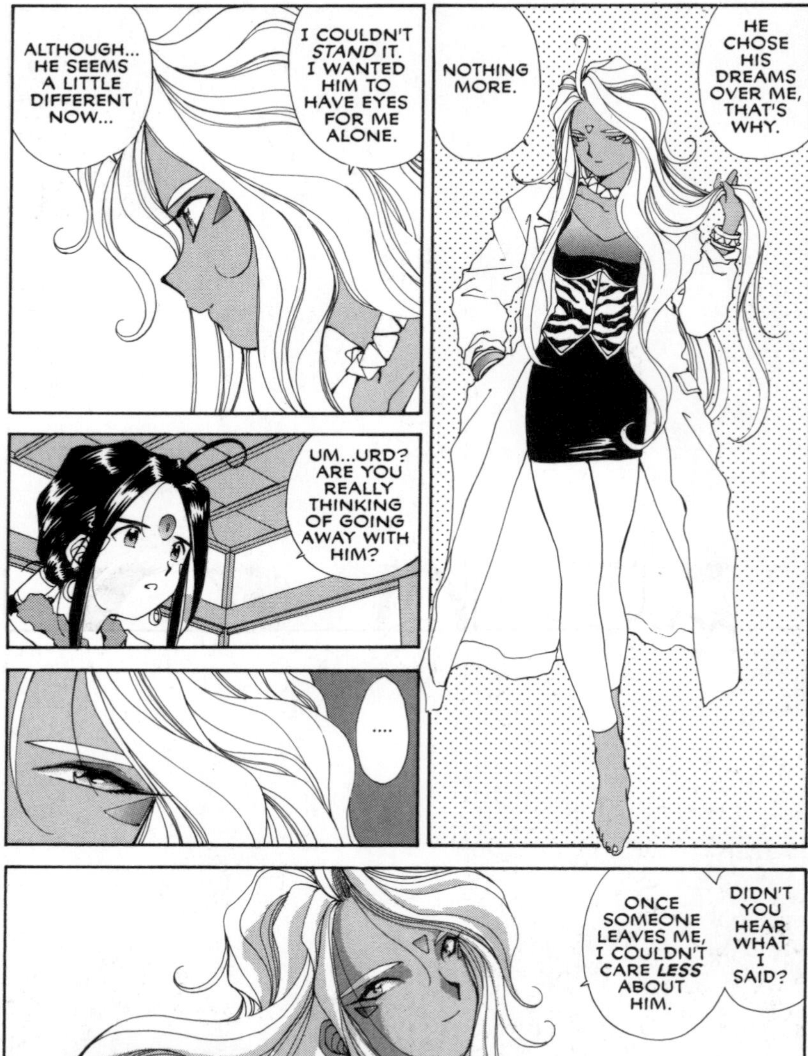
HE CHOSE HIS DREAMS OVER ME, THAT'S WHY.
NOTHING MORE.
I COULDN'T *STAND* IT. I WANTED HIM TO HAVE EYES FOR ME ALONE.
ALTHOUGH... HE SEEMS A LITTLE DIFFERENT NOW...
UM...URD? ARE YOU REALLY THINKING OF GOING AWAY WITH HIM?
....
DIDN'T YOU HEAR WHAT I SAID?
ONCE SOMEONE LEAVES ME, I COULDN'T CARE *LESS* ABOUT HIM.

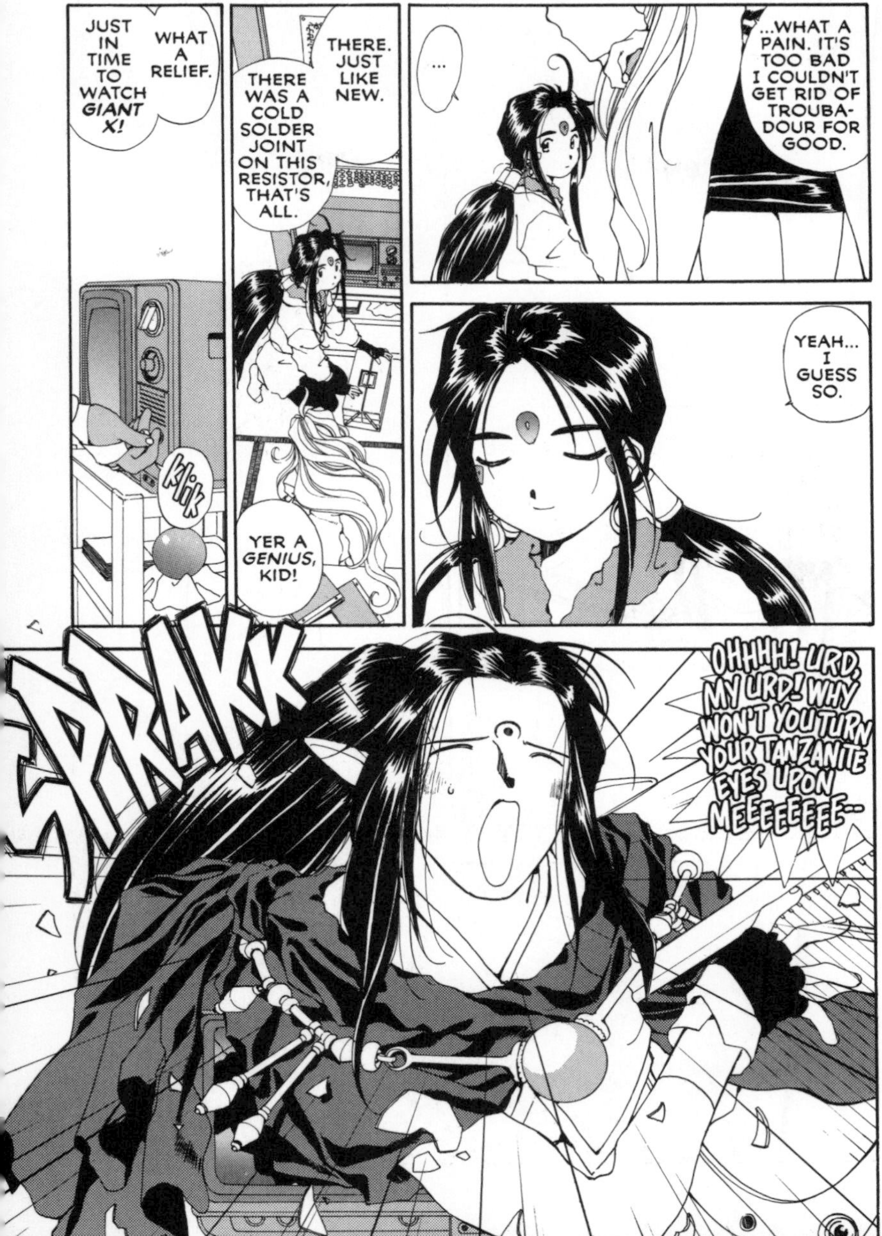
...WHAT A PAIN. IT'S TOO BAD I COULDN'T GET RID OF TROUBA-DOUR FOR GOOD.
...
YEAH... I GUESS SO.
THERE. JUST LIKE NEW.
THERE WAS A COLD SOLDER JOINT ON THIS RESISTOR, THAT'S ALL.
YER A *GENIUS*, KID!
WHAT A RELIEF.
JUST IN TIME TO WATCH *GIANT X!*
klik
OHHHH! URD, MY URD! WHY WON'T YOU TURN YOUR TANZANITE EYES UPON MEEEEEEE--
SPRAKK

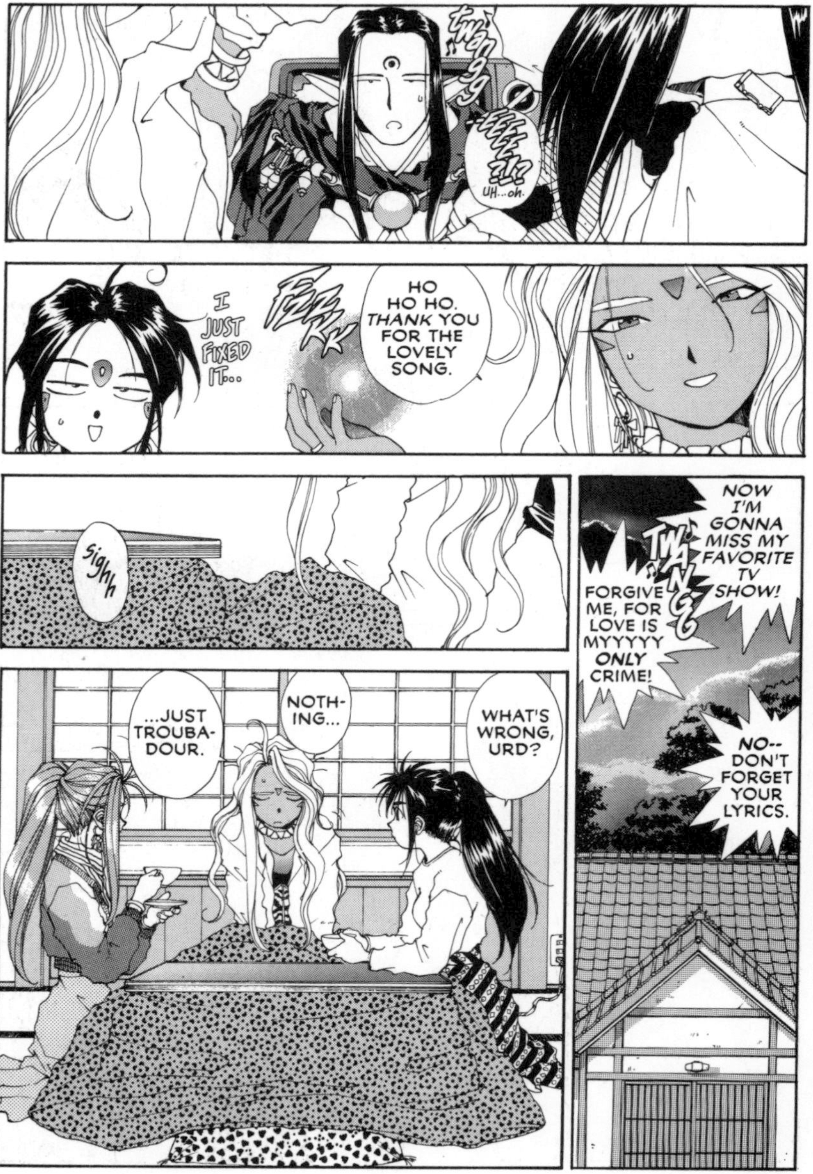
twanggg
EEEE!!?
UH...oh.
HO HO HO. *THANK* YOU FOR THE LOVELY SONG.
I JUST FIXED IT...
NOW I'M GONNA MISS MY FAVORITE TV SHOW!
TWANG
FORGIVE ME, FOR LOVE IS MYYYYY *ONLY* CRIME!
NO-- DON'T FORGET YOUR LYRICS.
sighh
WHAT'S WRONG, URD?
NOTH-ING...
...JUST TROUBA-DOUR.

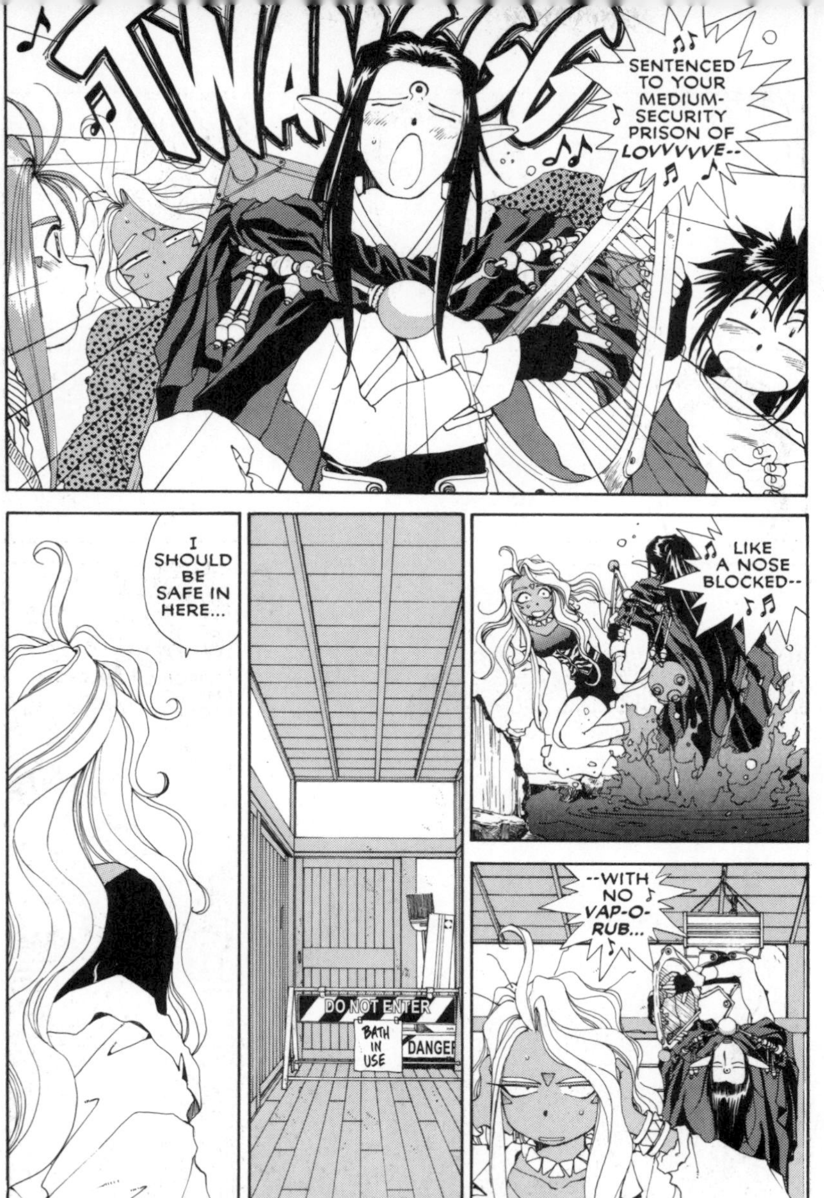
SENTENCED TO YOUR MEDIUM-SECURITY PRISON OF LOVVVVVE--
LIKE A NOSE BLOCKED--
--WITH NO VAP-O-RUB...
DO NOT ENTER
BATH IN USE
I SHOULD BE SAFE IN HERE...

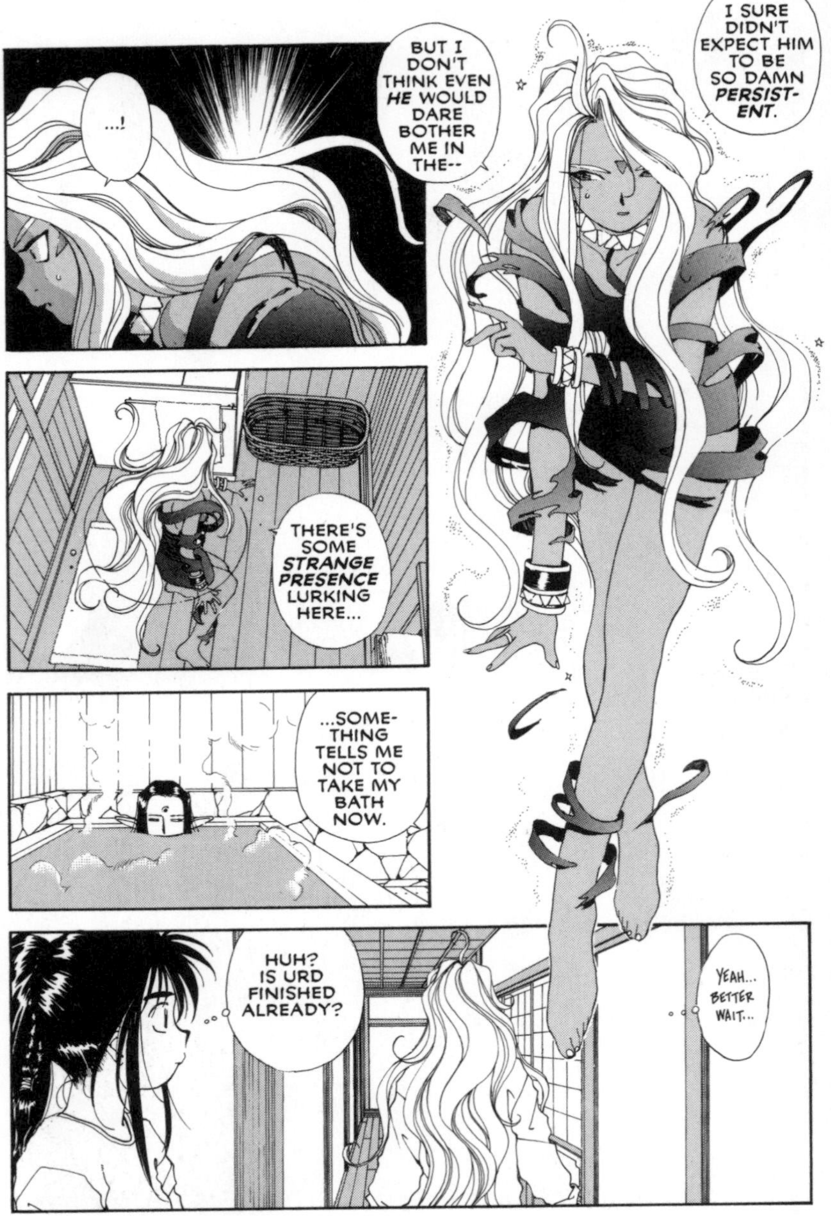
I SURE DIDN'T EXPECT HIM TO BE SO DAMN *PERSIST-ENT*.
BUT I DON'T THINK EVEN *HE* WOULD DARE BOTHER ME IN THE--
...!
THERE'S SOME *STRANGE PRESENCE* LURKING HERE...
...SOME-THING TELLS ME NOT TO TAKE MY BATH NOW.
YEAH... BETTER WAIT...
HUH? IS URD FINISHED ALREADY?

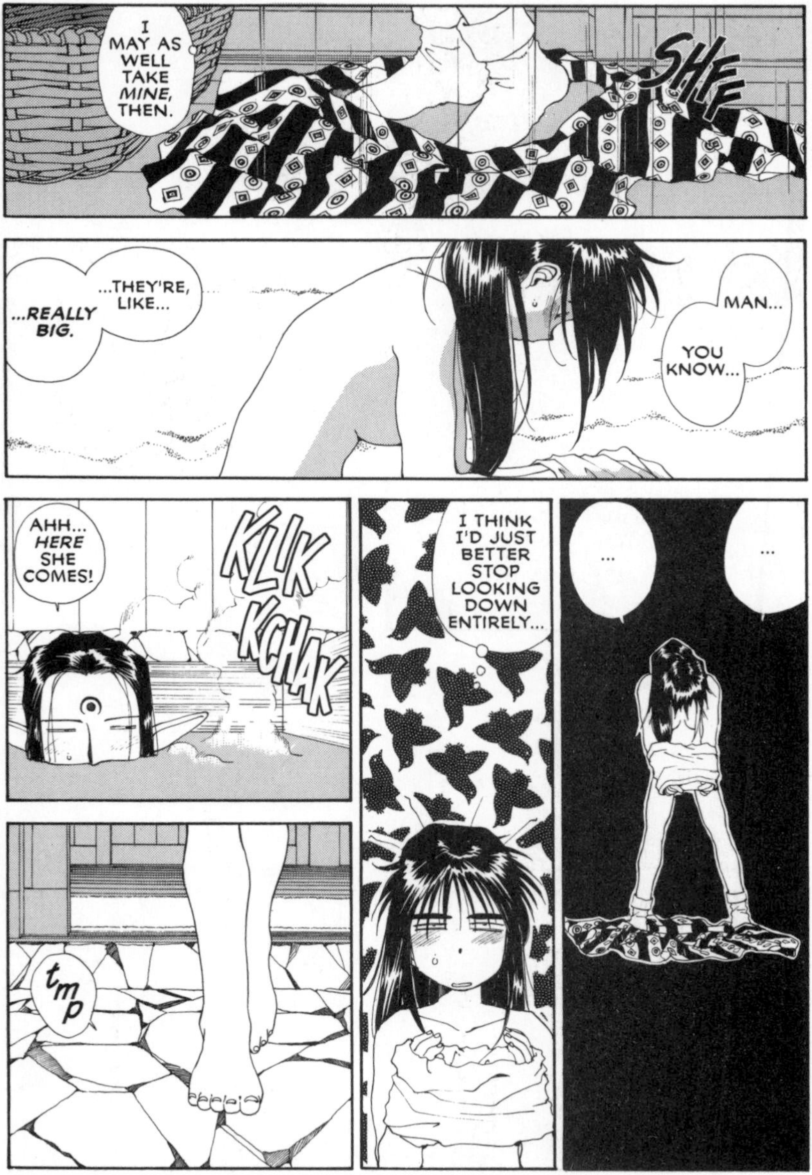
I MAY AS WELL TAKE *MINE*, THEN.
SHFF
MAN...
YOU KNOW...
...THEY'RE, LIKE...
...REALLY BIG.
...
...
I THINK I'D JUST BETTER STOP LOOKING DOWN ENTIRELY...
AHH... *HERE* SHE COMES!
KLIK
KCHAK
tmp

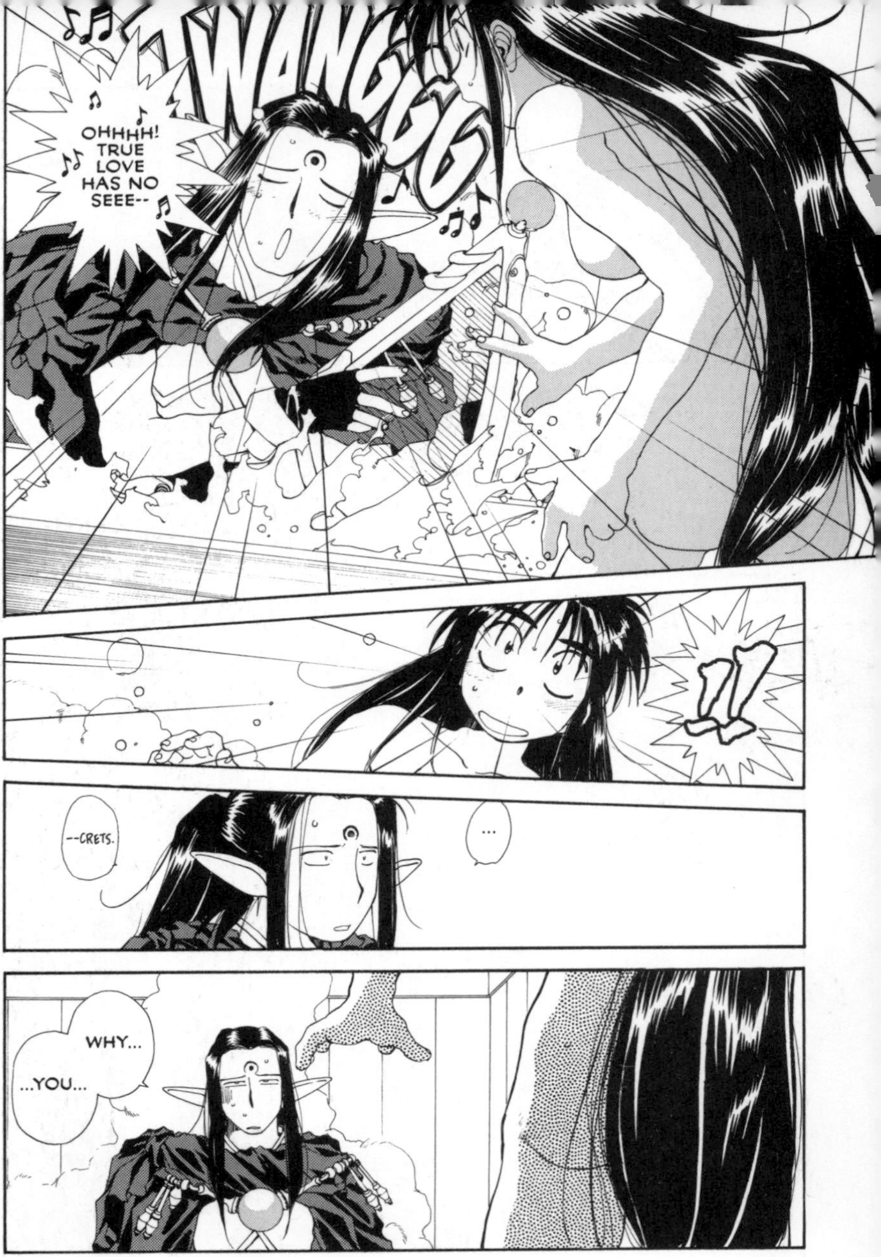
WANGGG
OHHHH! TRUE LOVE HAS NO SEEE--
...
--CRETS.
WHY...
...YOU...

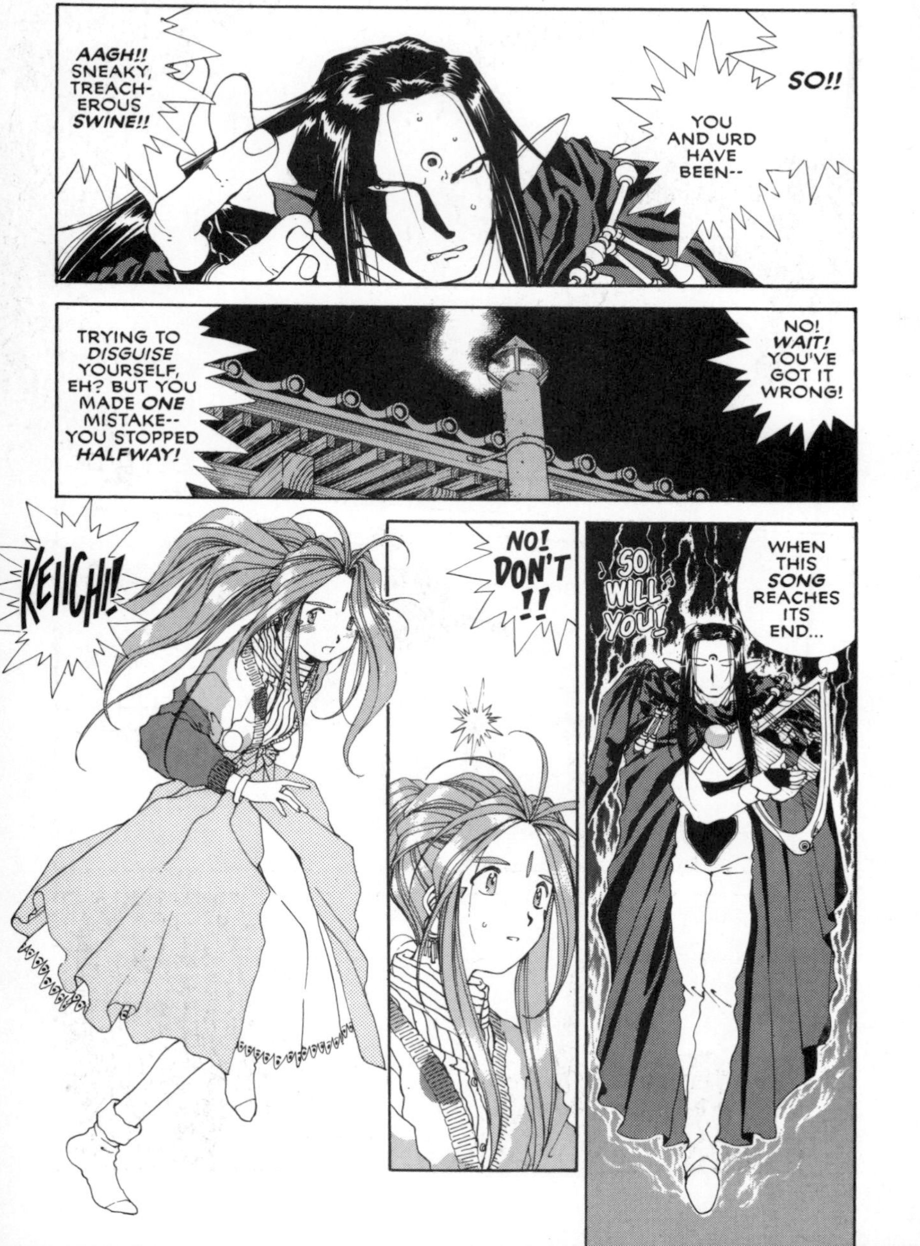
SO!!
YOU AND URD HAVE BEEN--
AAGH!! SNEAKY, TREACHEROUS SWINE!!
NO! WAIT! YOU'VE GOT IT WRONG!
TRYING TO DISGUISE YOURSELF, EH? BUT YOU MADE ONE MISTAKE-- YOU STOPPED HALFWAY!
WHEN THIS SONG REACHES ITS END...
SO WILL YOU!
NO! DON'T !!
KEIICHI!

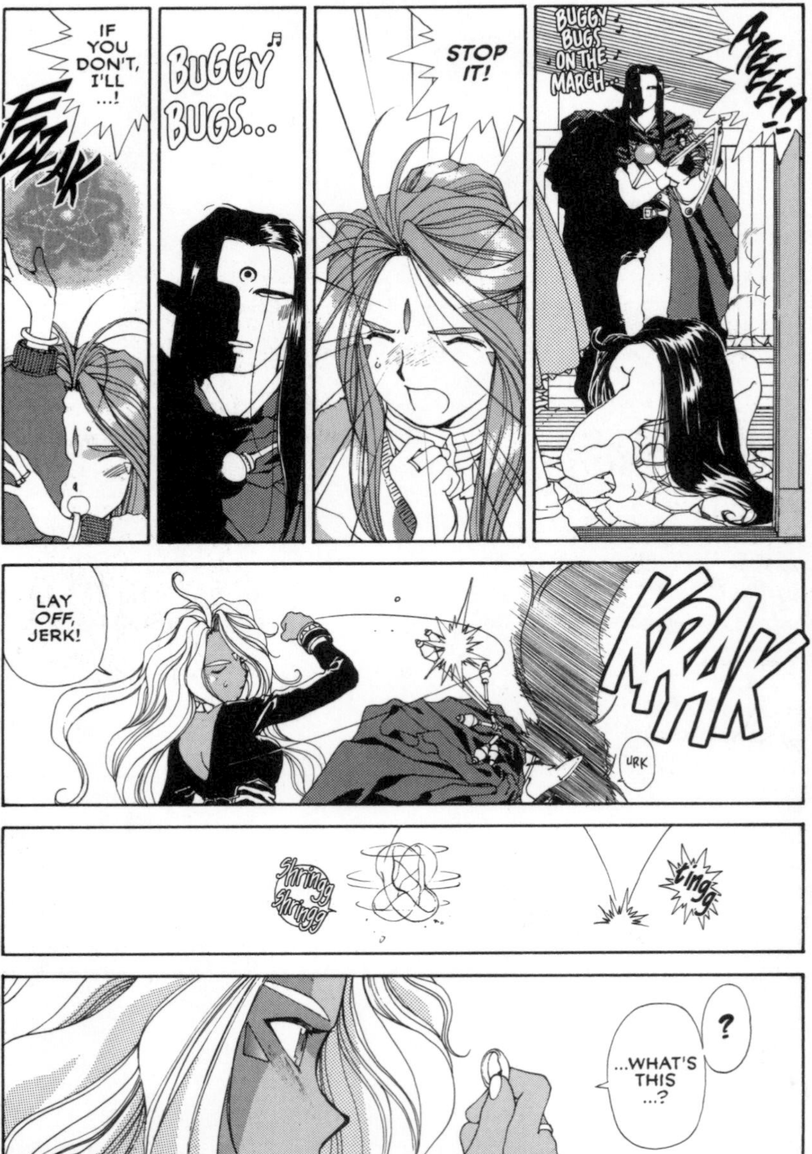
AIEEEE!!
BUGGY BUGS ON THE MARCH...
STOP IT!
BUGGY BUGS...
IF YOU DON'T, I'LL ...!
FZZZAK
KRAK
LAY OFF, JERK!
URK
tingg
Shringg Shringg
?
...WHAT'S THIS ...?

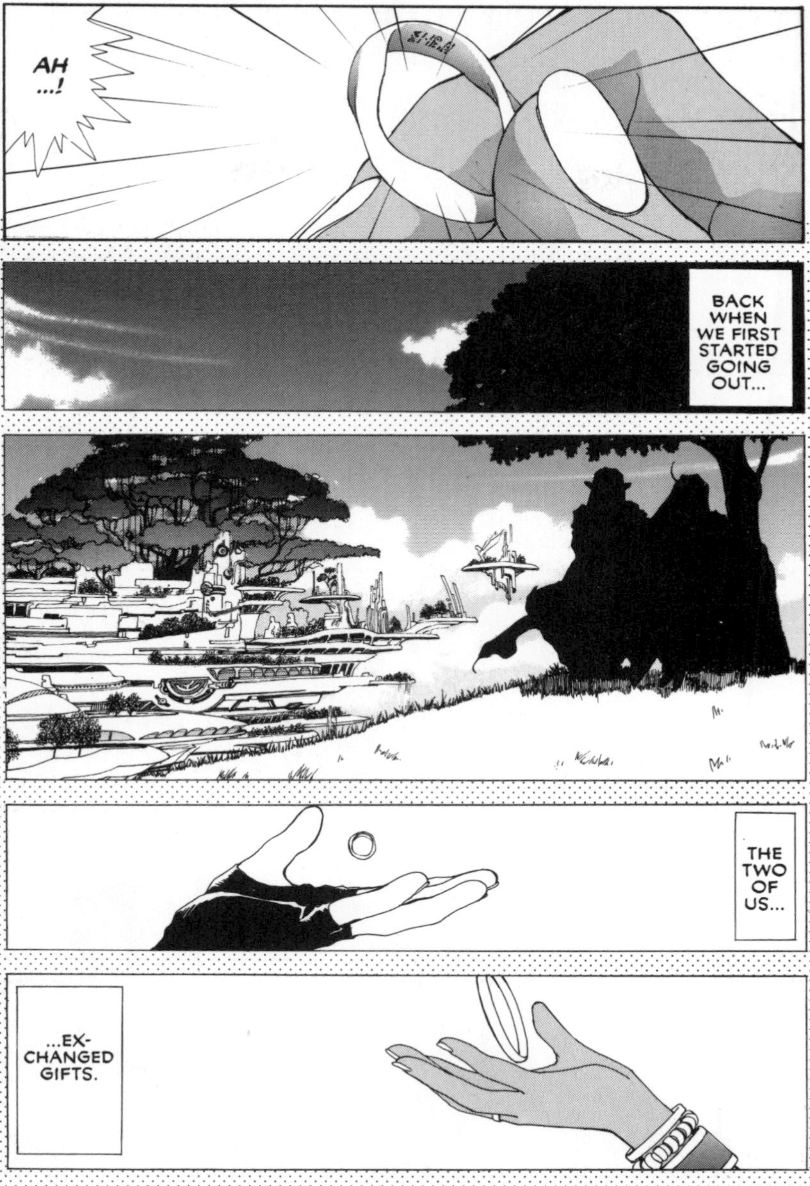
AH ...!
BACK WHEN WE FIRST STARTED GOING OUT...
THE TWO OF US...
...EX-CHANGED GIFTS.

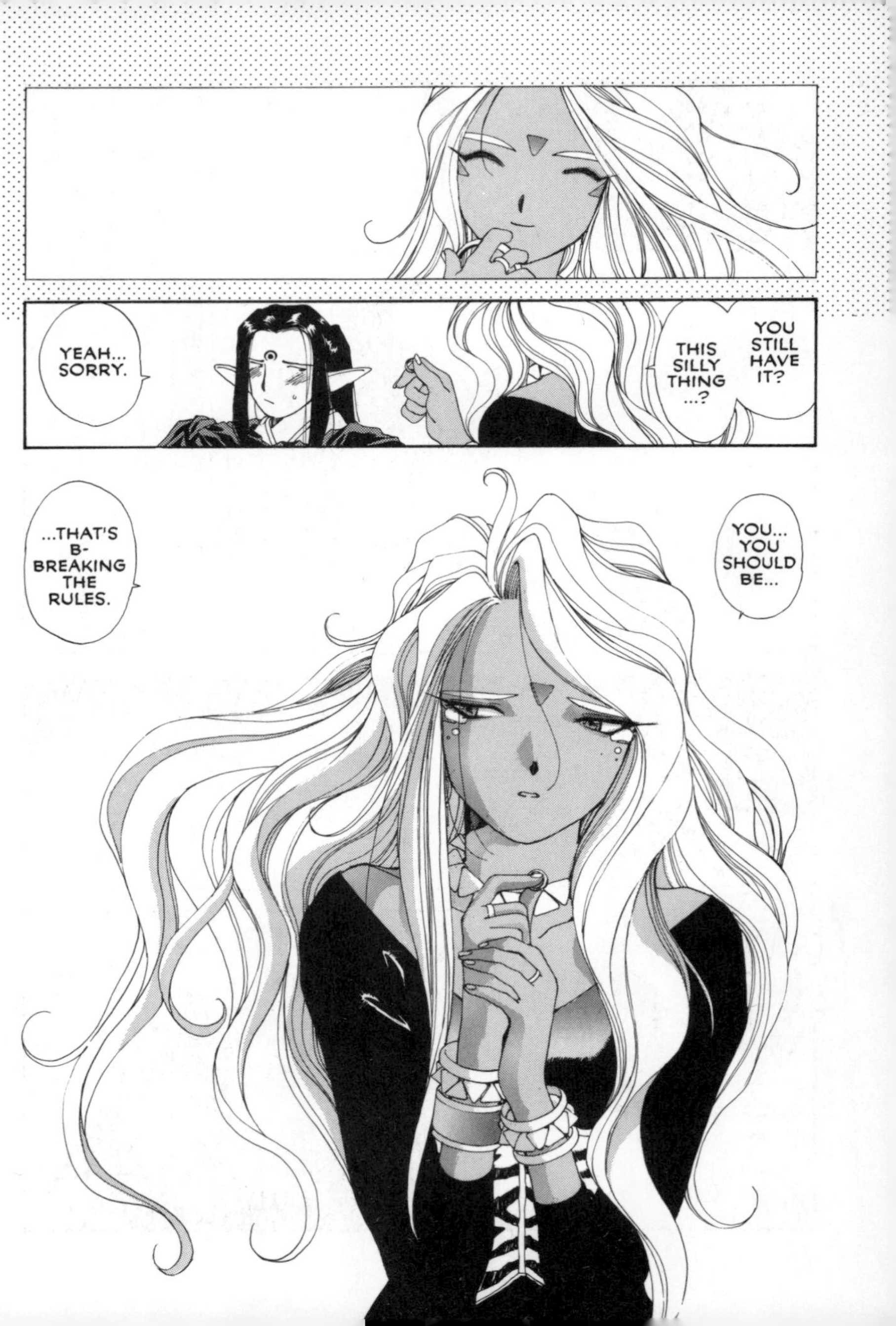
YOU STILL HAVE IT?
THIS SILLY THING ...?
YEAH... SORRY.
YOU... YOU SHOULD BE...
...THAT'S B-BREAKING THE RULES.

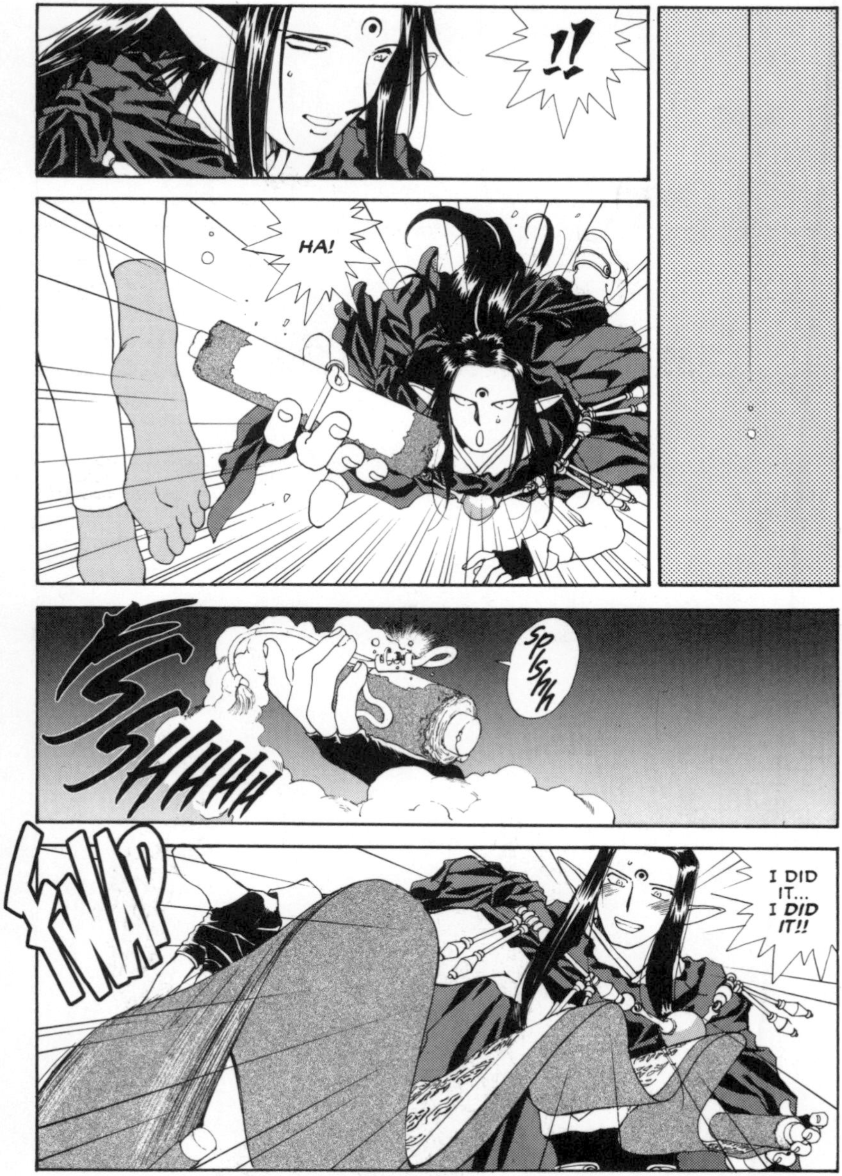
!!
HA!
SPISHH
SSHHHH
FWAP
I DID IT... I DID IT!!

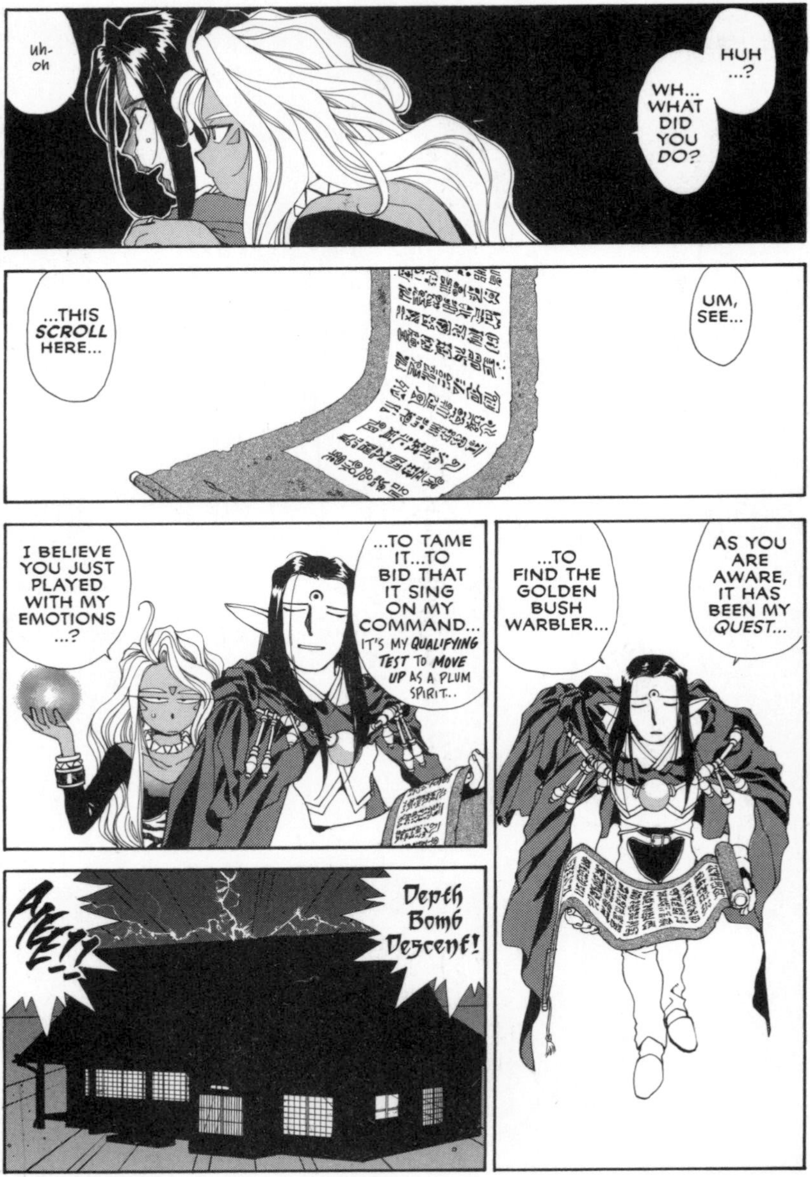
HUH ...?
WH... WHAT DID YOU DO?
uh-oh
UM, SEE...
...THIS SCROLL HERE...
AS YOU ARE AWARE, IT HAS BEEN MY QUEST...
...TO FIND THE GOLDEN BUSH WARBLER...
...TO TAME IT...TO BID THAT IT SING ON MY COMMAND...
IT'S MY QUALIFYING TEST TO MOVE UP AS A PLUM SPIRIT..
I BELIEVE YOU JUST PLAYED WITH MY EMOTIONS ...?
Depth Bomb Descent!
AIEE!!

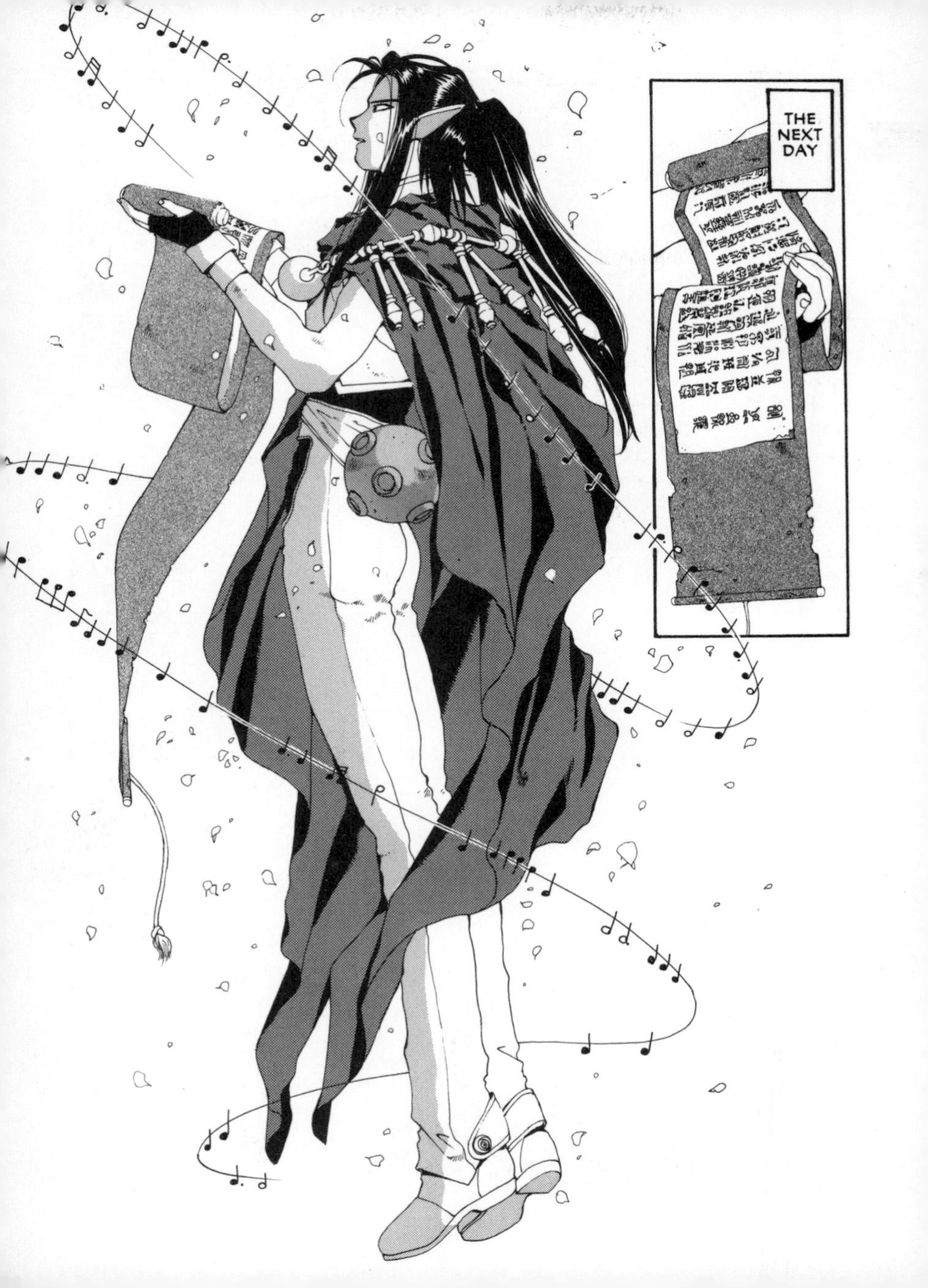
THE NEXT DAY

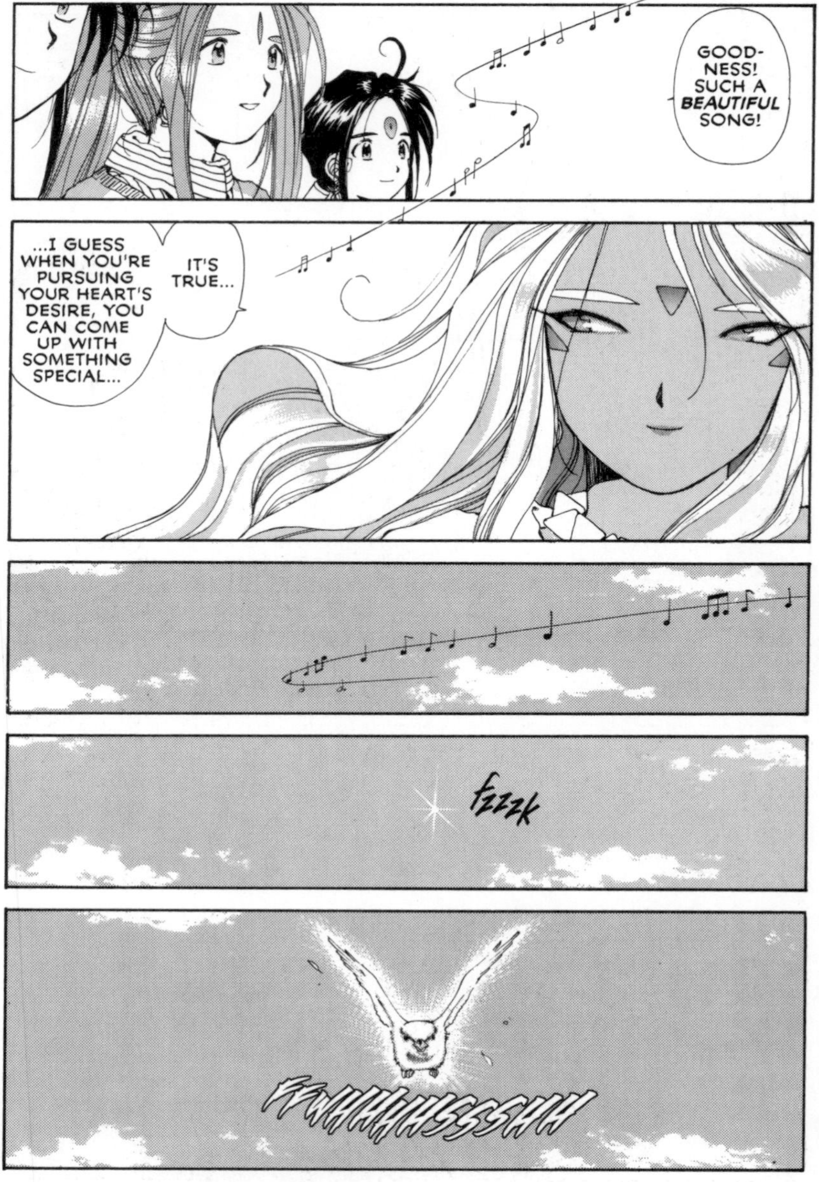
GOOD-NESS! SUCH A **BEAUTIFUL** SONG!
IT'S TRUE...
...I GUESS WHEN YOU'RE PURSUING YOUR HEART'S DESIRE, YOU CAN COME UP WITH SOMETHING SPECIAL...
fzzzk
FFWHHHHHSSSSHH

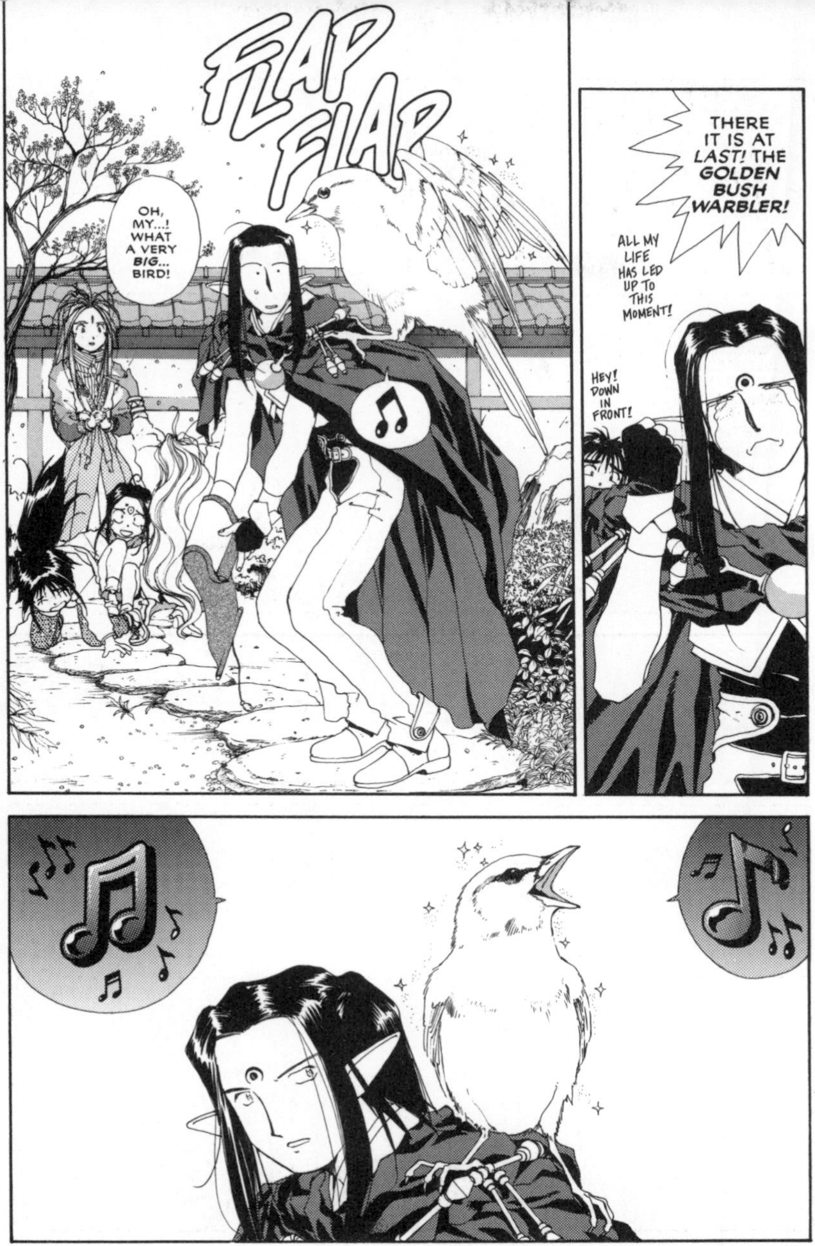
THERE IT IS AT LAST! THE GOLDEN BUSH WARBLER!
ALL MY LIFE HAS LED UP TO THIS MOMENT!
HEY! DOWN IN FRONT!
FLAP FLAP
OH, MY...! WHAT A VERY BIG... BIRD!

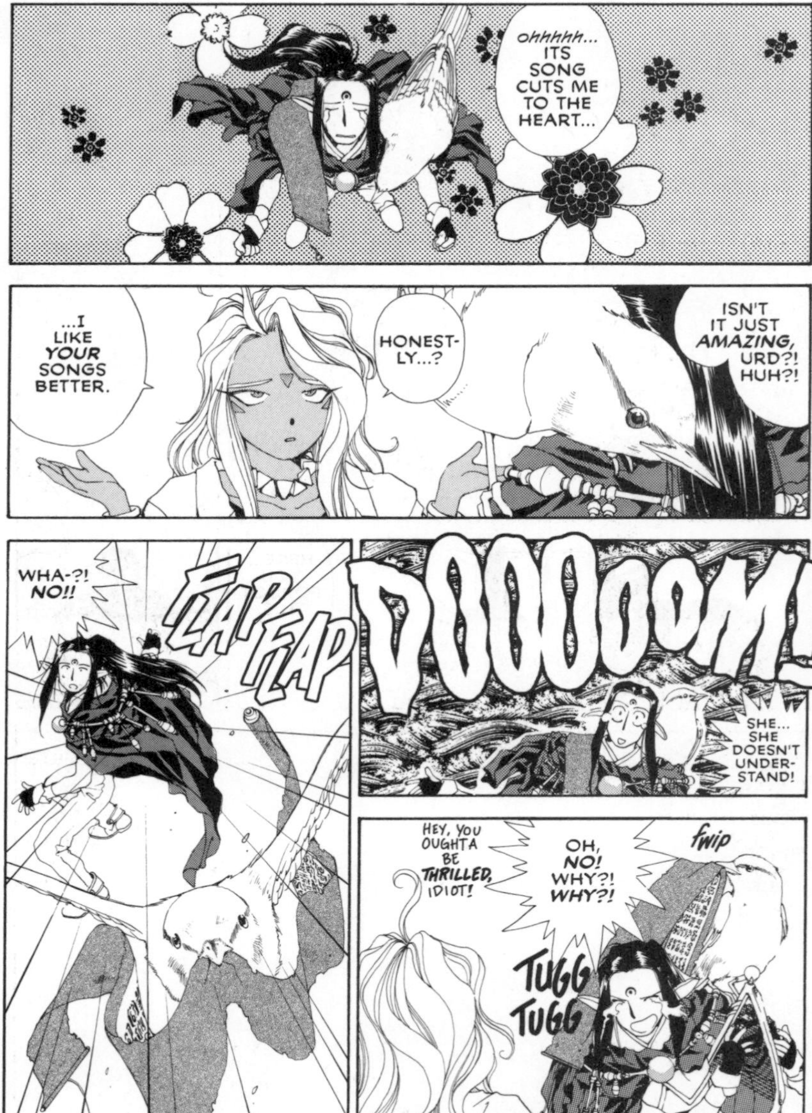

ohhhhh... ITS SONG CUTS ME TO THE HEART...
ISN'T IT JUST AMAZING, URD?! HUH?!
HONEST-LY...?
...I LIKE YOUR SONGS BETTER.
DOOOOOM!
SHE... SHE DOESN'T UNDER-STAND!
fwip
OH, NO! WHY?! WHY?!
HEY, YOU OUGHTA BE THRILLED, IDIOT!
TUGG TUGG
FLAP FLAP
WHA-?! NO!!

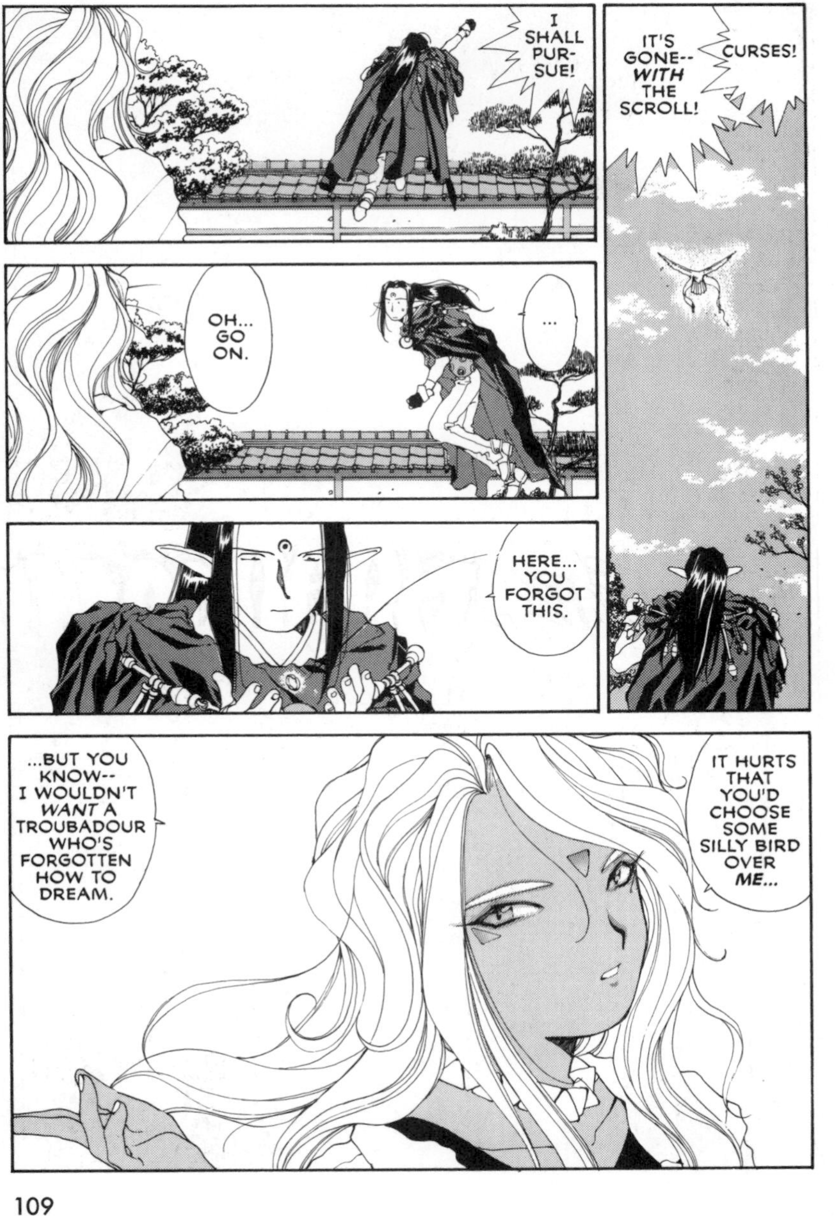
CURSES!
IT'S GONE--*WITH* THE SCROLL!
I SHALL PUR-SUE!
...
OH... GO ON.
HERE... YOU FORGOT THIS.
IT HURTS THAT YOU'D CHOOSE SOME SILLY BIRD OVER *ME*...
...BUT YOU KNOW-- I WOULDN'T *WANT* A TROUBADOUR WHO'S FORGOTTEN HOW TO DREAM.

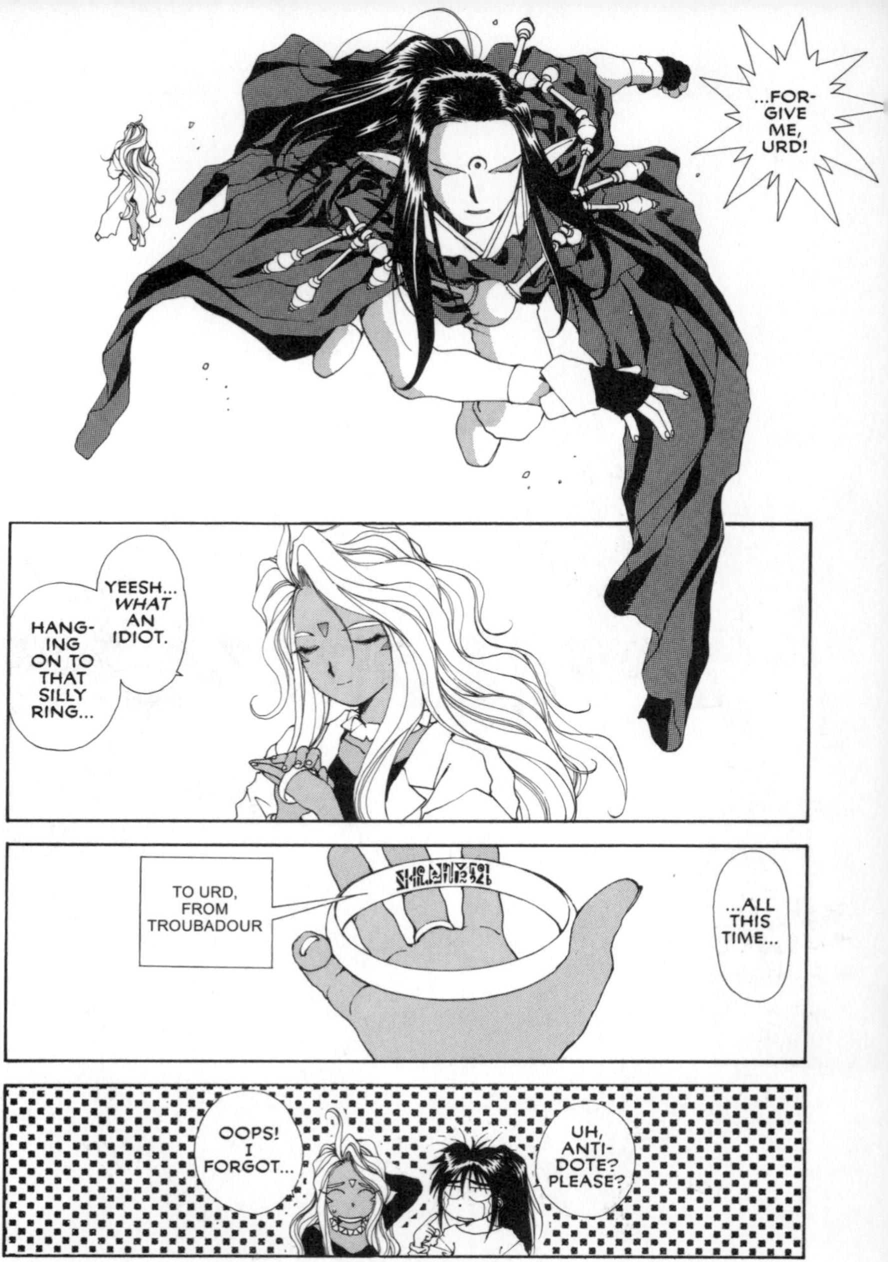
...FORGIVE ME, URD!
YEESH... *WHAT* AN IDIOT.
HANGING ON TO THAT SILLY RING...
...ALL THIS TIME...
TO URD, FROM TROUBADOUR
UH, ANTIDOTE? PLEASE?
OOPS! I FORGOT...

CHAPTER 56

It's Lonely at the Top

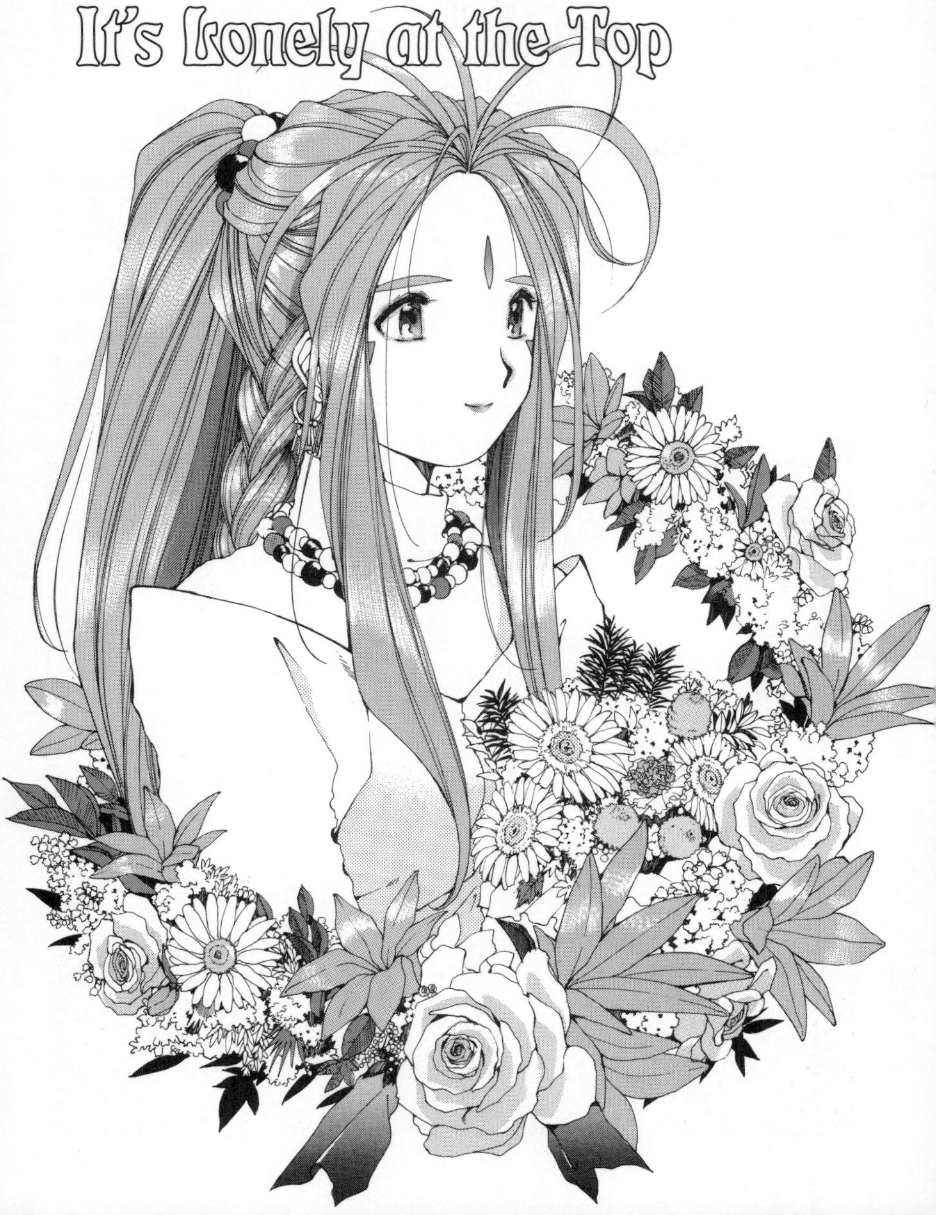

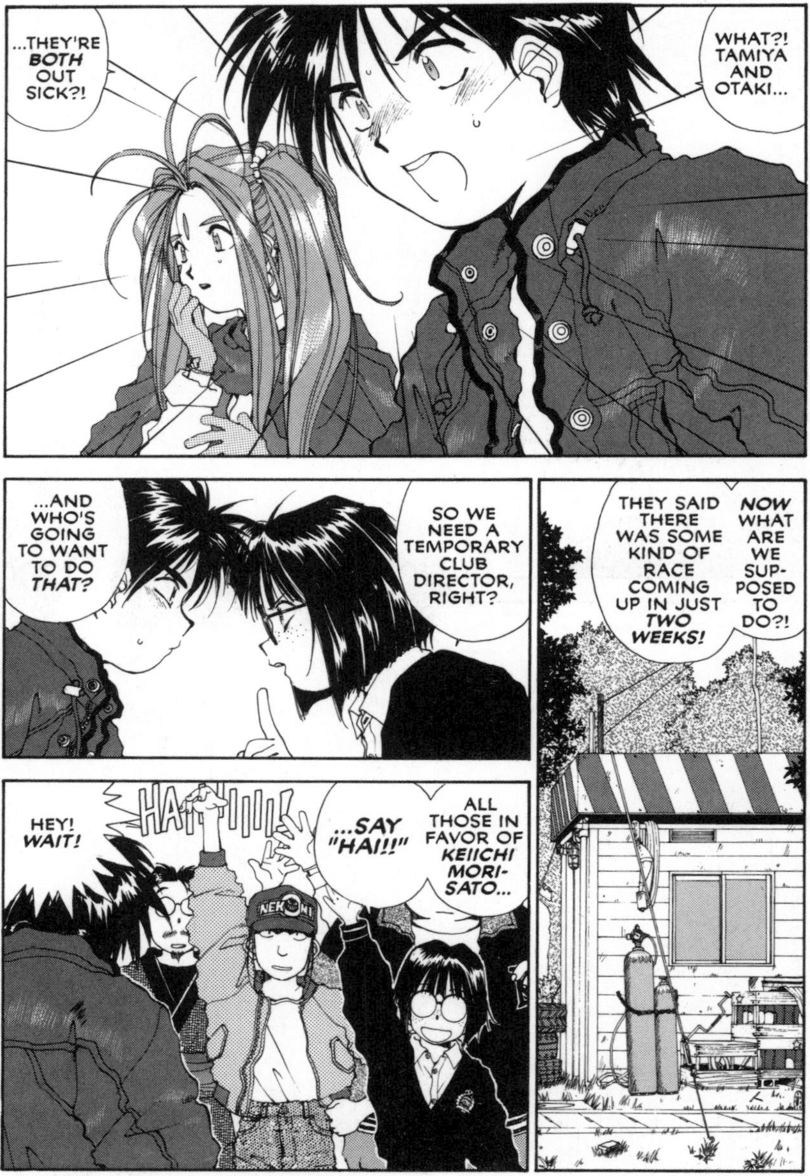
WHAT?! TAMIYA AND OTAKI...
...THEY'RE *BOTH* OUT SICK?!
NOW WHAT ARE WE SUP-POSED TO DO?!
THEY SAID THERE WAS SOME KIND OF RACE COMING UP IN JUST *TWO WEEKS!*
SO WE NEED A TEMPORARY CLUB DIRECTOR, RIGHT?
...AND WHO'S GOING TO WANT TO DO *THAT?*
ALL THOSE IN FAVOR OF *KEIICHI MORI-SATO...*
...SAY "HAI!!"
HAIIIIII!
HEY! *WAIT!*

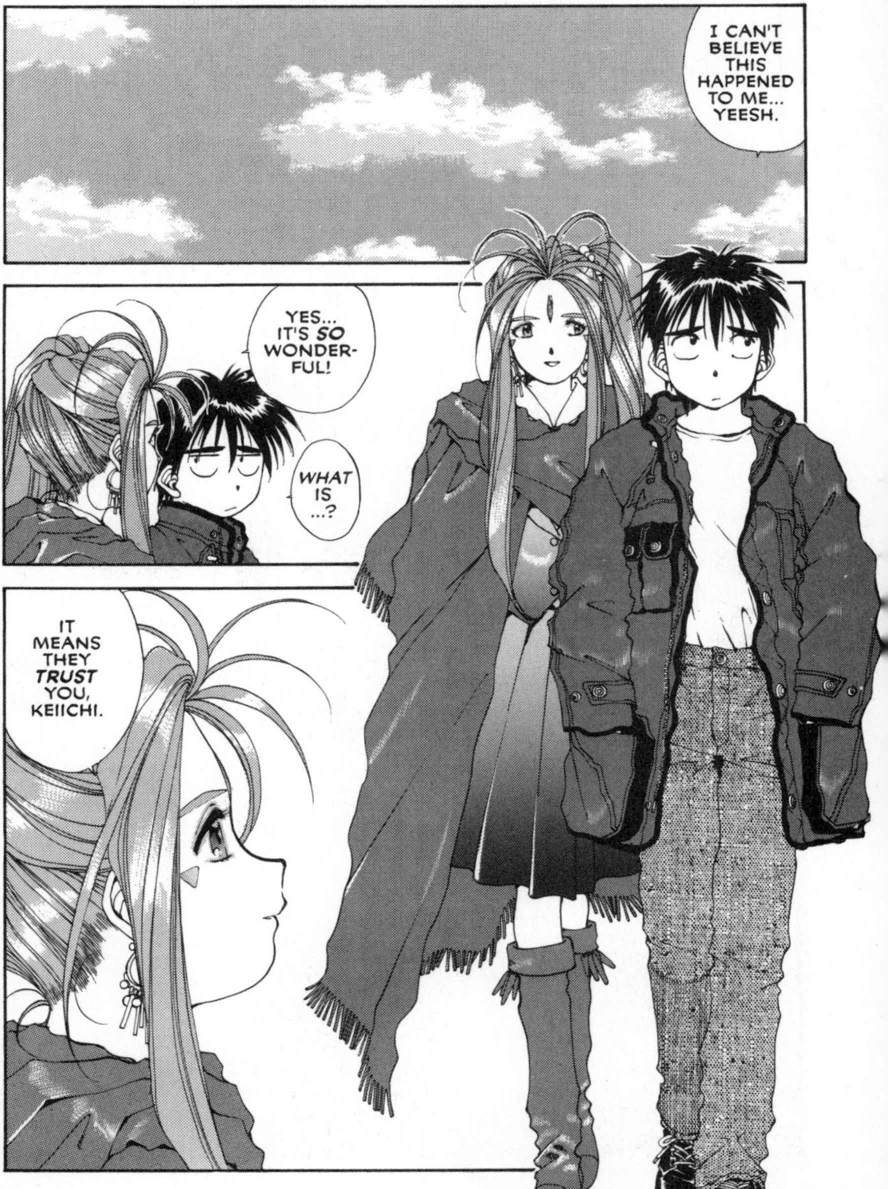
I CAN'T BELIEVE THIS HAPPENED TO ME... YEESH.
YES... IT'S *SO* WONDERFUL!
WHAT IS ...?
IT MEANS THEY ***TRUST*** YOU, KEIICHI.

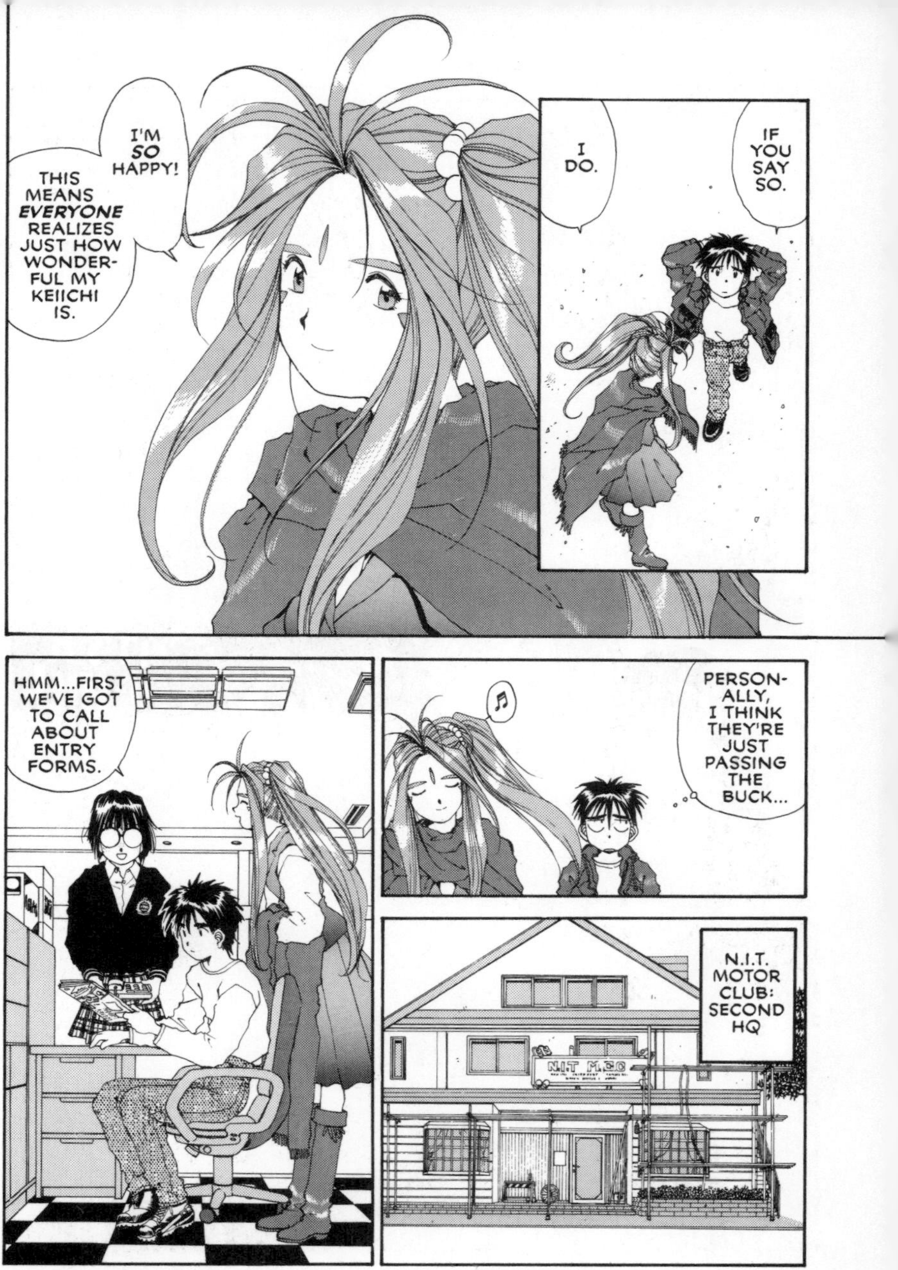
IF YOU SAY SO.
I DO.
I'M SO HAPPY!
THIS MEANS EVERYONE REALIZES JUST HOW WONDERFUL MY KEIICHI IS.
♫
PERSONALLY, I THINK THEY'RE JUST PASSING THE BUCK...
N.I.T. MOTOR CLUB: SECOND HQ
N.I.T M.C.C
HMM...FIRST WE'VE GOT TO CALL ABOUT ENTRY FORMS.

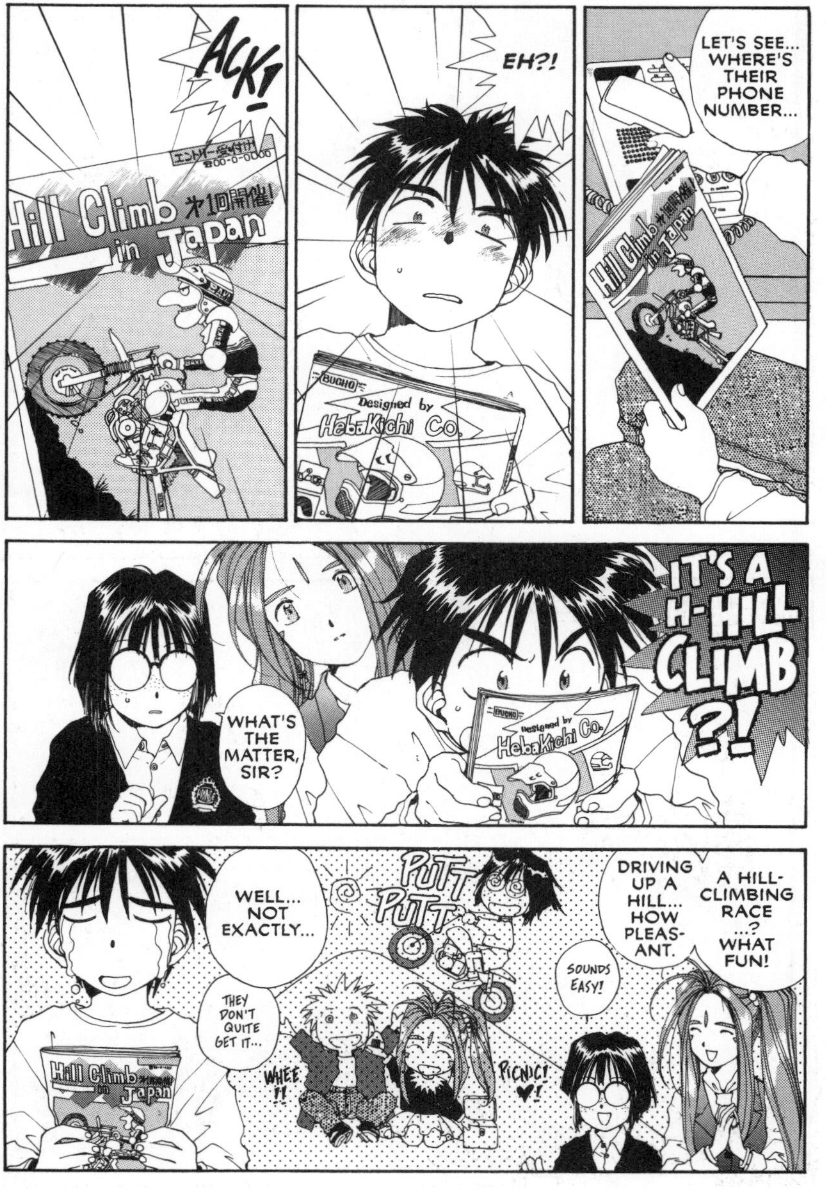
LET'S SEE... WHERE'S THEIR PHONE NUMBER...
Hill Climb in Japan
EH?!
Designed by HebaKichi Co.
ACK!
Hill Climb in Japan
IT'S A H-HILL CLIMB?!
Designed by HebaKichi Co.
WHAT'S THE MATTER, SIR?
A HILL-CLIMBING RACE ...? WHAT FUN!
DRIVING UP A HILL... HOW PLEASANT.
SOUNDS EASY!
PICNIC! ♥!
PUTT PUTT
WHEE!!
WELL... NOT EXACTLY...
THEY DON'T QUITE GET IT...
Hill Climb in Japan

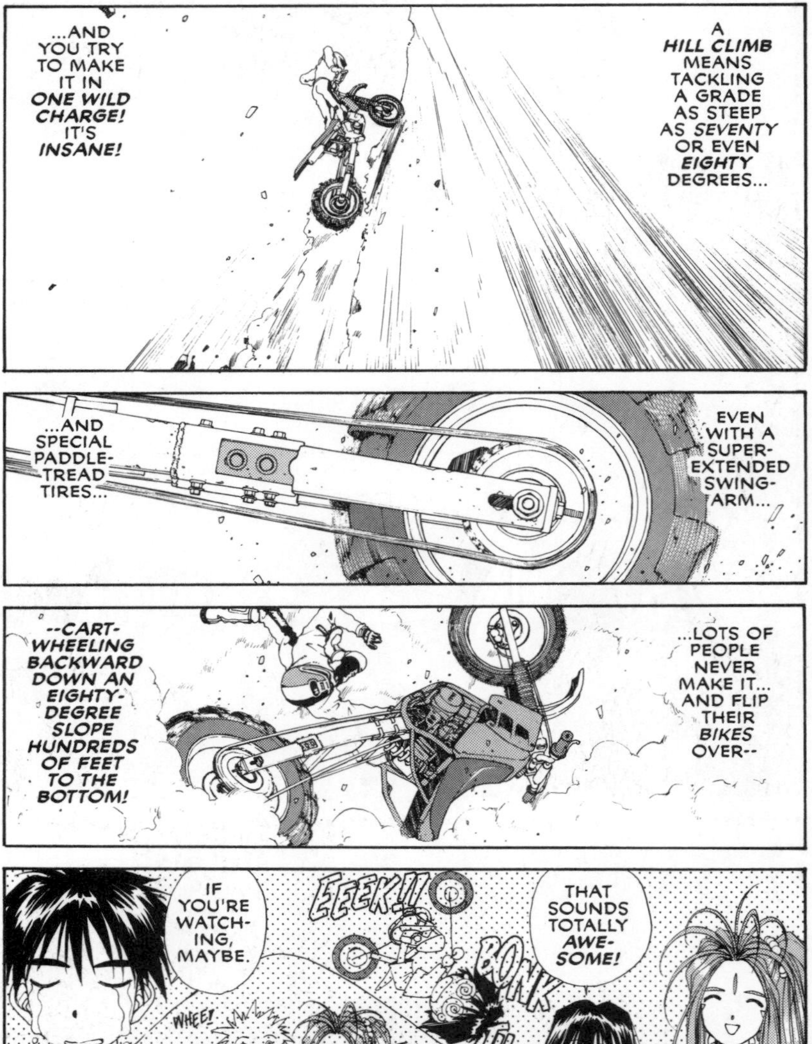

A HILL CLIMB MEANS TACKLING A GRADE AS STEEP AS SEVENTY OR EVEN EIGHTY DEGREES...
...AND YOU TRY TO MAKE IT IN ONE WILD CHARGE! IT'S INSANE!
EVEN WITH A SUPER-EXTENDED SWING-ARM...
...AND SPECIAL PADDLE-TREAD TIRES...
...LOTS OF PEOPLE NEVER MAKE IT... AND FLIP THEIR BIKES OVER--
--CART-WHEELING BACKWARD DOWN AN EIGHTY-DEGREE SLOPE HUNDREDS OF FEET TO THE BOTTOM!
THAT SOUNDS TOTALLY AWESOME!
BONK
THUD
EEEK!!
IF YOU'RE WATCHING, MAYBE.
TEA TIME!
WHEE!

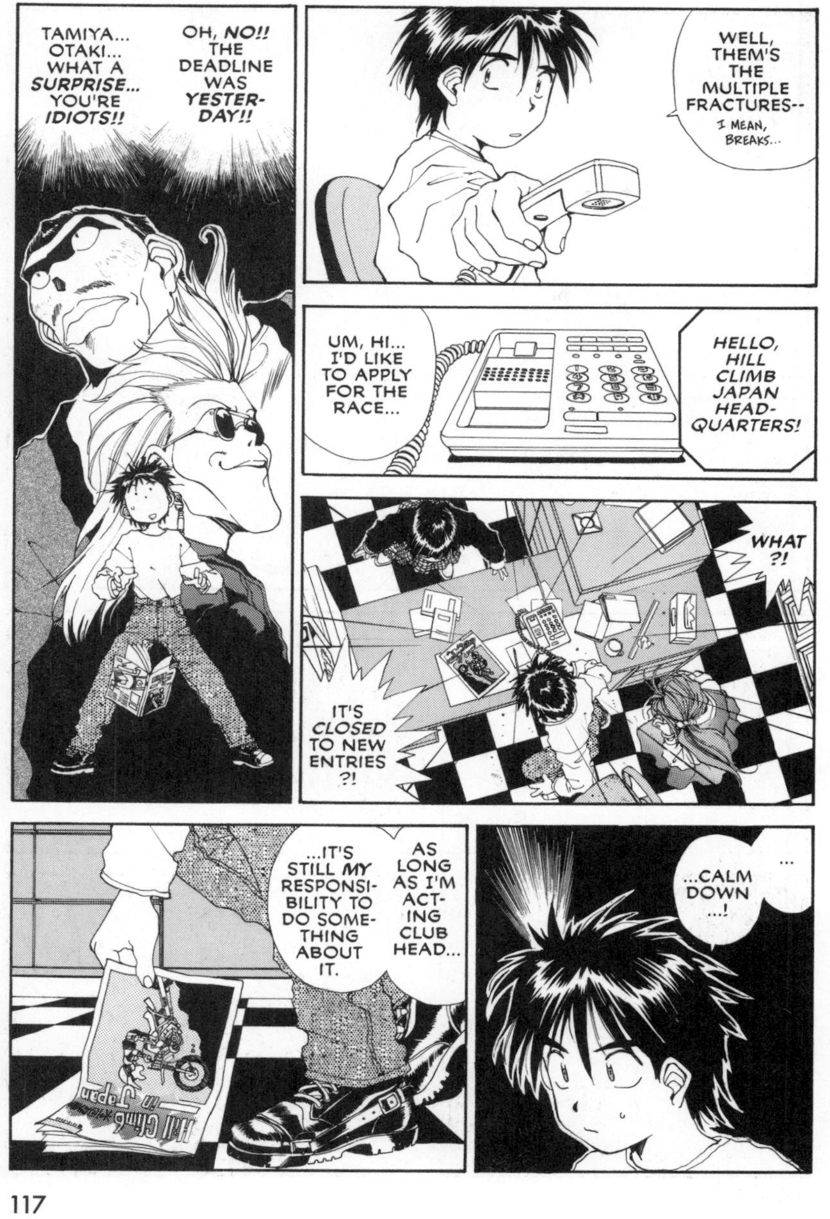
WELL, THEM'S THE MULTIPLE FRACTURES-- I MEAN, BREAKS...
HELLO, HILL CLIMB JAPAN HEAD-QUARTERS!
UM, HI... I'D LIKE TO APPLY FOR THE RACE...
WHAT?!
IT'S CLOSED TO NEW ENTRIES?!
OH, NO!! THE DEADLINE WAS YESTER-DAY!!
TAMIYA... OTAKI... WHAT A SURPRISE... YOU'RE IDIOTS!!
...
...CALM DOWN...!
AS LONG AS I'M ACT-ING CLUB HEAD...
...IT'S STILL MY RESPONSI-BILITY TO DO SOME-THING ABOUT IT.

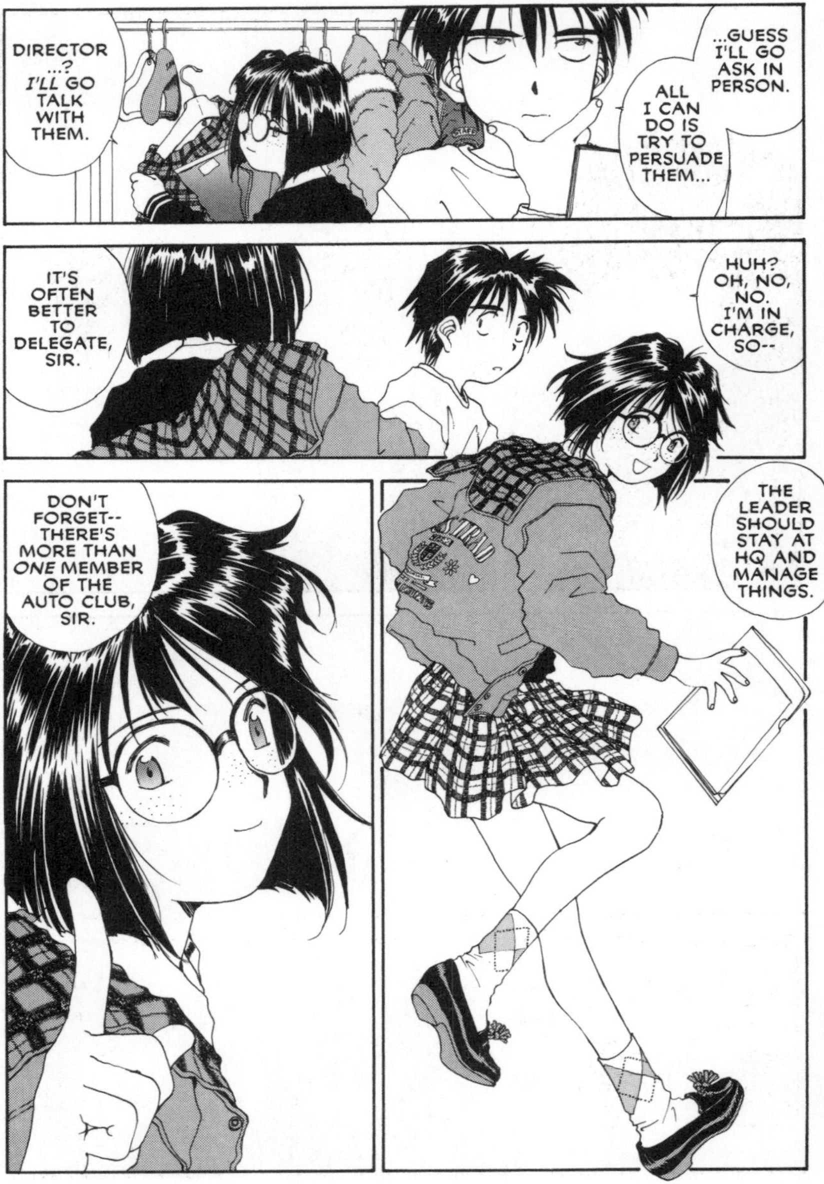
...GUESS I'LL GO ASK IN PERSON.
ALL I CAN DO IS TRY TO PERSUADE THEM...
DIRECTOR ...? *I'LL* GO TALK WITH THEM.
HUH? OH, NO, NO. I'M IN CHARGE, SO--
IT'S OFTEN BETTER TO DELEGATE, SIR.
THE LEADER SHOULD STAY AT HQ AND MANAGE THINGS.
DON'T FORGET-- THERE'S MORE THAN *ONE* MEMBER OF THE AUTO CLUB, SIR.

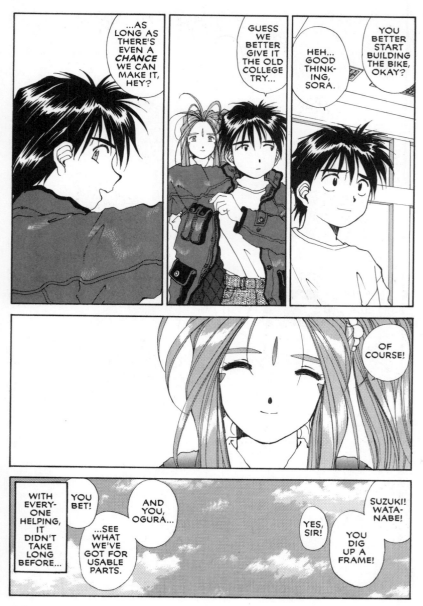

YOU BETTER START BUILDING THE BIKE, OKAY?
HEH... GOOD THINKING, SORA.
GUESS WE BETTER GIVE IT THE OLD COLLEGE TRY...
...AS LONG AS THERE'S EVEN A ***CHANCE*** WE CAN MAKE IT, HEY?
OF COURSE!
SUZUKI! WATANABE!
YOU DIG UP A FRAME!
YES, SIR!
AND YOU, OGURA...
...SEE WHAT WE'VE GOT FOR USABLE PARTS.
YOU BET!
WITH EVERYONE HELPING, IT DIDN'T TAKE LONG BEFORE...

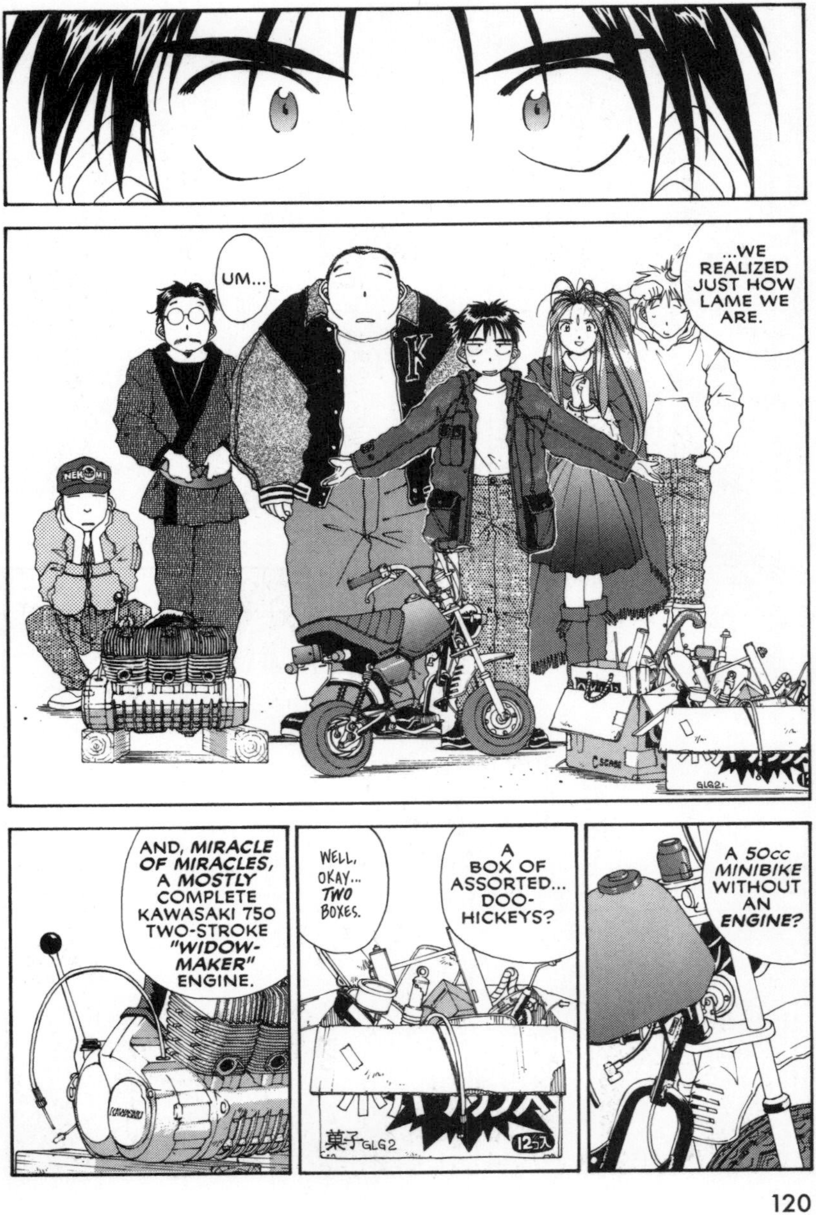
...WE REALIZED JUST HOW LAME WE ARE.
UM...
A 50cc MINIBIKE WITHOUT AN ENGINE?
A BOX OF ASSORTED... DOO-HICKEYS?
WELL, OKAY... TWO BOXES.
AND, MIRACLE OF MIRACLES, A MOSTLY COMPLETE KAWASAKI 750 TWO-STROKE "WIDOW-MAKER" ENGINE.

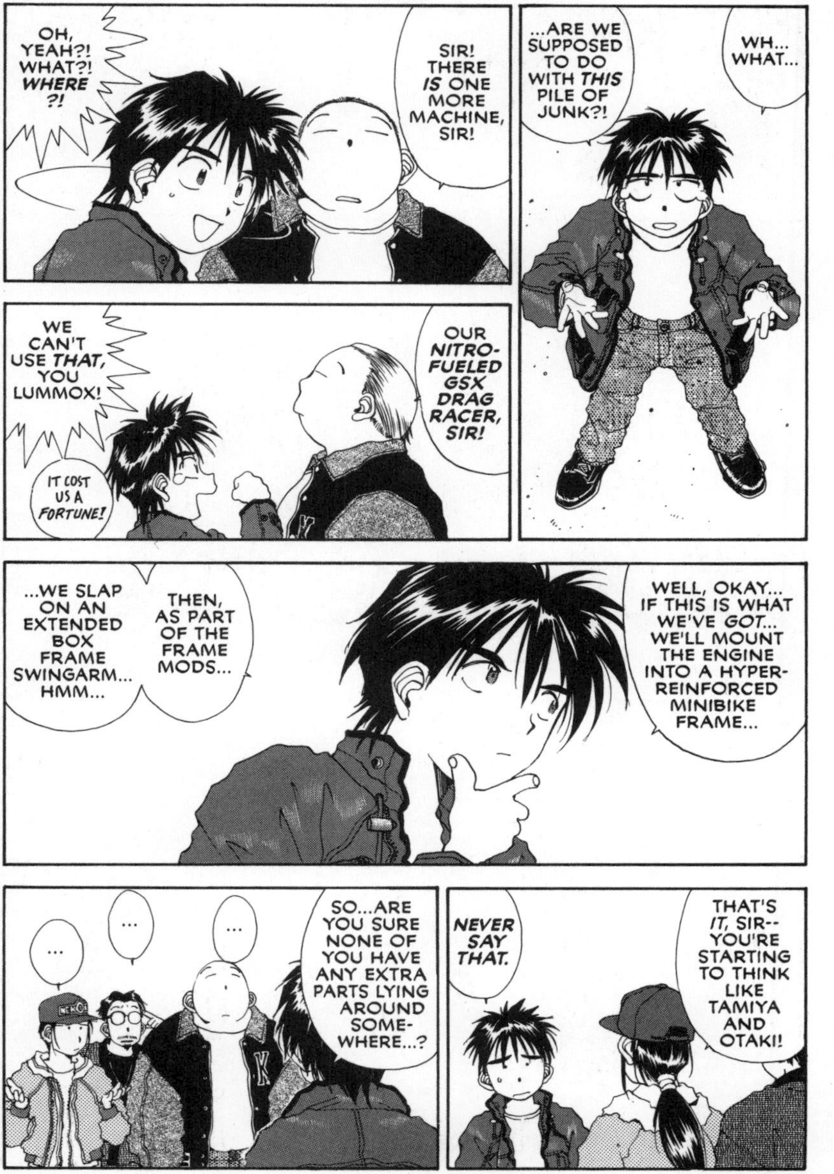
WH... WHAT...
...ARE WE SUPPOSED TO DO WITH *THIS* PILE OF JUNK?!
SIR! THERE *IS* ONE MORE MACHINE, SIR!
OH, YEAH?! WHAT?! *WHERE ?!*
OUR *NITRO-FUELED GSX DRAG RACER, SIR!*
WE CAN'T USE *THAT,* YOU LUMMOX!
IT COST US A *FORTUNE!*
WELL, OKAY... IF THIS IS WHAT WE'VE *GOT*... WE'LL MOUNT THE ENGINE INTO A HYPER-REINFORCED MINIBIKE FRAME...
THEN, AS PART OF THE FRAME MODS...
...WE SLAP ON AN EXTENDED BOX FRAME SWINGARM... HMM...
THAT'S *IT,* SIR-- YOU'RE STARTING TO THINK LIKE TAMIYA AND OTAKI!
NEVER SAY THAT.
SO...ARE YOU SURE NONE OF YOU HAVE ANY EXTRA PARTS LYING AROUND SOME-WHERE...?
...
...
...

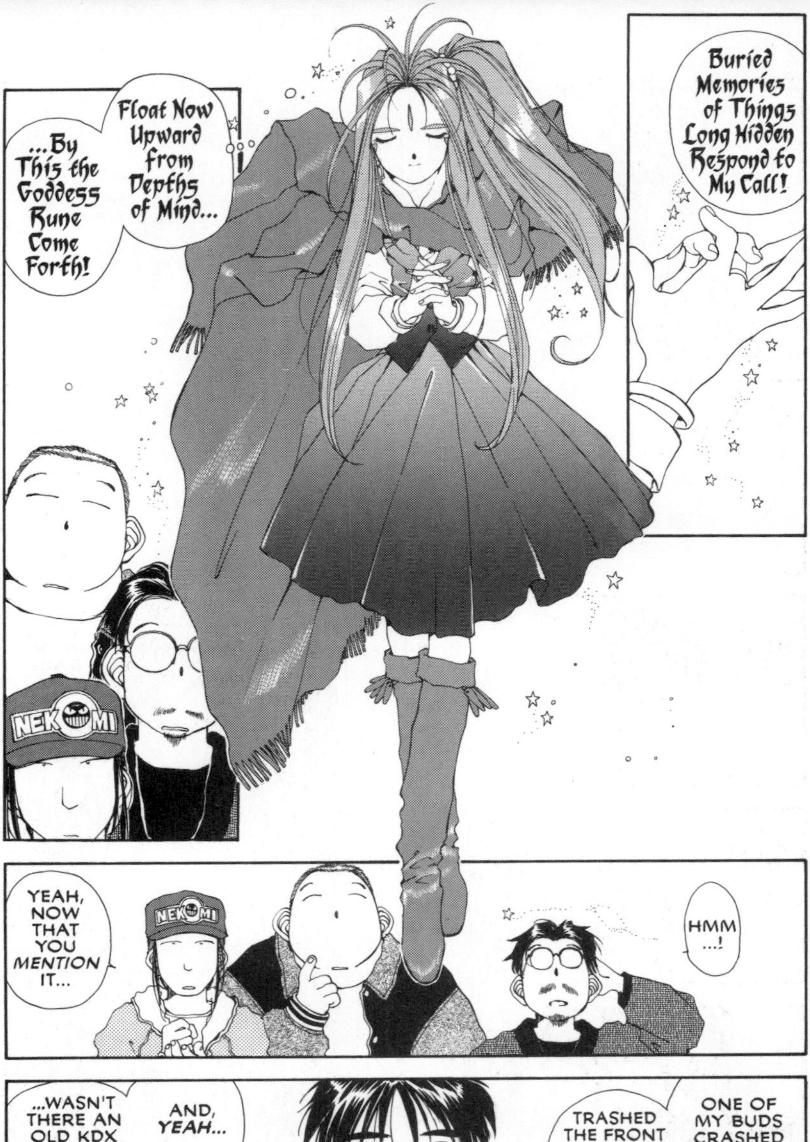
Buried Memories of Things Long Hidden Respond to My Call!
Float Now Upward from Depths of Mind...
...By This the Goddess Rune Come Forth!
NEKOMI
HMM ...!
YEAH, NOW THAT YOU *MENTION* IT...
NEKOMI
ONE OF MY BUDS CRASHED OUT LAST FALL.
TRASHED THE FRONT END, BUT HE'S GOT THE REAR SUSPENSION HANGING AROUND.
AND, *YEAH*...
...WASN'T THERE AN OLD KDX FORK AND TRIPLE-CLAMP UNDER THOSE BOXES IN THE WARE-HOUSE...?

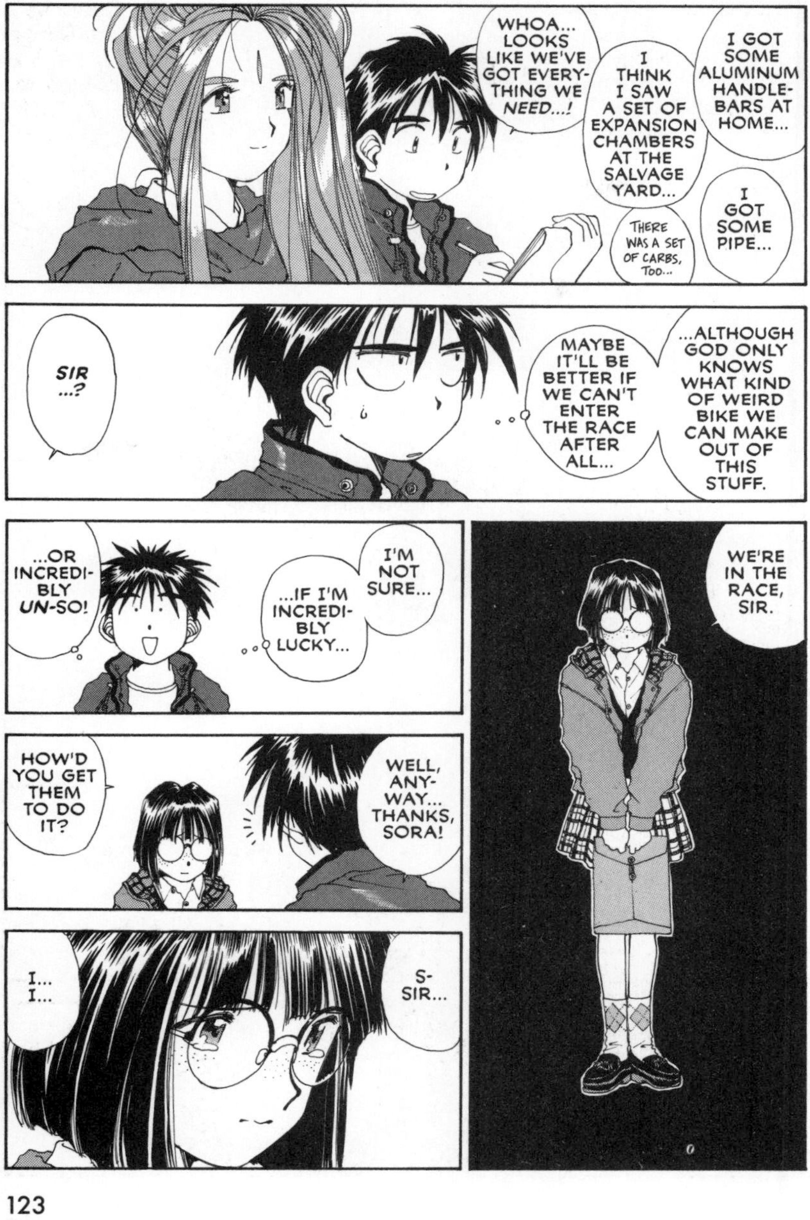
I GOT SOME ALUMINUM HANDLEBARS AT HOME...
I GOT SOME PIPE...
I THINK I SAW A SET OF EXPANSION CHAMBERS AT THE SALVAGE YARD...
THERE WAS A SET OF CARBS, TOO...
WHOA... LOOKS LIKE WE'VE GOT EVERYTHING WE *NEED*...!
...ALTHOUGH GOD ONLY KNOWS WHAT KIND OF WEIRD BIKE WE CAN MAKE OUT OF THIS STUFF.
MAYBE IT'LL BE BETTER IF WE CAN'T ENTER THE RACE AFTER ALL...
SIR ...?
WE'RE IN THE RACE, SIR.
I'M NOT SURE...
...IF I'M INCREDIBLY LUCKY...
...OR INCREDIBLY *UN*-SO!
WELL, ANYWAY... THANKS, SORA!
HOW'D YOU GET THEM TO DO IT?
S-SIR...
I... I...

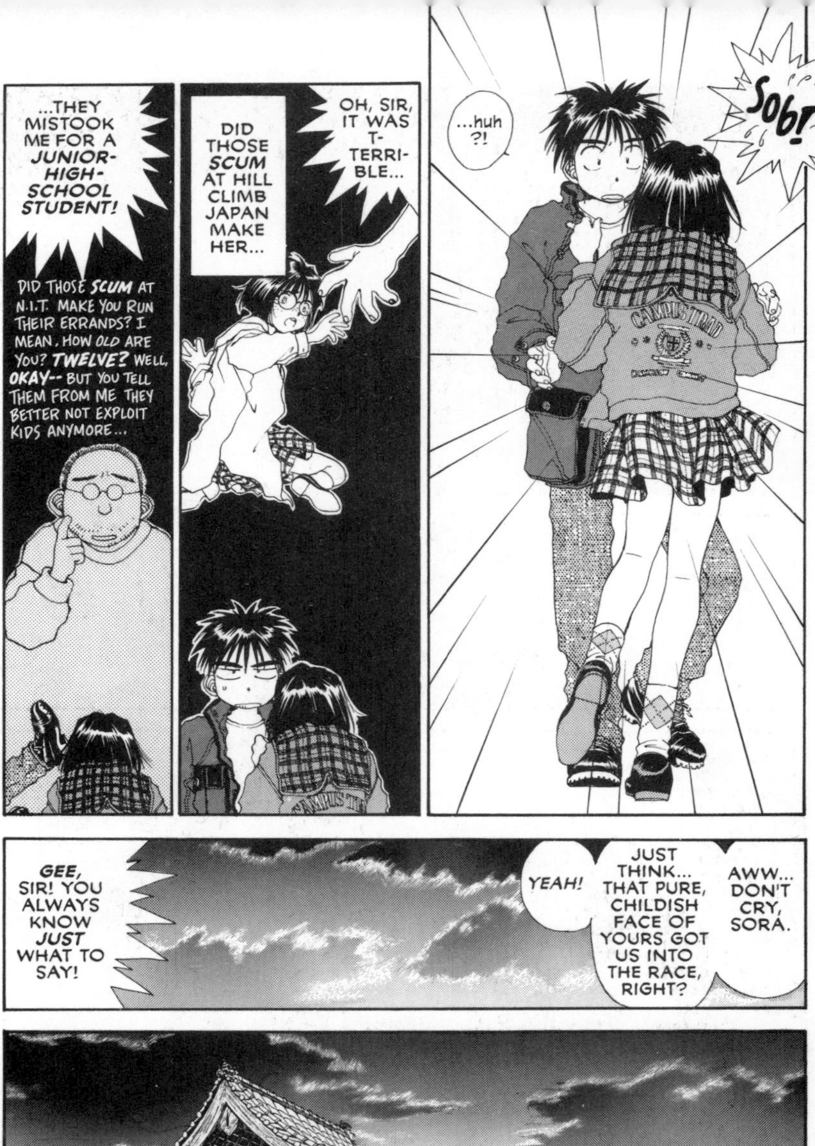
SOB!
...huh ?!
OH, SIR, IT WAS T-TERRIBLE...
DID THOSE SCUM AT HILL CLIMB JAPAN MAKE HER...
...THEY MISTOOK ME FOR A JUNIOR-HIGH-SCHOOL STUDENT!
DID THOSE SCUM AT N.I.T. MAKE YOU RUN THEIR ERRANDS? I MEAN, HOW OLD ARE YOU? TWELVE? WELL, OKAY-- BUT YOU TELL THEM FROM ME THEY BETTER NOT EXPLOIT KIDS ANYMORE...
AWW... DON'T CRY, SORA.
JUST THINK... THAT PURE, CHILDISH FACE OF YOURS GOT US INTO THE RACE, RIGHT?
YEAH!
GEE, SIR! YOU ALWAYS KNOW JUST WHAT TO SAY!

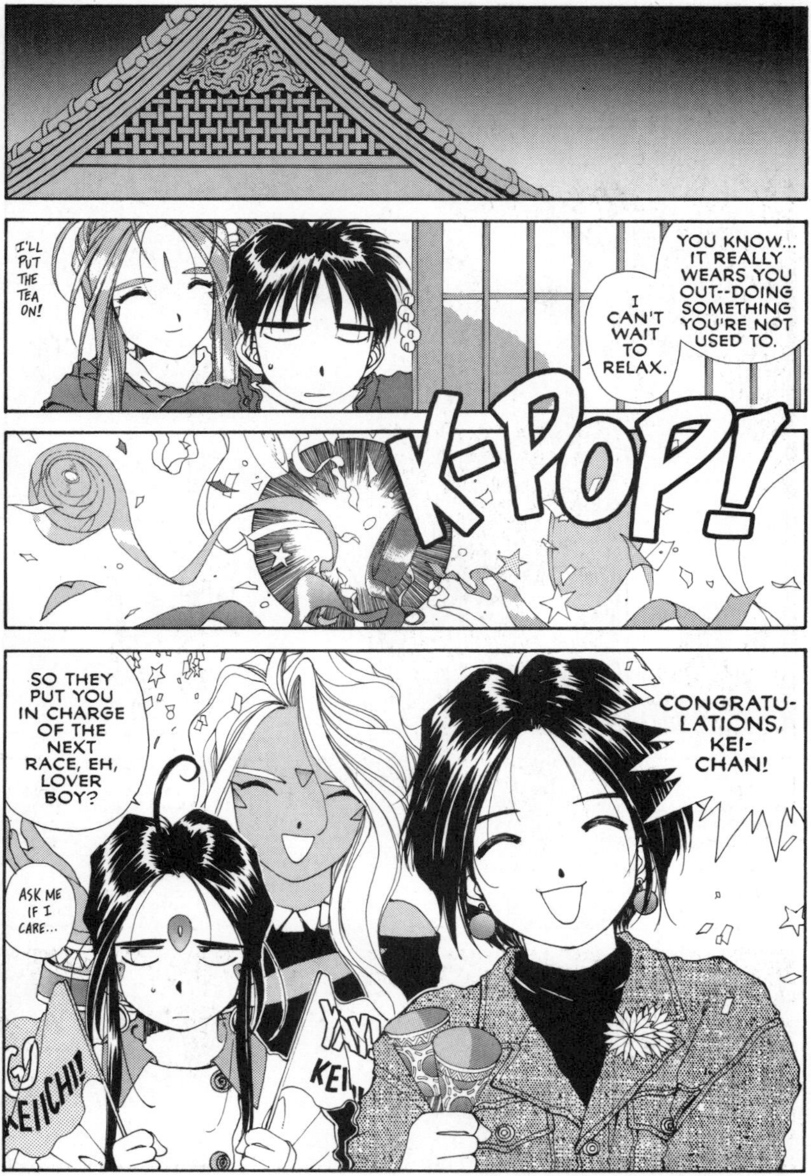
YOU KNOW... IT REALLY WEARS YOU OUT--DOING SOMETHING YOU'RE NOT USED TO.
I CAN'T WAIT TO RELAX.
I'LL PUT THE TEA ON!
K-POP!
CONGRATULATIONS, KEI-CHAN!
SO THEY PUT YOU IN CHARGE OF THE NEXT RACE, EH, LOVER BOY?
ASK ME IF I CARE...
YAY!
KEIICHI!

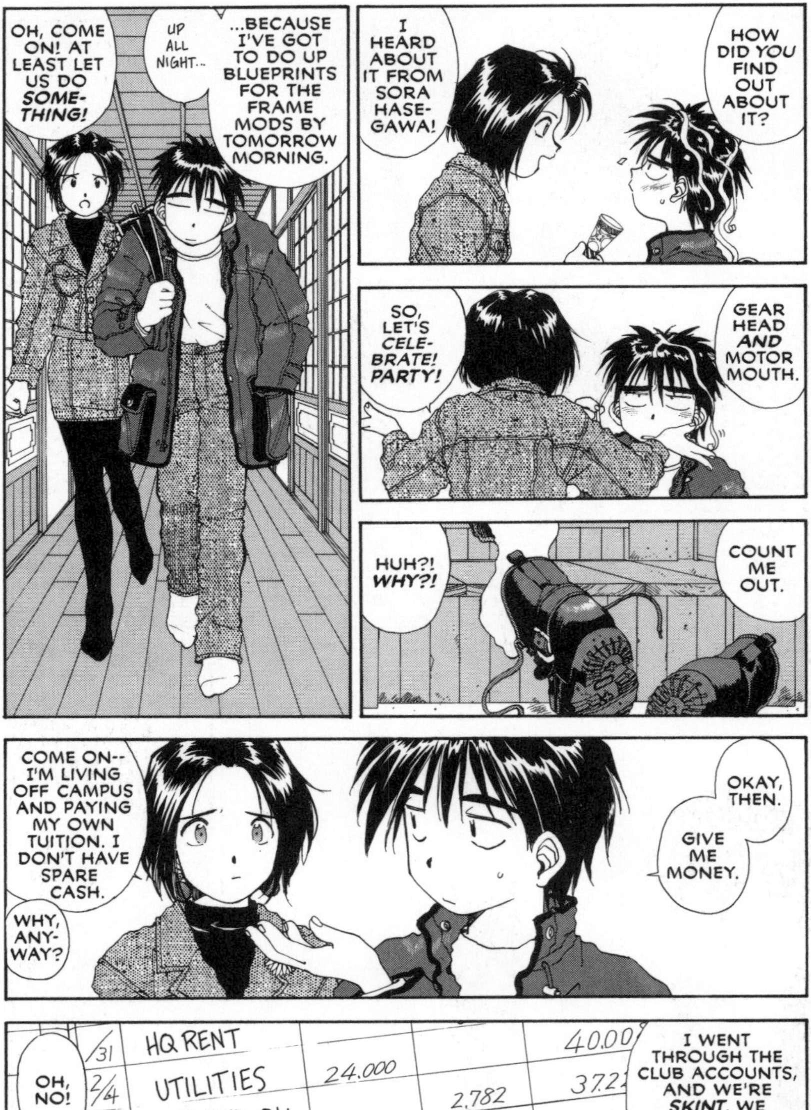
HOW DID YOU FIND OUT ABOUT IT?
I HEARD ABOUT IT FROM SORA HASEGAWA!
GEAR HEAD AND MOTOR MOUTH.
SO, LET'S CELEBRATE! PARTY!
COUNT ME OUT.
HUH?! WHY?!
...BECAUSE I'VE GOT TO DO UP BLUEPRINTS FOR THE FRAME MODS BY TOMORROW MORNING.
UP ALL NIGHT...
OH, COME ON! AT LEAST LET US DO SOMETHING!
OKAY, THEN. GIVE ME MONEY.
COME ON-- I'M LIVING OFF CAMPUS AND PAYING MY OWN TUITION. I DON'T HAVE SPARE CASH.
WHY, ANYWAY?
I WENT THROUGH THE CLUB ACCOUNTS, AND WE'RE SKINT. WE HAVE EXACTLY 218 YEN LEFT.
HQ RENT
UTILITIES
24,000
2,782
GAS AND OIL
24,921
OH, NO!

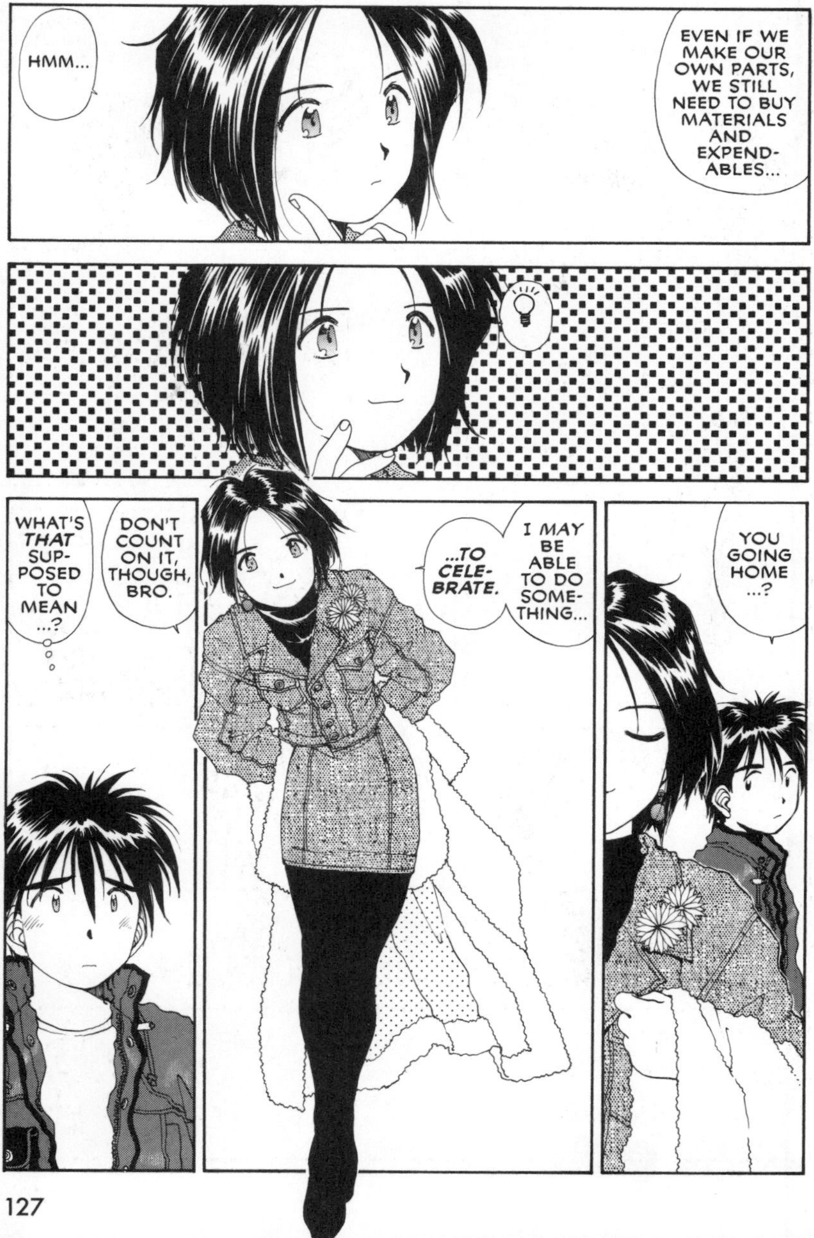
EVEN IF WE MAKE OUR OWN PARTS, WE STILL NEED TO BUY MATERIALS AND EXPEND-ABLES...
HMM...
YOU GOING HOME ...?
I *MAY* BE ABLE TO DO SOME-THING...
...TO CELE-BRATE.
DON'T COUNT ON IT, THOUGH, BRO.
WHAT'S *THAT* SUP-POSED TO MEAN ...?

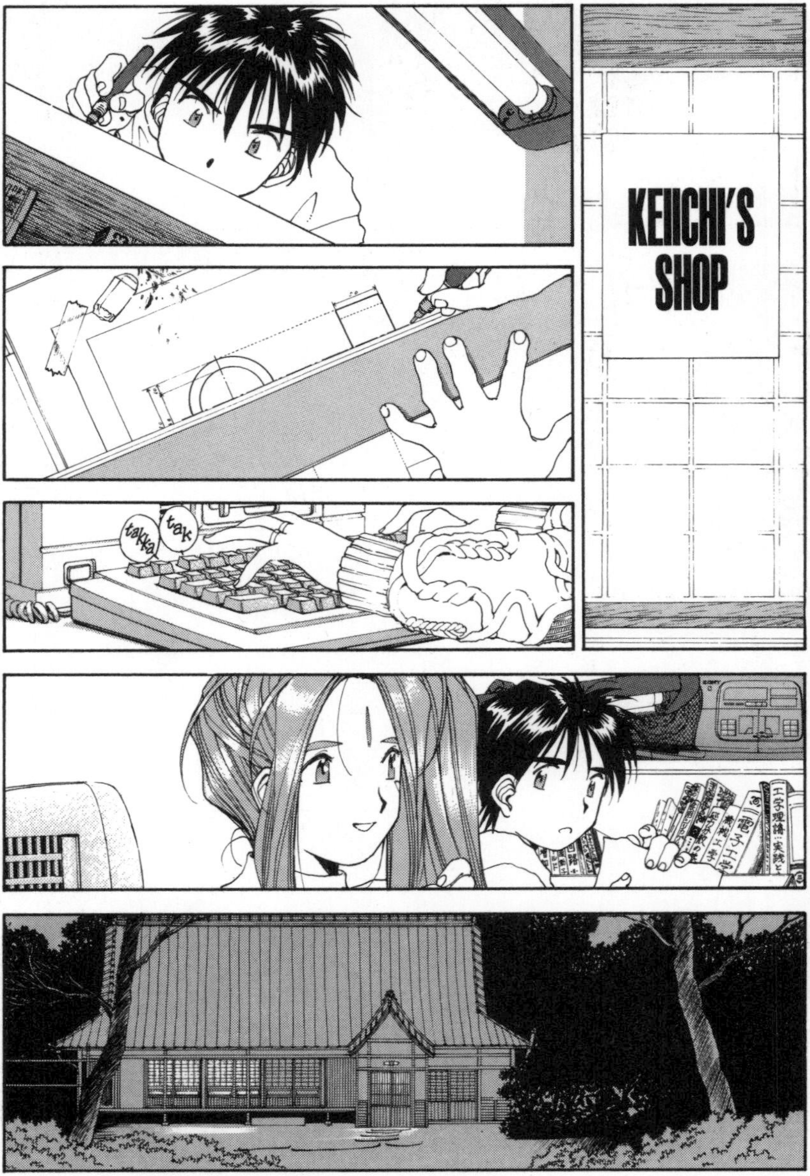
KEIICHI'S SHOP
tak
takka

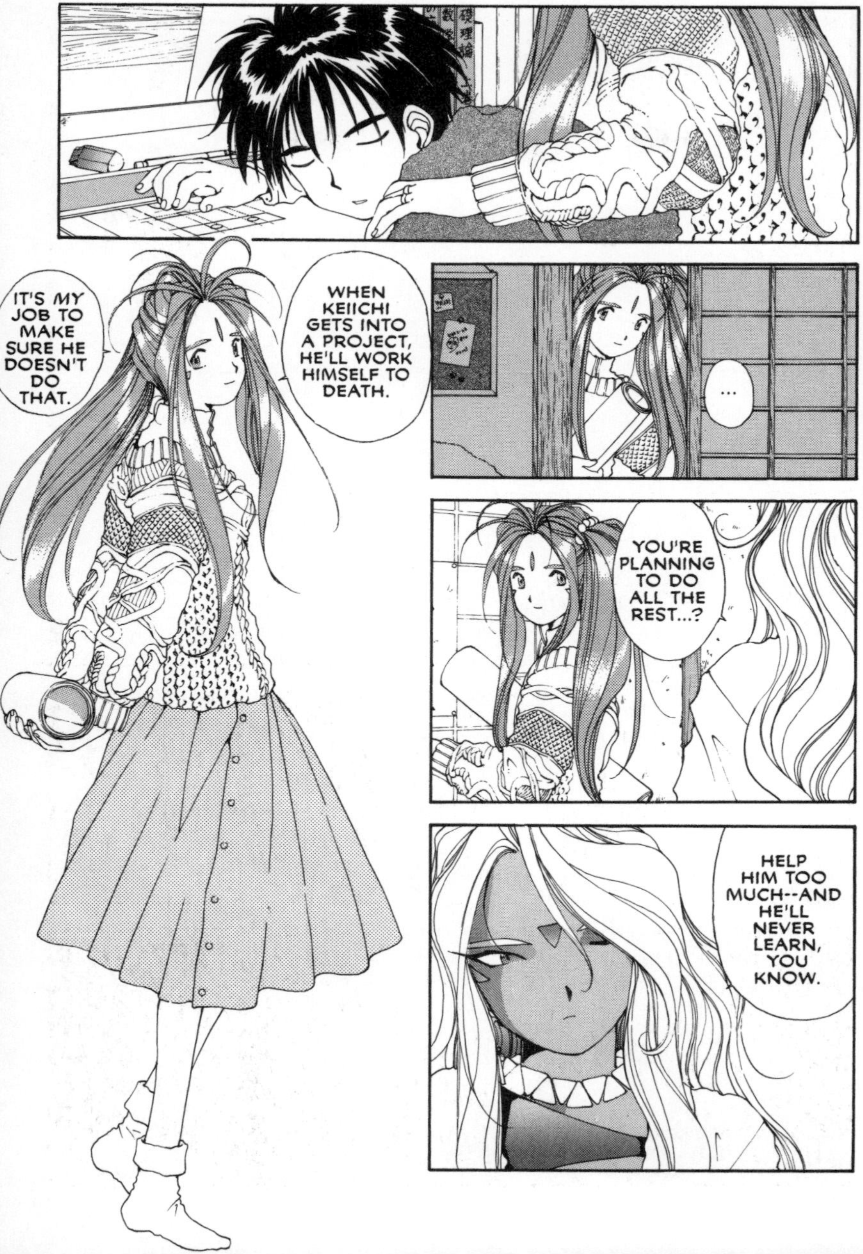
...
YOU'RE PLANNING TO DO ALL THE REST...?
HELP HIM TOO MUCH--AND HE'LL NEVER LEARN, YOU KNOW.
WHEN KEIICHI GETS INTO A PROJECT, HE'LL WORK HIMSELF TO DEATH.
IT'S MY JOB TO MAKE SURE HE DOESN'T DO THAT.

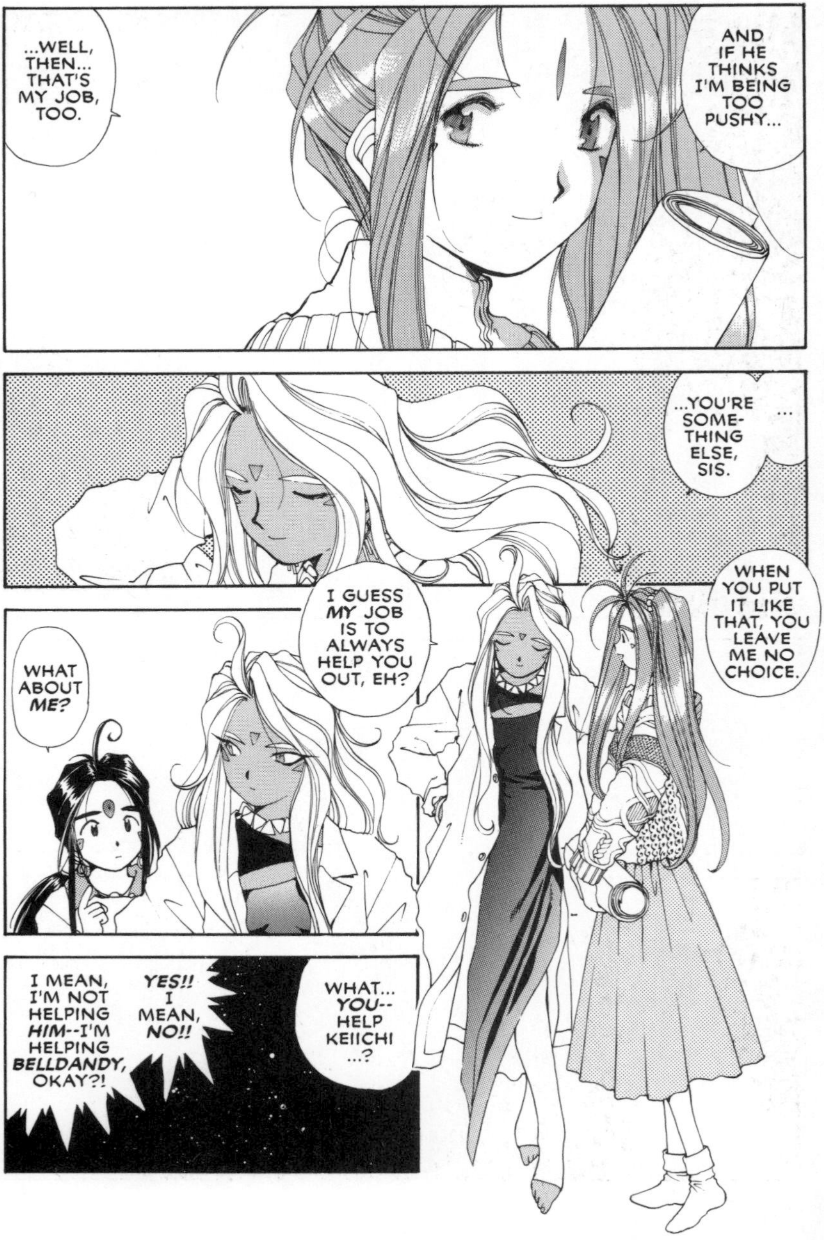
AND IF HE THINKS I'M BEING TOO PUSHY...
...WELL, THEN... THAT'S MY JOB, TOO.
...YOU'RE SOME-THING ELSE, SIS.
...
WHEN YOU PUT IT LIKE THAT, YOU LEAVE ME NO CHOICE.
I GUESS *MY* JOB IS TO ALWAYS HELP YOU OUT, EH?
WHAT ABOUT *ME?*
WHAT... *YOU*-- HELP KEIICHI ...?
YES!! I MEAN, *NO!!*
I MEAN, I'M NOT HELPING *HIM*--I'M HELPING *BELLDANDY*, OKAY?!

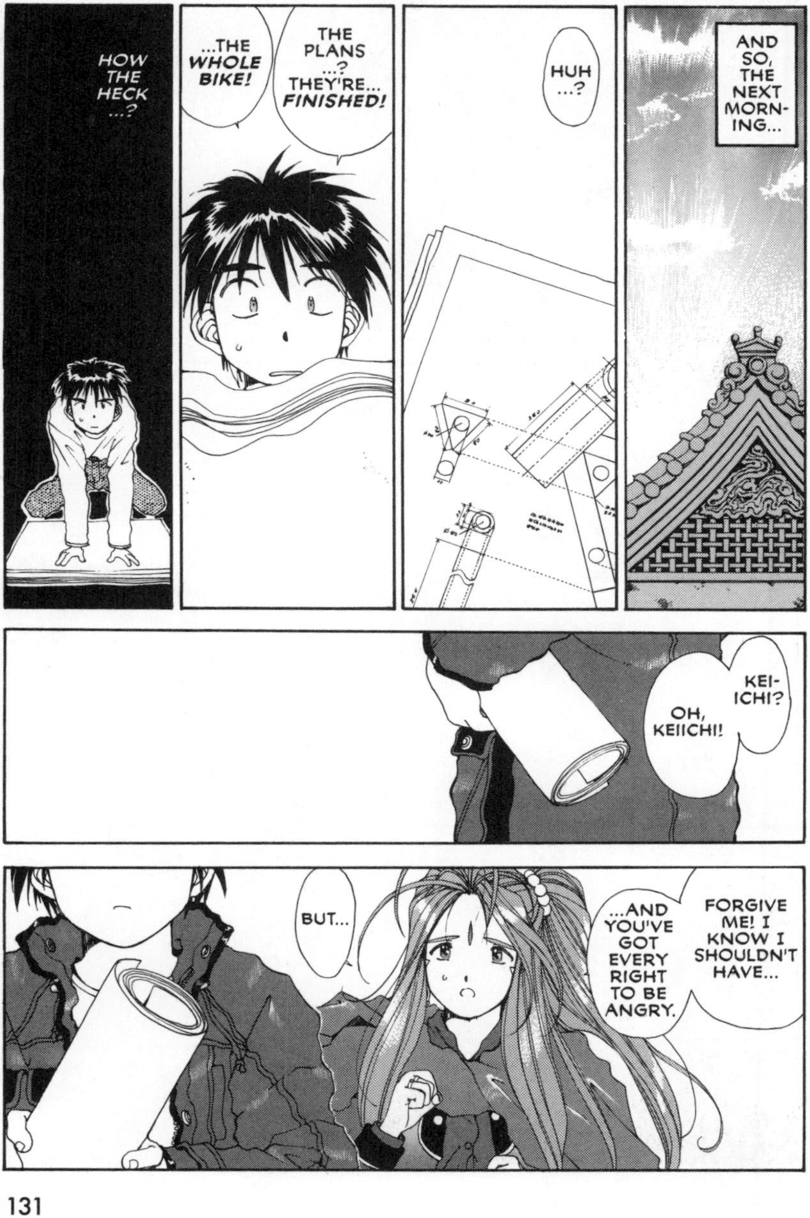
AND SO, THE NEXT MORNING...
HUH...?
THE PLANS...? THEY'RE... *FINISHED!*
...THE *WHOLE* BIKE!
HOW THE HECK...?
KEI-ICHI?
OH, KEIICHI!
FORGIVE ME! I KNOW I SHOULDN'T HAVE...
...AND YOU'VE GOT EVERY RIGHT TO BE ANGRY.
BUT...

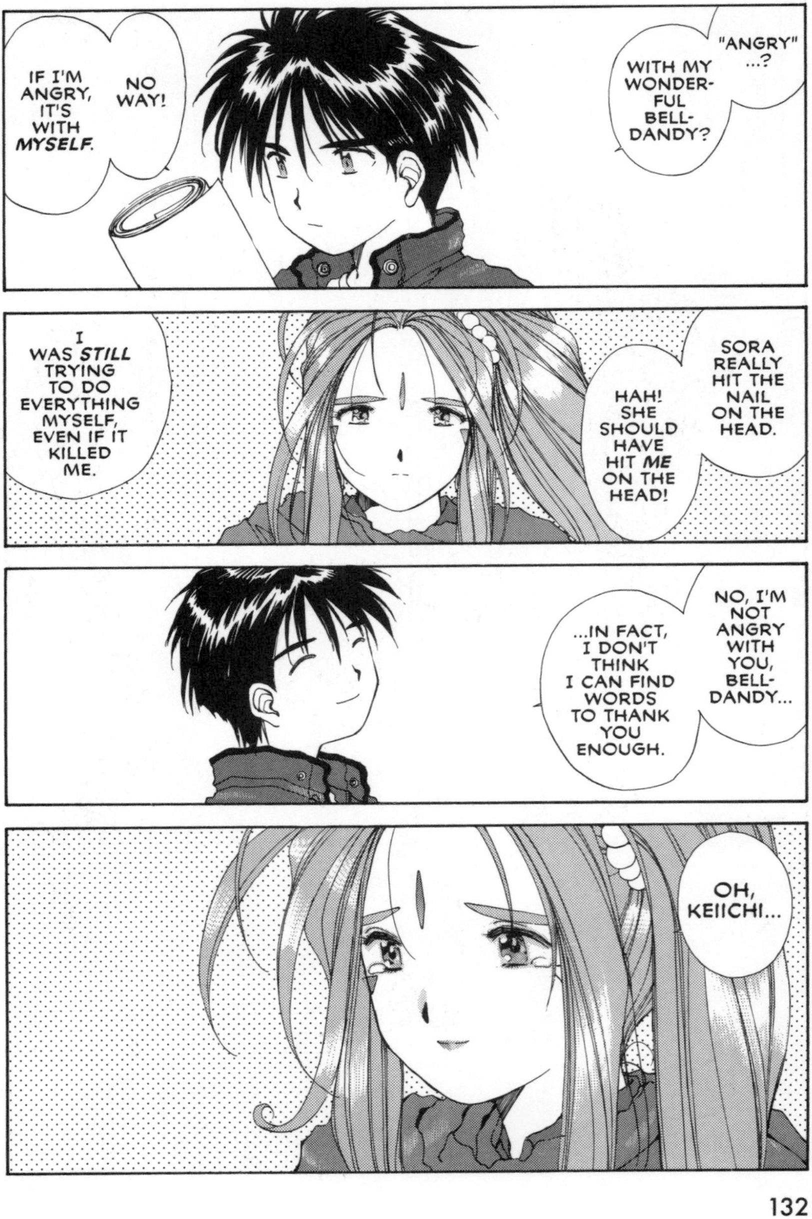
"ANGRY" ...?
WITH MY WONDER-FUL BELL-DANDY?
NO WAY!
IF I'M ANGRY, IT'S WITH *MYSELF*.
SORA REALLY HIT THE NAIL ON THE HEAD.
HAH! SHE SHOULD HAVE HIT *ME* ON THE HEAD!
I WAS *STILL* TRYING TO DO EVERYTHING MYSELF, EVEN IF IT KILLED ME.
NO, I'M NOT ANGRY WITH YOU, BELL-DANDY...
...IN FACT, I DON'T THINK I CAN FIND WORDS TO THANK YOU ENOUGH.
OH, KEIICHI...

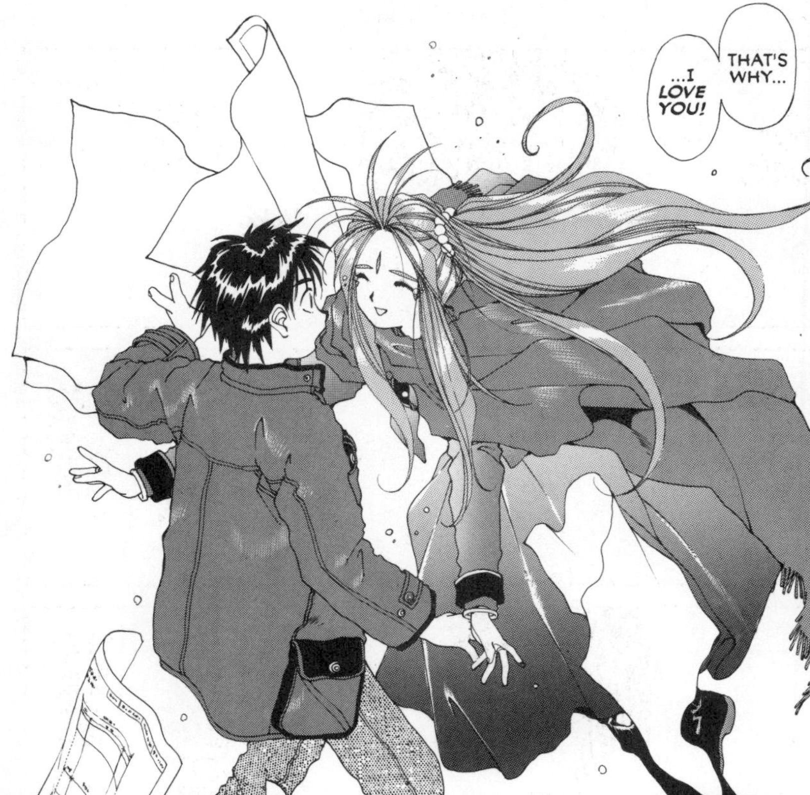
THAT'S WHY...
...I LOVE YOU!

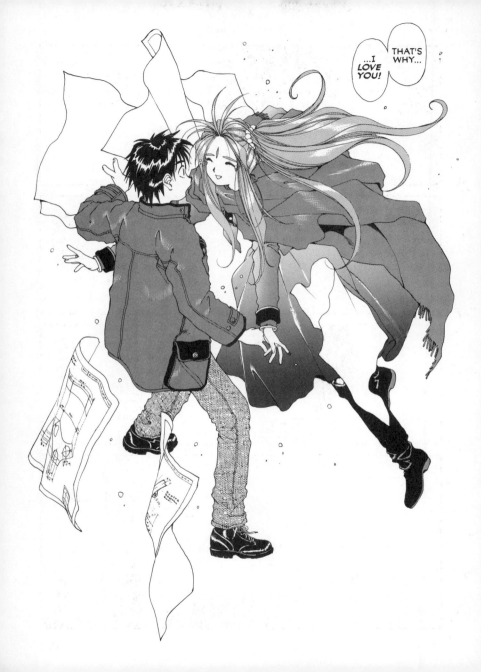

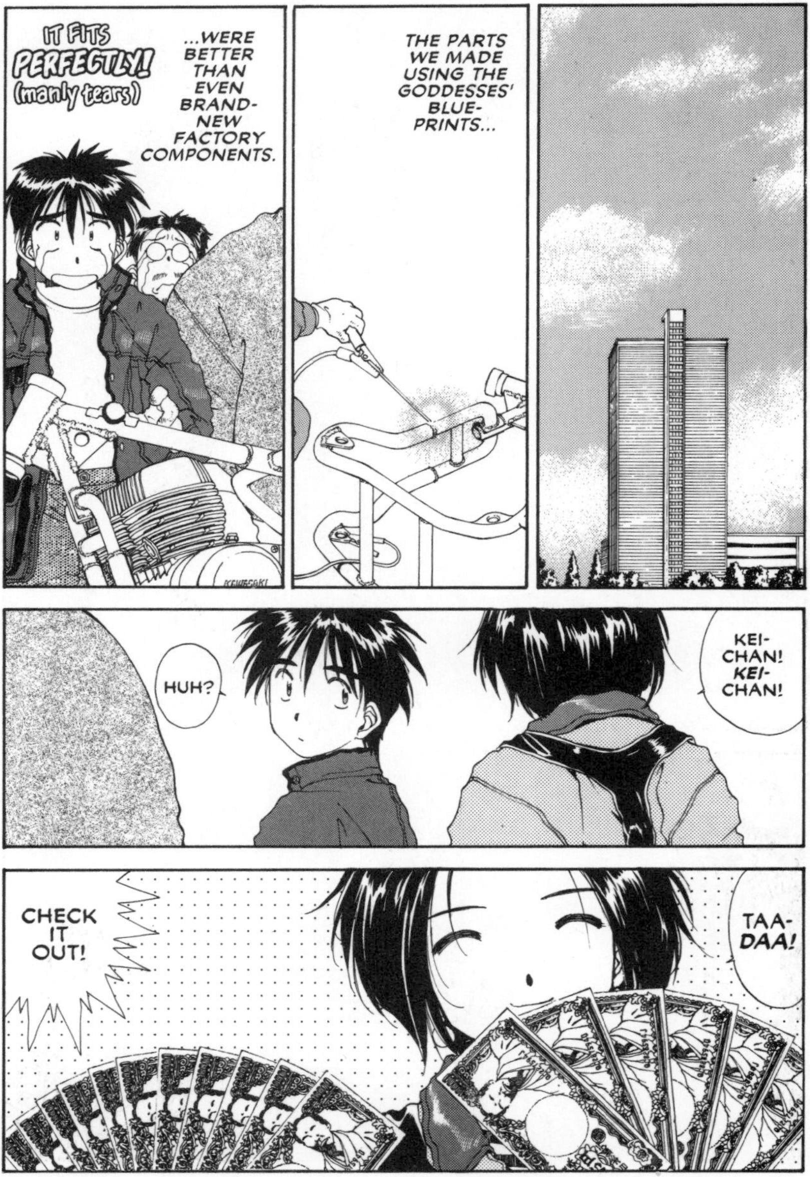
THE PARTS WE MADE USING THE GODDESSES' BLUE-PRINTS...
...WERE BETTER THAN EVEN BRAND-NEW FACTORY COMPONENTS.
IT FITS PERFECTLY! (manly tears)
KEI-CHAN! KEI-CHAN!
HUH?
TAA-DAA!
CHECK IT OUT!

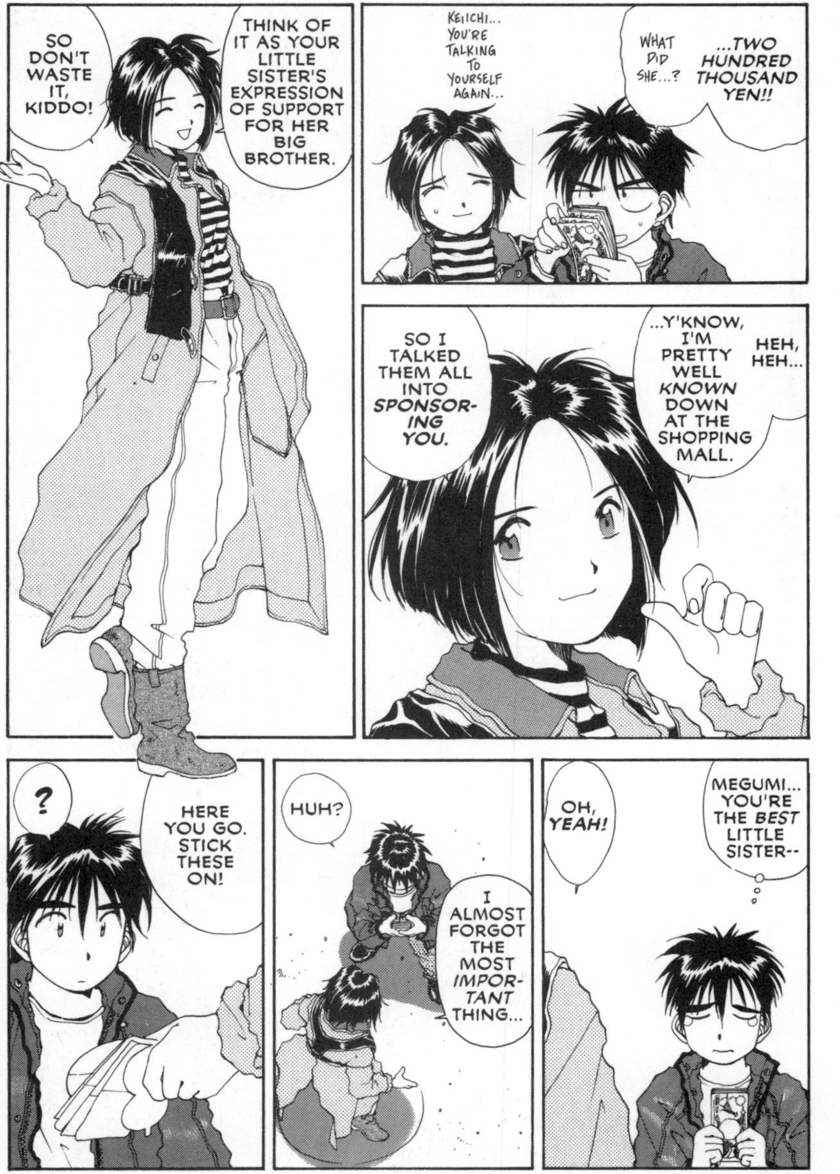
...TWO HUNDRED THOUSAND YEN!!
WHAT DID SHE...?
KEIICHI... YOU'RE TALKING TO YOURSELF AGAIN...
...Y'KNOW, I'M PRETTY WELL *KNOWN* DOWN AT THE SHOPPING MALL.
HEH, HEH...
SO I TALKED THEM ALL INTO *SPONSORING* YOU.
THINK OF IT AS YOUR LITTLE SISTER'S EXPRESSION OF SUPPORT FOR HER BIG BROTHER.
SO DON'T WASTE IT, KIDDO!
MEGUMI... YOU'RE THE *BEST* LITTLE SISTER--
OH, *YEAH!*
I ALMOST FORGOT THE MOST *IMPORTANT* THING...
HUH?
HERE YOU GO. STICK THESE ON!
?

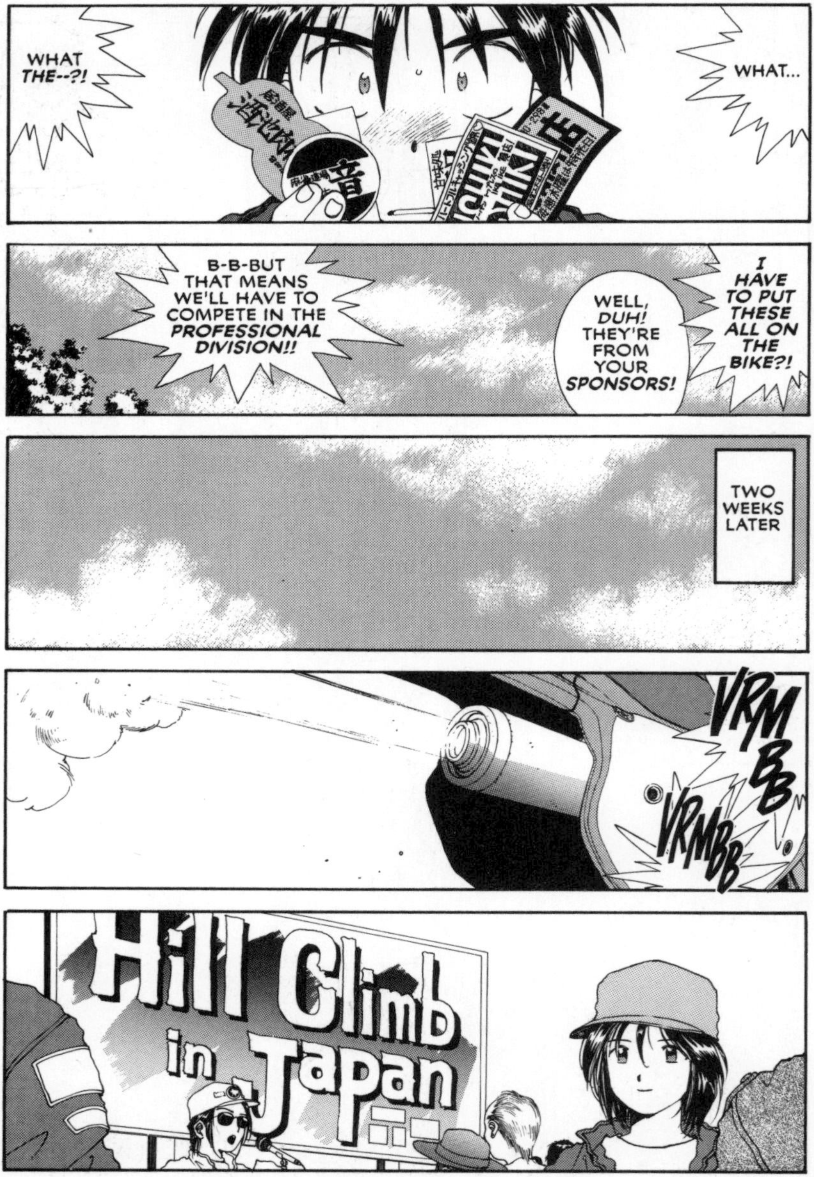
WHAT...
WHAT THE--?!
I HAVE TO PUT THESE ALL ON THE BIKE?!
WELL, DUH! THEY'RE FROM YOUR SPONSORS!
B-B-BUT THAT MEANS WE'LL HAVE TO COMPETE IN THE PROFESSIONAL DIVISION!!
TWO WEEKS LATER
VRMBB
VRMBB
Hill Climb in Japan

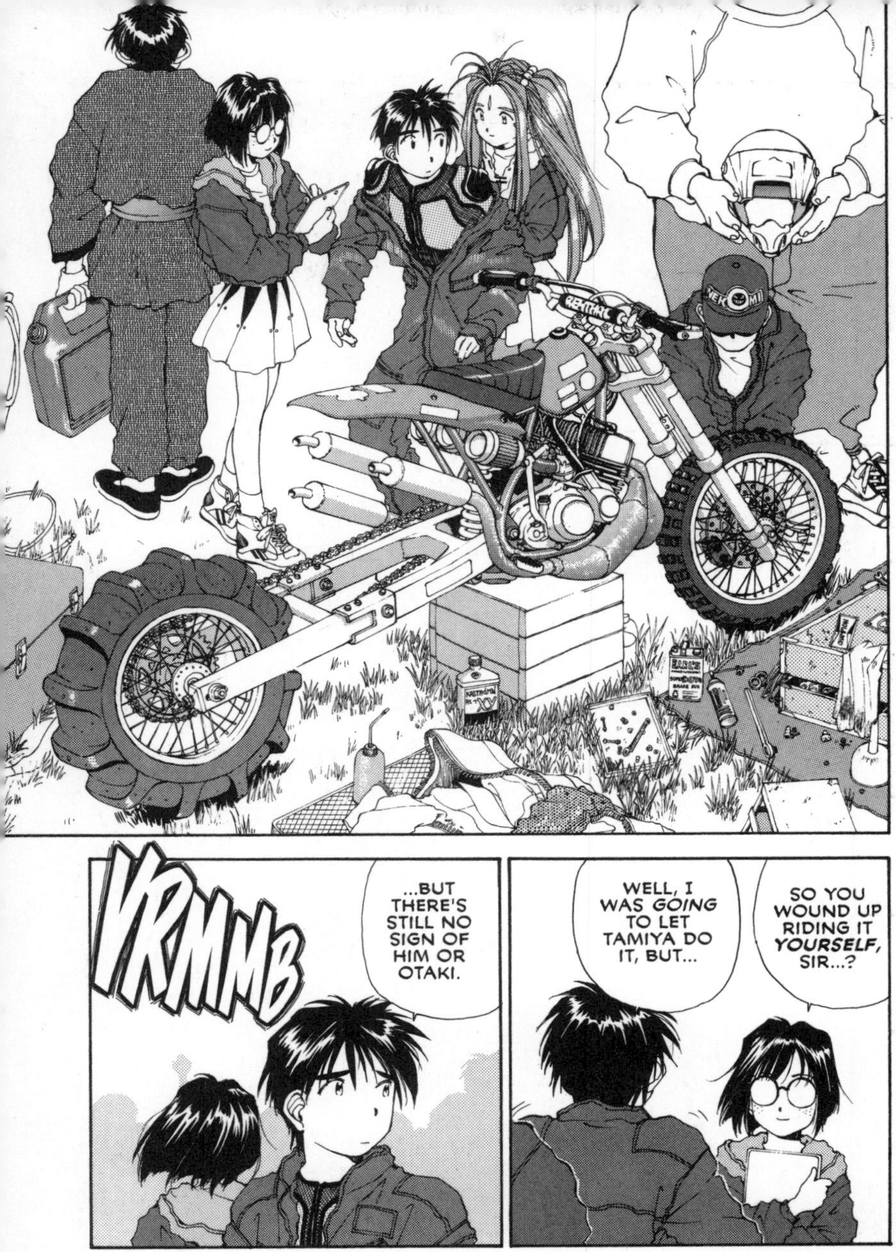
SO YOU WOUND UP RIDING IT *YOURSELF,* SIR...?
WELL, I WAS *GOING* TO LET TAMIYA DO IT, BUT...
...BUT THERE'S STILL NO SIGN OF HIM OR OTAKI.
VRMMB

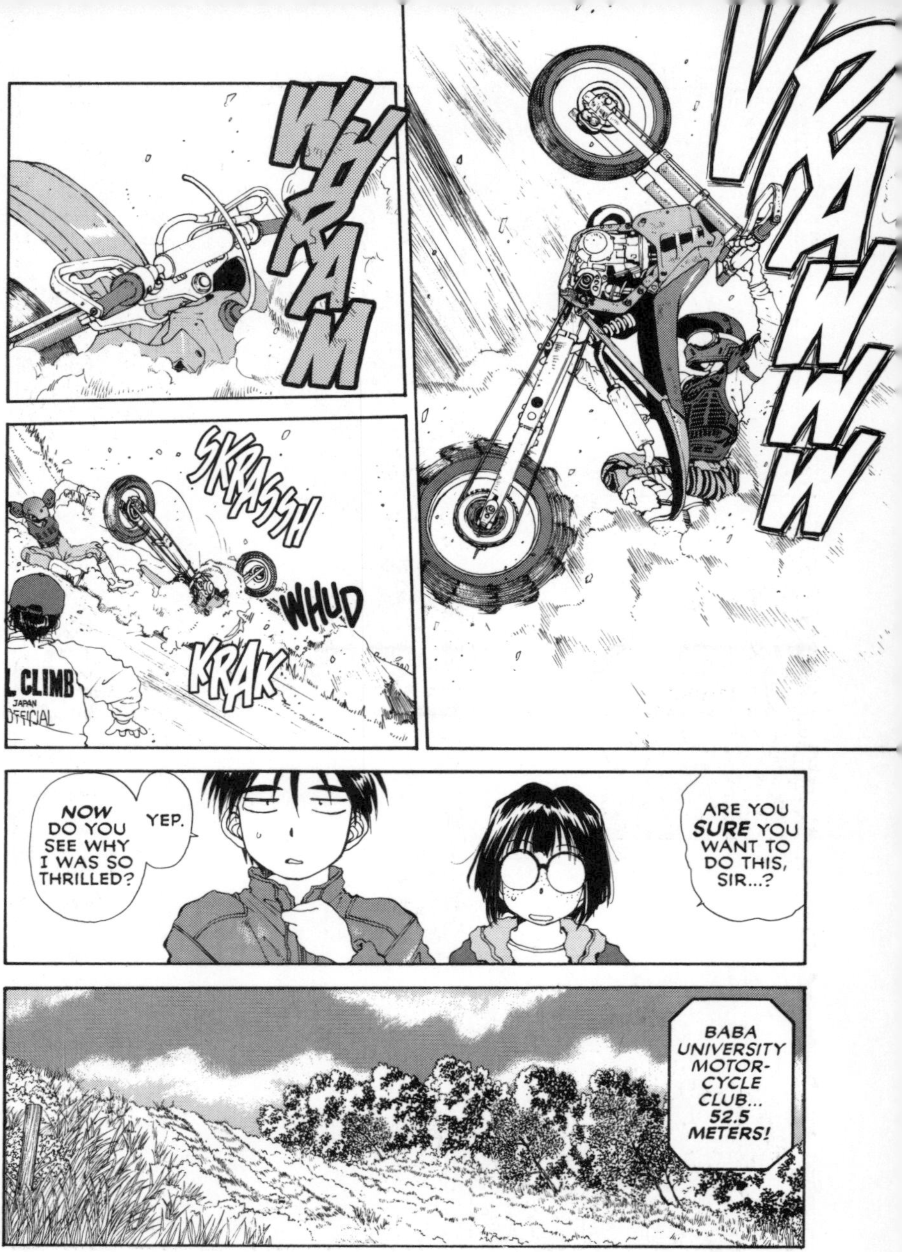
VRAAWWWW
WHAAM
SKRASSH
WHUD
KRAK
L CLIMB
JAPAN
OFFICIAL
ARE YOU SURE YOU WANT TO DO THIS, SIR...?
NOW DO YOU SEE WHY I WAS SO THRILLED?
YEP.
BABA UNIVERSITY MOTOR-CYCLE CLUB... 52.5 METERS!

AND BEST RUN OF THE DAY STANDS AT 102.3 METERS! SO FAR NO TEAM HAS MADE IT TO THE TOP!
AND NOW, ENTRY ONE-ONE-NINE... THE NEKOMI INSTITUTE OF TECHNOLOGY MOTOR CLUB...
...PLEASE TAKE YOUR PLACE AT THE STARTING LINE!
THAT'S NOT A HILL-- IT'S A PRECI-PICE!
CAN I REALLY MAKE IT...?
smak

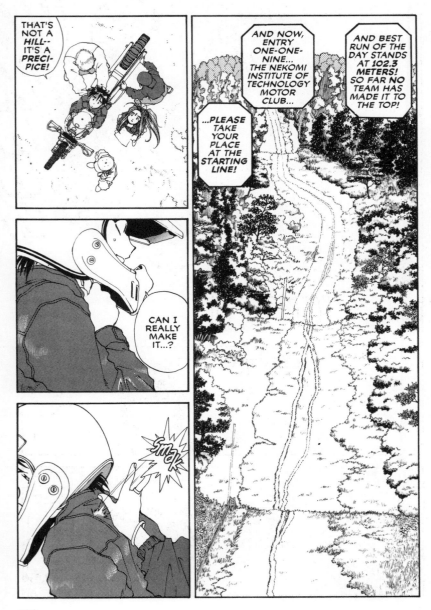

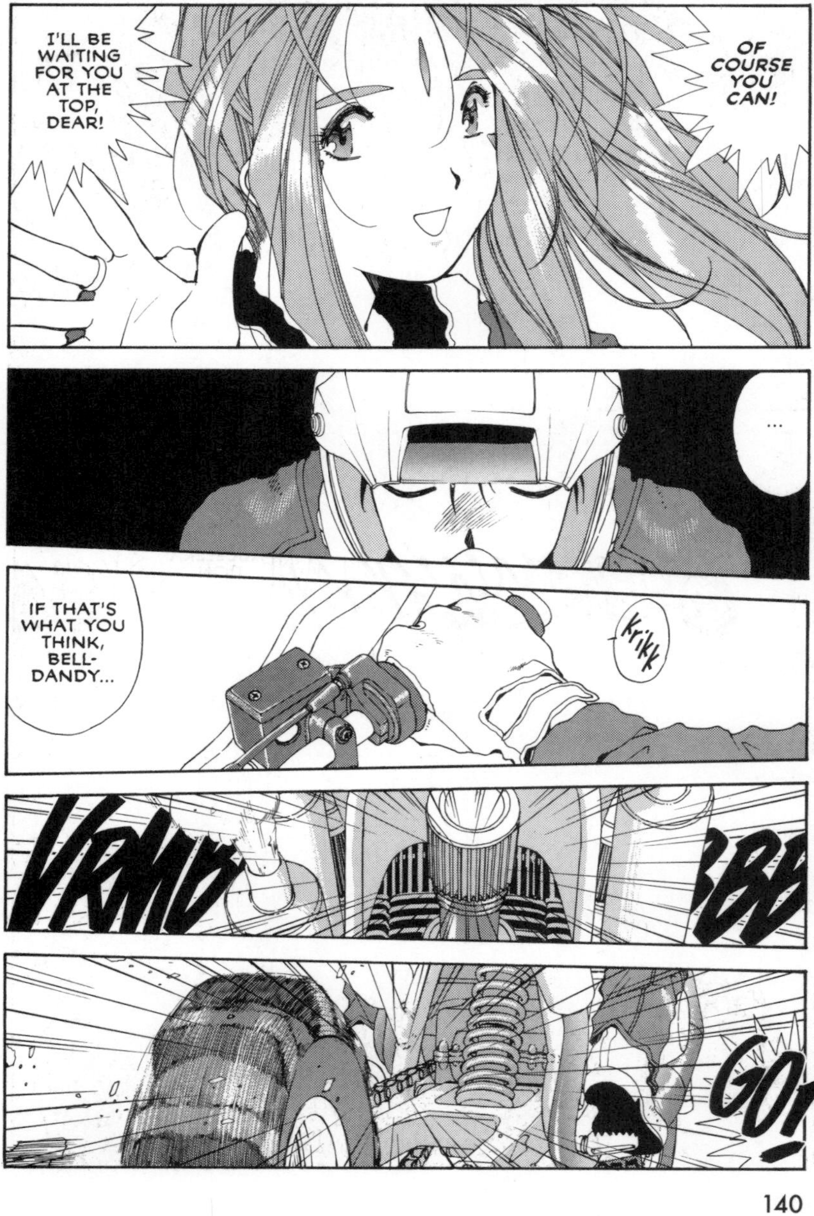
OF COURSE YOU CAN!
I'LL BE WAITING FOR YOU AT THE TOP, DEAR!
...
krikk
IF THAT'S WHAT YOU THINK, BELL-DANDY...
GO!

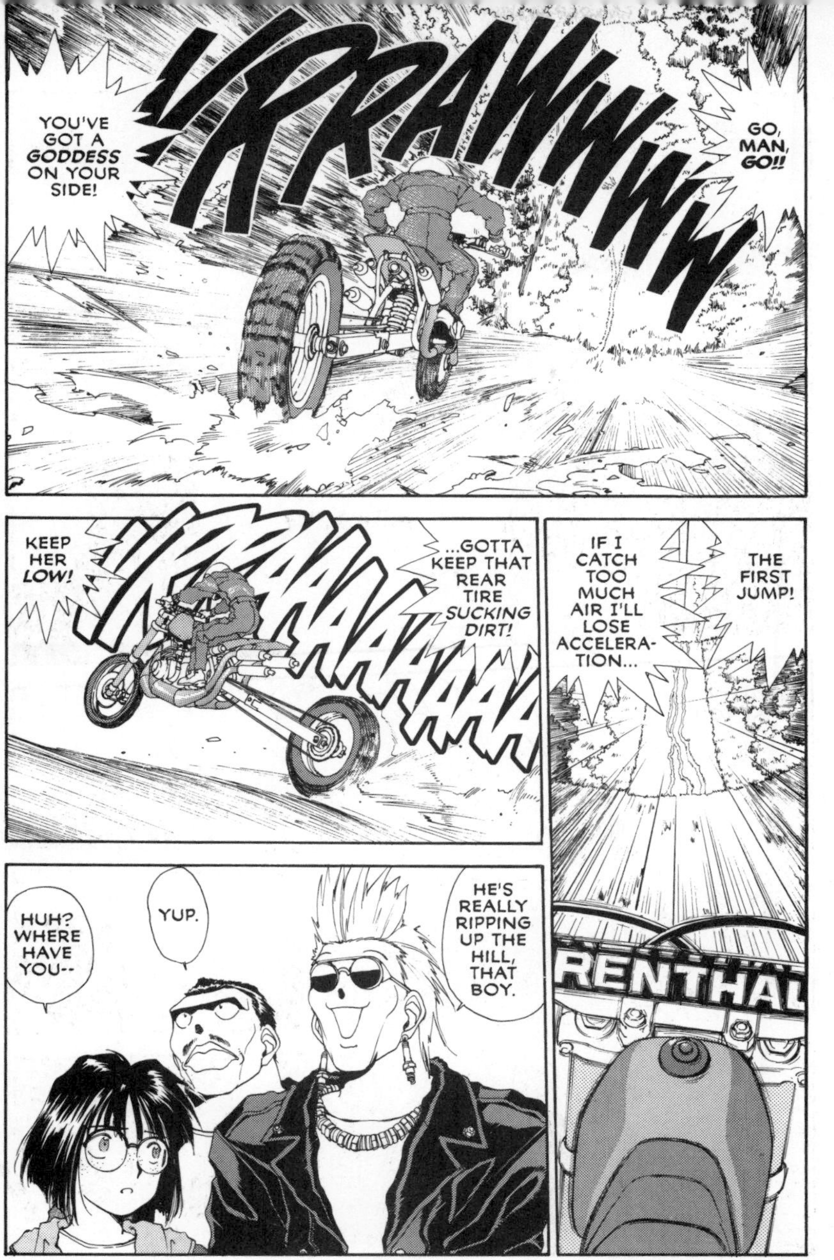
GO, MAN, *GO!!*
VRRAWWWWWW
YOU'VE GOT A *GODDESS* ON YOUR SIDE!
THE FIRST JUMP!
IF I CATCH TOO MUCH AIR I'LL LOSE ACCELERATION...
RENTHAL
...GOTTA KEEP THAT REAR TIRE *SUCKING DIRT!*
VRRAAAAAAAA
KEEP HER *LOW!*
HE'S REALLY RIPPING UP THE HILL, THAT BOY.
YUP.
HUH? WHERE HAVE YOU--

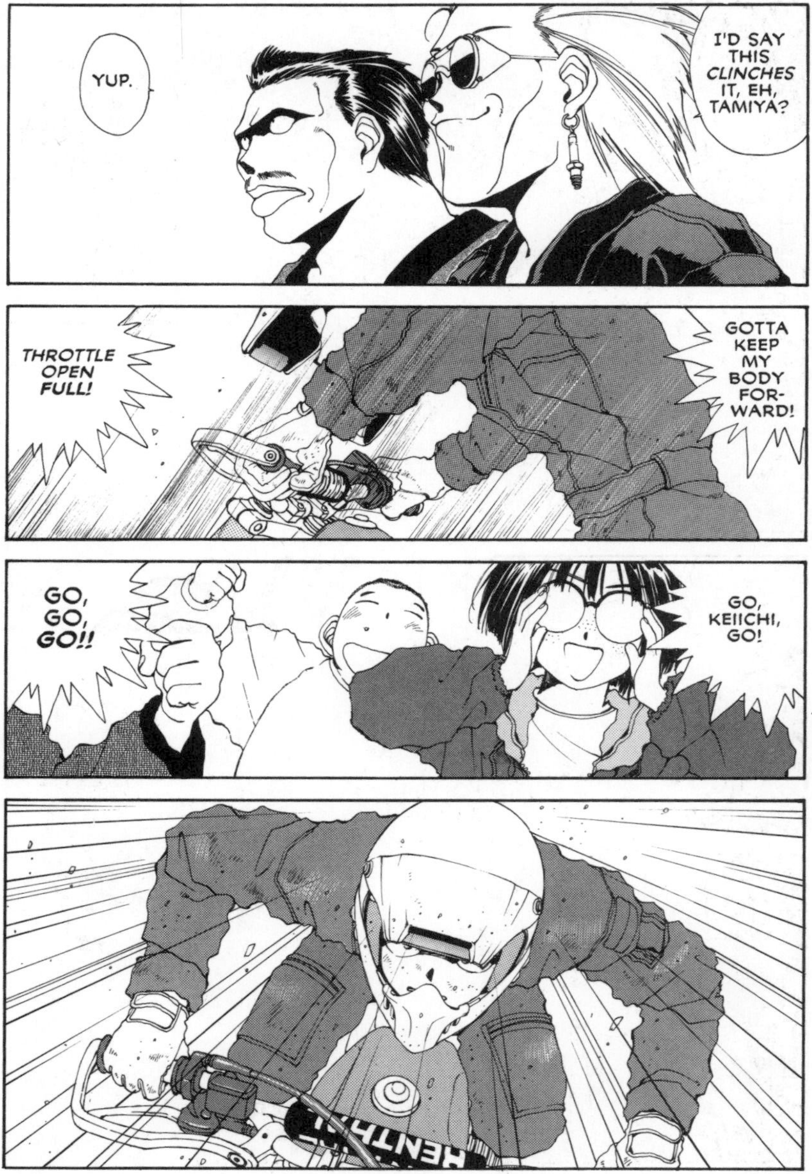
I'D SAY THIS *CLINCHES* IT, EH, TAMIYA?
YUP.
GOTTA KEEP MY BODY FOR-WARD!
THROTTLE OPEN FULL!
GO, KEIICHI, GO!
GO, GO, **GO!!**

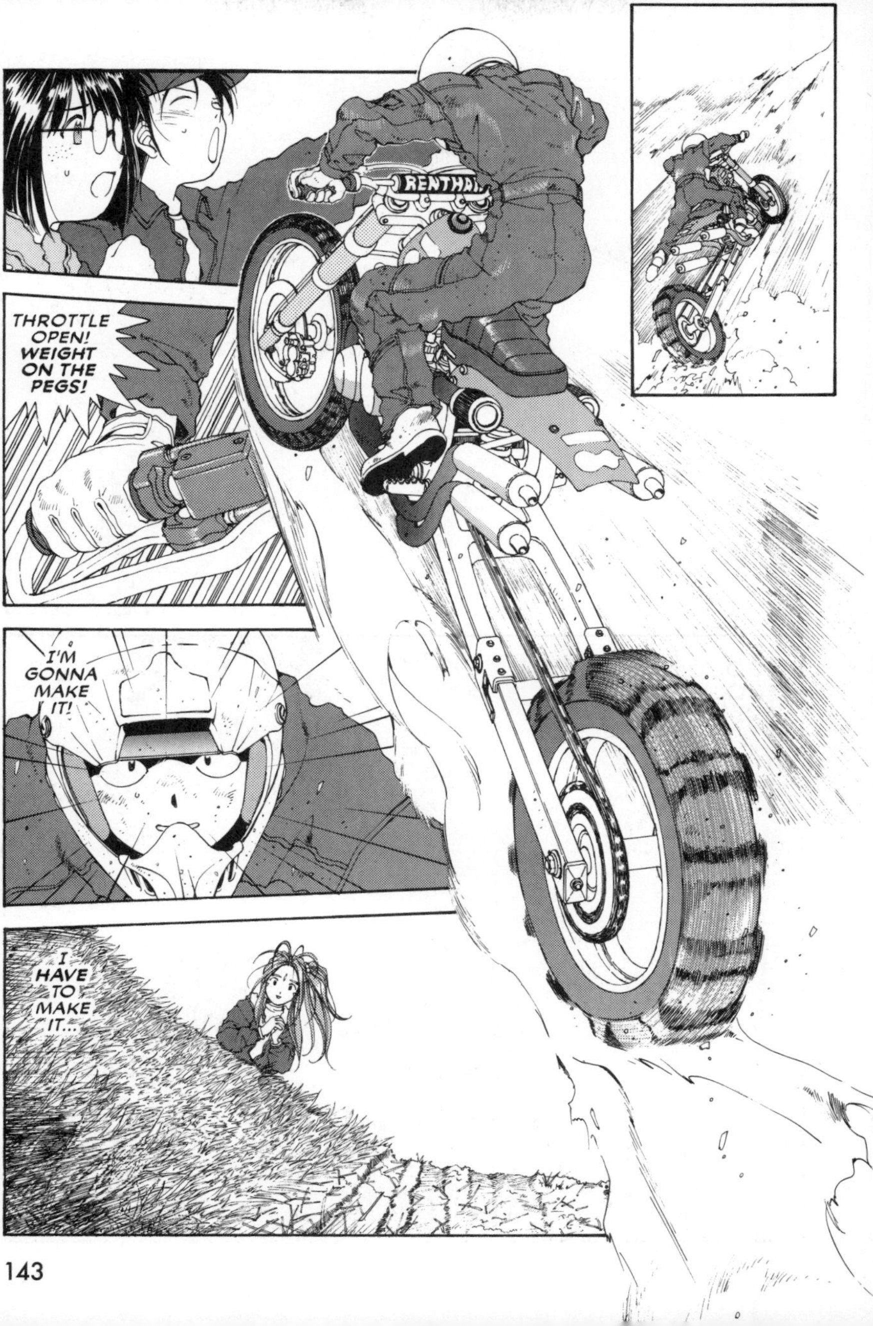
THROTTLE OPEN! WEIGHT ON THE PEGS!
I'M GONNA MAKE IT!
I HAVE TO MAKE IT...

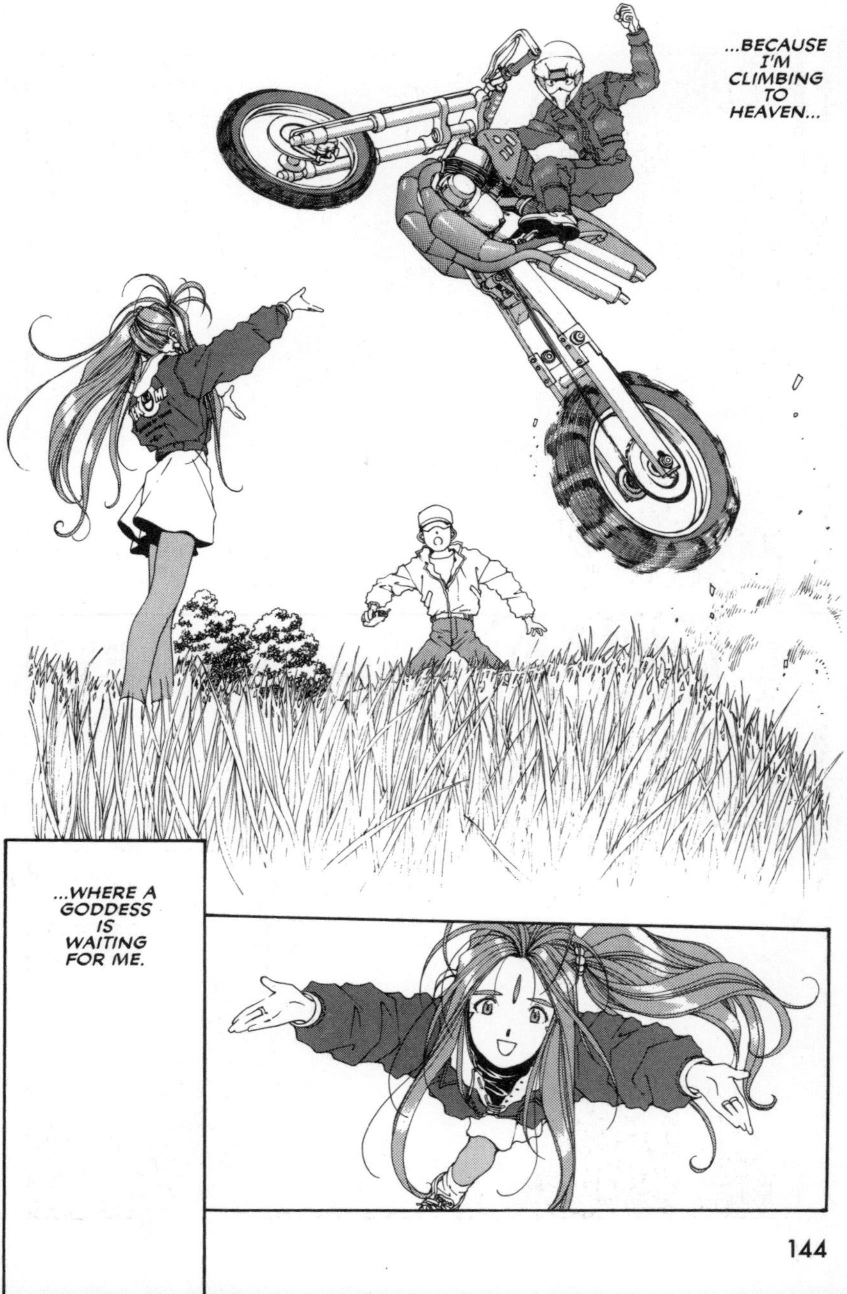
...BECAUSE I'M CLIMBING TO HEAVEN...
...WHERE A GODDESS IS WAITING FOR ME.

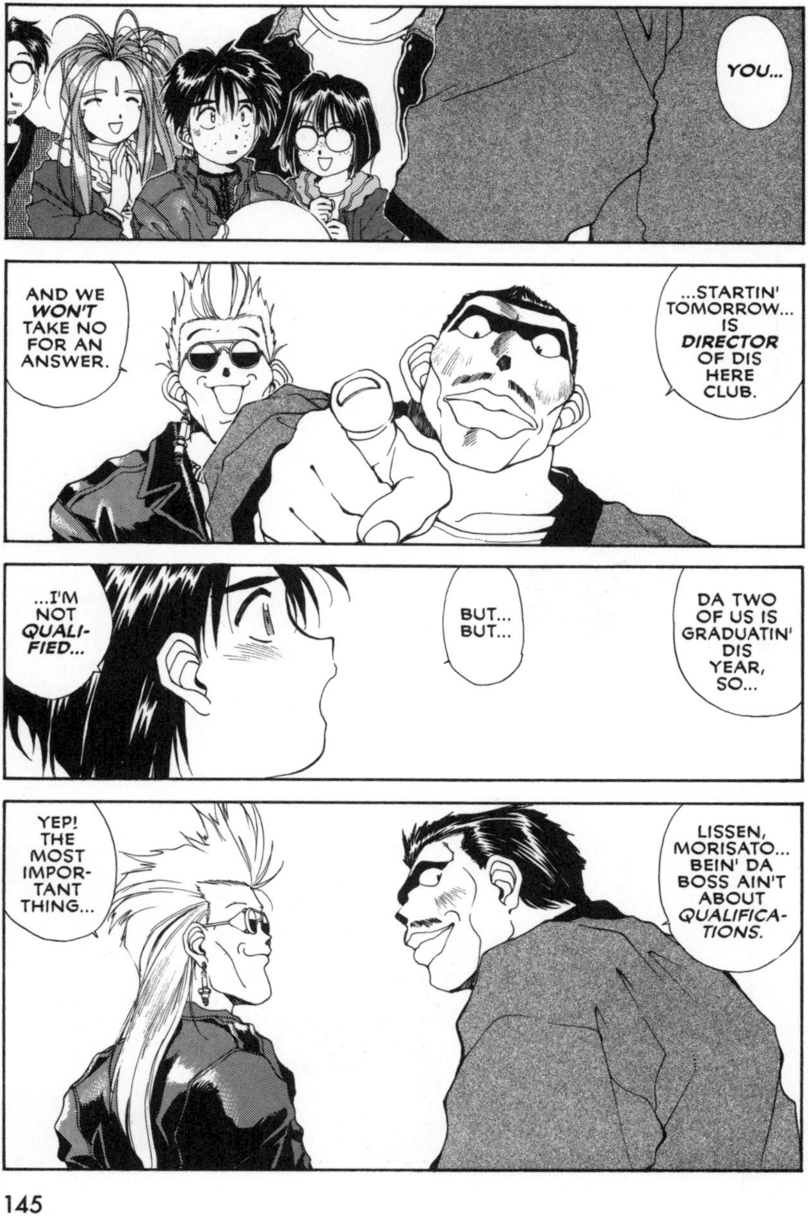
YOU...
...STARTIN' TOMORROW... IS DIRECTOR OF DIS HERE CLUB.
AND WE WON'T TAKE NO FOR AN ANSWER.
DA TWO OF US IS GRADUATIN' DIS YEAR, SO...
BUT... BUT...
...I'M NOT QUALIFIED...
LISSEN, MORISATO... BEIN' DA BOSS AIN'T ABOUT QUALIFICATIONS.
YEP! THE MOST IMPORTANT THING...

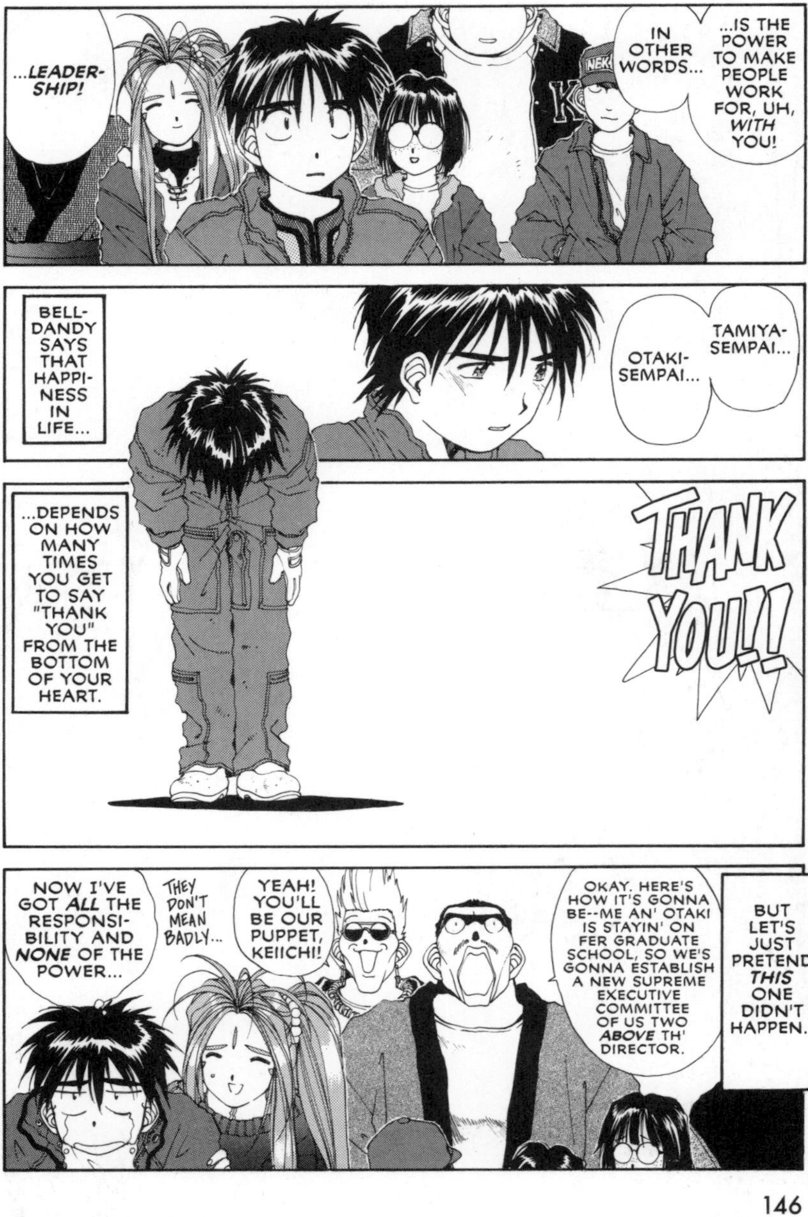
...IS THE POWER TO MAKE PEOPLE WORK FOR, UH, *WITH* YOU!
IN OTHER WORDS...
...*LEADER-SHIP!*
TAMIYA-SEMPAI...
OTAKI-SEMPAI...
BELL-DANDY SAYS THAT HAPPI-NESS IN LIFE...
THANK YOU!!
...DEPENDS ON HOW MANY TIMES YOU GET TO SAY "THANK YOU" FROM THE BOTTOM OF YOUR HEART.
BUT LET'S JUST PRETEND *THIS* ONE DIDN'T HAPPEN.
OKAY. HERE'S HOW IT'S GONNA BE--ME AN' OTAKI IS STAYIN' ON FER GRADUATE SCHOOL, SO WE'S GONNA ESTABLISH A NEW SUPREME EXECUTIVE COMMITTEE OF US TWO *ABOVE* TH' DIRECTOR.
YEAH! YOU'LL BE OUR PUPPET, KEIICHI!
THEY DON'T MEAN BADLY...
NOW I'VE GOT *ALL* THE RESPONSI-BILITY AND *NONE* OF THE POWER...

CHAPTER 57

Tainted God

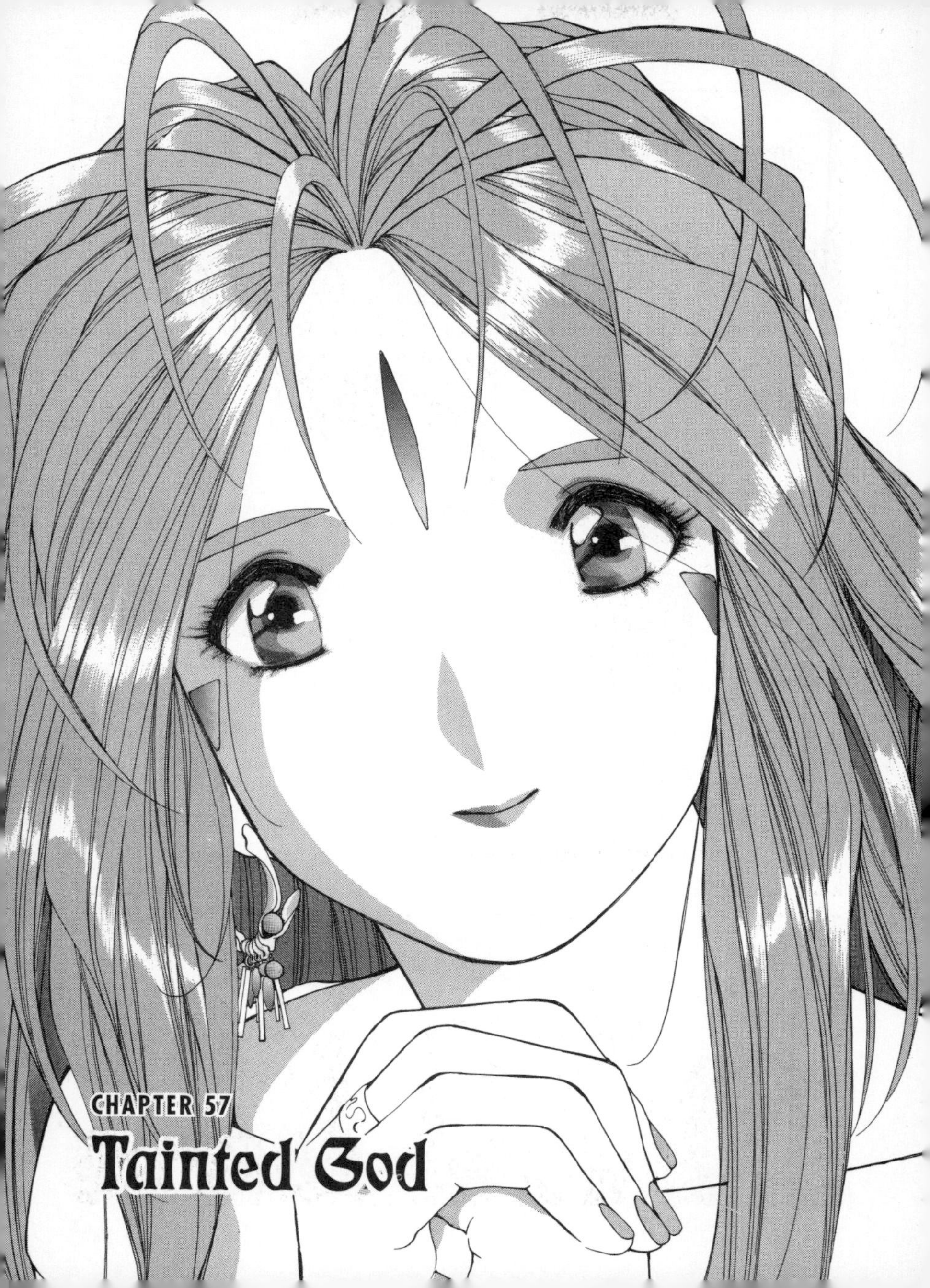

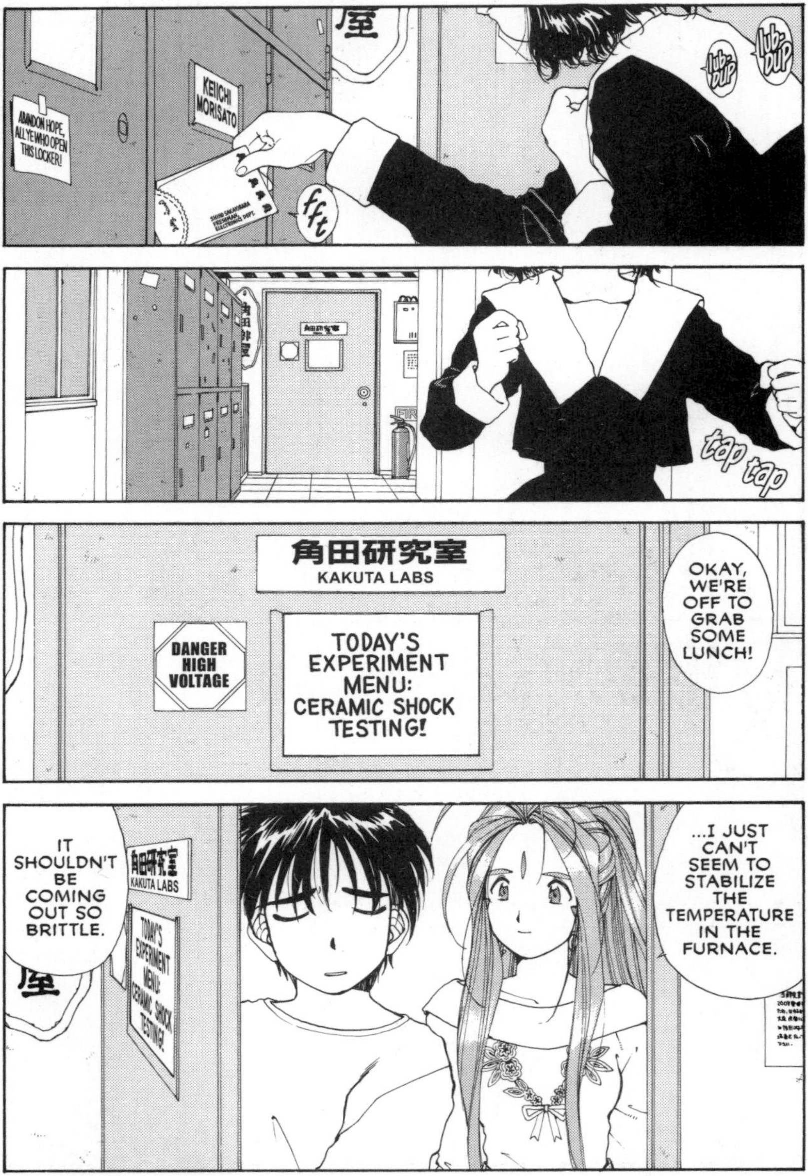
lub-DUP
lub-DUP
KEIICHI MORISATO
ABANDON HOPE, ALL YE WHO OPEN THIS LOCKER!
fft
tap tap
OKAY, WE'RE OFF TO GRAB SOME LUNCH!
角田研究室
KAKUTA LABS
TODAY'S EXPERIMENT MENU: CERAMIC SHOCK TESTING!
DANGER HIGH VOLTAGE
...I JUST CAN'T SEEM TO STABILIZE THE TEMPERATURE IN THE FURNACE.
IT SHOULDN'T BE COMING OUT SO BRITTLE.
角田研究室
KAKUTA LABS
TODAY'S EXPERIMENT MENU: CERAMIC SHOCK TESTING!

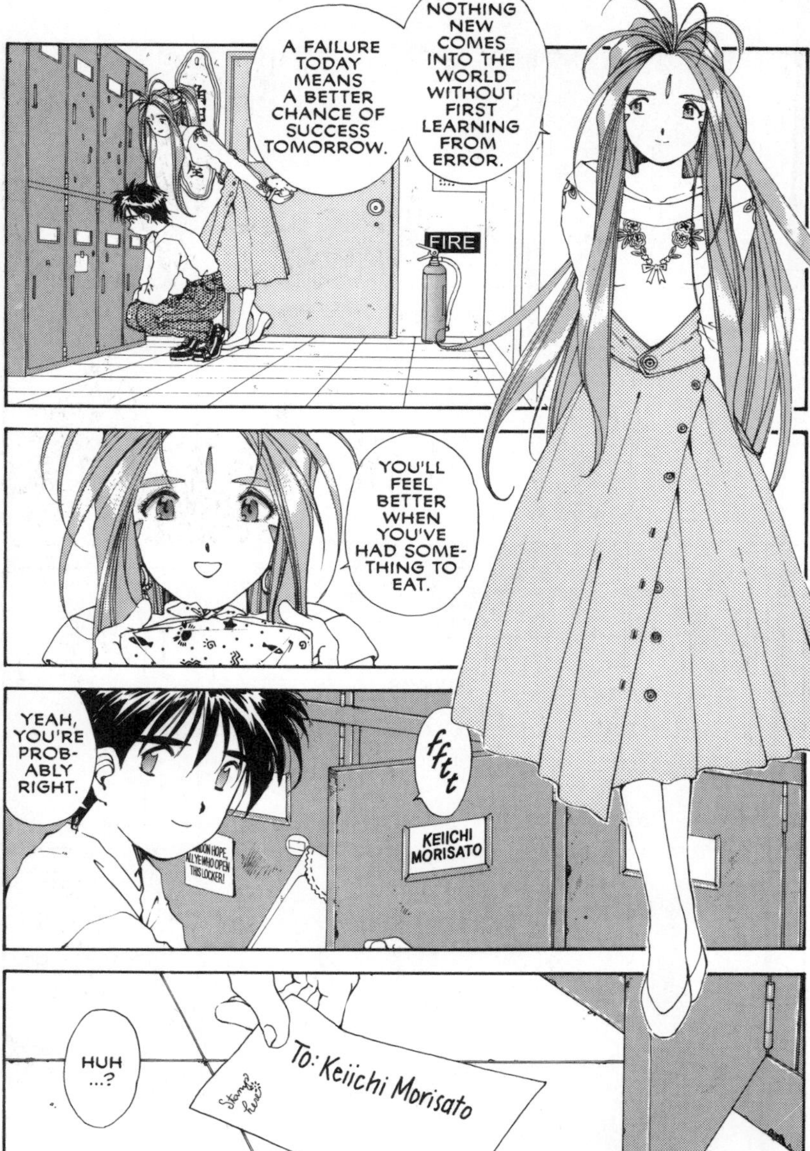
NOTHING NEW COMES INTO THE WORLD WITHOUT FIRST LEARNING FROM ERROR.
A FAILURE TODAY MEANS A BETTER CHANCE OF SUCCESS TOMORROW.
FIRE
YOU'LL FEEL BETTER WHEN YOU'VE HAD SOME-THING TO EAT.
fttt
KEIICHI MORISATO
YEAH, YOU'RE PROB-ABLY RIGHT.
To: Keiichi Morisato
Stamp here
HUH ...?

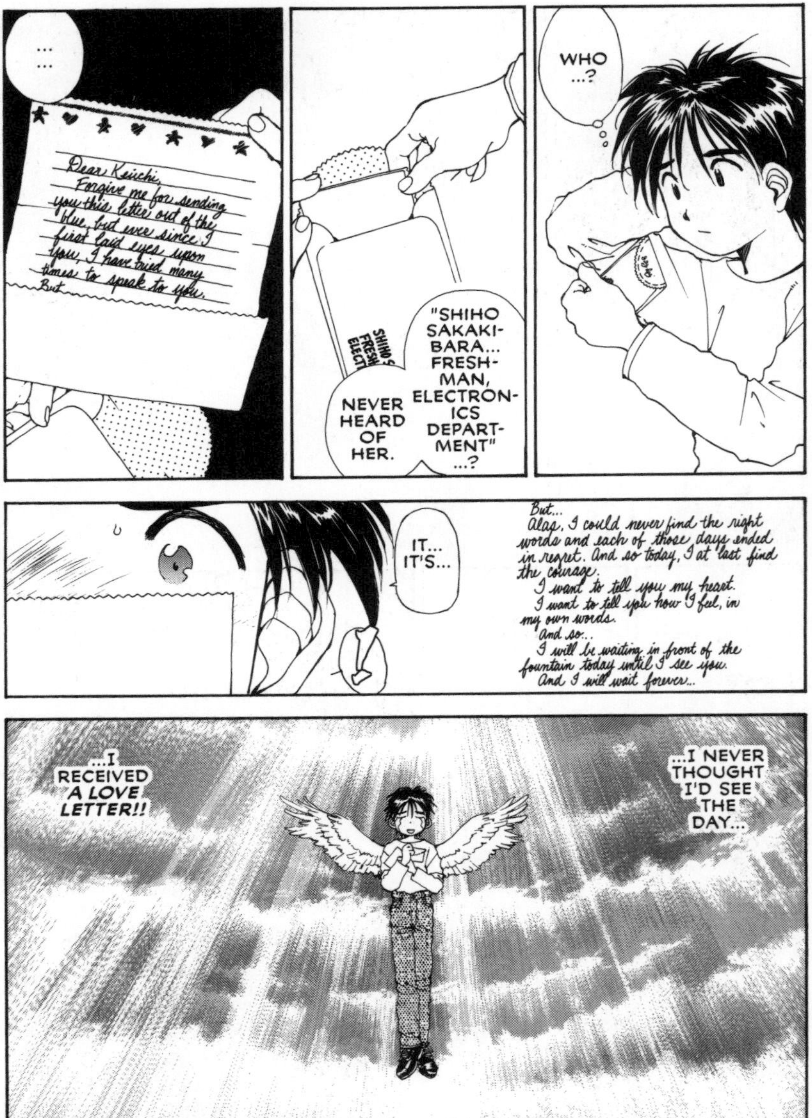
WHO ...?
"SHIHO SAKAKIBARA... FRESHMAN, ELECTRONICS DEPARTMENT" ...?
NEVER HEARD OF HER.
... ...
Dear Keiichi,
Forgive me for sending you this letter out of the blue, but ever since I first laid eyes upon you, I have tried many times to speak to you.
But...
But...
Alas, I could never find the right words and each of those days ended in regret. And so today, I at last find the courage.
I want to tell you my heart.
I want to tell you how I feel, in my own words.
And so..
I will be waiting in front of the fountain today until I see you.
And I will wait forever...
IT... IT'S...
...I NEVER THOUGHT I'D SEE THE DAY...
...I RECEIVED A LOVE LETTER!!

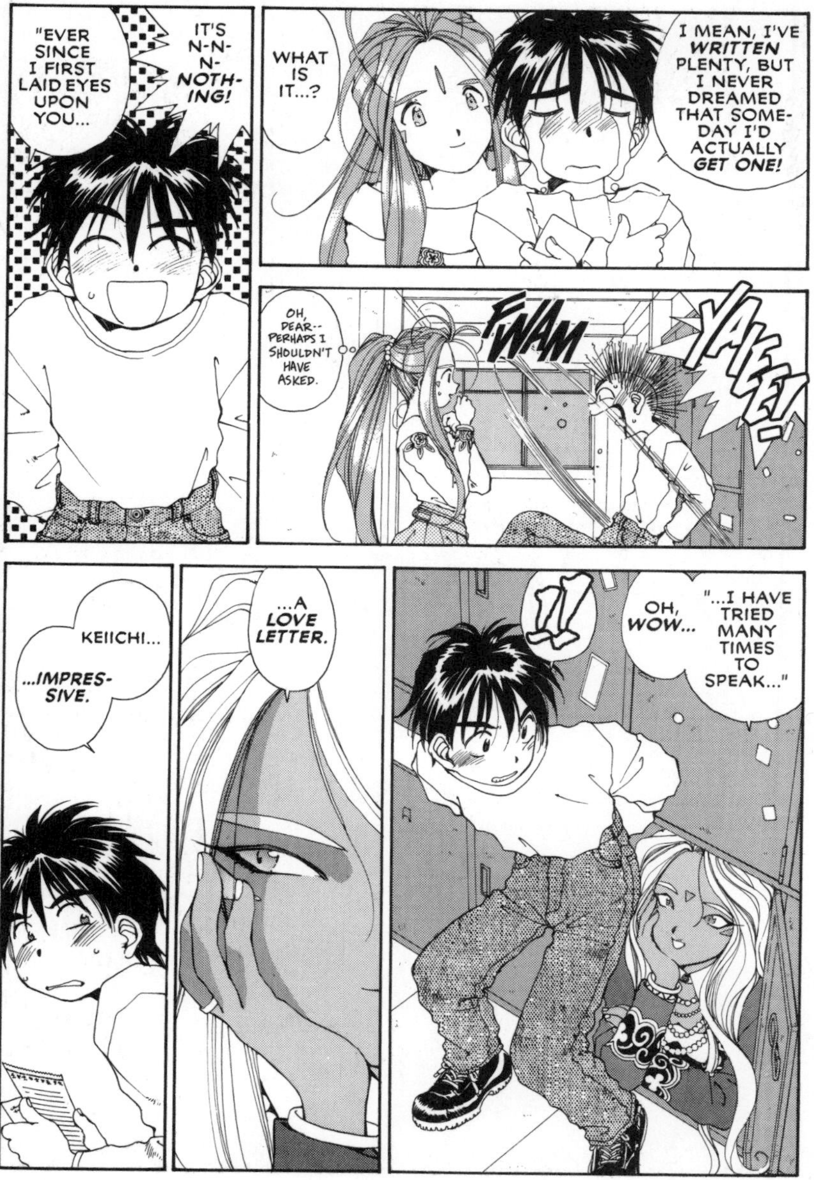

I MEAN, I'VE WRITTEN PLENTY, BUT I NEVER DREAMED THAT SOMEDAY I'D ACTUALLY GET ONE!
WHAT IS IT...?
YAEEE!
FWAM
OH, DEAR-- PERHAPS I SHOULDN'T HAVE ASKED.
IT'S N-N-N-NOTHING!
"EVER SINCE I FIRST LAID EYES UPON YOU...
"...I HAVE TRIED MANY TIMES TO SPEAK..."
OH, WOW...
...A LOVE LETTER.
KEIICHI...
...IMPRESSIVE.

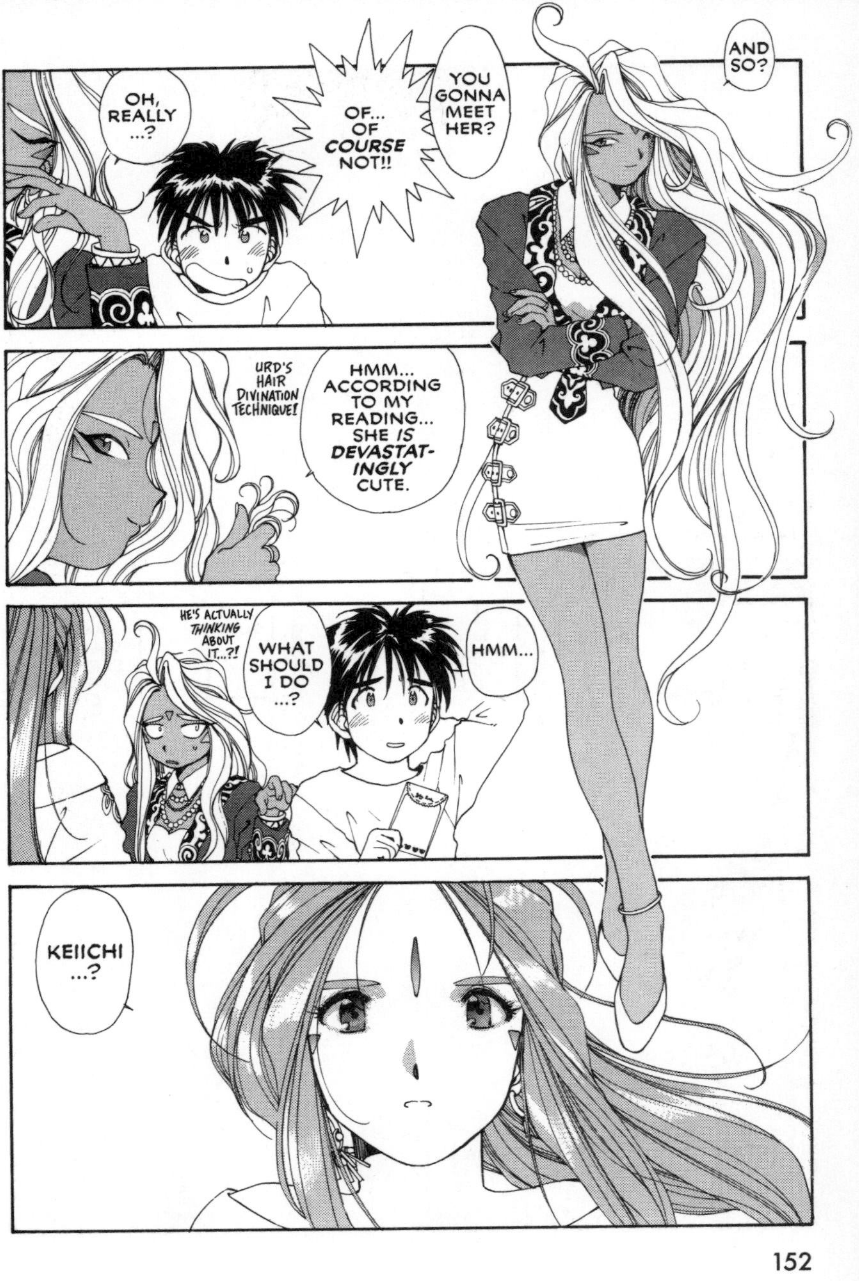
AND SO?
YOU GONNA MEET HER?
OF... OF *COURSE* NOT!!
OH, REALLY ...?
HMM... ACCORDING TO MY READING... SHE *IS* *DEVASTATINGLY* CUTE.
URD'S HAIR DIVINATION TECHNIQUE!
HMM...
WHAT SHOULD I DO ...?
HE'S ACTUALLY *THINKING* ABOUT IT...?!
KEIICHI ...?

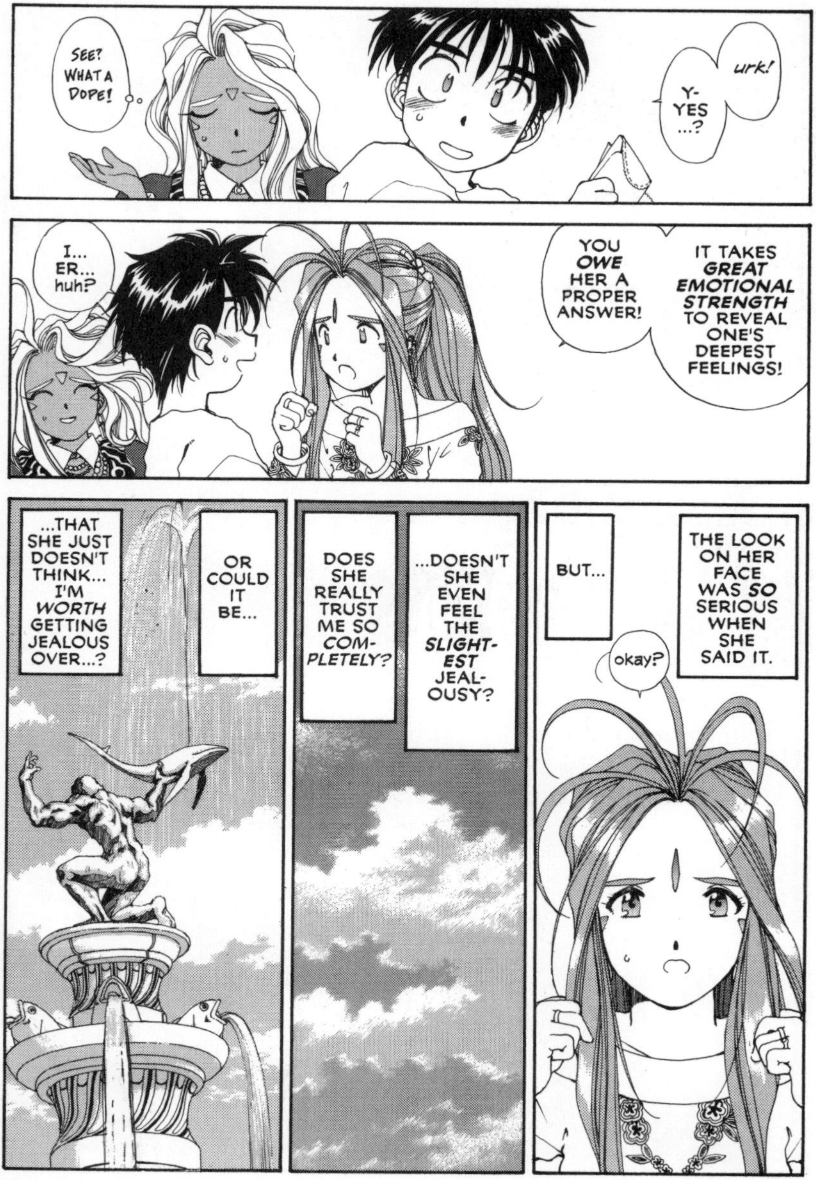
urk!
Y-YES ...?
SEE? WHAT A DOPE!
IT TAKES GREAT EMOTIONAL STRENGTH TO REVEAL ONE'S DEEPEST FEELINGS!
YOU OWE HER A PROPER ANSWER!
I... ER... huh?
THE LOOK ON HER FACE WAS SO SERIOUS WHEN SHE SAID IT.
BUT...
okay?
...DOESN'T SHE EVEN FEEL THE SLIGHT-EST JEAL-OUSY?
DOES SHE REALLY TRUST ME SO COM-PLETELY?
OR COULD IT BE...
...THAT SHE JUST DOESN'T THINK... I'M WORTH GETTING JEALOUS OVER...?

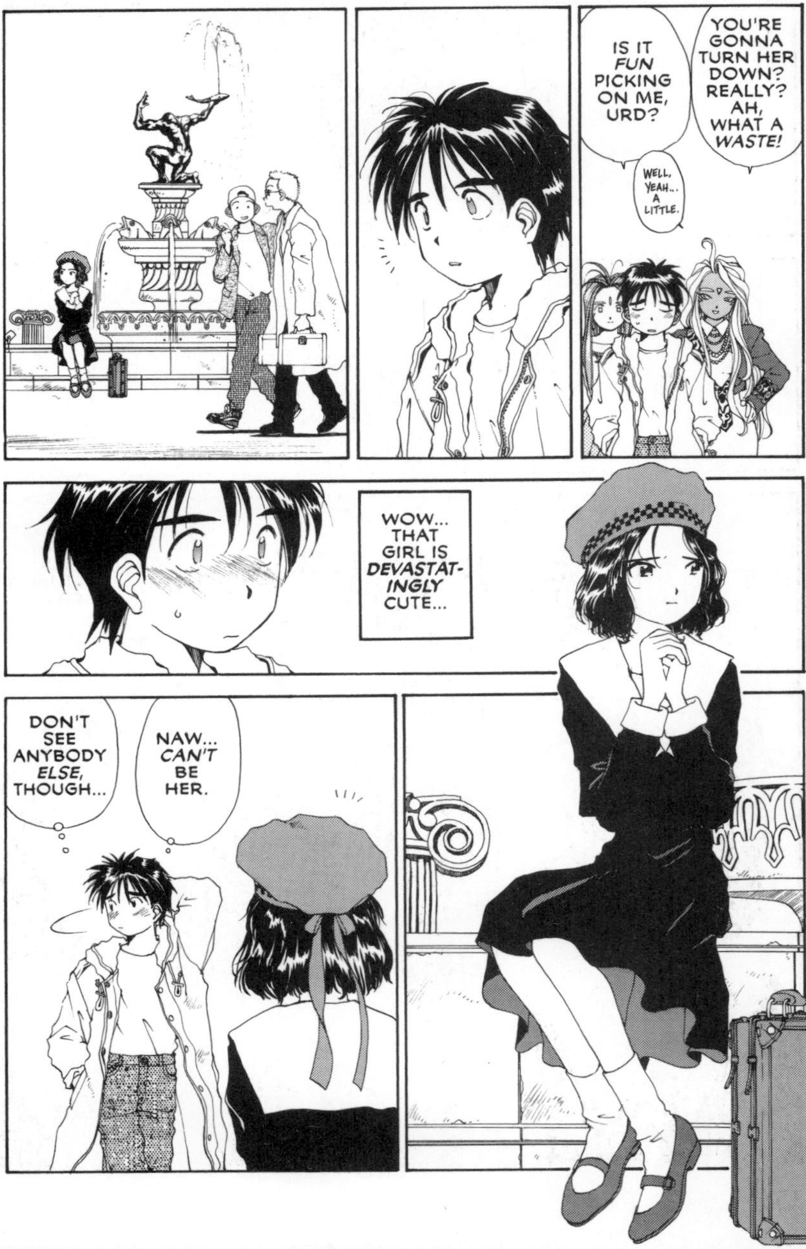
YOU'RE GONNA TURN HER DOWN? REALLY? AH, WHAT A *WASTE!*
IS IT *FUN* PICKING ON ME, URD?
WELL, YEAH... A LITTLE.
WOW... THAT GIRL IS ***DEVASTATINGLY*** CUTE...
NAW... *CAN'T* BE HER.
DON'T SEE ANYBODY *ELSE*, THOUGH...

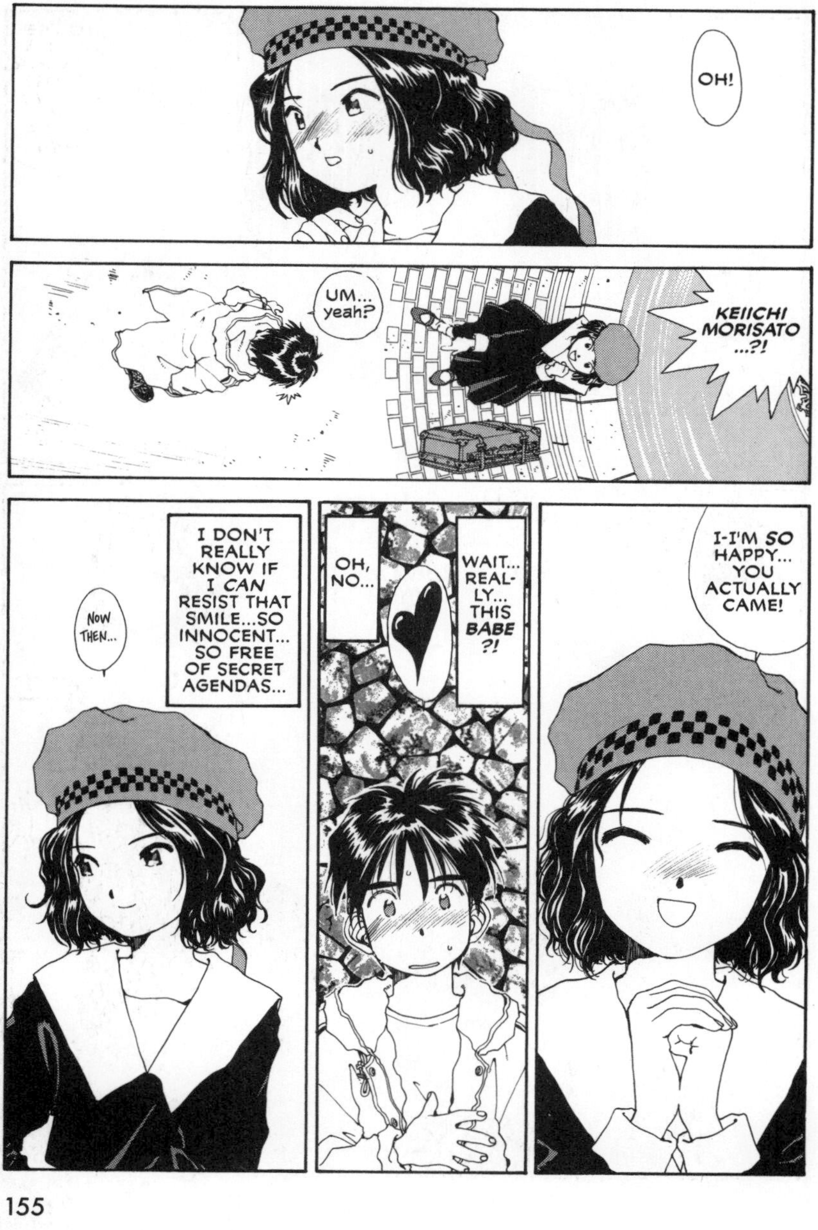
OH!
KEIICHI MORISATO ...?!
UM... yeah?
I-I'M SO HAPPY... YOU ACTUALLY CAME!
WAIT... REALLY... THIS BABE?!
OH, NO...
I DON'T REALLY KNOW IF I CAN RESIST THAT SMILE...SO INNOCENT... SO FREE OF SECRET AGENDAS...
NOW THEN...

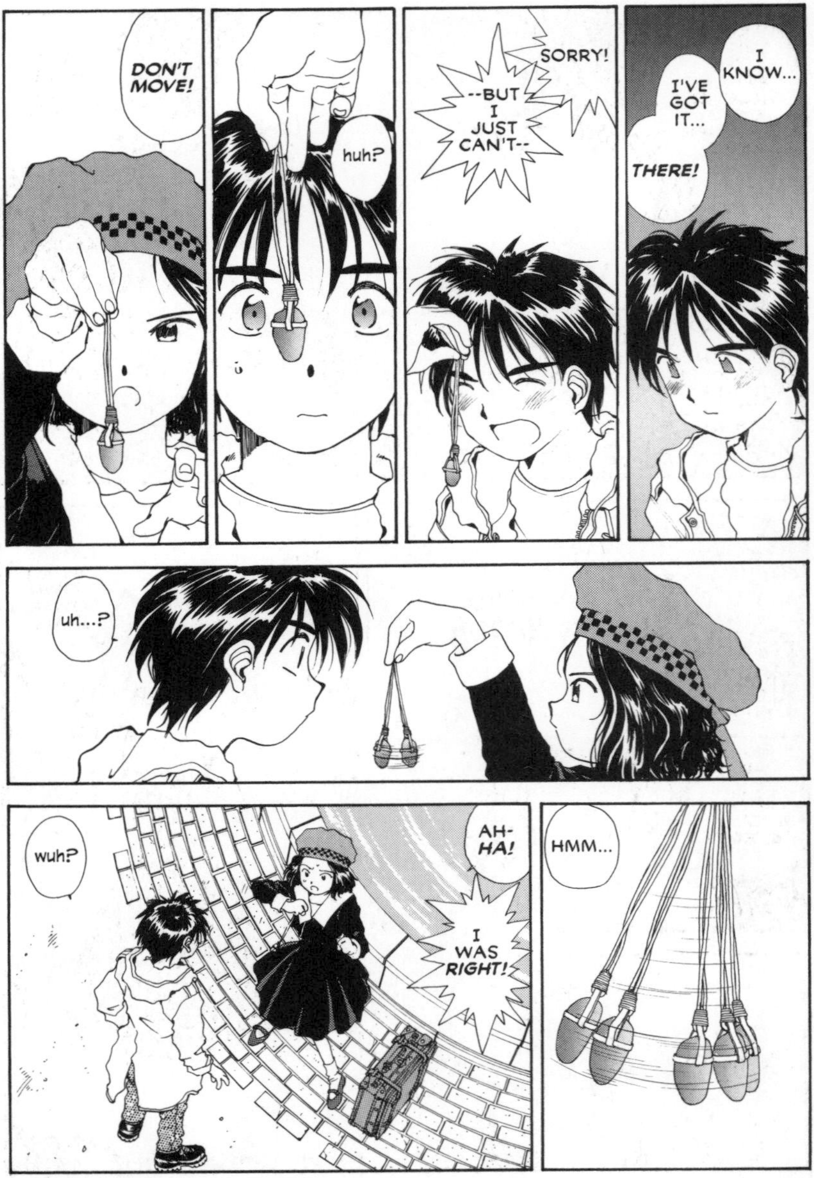
I KNOW...
I'VE GOT IT...
THERE!
SORRY!
--BUT I JUST CAN'T--
huh?
DON'T MOVE!
uh...?
HMM...
AH-HA!
I WAS RIGHT!
wuh?

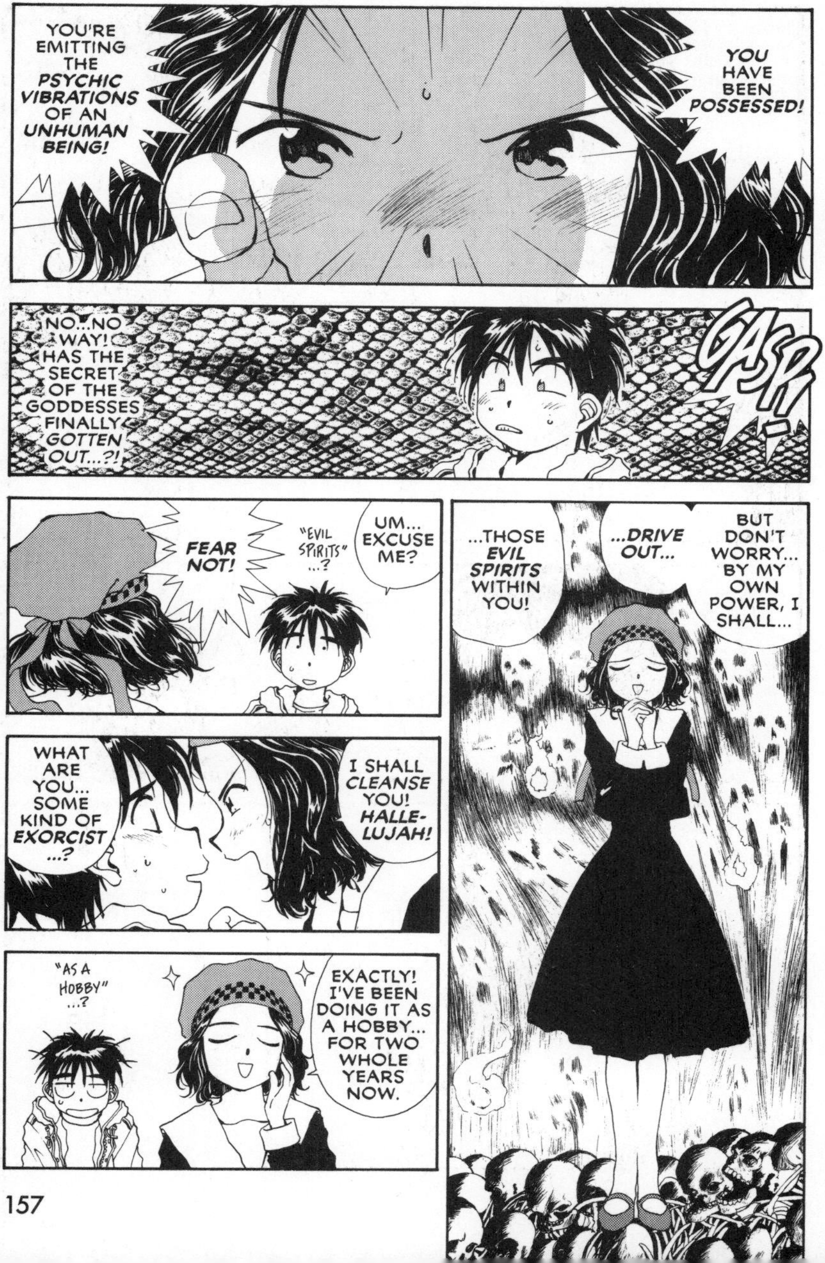
YOU HAVE BEEN POSSESSED!
YOU'RE EMITTING THE PSYCHIC VIBRATIONS OF AN UNHUMAN BEING!
GASP!
NO...NO WAY! HAS THE SECRET OF THE GODDESSES FINALLY GOTTEN OUT...?!
BUT DON'T WORRY... BY MY OWN POWER, I SHALL...
...DRIVE OUT...
...THOSE EVIL SPIRITS WITHIN YOU!
UM... EXCUSE ME?
"EVIL SPIRITS" ...?
FEAR NOT!
I SHALL CLEANSE YOU! HALLE-LUJAH!
WHAT ARE YOU... SOME KIND OF EXORCIST ...?
EXACTLY! I'VE BEEN DOING IT AS A HOBBY... FOR TWO WHOLE YEARS NOW.
"AS A HOBBY" ...?

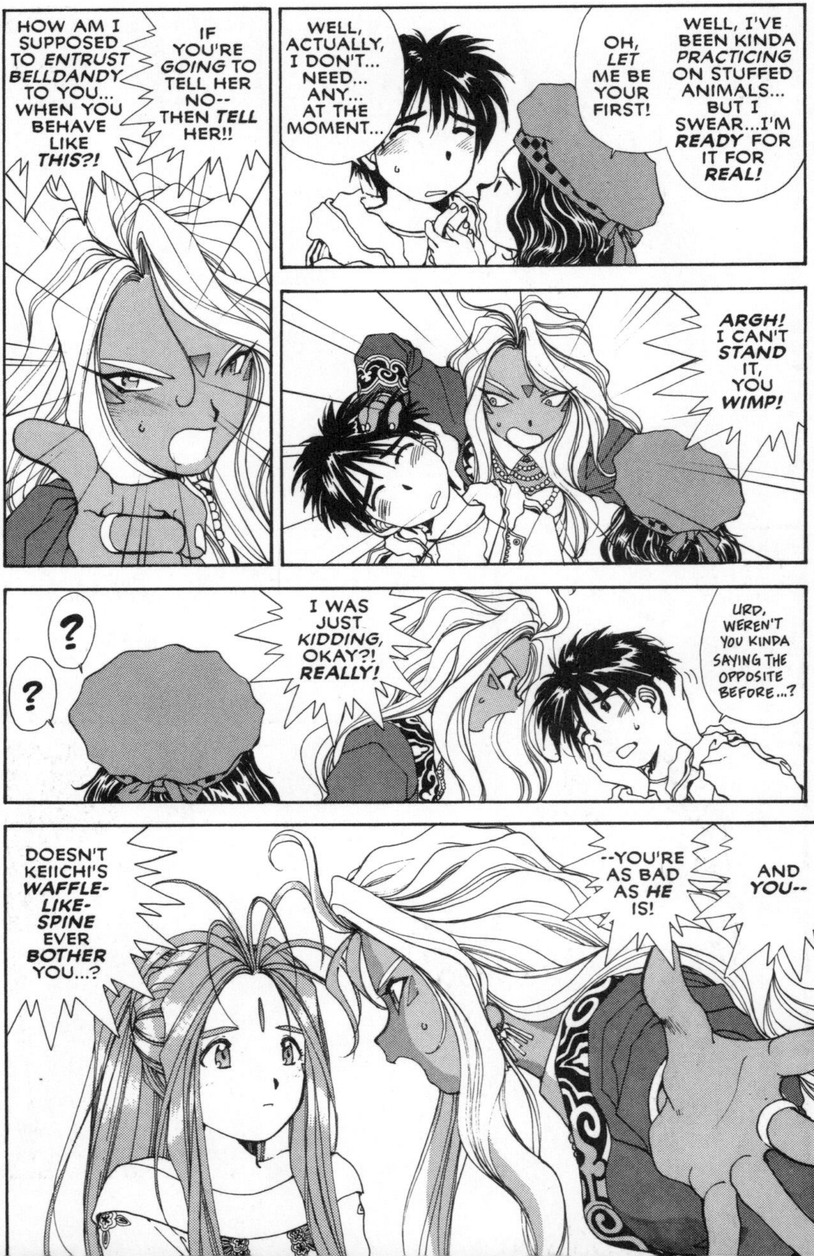
WELL, I'VE BEEN KINDA PRACTICING ON STUFFED ANIMALS... BUT I SWEAR...I'M READY FOR IT FOR REAL!
OH, LET ME BE YOUR FIRST!
WELL, ACTUALLY, I DON'T... NEED... ANY... AT THE MOMENT...
ARGH! I CAN'T STAND IT, YOU WIMP!
IF YOU'RE GOING TO TELL HER NO-- THEN TELL HER!!
HOW AM I SUPPOSED TO ENTRUST BELLDANDY TO YOU... WHEN YOU BEHAVE LIKE THIS?!
URD, WEREN'T YOU KINDA SAYING THE OPPOSITE BEFORE...?
I WAS JUST KIDDING, OKAY?! REALLY!
?
?
AND YOU--
--YOU'RE AS BAD AS HE IS!
DOESN'T KEIICHI'S WAFFLE-LIKE-SPINE EVER BOTHER YOU...?

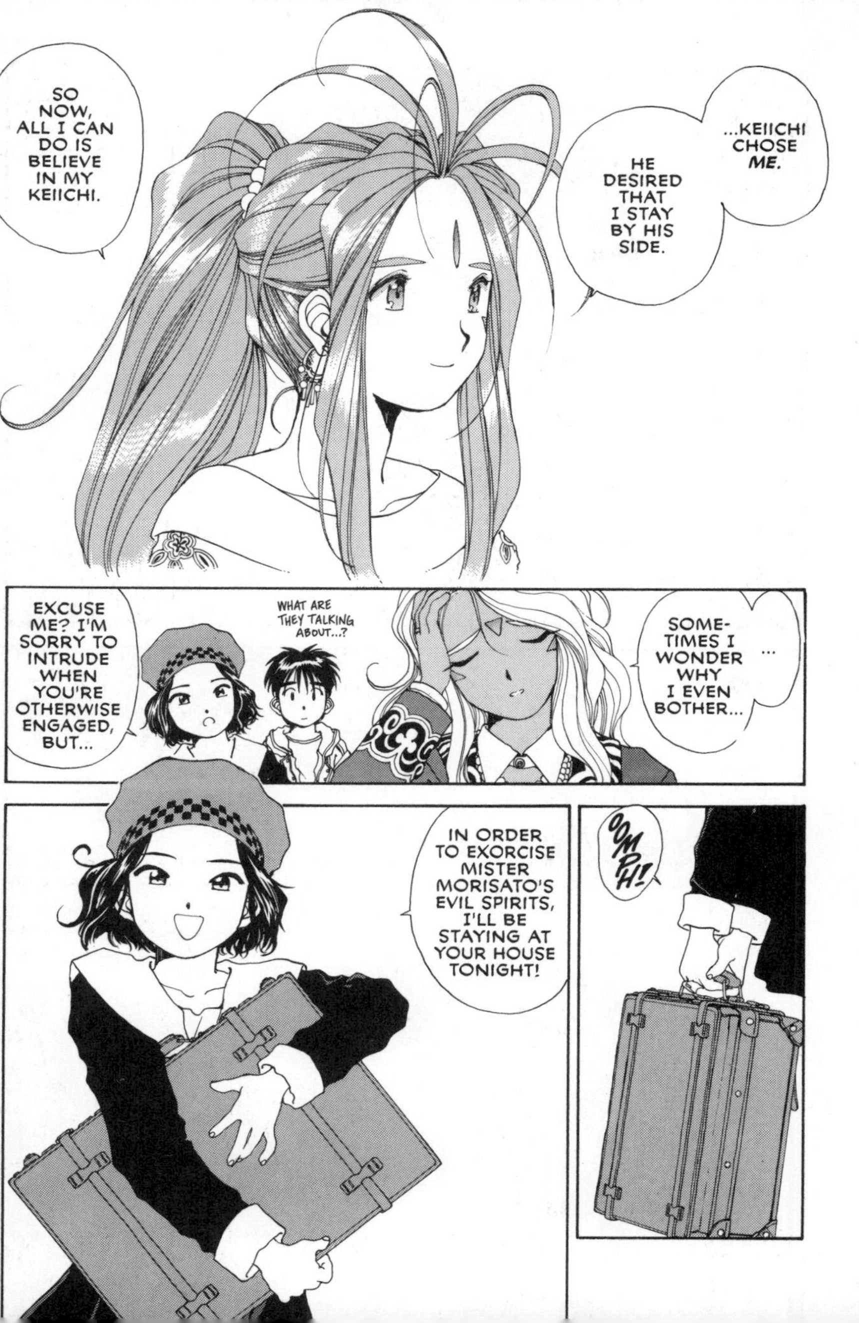
...KEIICHI CHOSE *ME.*
HE DESIRED THAT I STAY BY HIS SIDE.
SO NOW, ALL I CAN DO IS BELIEVE IN MY KEIICHI.
SOME-TIMES I WONDER WHY I EVEN BOTHER...
...
WHAT ARE THEY TALKING ABOUT...?
EXCUSE ME? I'M SORRY TO INTRUDE WHEN YOU'RE OTHERWISE ENGAGED, BUT...
OOMPH!
IN ORDER TO EXORCISE MISTER MORISATO'S EVIL SPIRITS, I'LL BE STAYING AT YOUR HOUSE TONIGHT!

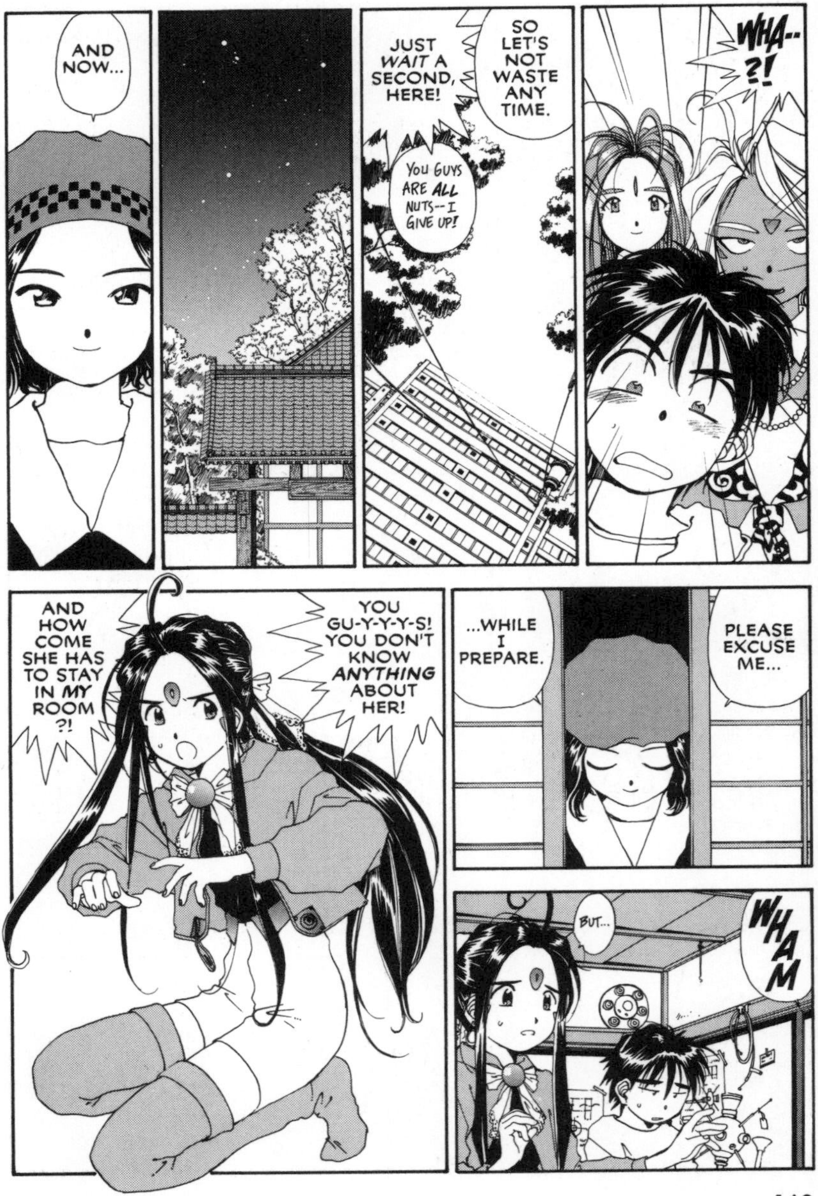
WHA-- ?!
SO LET'S NOT WASTE ANY TIME.
JUST WAIT A SECOND, HERE!
YOU GUYS ARE ALL NUTS-- I GIVE UP!
AND NOW...
PLEASE EXCUSE ME...
...WHILE I PREPARE.
WHAM
BUT...
YOU GU-Y-Y-Y-S! YOU DON'T KNOW ANYTHING ABOUT HER!
AND HOW COME SHE HAS TO STAY IN MY ROOM ?!

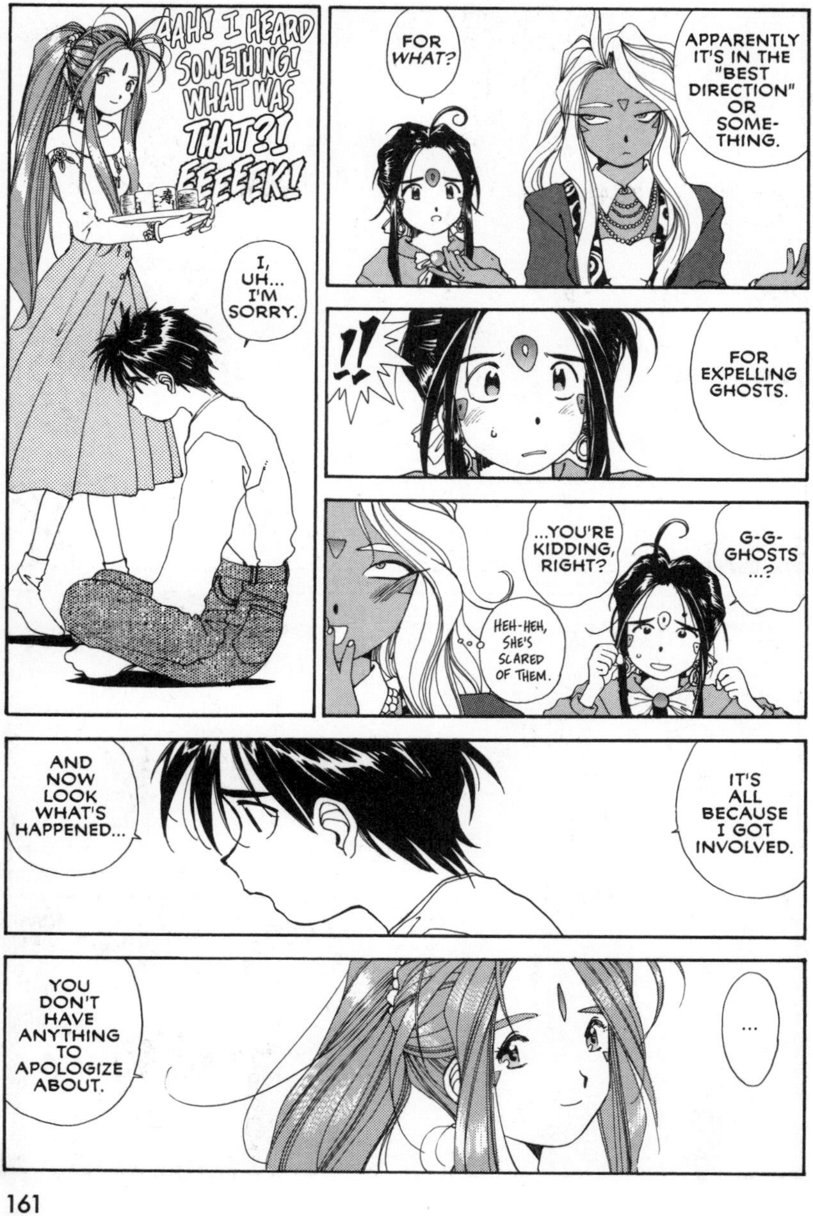
APPARENTLY IT'S IN THE "BEST DIRECTION" OR SOME- THING.
FOR WHAT?
FOR EXPELLING GHOSTS.
!!
G-G- GHOSTS ...?
...YOU'RE KIDDING, RIGHT?
HEH-HEH, SHE'S SCARED OF THEM.
AAH! I HEARD SOMETHING! WHAT WAS THAT?! EEEEEK!
I, UH... I'M SORRY.
IT'S ALL BECAUSE I GOT INVOLVED.
AND NOW LOOK WHAT'S HAPPENED...
...
YOU DON'T HAVE ANYTHING TO APOLOGIZE ABOUT.

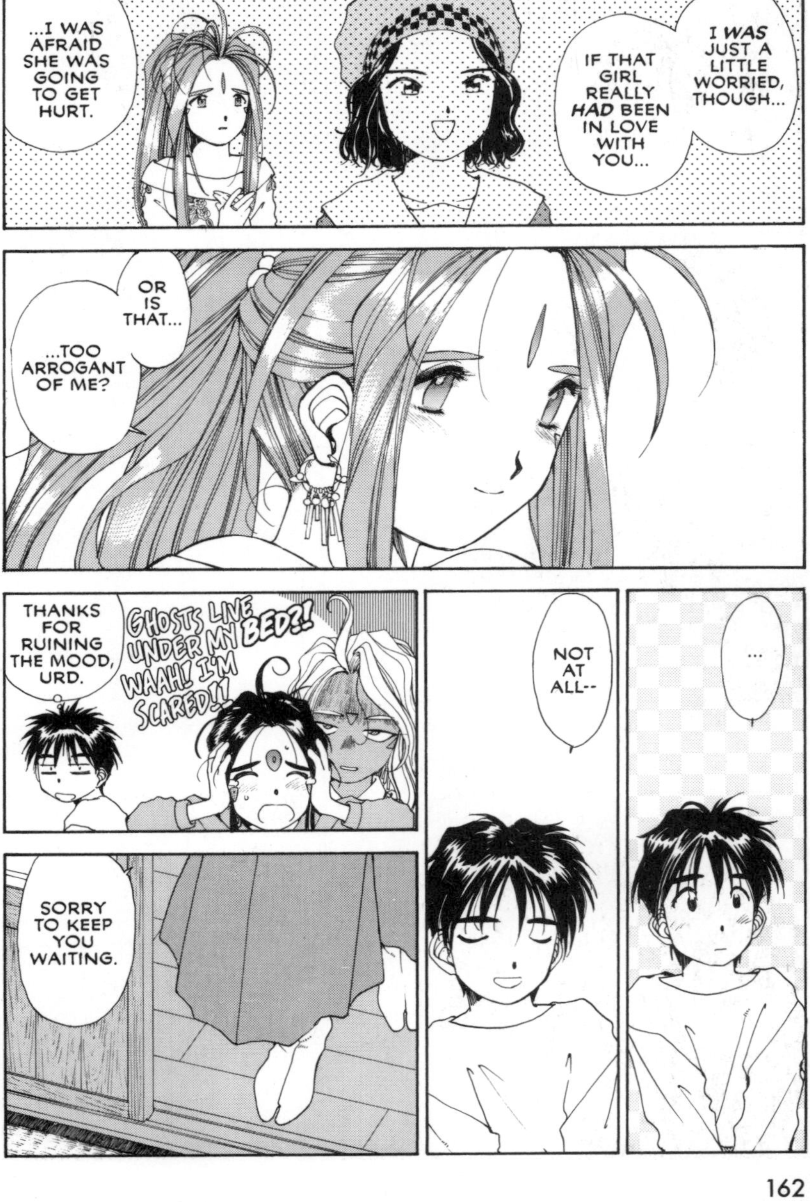
I *WAS* JUST A LITTLE WORRIED, THOUGH...
IF THAT GIRL REALLY *HAD* BEEN IN LOVE WITH YOU...
...I WAS AFRAID SHE WAS GOING TO GET HURT.
OR IS THAT...
...TOO ARROGANT OF ME?
...
NOT AT ALL--
GHOSTS LIVE UNDER MY BED?! WAAH! I'M SCARED!!
THANKS FOR RUINING THE MOOD, URD.
SORRY TO KEEP YOU WAITING.

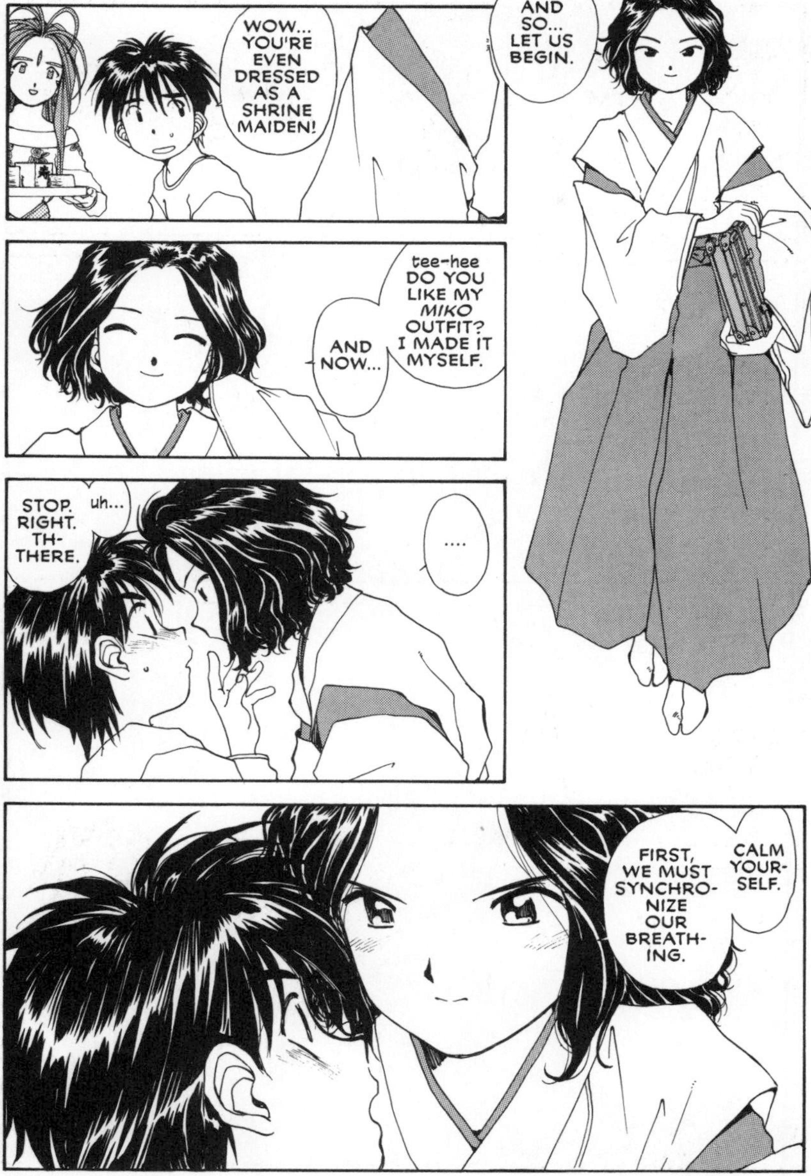

AND SO... LET US BEGIN.
WOW... YOU'RE EVEN DRESSED AS A SHRINE MAIDEN!
tee-hee DO YOU LIKE MY *MIKO* OUTFIT? I MADE IT MYSELF.
AND NOW...
....
uh...
STOP. RIGHT. TH-THERE.
CALM YOURSELF.
FIRST, WE MUST SYNCHRONIZE OUR BREATHING.

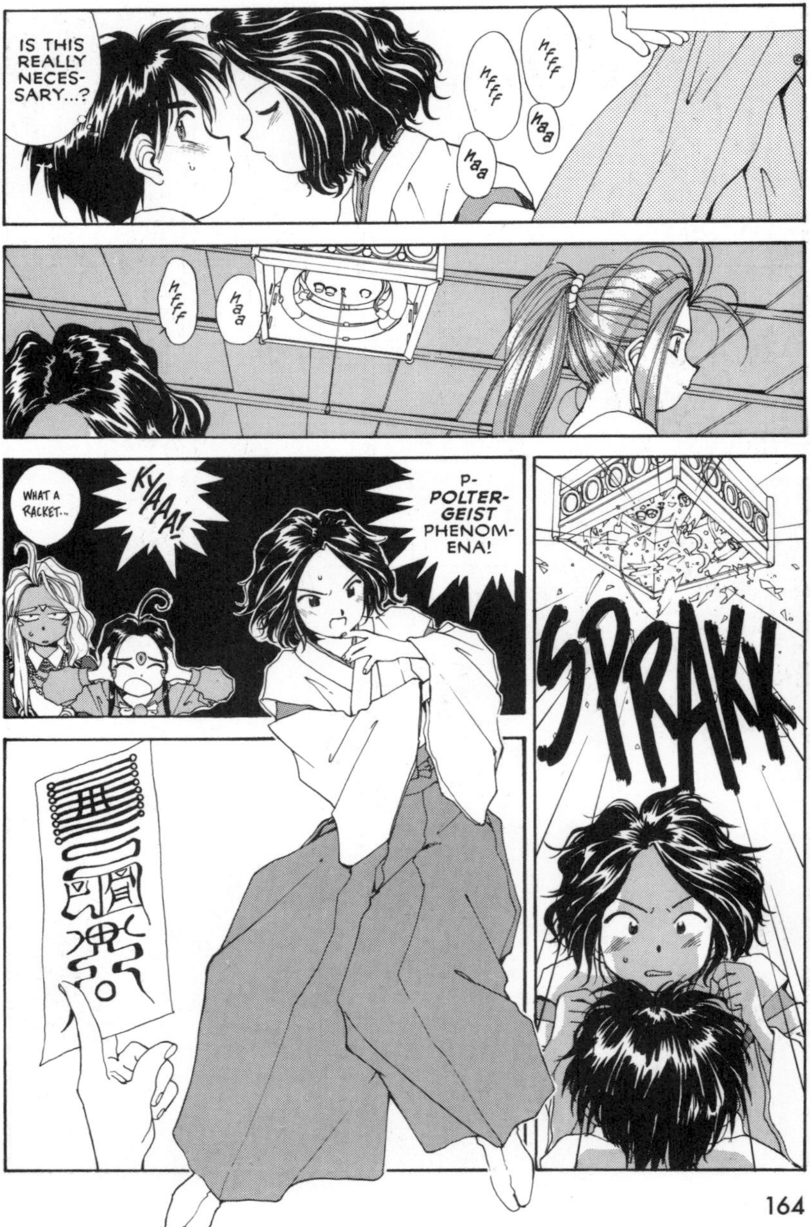
nfff
nfff
naa
naa
IS THIS REALLY NECES-SARY...?
nfff
naa
SPRAKK
P-POLTER-GEIST PHENOM-ENA!
KYAAAA!
WHAT A RACKET...

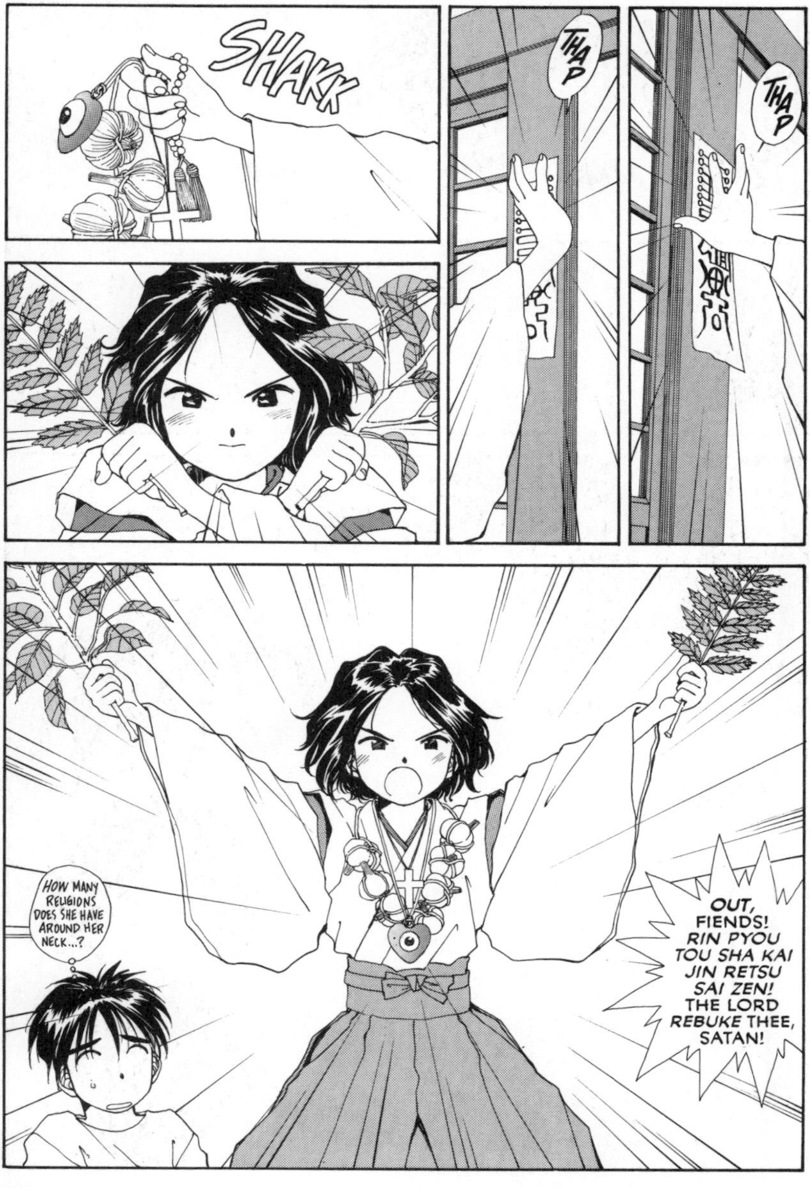
THAP
THAP
SHAKK
OUT, FIENDS! RIN PYOU TOU SHA KAI JIN RETSU SAI ZEN! THE LORD REBUKE THEE, SATAN!
HOW MANY RELIGIONS DOES SHE HAVE AROUND HER NECK...?

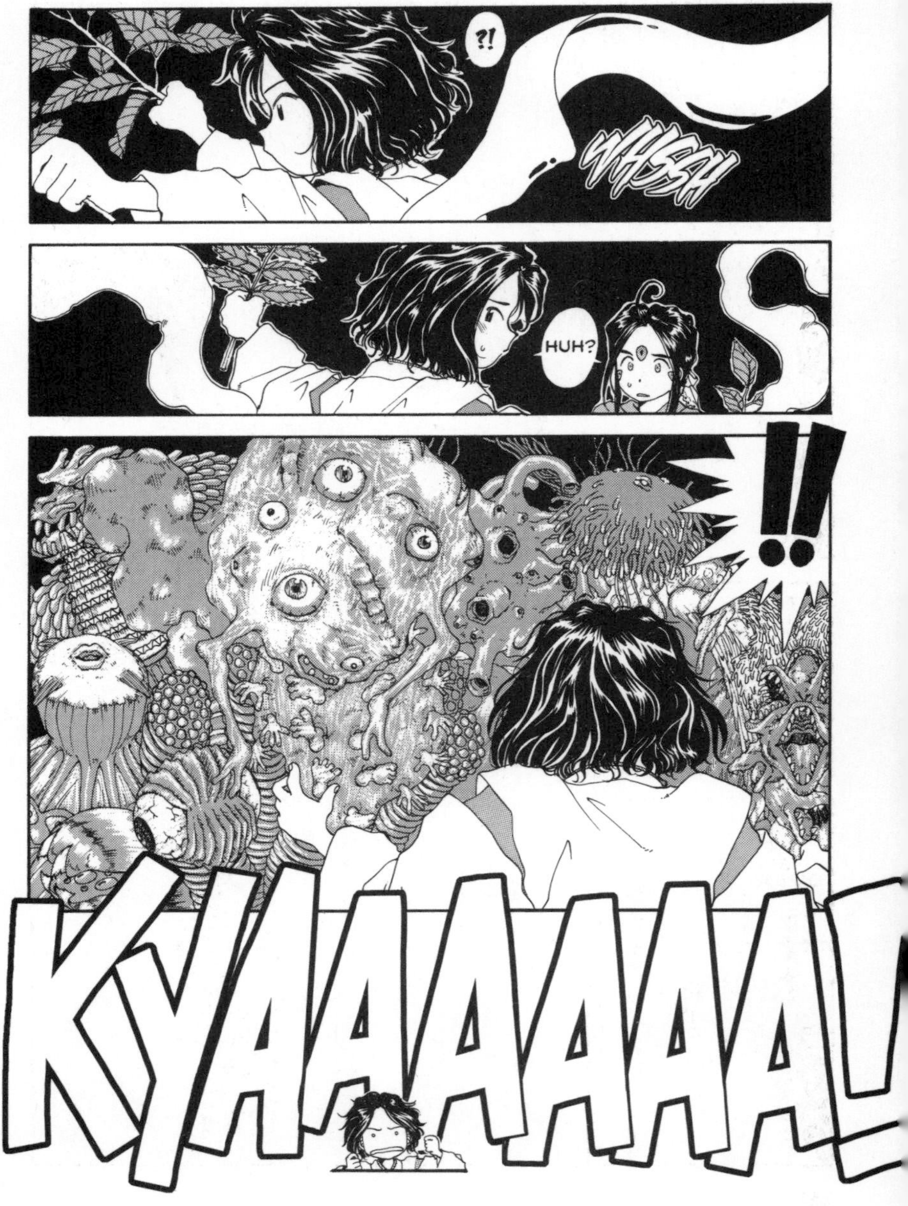

WHSSH
?!
HUH?
!!
KYAAAAAA!

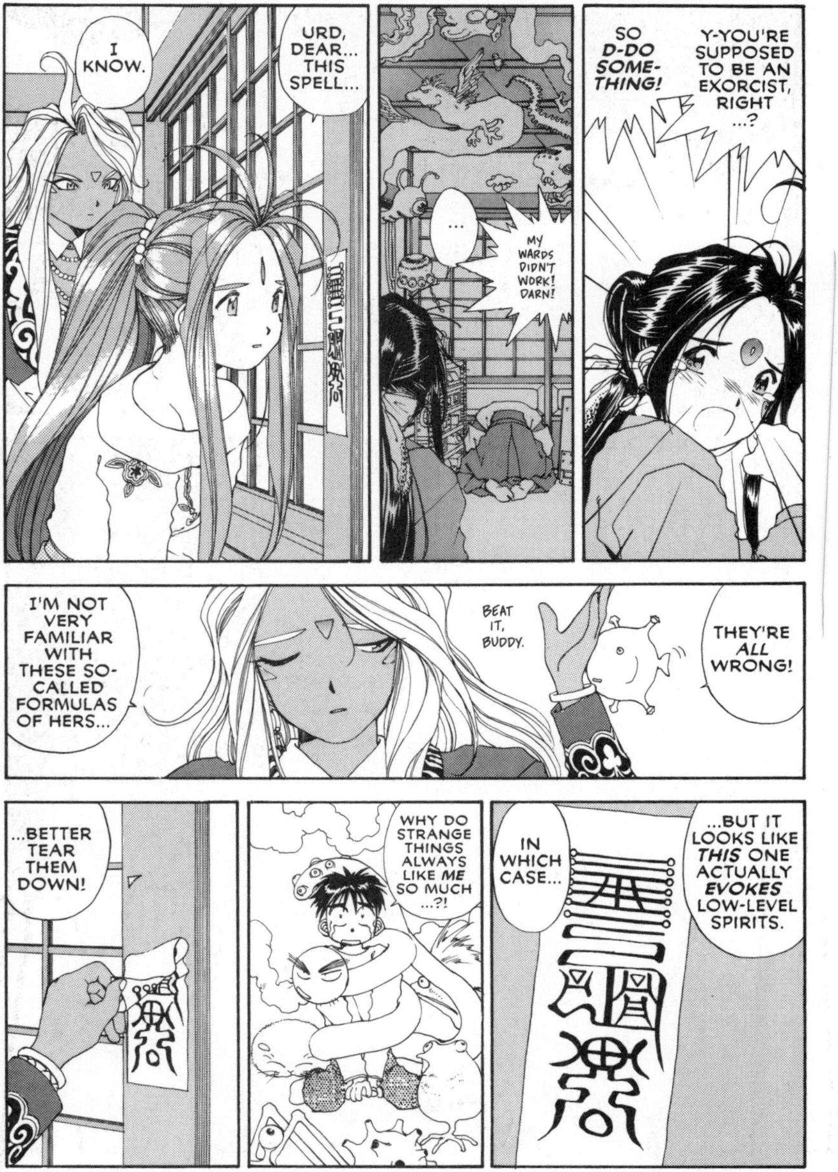
Y-YOU'RE SUPPOSED TO BE AN EXORCIST, RIGHT ...?
SO D-DO SOME-THING!
MY WARDS DIDN'T WORK! DARN!
...
URD, DEAR... THIS SPELL...
I KNOW.
THEY'RE ALL WRONG!
BEAT IT, BUDDY.
I'M NOT VERY FAMILIAR WITH THESE SO-CALLED FORMULAS OF HERS...
...BUT IT LOOKS LIKE THIS ONE ACTUALLY EVOKES LOW-LEVEL SPIRITS.
IN WHICH CASE...
WHY DO STRANGE THINGS ALWAYS LIKE ME SO MUCH ...?!
...BETTER TEAR THEM DOWN!

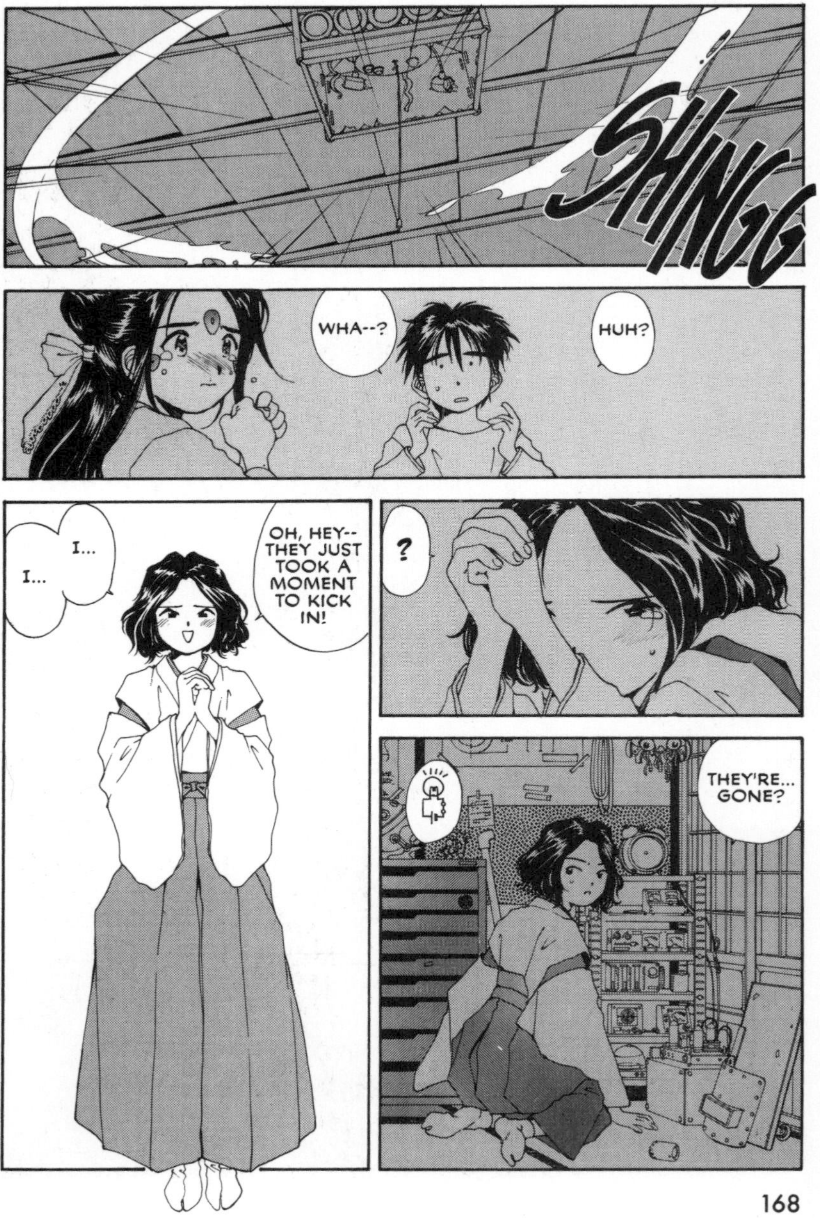
SHINGG
HUH?
WHA--?
?
THEY'RE... GONE?
OH, HEY-- THEY JUST TOOK A MOMENT TO KICK IN!
I... I...

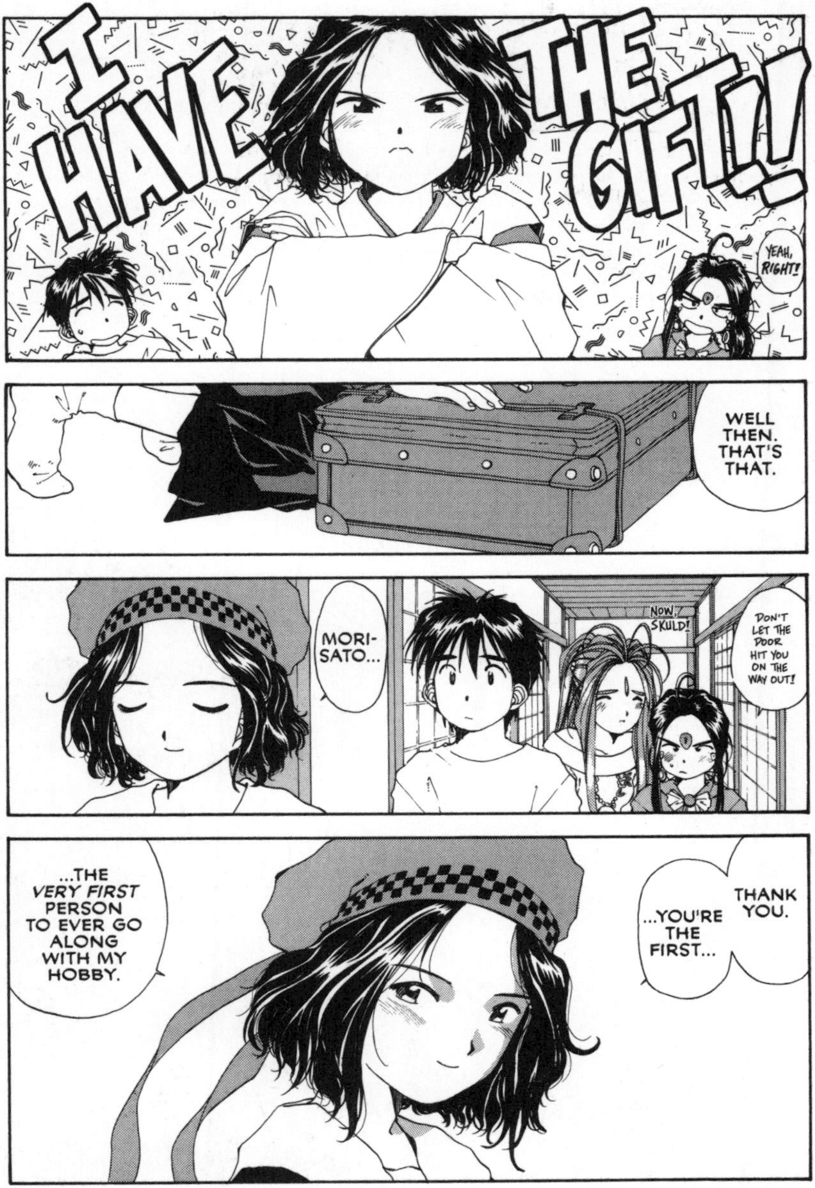
I HAVE THE GIFT!!
YEAH, RIGHT!
WELL THEN. THAT'S THAT.
DON'T LET THE DOOR HIT YOU ON THE WAY OUT!
NOW, SKULD!
MORI-SATO...
THANK YOU.
...YOU'RE THE FIRST...
...THE *VERY FIRST* PERSON TO EVER GO ALONG WITH MY HOBBY.

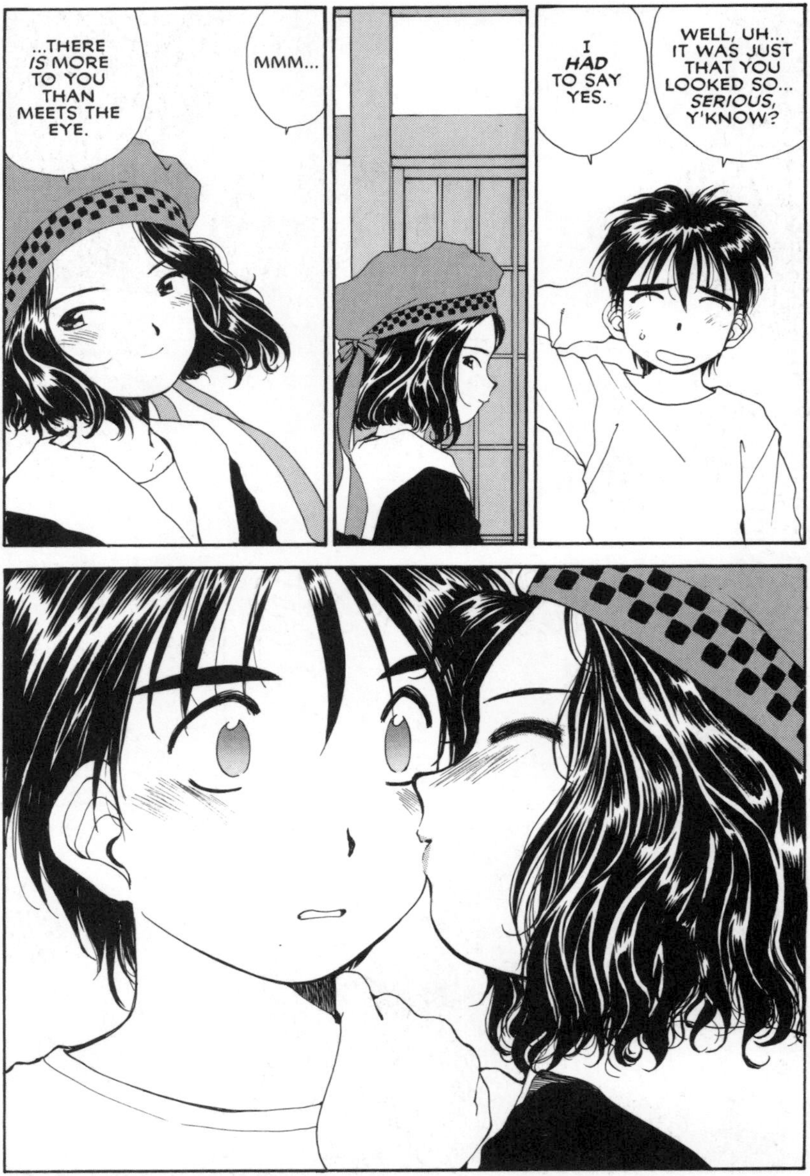
WELL, UH... IT WAS JUST THAT YOU LOOKED SO... *SERIOUS,* Y'KNOW?
I *HAD* TO SAY YES.
MMM...
...THERE *IS* MORE TO YOU THAN MEETS THE EYE.

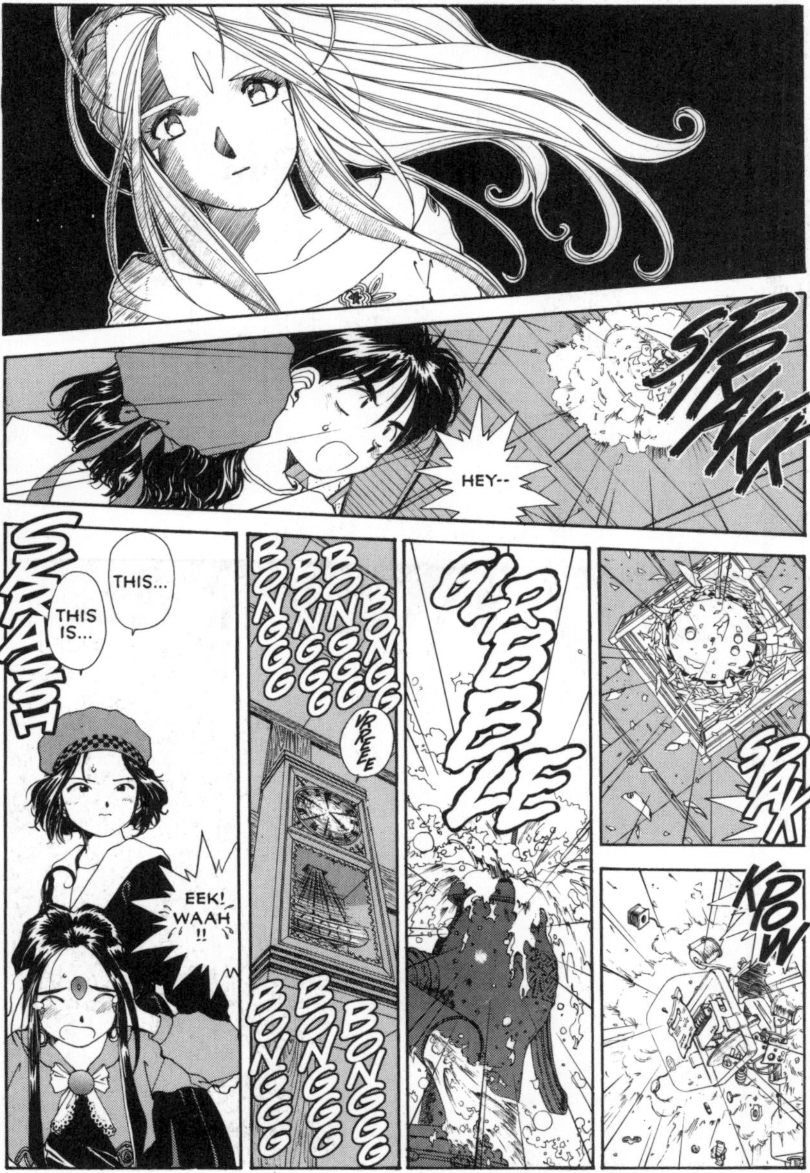

SPRAKK
HEY--
SPAK
KPOW
GLRBBLE
BONGGG BONGGGG BONGGGG BONGGG
VRREEE
BONGGGG BONGGGG BONGGGG
SPRAASH
THIS...
THIS IS...
EEK! WAAH!!

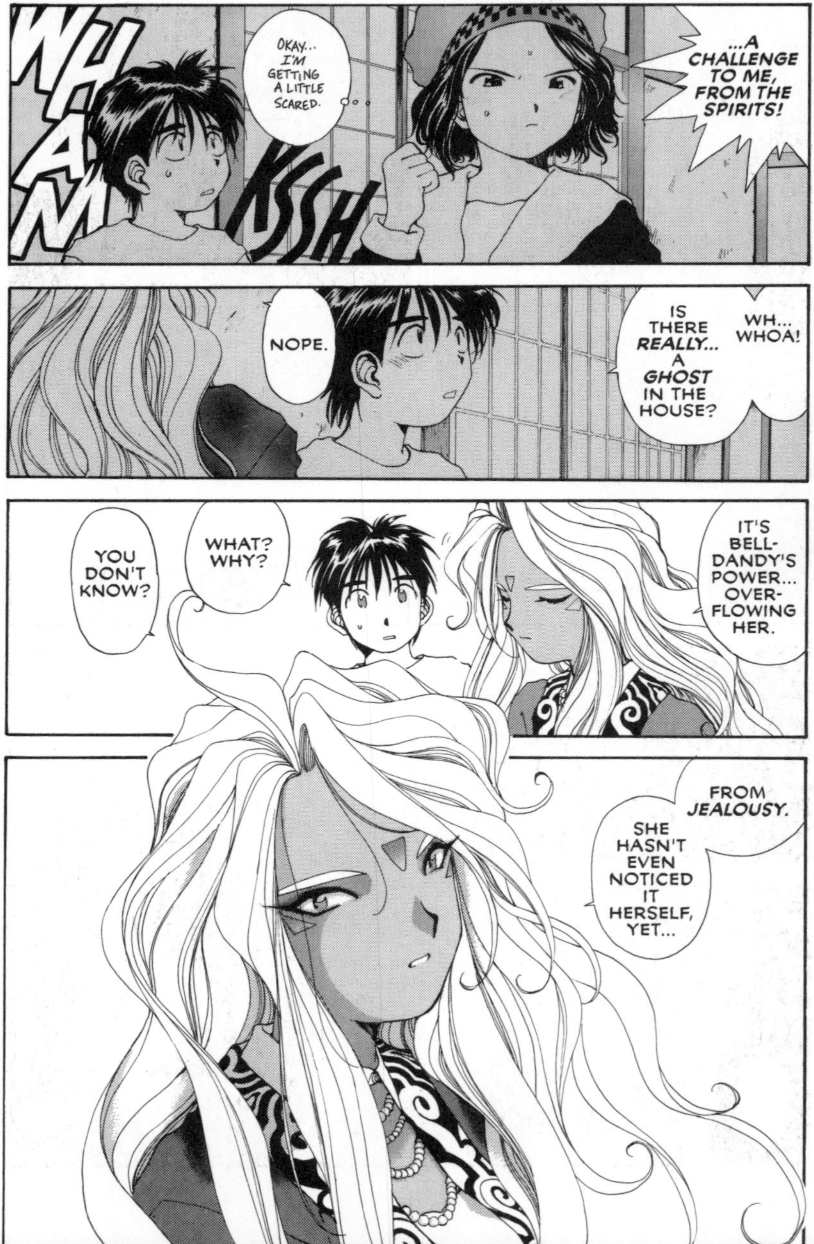
...A CHALLENGE TO ME, FROM THE SPIRITS!
OKAY... I'M GETTING A LITTLE SCARED.
KSSH
WHAM
WH... WHOA!
IS THERE *REALLY*... A *GHOST* IN THE HOUSE?
NOPE.
IT'S BELL-DANDY'S POWER... OVER-FLOWING HER.
WHAT? WHY?
YOU DON'T KNOW?
FROM *JEALOUSY.*
SHE HASN'T EVEN NOTICED IT HERSELF, YET...

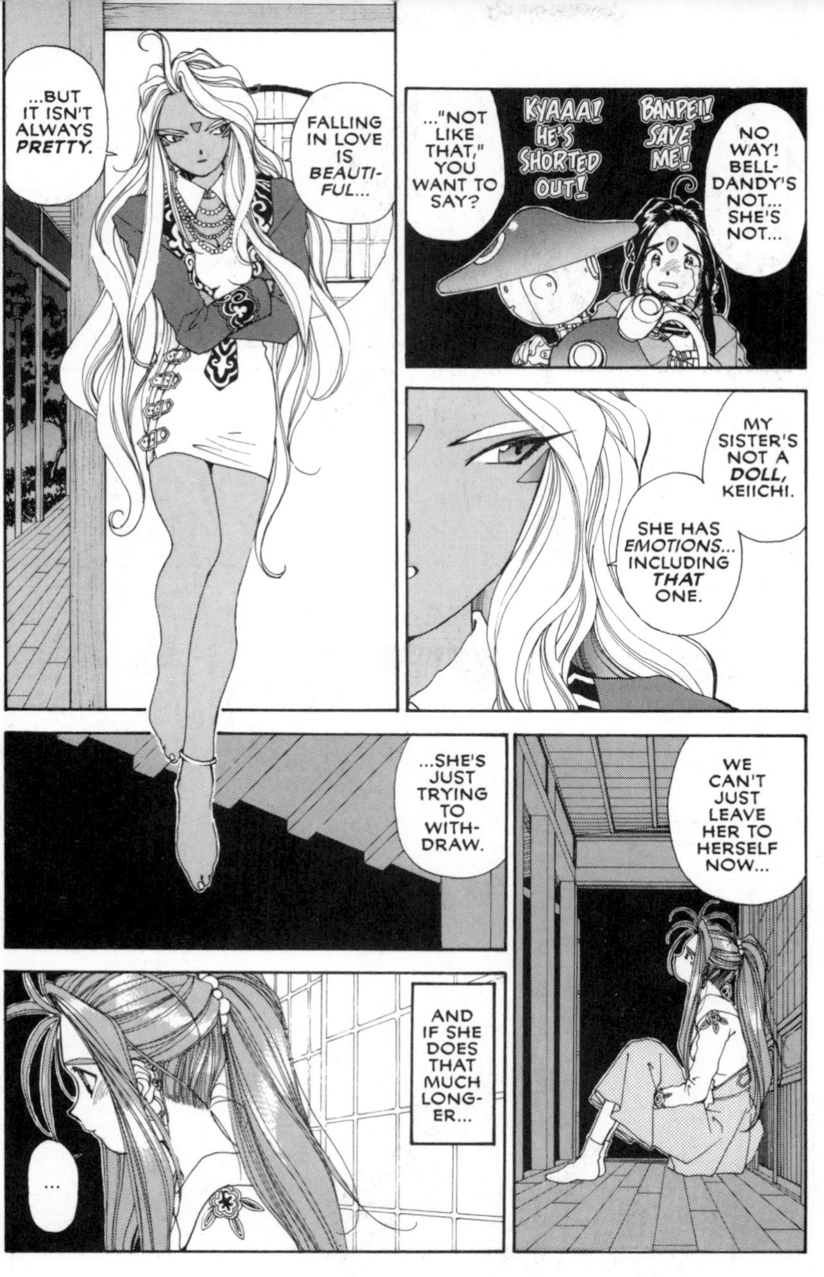
NO WAY! BELL-DANDY'S NOT... SHE'S NOT...
BANPEI!! SAVE ME!
KYAAA! HE'S SHORTED OUT!
..."NOT LIKE THAT," YOU WANT TO SAY?
MY SISTER'S NOT A *DOLL,* KEIICHI.
SHE HAS *EMOTIONS*... INCLUDING *THAT* ONE.
FALLING IN LOVE IS *BEAUTI-FUL*...
...BUT IT ISN'T ALWAYS *PRETTY.*
WE CAN'T JUST LEAVE HER TO HERSELF NOW...
...SHE'S JUST TRYING TO WITH-DRAW.
AND IF SHE DOES THAT MUCH LONG-ER...
...

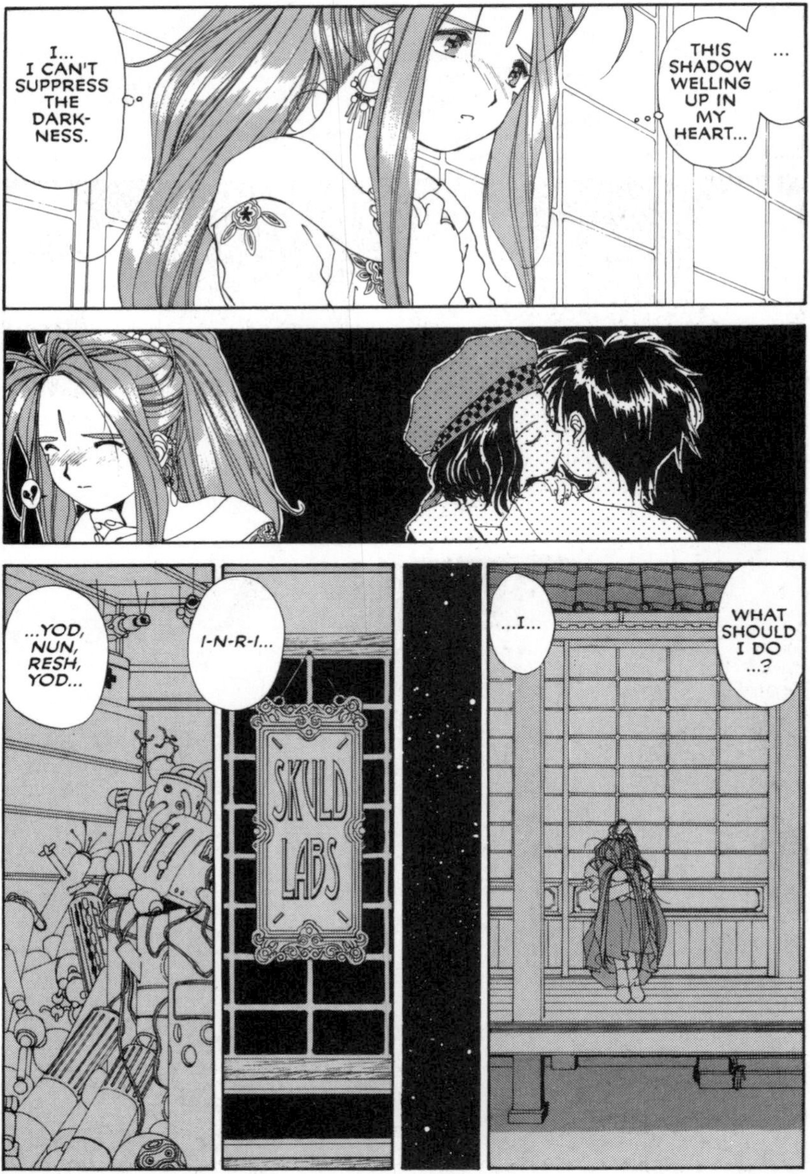

... THIS SHADOW WELLING UP IN MY HEART...
I... I CAN'T SUPPRESS THE DARKNESS.
WHAT SHOULD I DO ...?
...I...
I-N-R-I...
...YOD, NUN, RESH, YOD...
SKULD LABS

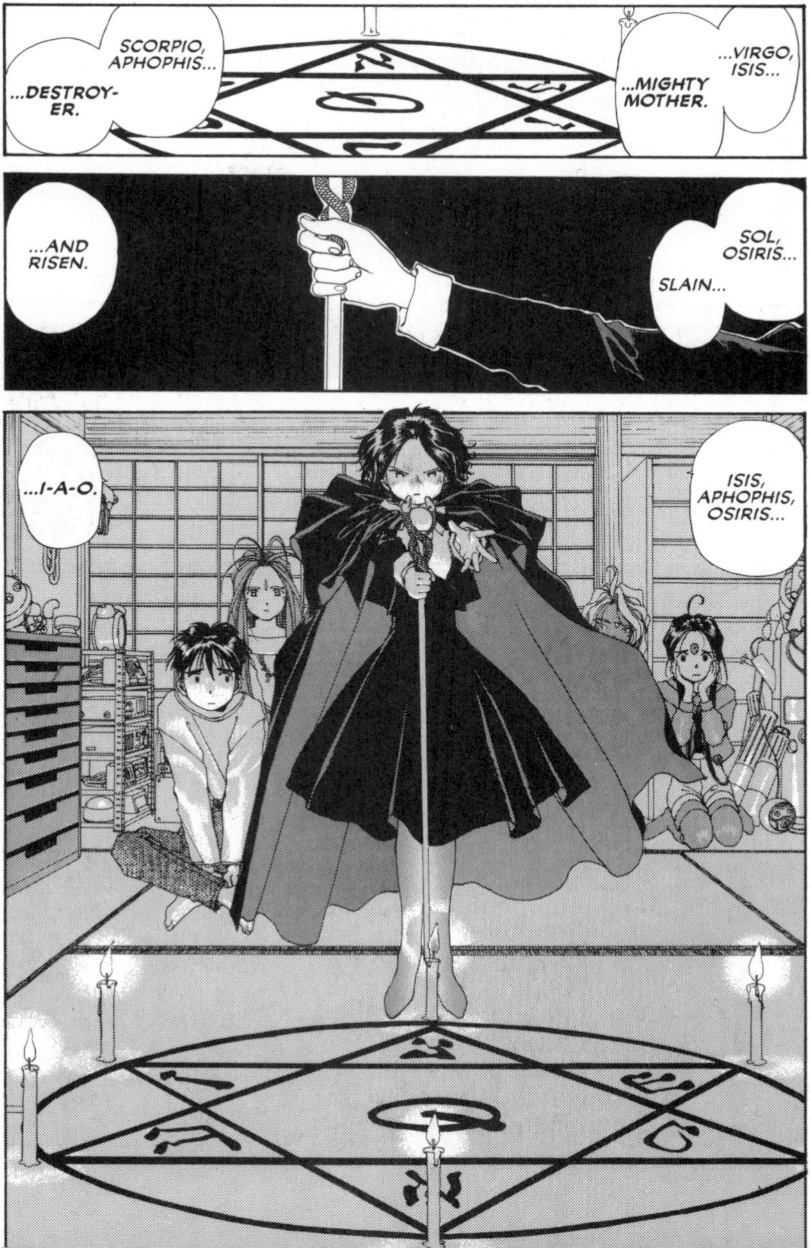
...VIRGO, ISIS...
...MIGHTY MOTHER.
SCORPIO, APHOPHIS...
...DESTROY-ER.
SOL, OSIRIS...
SLAIN...
...AND RISEN.
ISIS, APHOPHIS, OSIRIS...
...I-A-O.

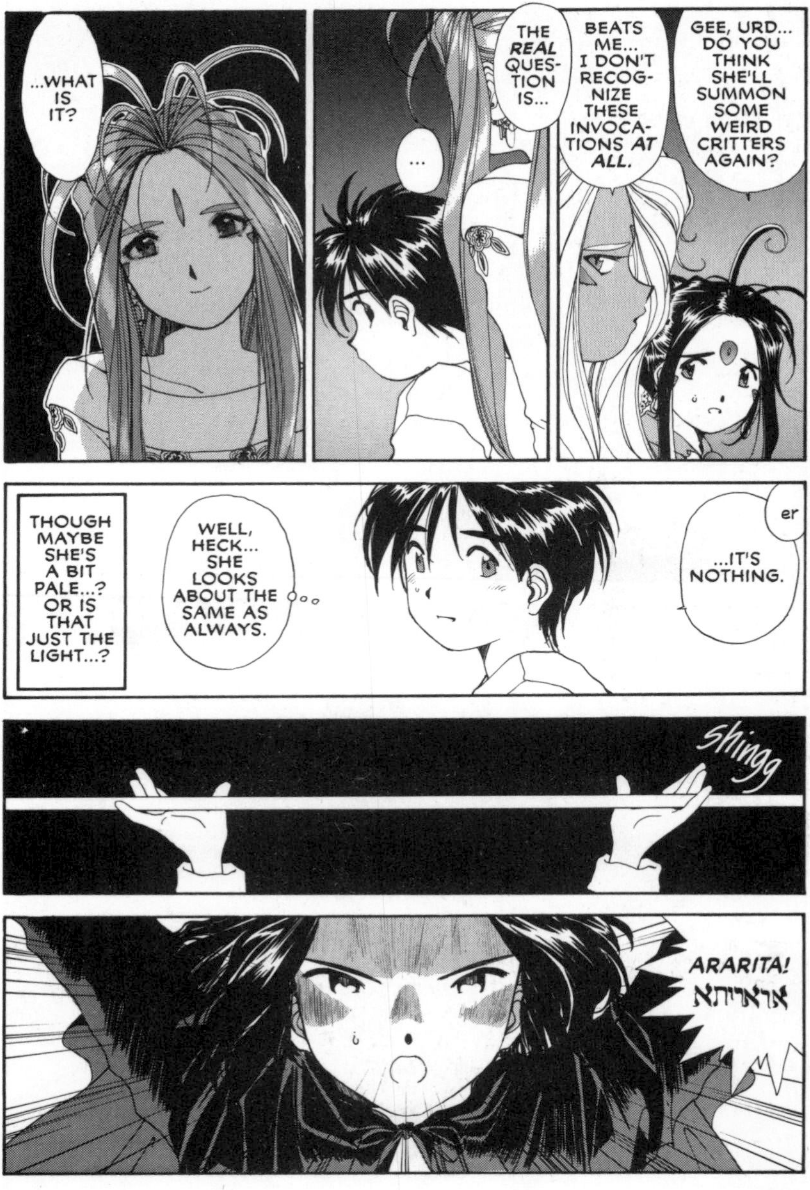
GEE, URD... DO YOU THINK SHE'LL SUMMON SOME WEIRD CRITTERS AGAIN?
BEATS ME... I DON'T RECOGNIZE THESE INVOCATIONS *AT ALL.*
THE *REAL* QUESTION IS...
...
...WHAT IS IT?
er
...IT'S NOTHING.
WELL, HECK... SHE LOOKS ABOUT THE SAME AS ALWAYS.
THOUGH MAYBE SHE'S A BIT PALE...? OR IS THAT JUST THE LIGHT...?
shingg
ARARITA!
אראריתא

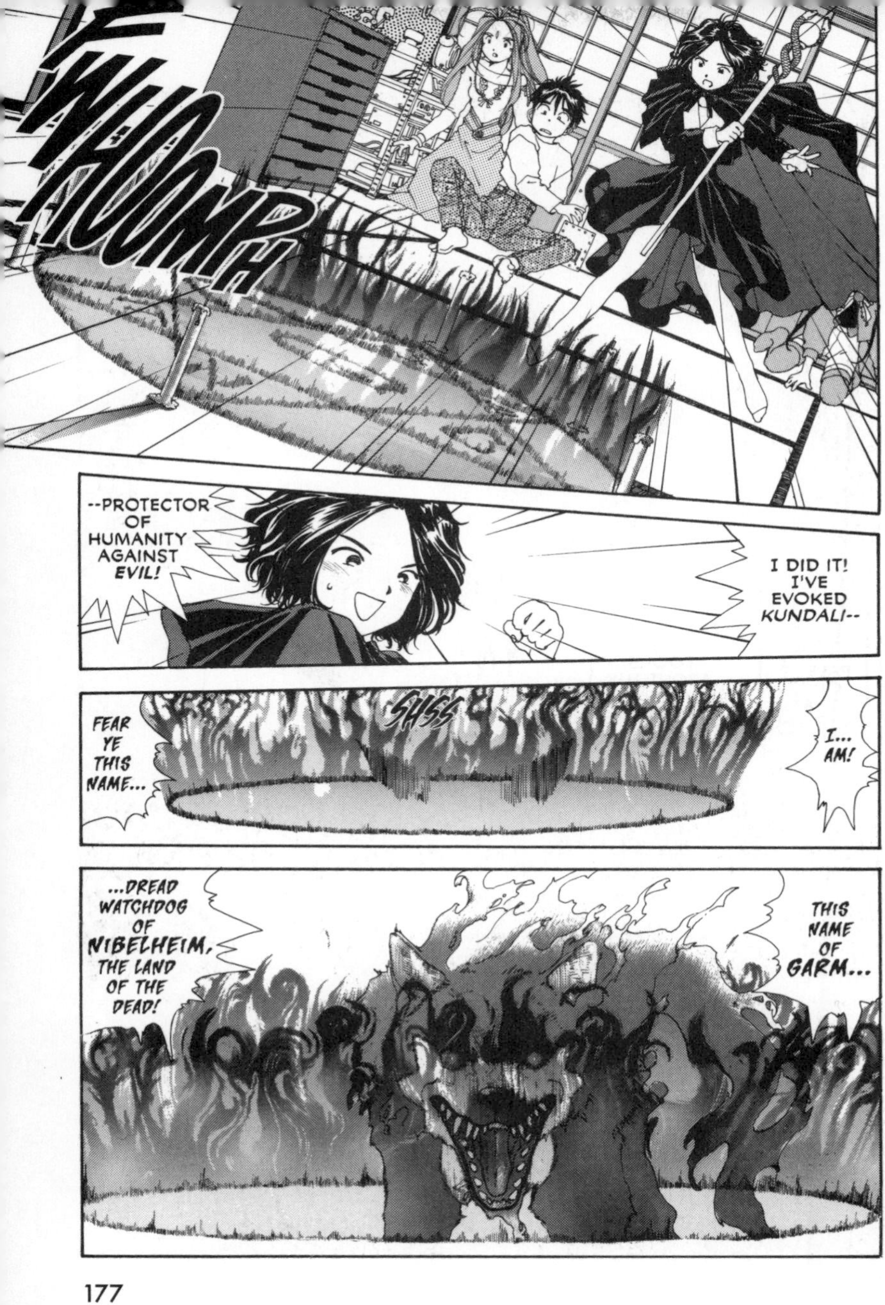
FWHOOMPH
I DID IT! I'VE EVOKED KUNDALI--
--PROTECTOR OF HUMANITY AGAINST EVIL!
SHSS
I... AM!
FEAR YE THIS NAME...
THIS NAME OF GARM...
...DREAD WATCHDOG OF NIBELHEIM, THE LAND OF THE DEAD!

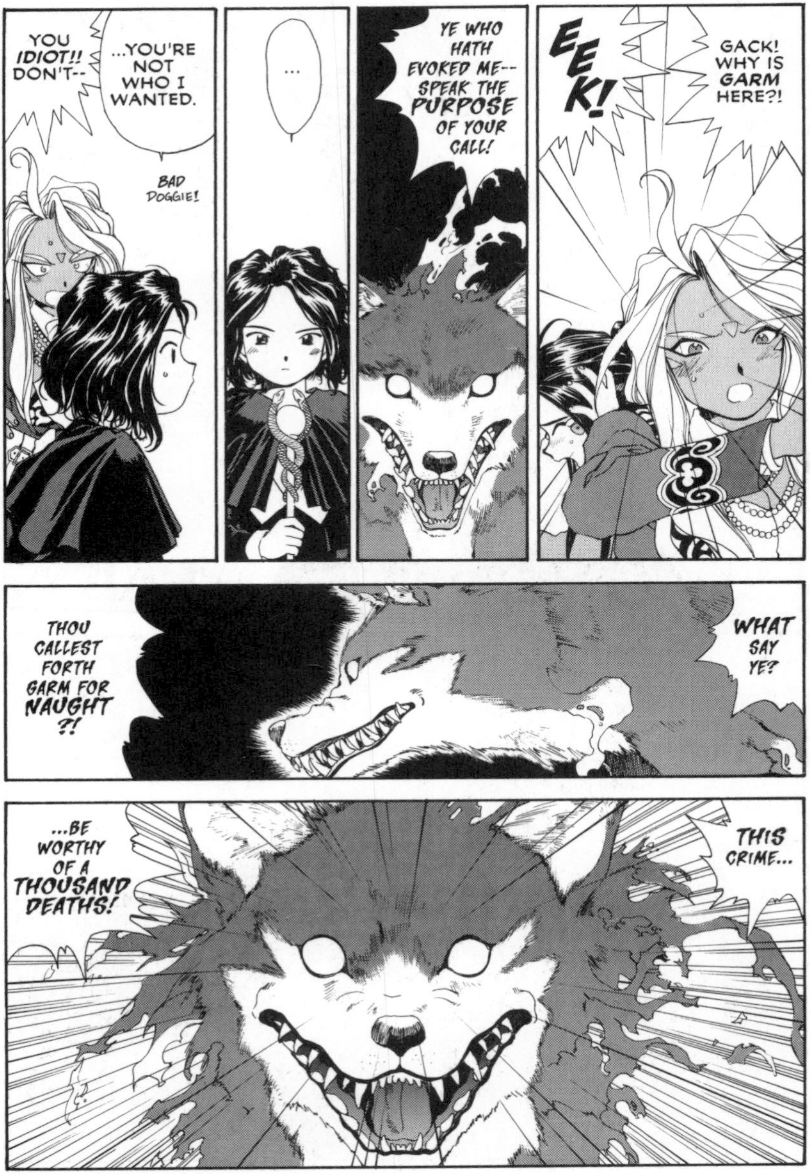
GACK! WHY IS GARM HERE?!
EEK!
YE WHO HATH EVOKED ME-- SPEAK THE PURPOSE OF YOUR CALL!
...
...YOU'RE NOT WHO I WANTED.
YOU IDIOT!! DON'T--
BAD DOGGIE!
WHAT SAY YE?
THOU CALLEST FORTH GARM FOR NAUGHT ?!
THIS CRIME...
...BE WORTHY OF A THOUSAND DEATHS!

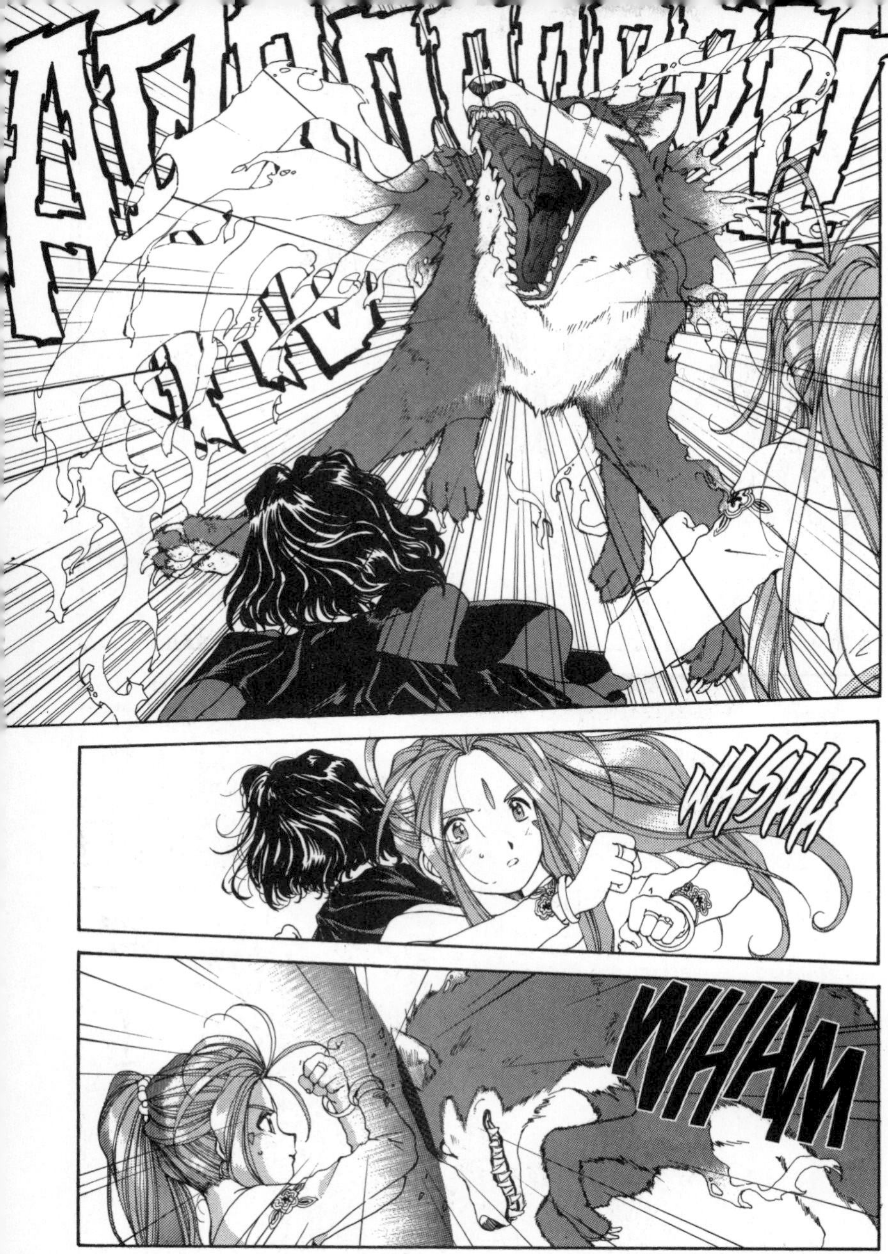
WHSHH
WHAM

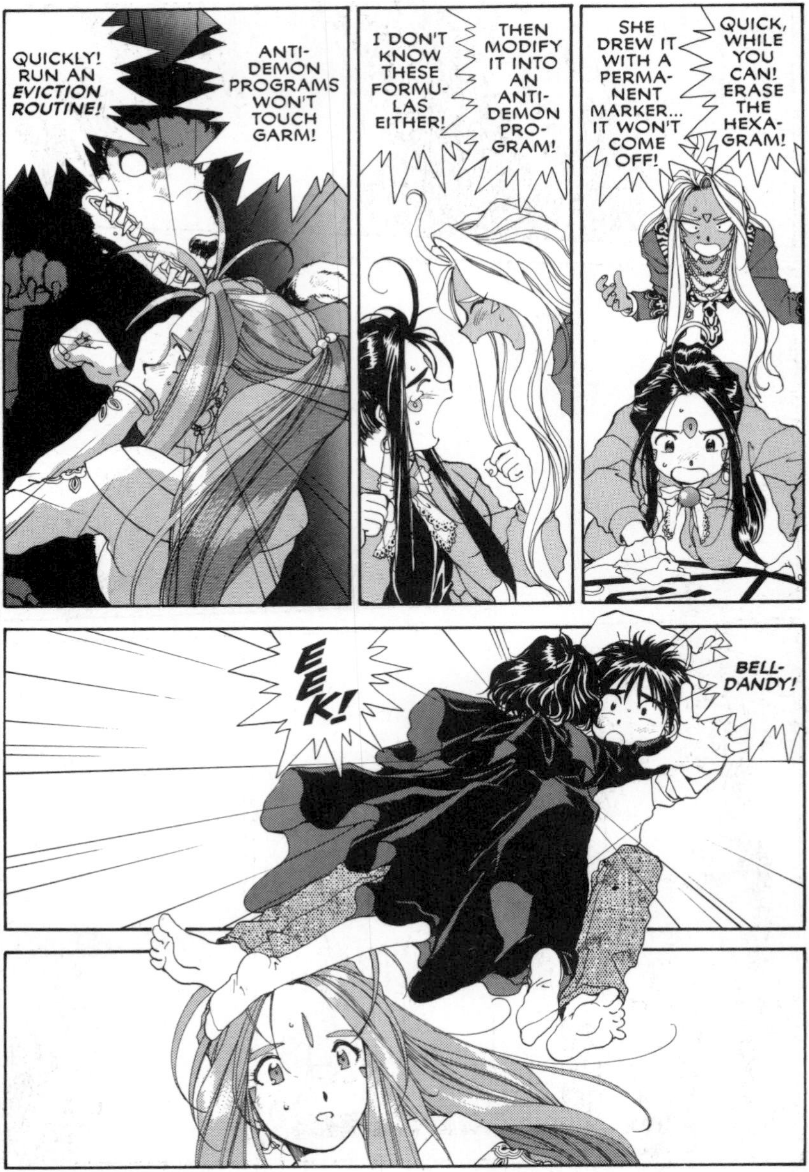
QUICK, WHILE YOU CAN! ERASE THE HEXA-GRAM!
SHE DREW IT WITH A PERMA-NENT MARKER... IT WON'T COME OFF!
THEN MODIFY IT INTO AN ANTI-DEMON PRO-GRAM!
I DON'T KNOW THESE FORMU-LAS EITHER!
ANTI-DEMON PROGRAMS WON'T TOUCH GARM!
QUICKLY! RUN AN *EVICTION ROUTINE!*
BELL-DANDY!
EEK!

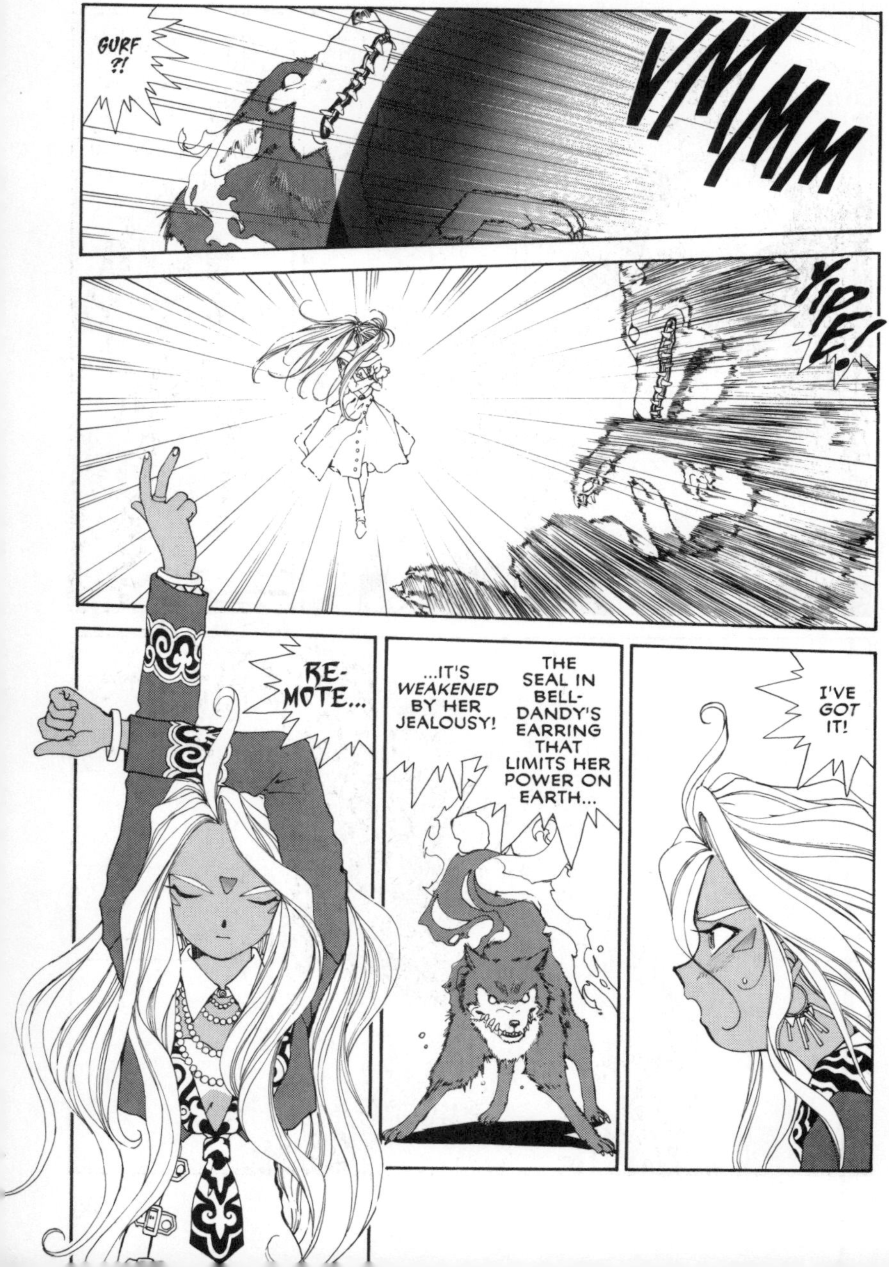
VMMM
GURF ?!
YIPE!
I'VE GOT IT!
THE SEAL IN BELL-DANDY'S EARRING THAT LIMITS HER POWER ON EARTH...
...IT'S *WEAKENED* BY HER JEALOUSY!
RE-MOTE...

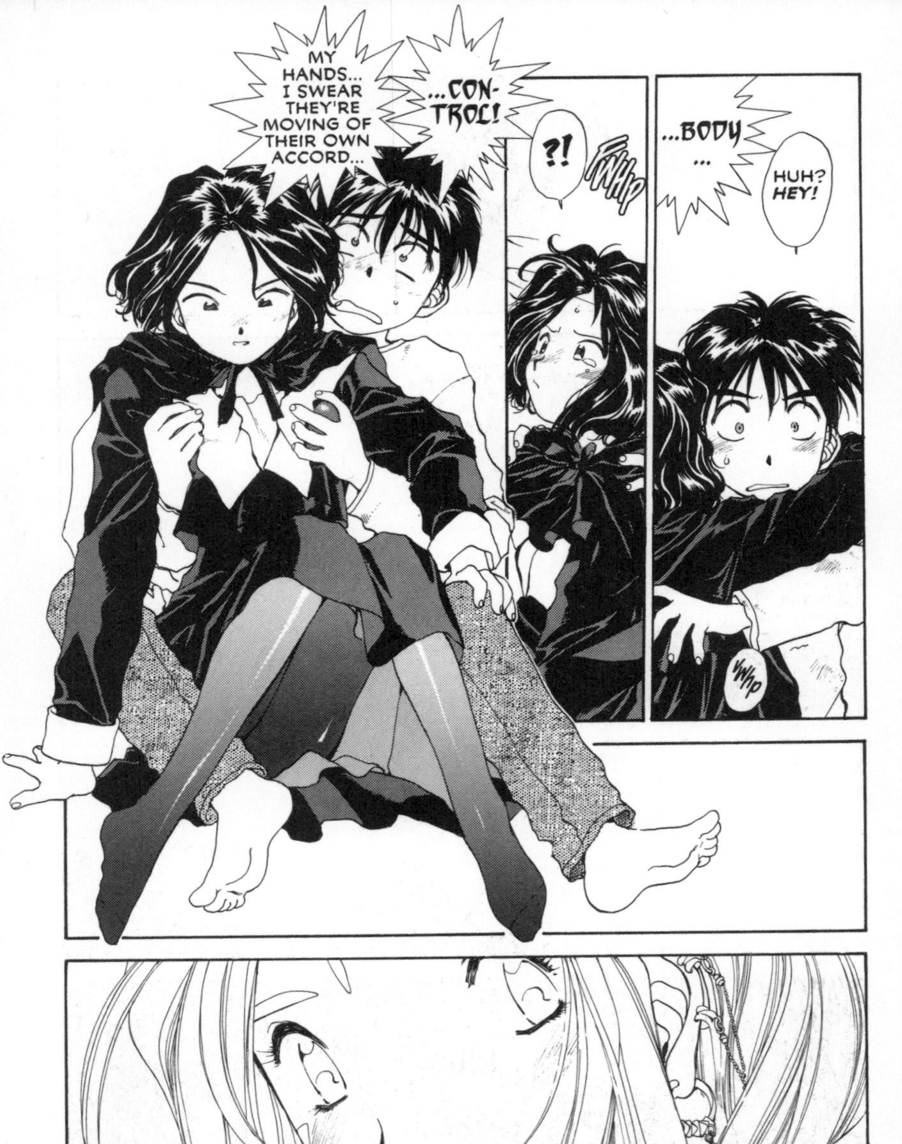
...BODY ...
HUH? HEY!
VWHP
?!
FWHIP
...CON-TROL!
MY HANDS... I SWEAR THEY'RE MOVING OF THEIR OWN ACCORD...

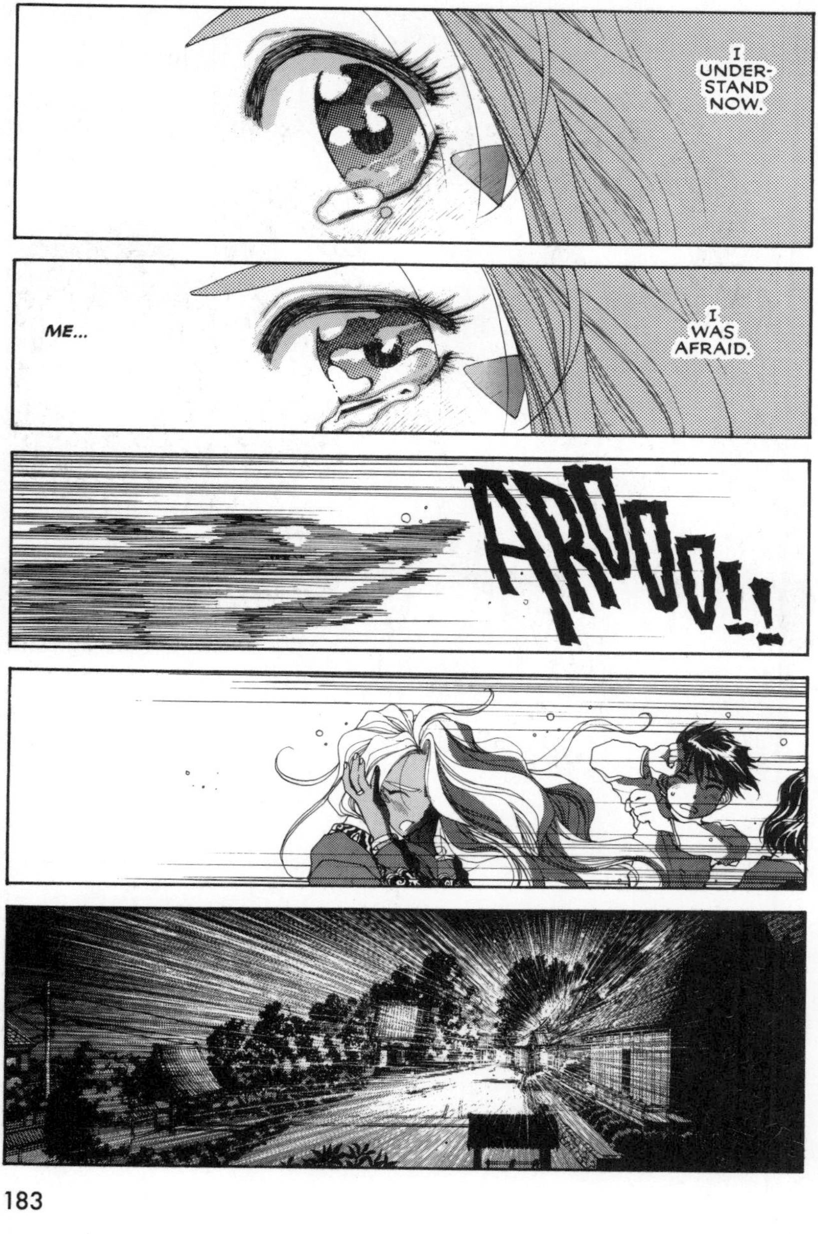
I UNDER-STAND NOW.
I WAS AFRAID.
ME...
AROOO!!

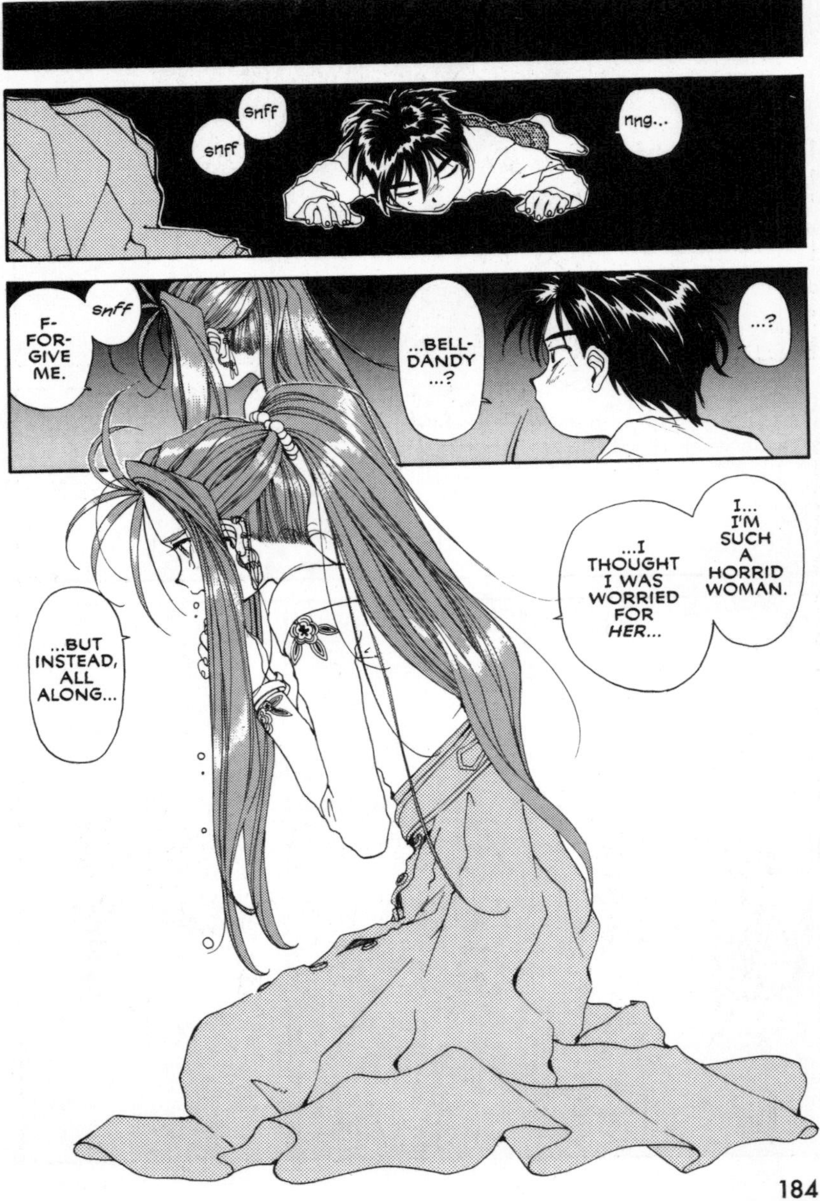
nng...
snff
snff
...?
...BELL-DANDY ...?
snff
F-FORGIVE ME.
I... I'M SUCH A HORRID WOMAN.
...I THOUGHT I WAS WORRIED FOR *HER*...
...BUT INSTEAD, ALL ALONG...

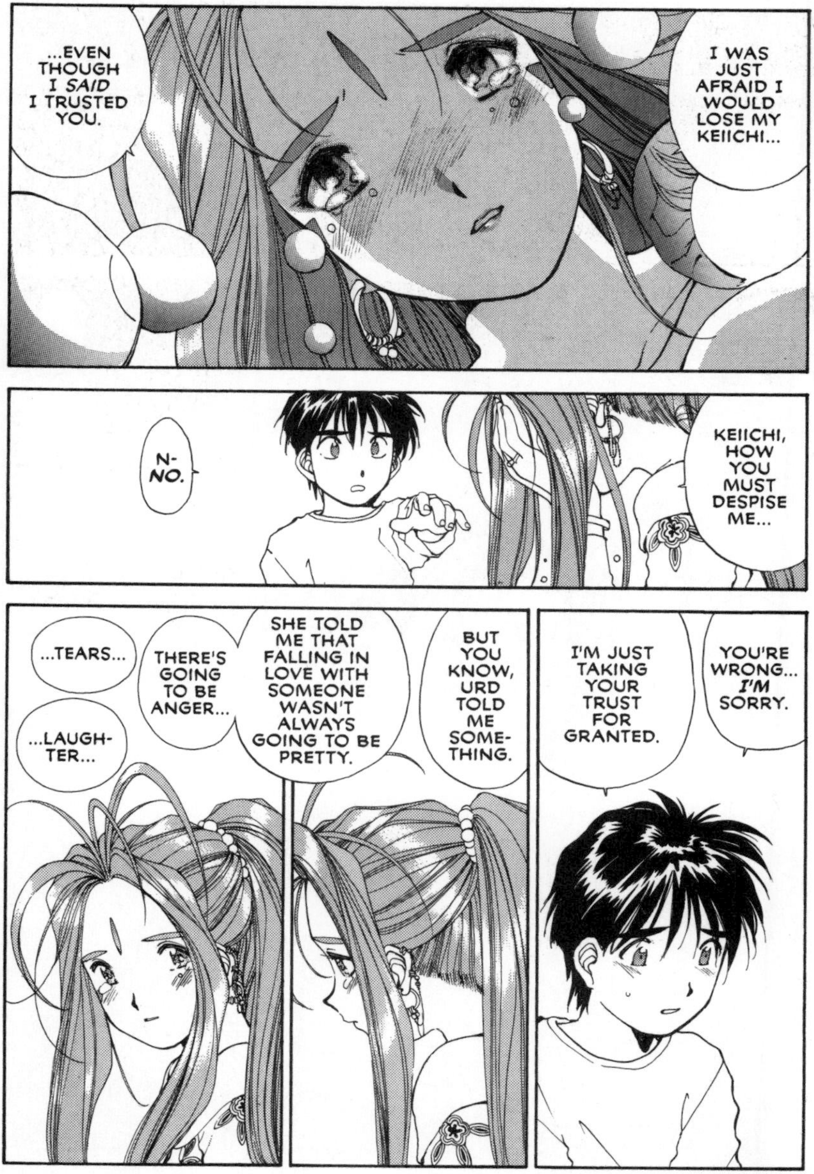
I WAS JUST AFRAID I WOULD LOSE MY KEIICHI...
...EVEN THOUGH I *SAID* I TRUSTED YOU.
KEIICHI, HOW YOU MUST DESPISE ME...
N-*NO.*
YOU'RE WRONG... *I'M* SORRY.
I'M JUST TAKING YOUR TRUST FOR GRANTED.
BUT YOU KNOW, URD TOLD ME SOME-THING.
SHE TOLD ME THAT FALLING IN LOVE WITH SOMEONE WASN'T ALWAYS GOING TO BE PRETTY.
THERE'S GOING TO BE ANGER...
...TEARS...
...LAUGH-TER...

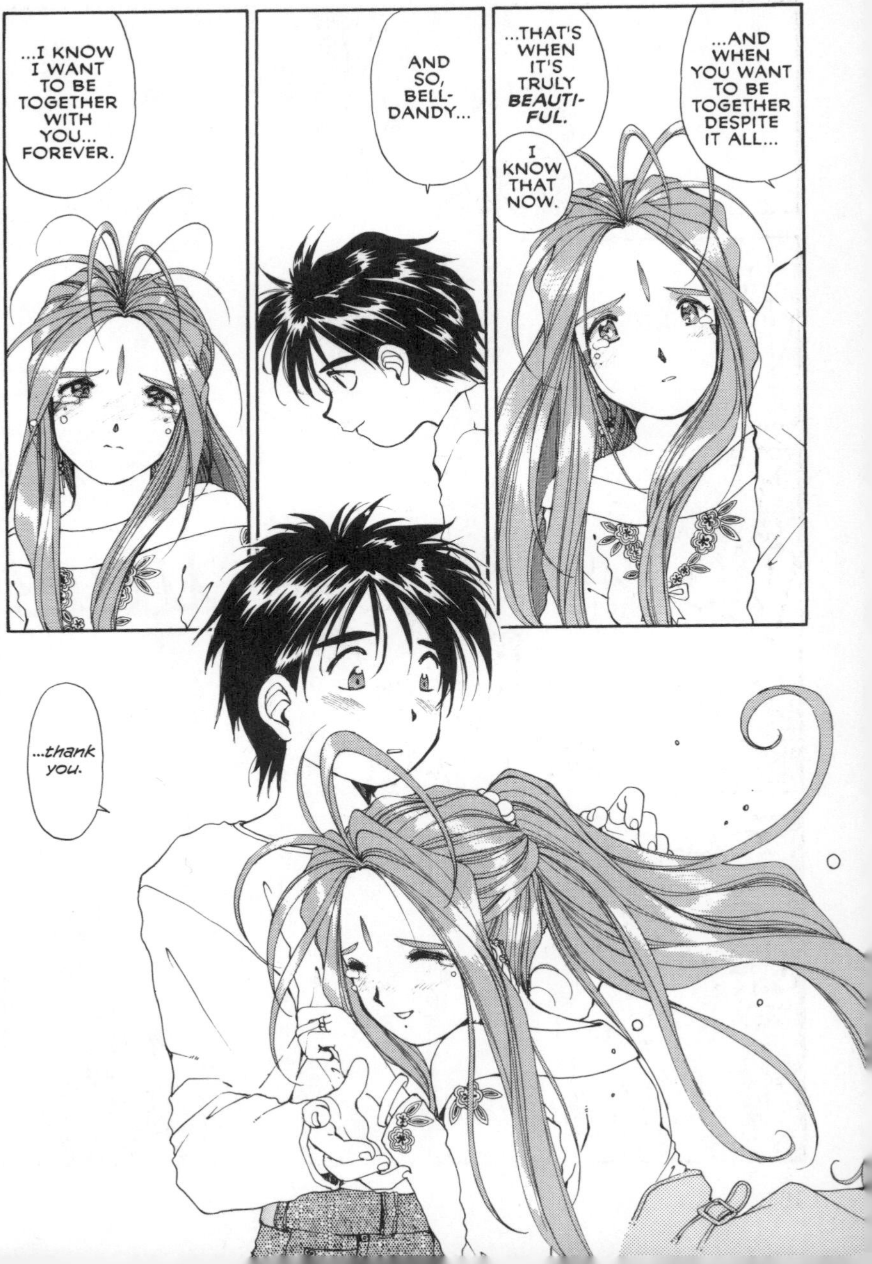
...AND WHEN YOU WANT TO BE TOGETHER DESPITE IT ALL...
...THAT'S WHEN IT'S TRULY *BEAUTIFUL.*
I KNOW THAT NOW.
AND SO, BELL-DANDY...
...I KNOW I WANT TO BE TOGETHER WITH YOU... FOREVER.
...thank you.

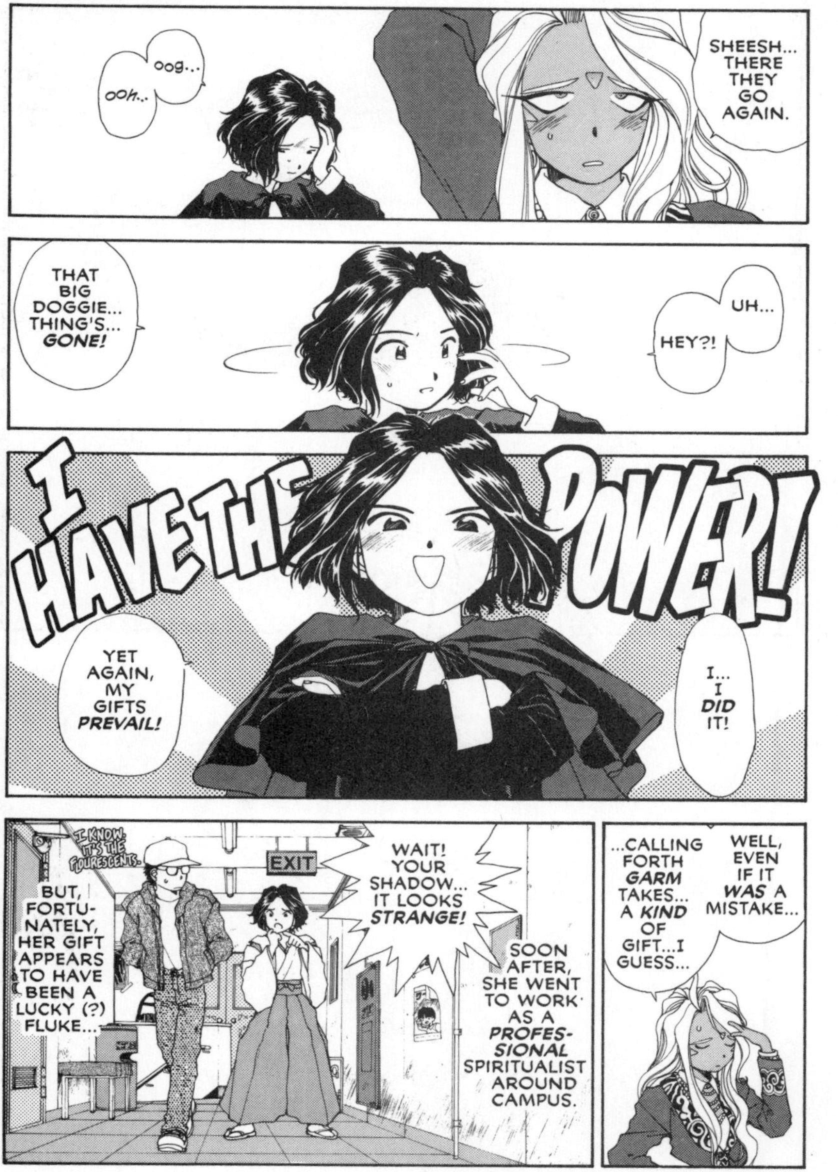
SHEESH... THERE THEY GO AGAIN.
oog...
ooh..
UH...
HEY?!
THAT BIG DOGGIE... THING'S... GONE!
I HAVE THE POWER!
I... I DID IT!
YET AGAIN, MY GIFTS PREVAIL!
WELL, EVEN IF IT WAS A MISTAKE...
...CALLING FORTH GARM TAKES... A KIND OF GIFT...I GUESS...
WAIT! YOUR SHADOW... IT LOOKS STRANGE!
EXIT
SOON AFTER, SHE WENT TO WORK AS A PROFESSIONAL SPIRITUALIST AROUND CAMPUS.
I KNOW. IT'S THE FLOURESCENTS.
BUT, FORTUNATELY, HER GIFT APPEARS TO HAVE BEEN A LUCKY (?) FLUKE...

THE ADVENTURES OF MINI-URD

NINJA-FORTIFIED

◇ IS THE MISO SOUP IN *YOUR* HOUSE SAFE? ◇

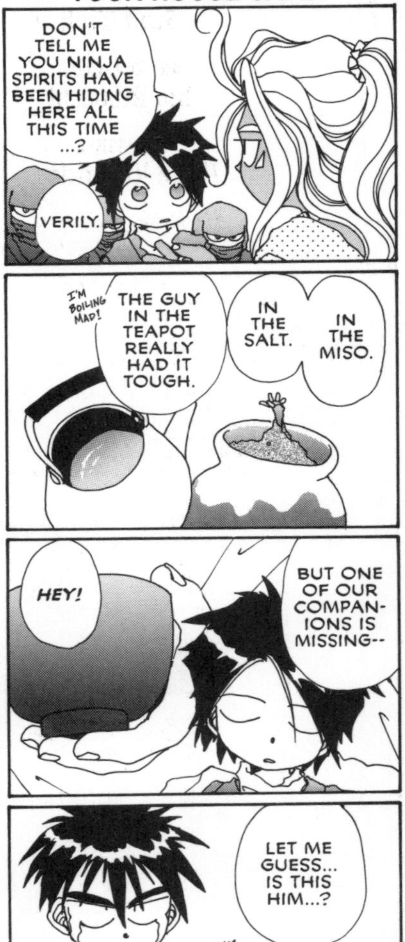
DON'T TELL ME YOU NINJA SPIRITS HAVE BEEN HIDING HERE ALL THIS TIME ...?
VERILY.
IN THE MISO.
IN THE SALT.
THE GUY IN THE TEAPOT REALLY HAD IT TOUGH.
I'M BOILING MAD!
BUT ONE OF OUR COMPANIONS IS MISSING--
HEY!
LET ME GUESS... IS THIS HIM...?
urk!
umm...

◇ WARNING: EXCESSIVE SUBDIVISION CAN BE HAZARDOUS TO YOUR HEALTH ◇

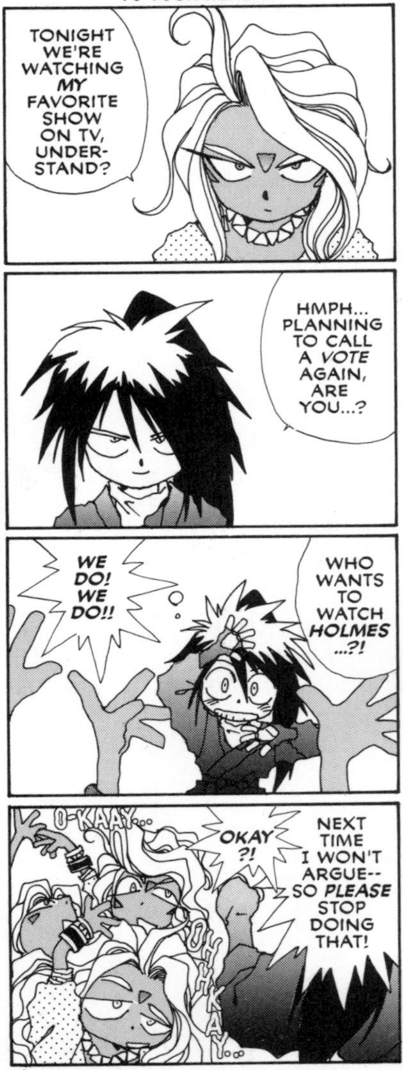
TONIGHT WE'RE WATCHING *MY* FAVORITE SHOW ON TV, UNDERSTAND?
HMPH... PLANNING TO CALL A *VOTE* AGAIN, ARE YOU...?
WHO WANTS TO WATCH *HOLMES* ...?!
WE DO! WE DO!!
NEXT TIME I WON'T ARGUE-- SO *PLEASE* STOP DOING THAT!
OKAY ?!
O-KAAY...

▲ SUBDIVIDED INTO TOO MANY COPIES...

EDITOR
Carl Gustav Horn

DESIGNER
Scott Cook

ART DIRECTOR
Lia Ribacchi

PUBLISHER
Mike Richardson

English-language version
produced by Dark Horse Comics

Published by Dark Horse Manga
a division of Dark Horse Comics, Inc.
10956 SE Main Street
Milwaukie, OR 97222
www.darkhorse.com

To find a comics shop in your area,
call the Comic Shop Locator Service
toll-free at 1-888-266-4226

First edition: June 2008
ISBN 978-1-59307-970-3

1 3 5 7 9 10 8 6 4 2

Printed in Canada

letters to the
ENCHANTRESS

10956 SE Main Street, Milwaukie, Oregon 97222
omg@darkhorse.com • www.darkhorse.com

NOTE: Full addresses and e-mail addresses will not be printed, unless you ask! All fan art-work, letters, and e-mails submitted become the property of Dark Horse Comics.

We've been seeing a lot of Urd lately (in fact, Keiichi got to see her in a way granted few mortals in Vol. 8) so perhaps the new fan art we've received should be no surprise. The artist, William Levy, tells us below:

Dear *OMG* staff,
    Really enjoying the new format; can't wait to see how the latest cliffhanger turns out. I'm also enjoying learning more about the extended family. Enclosed is a piece I drew based on *OMG*; Urd, who pro-tects my laptop from malicious influences. Works so far, anyway.

Better than any spyware: Goddessware!

Keep up the good work,
William Levy
Louisville, KY
(via e-mail)

That piece, of course, is just on the next page over! When you combine her skill at programming with her extreme nosiness, Urd is indeed the divine embodiment of spyware—if you remember back in Vol. 2, her very first conversation with Bell and Keiichi was devoted to a surveillance report on their relationship! But if you don't mind my saying so, you've probably chosen exactly the wrong volume to reveal you're a man with an interest in Urd. Buggy bugs on the march, is what I'm trying to say. Buggy bugs . . .

Just kidding. Don't be afraid of some long-eared manga bard casting *Creeping Doom* upon you—everyone, keep send-ing in your art and letters! And the rea-son you shouldn't be afraid, of course, is that bards can't cast druid spells that high a level. At least, I think they can't. I'd ask Gombos, but he's in Japan right now.
—CGH

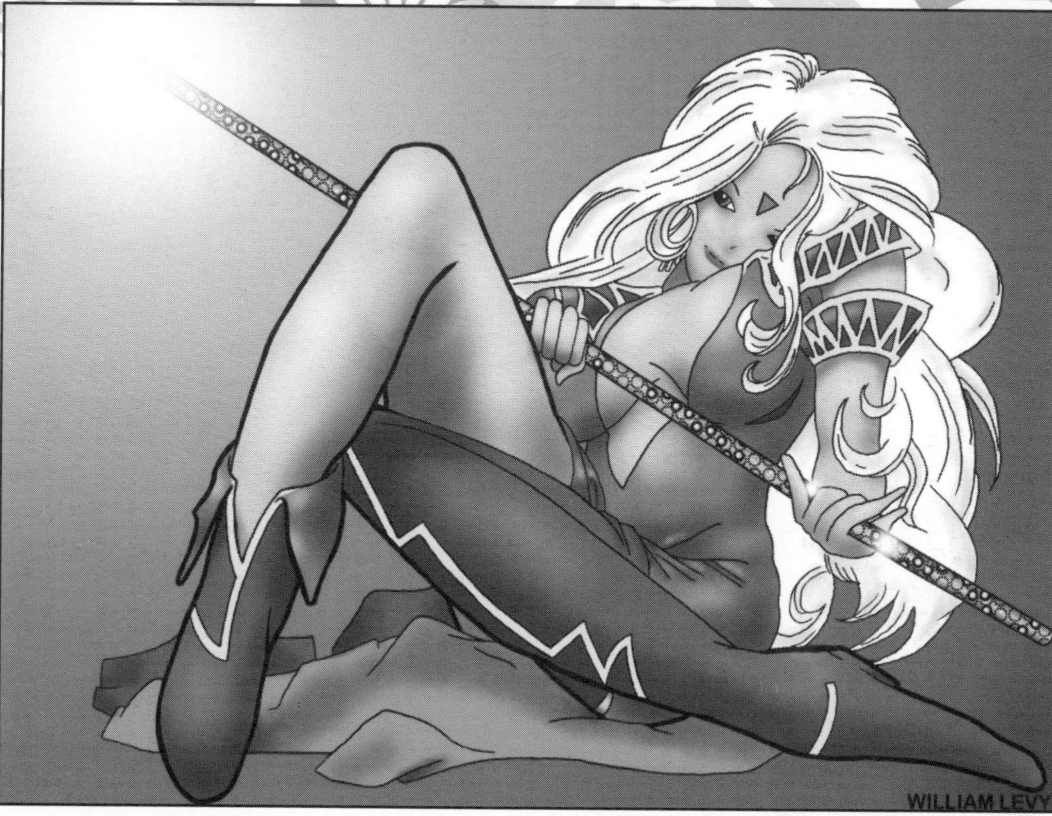
WILLIAM LEVY

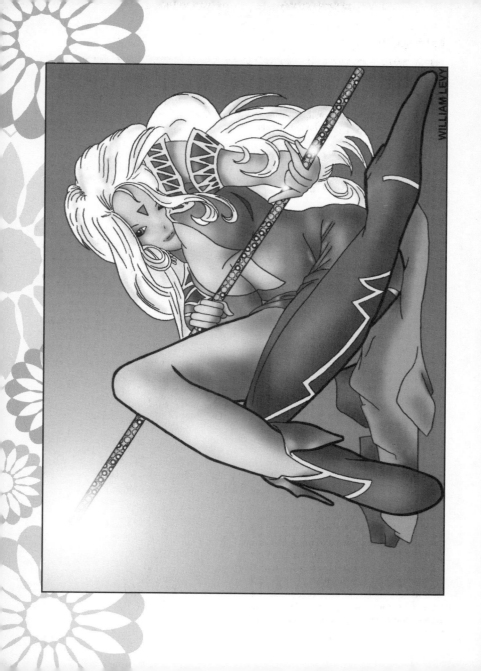

Creator Kosuke Fujishima in 1993!

His message to fans in the original Japanese *Oh My Goddess!* Vol. 9:

Hey, everyone, it's been a while! It's me yet again, with a new machine that I'm here to introduce—so just stick with me here. This time I'm showing off the Japan Express Hikari-go, capable of reaching speeds of over 250 km/h. For some reason, there's something that strikes me as really cute about its body. It gets very good fuel economy, and it only costs 100 yen per ride. Admittedly it has a label saying, "Adults, Please Don't Ride This," but I've never been much for the fine print. Next time, I'll show you the private helicopter that I bought.

AN ALL-NEW NOVEL BASED ON THE HIT MANGA AND ANIME!

OH MY GODDESS!
— FIRST END —

WRITTEN BY
YUMI TOHMA

WITH ILLUSTRATIONS BY
KOSUKE FUJISHIMA AND HIDENORI MATSUBARA

Keiichi Morisato was a typical college student—a failure with women, he was struggling to get through his classes and in general living a pretty nondescript life. That is, until he dialed a wrong number and accidentally summoned the goddess Belldandy. Not believing Belldandy was a goddess and that she could grant his every wish, Keiichi wished for her to stay with him forever. As they say, be careful what you wish for! Now bound to Earth and at Keiichi's side for life, the lives of this goddess and human will never be the same again!

ISBN 978-1-59582-137-9 | $14.95

DARK
HORSE
BOOKS

darkhorse.com

AVAILABLE AT YOUR LOCAL COMICS SHOP OR BOOKSTORE
To find a comics shop in your area, call 1.888.266.4226. For more information or to order direct: •On the web: darkhorse.com •E-mail: mailorder@darkhorse.com •Phone: 1.800.862.0052 Mon.–Fri. 9 AM to 5 PM Pacific Time.

Oh My Goddess!: First End © 2006, 2007 Yumi Tohma/Kosuke Fujishima. All rights reserved. First published in Japan in 2006 by Kodansha Ltd., Tokyo. Publication rights for this English edition arranged through Kodansha Ltd. Dark Horse Books® and the Dark Horse logo are registered trademarks of Dark Horse Comics, Inc. All rights reserved. (BL7056)

Kosuke Fujishima's Oh My Goddess!

Dark Horse is proud to re-present *Oh My Goddess!* in the much-requested, affordable, Japanese-reading, right-to-left format, complete with color sections, informative bonus notes, and your letters!

Volume 1
ISBN: 978-1-59307-387-9

Volume 2
ISBN: 978-1-59307-457-9

Volume 3
ISBN: 978-1-59307-539-2

Volume 4
ISBN: 978-1-59307-623-8

Volume 5
ISBN: 978-1-59307-708-2

Volume 6
ISBN: 978-1-59307-772-3

Volume 7
ISBN: 978-1-59307-850-8

Volume 8
ISBN: 978-1-59307-889-8

Volume 22
ISBN: 978-1-59307-400-5

Volume 23
ISBN: 978-1-59307-463-0

Volume 24
ISBN: 978-1-59307-545-3

Volume 25
ISBN: 978-1-59307-644-3

Volume 26
ISBN: 978-1-59307-715-0

Volume 27
ISBN: 978-1-59307-788-4

Volume 28
ISBN: 978-1-59307-857-7

$10.95 each!

AVAILABLE AT YOUR LOCAL COMICS SHOP OR BOOKSTORE
*To find a comics shop in your area, call 1-888-266-4226

For more information or to order direct: •On the web: darkhorse.com
•E-mail: mailorder@darkhorse.com
•Phone: 1-800-862-0052 Mon.–Fri. 9 AM to 5 PM Pacific Time.

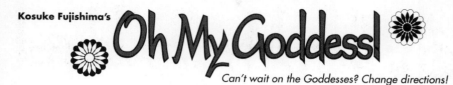

Kosuke Fujishima's

Oh My Goddess!

Can't wait on the Goddesses? Change directions!

Just gotten into the new unflopped editions of *Oh My Goddess!*, and found you can't wait to see what happens next? Have no fear! The first ***20 volumes*** of *Oh My Goddess!* are available ***right now*** in Western-style editions! Released between 1994 and 2005, our *OMG!* Western-style volumes feature premium paper, and pages 40% larger than those of the unflopped editions! If you've already got some of the unflopped volumes and want to know which Western-style ones to get to catch up, check out darkhorse.com's "Manga Zone" for a complete breakdown of how the editions compare!

Vol. 1: Wrong Number
ISBN: 1-56971-669-2 / $13.95

Vol. 2: Leader of the Pack
ISBN: 1-56971-764-8 / $13.95

Vol. 3: Final Exam
ISBN: 1-56971-765-6 / $13.95

Vol. 4: Love Potion No. 9
ISBN: 1-56971-252-2 / $14.95

Vol. 5: Sympathy for the Devil
ISBN: 1-56971-329-4 / $13.95

Vol. 6: Terrible Master Urd
ISBN: 1-56971-369-3 / $14.95

Vol. 7: The Queen of Vengeance
ISBN: 1-56971-431-2 / $13.95

Vol. 8: Mara Strikes Back!
ISBN: 1-56971-449-5 / $14.95

Vol. 9: Ninja Master
ISBN: 1-56971-474-6 / $13.95

Vol. 10: Miss Keiichi
ISBN: 1-56971-522-X / $16.95

Vol. 11: The Devil in Miss Urd
ISBN: 1-56971-540-8 / $14.95

Vol. 12: The Fourth Goddess
ISBN: 1-56971-551-3 / $18.95

Vol. 13: Childhood's End
ISBN: 1-56971-685-4/ $15.95

Vol. 14: Queen Sayoko
ISBN: 1-56971-766-4 / $16.95

Vol. 15: Hand in Hand
ISBN: 1-56971-921-7 / $17.95

Vol. 16: Mystery Child
ISBN: 1-56971-950-0 / $18.95

Vol. 17: Traveler
ISBN: 1-56971-986-1 / $17.95

Vol. 18: The Phantom Racer
ISBN: 1-59307-217-1 / $17.95

Vol. 19/20: Sora Unchained
ISBN: 1-59307-316-X / $18.95

Adventures of the Mini-Goddesses
ISBN: 1-56971-421-5 / $9.95

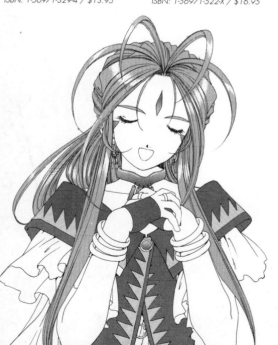

AVAILABLE AT YOUR LOCAL COMICS SHOP OR BOOKSTORE
*To find a comics shop in your area, call 1-888-266-4226

For more information or to order direct:
- On the web: darkhorse.com
- E-mail: mailorder@darkhorse.com
- Phone: 1-800-862-0052 Mon.-Fri. 9 A.M. to 5 P.M. Pacific Time.

【ㅗ爪ハ人ㄑ彐ータㅅㅗ】
translucent

Can you see right through her?

By Kazuhiro Okamoto

Shizuka is an introverted girl dealing with schoolwork, boys, and a medical condition that begins to turn her invisible! She finds support with Mamoru, a boy who is falling for Shizuka despite her condition, and with Keiko, a woman who suffers from this illness and has finally turned *completely* invisible! *Translucent's* exploration of what people see, what people think they see, and what people wish to see in themselves and others makes for an emotionally sensitive manga peppered with moments of surprising humor, heartbreak, and drama.

VOLUME 1
ISBN: 978-1-59307-647-4

VOLUME 2
ISBN: 978-1-59307-677-1

VOLUME 3
ISBN: 978-1-59307-679-5

$9.95 Each!

Previews for *TRANSLUCENT* and other DARK HORSE MANGA titles can be found at darkhorse.com!